THE GENIUS OF ITALY

THE GENIUS OF ITALY

by

LEONARDO OLSCHKI

LONDON
VICTOR GOLLANCZ LTD
1950

PRINTED IN GREAT BRITAIN BY
WE AND BRYDONE PRINTERS LIMITED, LONDON, N.W.10

THIS book contains a series of independent essays devoted to the fundamental aspects of Italian civilization from its origins in the Middle Ages to modern times. These essays are intended to describe the harmonious and dissonant developments in Italian life, art, and thought. In this new historical and critical appreciation of the individual, regional, and national accomplishments of Italy, the customary patterns of rise and fall, of primitivism and maturity, of renascence and decadence have been abandoned. They are replaced by an evaluation of the dominant expressions of national life in the different periods of its millenarian development.

In the gradual shifting of its creative energies from one field of human activity to another the potential vitality of a nation remains unchanged. Its manifestations may be determined or limited by natural, spiritual, political, or social conditions and contingencies, but on the whole they appear equivalent from the point of view of their function in the total structure of national life and civilization. In their earliest outbursts, between A.D. 1000 and 1250, the vital energies of the Italian people were concentrated on building up a new society represented by original political institutions, new juridical systems, and revolutionary religious movements. With Dante and Petrarca, poetry took the lead in the subsequent era of declining political passions. After 1400 the figurative arts attained a supremacy over literary concerns and public interests. In the century of Machiavelli, Bruno, and Galileo philosophical fervor and scientific enthusiasm directed the creative forces of the nation.

When the spiritual police of the Counter-Reformation arrested these powerful currents of secular thought, Italian vitality broke out in torrents of music that undermined the spiritual foundations and shook the moral structure of the nation. In the nineteenth century the ideal of a national and political brotherhood prevailed over all other individual and collective sentiments and inspired equally poetry and action in a general effort toward that common goal. The preference given by natives and foreigners to the one or the other of these great accomplishments does not imply a definitive judgment concerning their value and importance. A synoptical view of the life of a nation in its totality will help the professional historian and the general reader to discover in new trends and achievements the imperishable mark of the past.

The present book, however, was not written to support a thesis or to develop a new philosophy. The author's aim has been to revise and revive from firsthand knowledge of sources and documents, and from a direct experience of the country and of its people, the facts and events described in many monographs and manuals devoted to Italian history and culture. This book intends to initiate the general reader and the specialized student into a better understanding and a historical appreciation of a living civilization considered in all its decisive manifestations and in the accomplishments of its leading men.

L. O.

Berkeley, California

Table of Contents

THE GENIUS OF ITALY

I. *The Italian Landscape: Man and Soil*

SINCE time immemorial man has collaborated with nature in shaping the soil and landscape of Italy. Everywhere physical and human geography melt into one. For a true understanding of Italy's natural physiognomy, the geographical descriptions and the scientific statements must be integrated with the image created by artists and poets who discovered its transcendent charm. Science and history yield methodical knowledge of those same aspects and scenes that poetry interprets and the fine arts illustrate. Without the contribution of an inspired vision of reality, science is blind and nature is dead:

> *Salve sacra parens frugum Saturnia tellus!*
> 'Hail, land of Saturn, sacred mother of earth's fruits.'
> (Virgil, *Georgica* II, 175)

With this saturnian country the gods were generous but not lavish. Nowhere does the peninsula reveal the bare and rocky ridges and plateaus characteristic of the eastern Adriatic coast from Istria down to Albania, Epirus, and Greece. Italy has no such forbidding wilderness as the French *Massif Central* or the vast desert regions of the Spanish *Meseta*. From the hilly Sub-Alpine fringe down to the coast of Sicily, certain common physiographical and climatic features compose the most diversified natural aspects into a homogeneous geographical picture. This natural unity is emphasized by what has been called the insular character of Italy, bounded on three sides by the sea and on the north cut off from Europe by the lofty barrier of the Alps. Since

3

prehistoric times, man has crossed these barriers and finally abolished all natural obstacles to human intercourse. Yet Italy remains an island, homogeneous both in natural and human climate.

From the rounded Sub-Alpine and Apennine ridges and slopes, where migratory shepherds drive the herd to pasture in summertime, down to the verdant regions of the peninsula, only few and sparse areas of Italy are naturally unfit for human life. With little exaggeration it can be said that man, more than nature, is responsible for the fallow and uncultivated land and the thinly settled regions of continental and insular Italy. The naval development of Rome from the destruction of Carthage to the era of imperial expansion led to the deforestation of the Apennine heights. The process was completed in the course of the Middle Ages by the shipbuilders of Venice, Pisa, Genoa, and Amalfi. Since then the erosion of the unprotected soil has made a stony waste of the mountainous regions once covered, like the Calabrian Sila of today, by luxuriant forests. Large flocks of goats and sheep have completed the age-old process of deforestation by gnawing away the fresh shoots of deciduous plants tenaciously reburgeoning under a merciful sun.

Political events and social conditions have likewise transformed the interior of Sicily, once the granary of Rome, and vast sections of southern Italy, praised in antiquity for their fertility, into barren, fever-stricken, depopulated areas. The agrarian backwardness, characteristic of the country to the south of the Tuscan-Umbrian border, including the main Italian islands, subsists on the improvident methods of large estate owners, who have no interest in modernizing agricultural methods or in improving conditions among the impoverished population. The proponents of agrarian reform in the south have never been able to find, in a poor country, the huge capital needed for the regeneration of vast regions neglected by man and ravaged by nature. The successful commercial activity of the wine, citrus and olive growers along the luxuriant coastal regions of southern Italy and Sicily has had no noticeable influence on the customary apathy of their rural neighbors of the interior. The wish that moves mountains is helpless where man and soil have become equally torpid and recalcitrant.

Other districts of Italy have become unproductive at different epochs, largely through natural causes. Here man accepted the challenge and fought against the destructive power of nature. The Pontine marshes, the vast swamps of Lombardy, Venetia, Tuscany, and of the principal rivers, have always stimulated human determination and ingenuity. The history of the repeated attempts to redeem those lands from desolation reveals a moral courage and an intellectual effort that transcended the economic interest involved. Leonardo da Vinci created the modern system of irrigation in the Lombard plain; Galileo conceived the project of draining the marshy valleys of Tuscany; and since ancient times countless other men of versatile talents have collaborated in similar undertakings. More recently epidemics have been prevented through impressive systems of aqueducts inspired by an unforgotten Roman tradition. The 'Bonifiche' around the Po Delta restored vast tracts of scorched or swampy land to cultivation. Behind these efforts lay the same determination and almost religious spirit that inspired the construction of the consular highways of ancient Rome and endowed with almost divine power the 'pontifex,' or bridgemaker, who came to be regarded as the highest moral and intellectual authority of a community, and finally of mankind itself.

In almost every part of the country, a rugged district of stony hills or rocky mountains breaks the continuity of intensively cultivated areas or wooded ranges. From these dispersed masses of crystalline or granitic rocks, of Triassic limestone or sedimentary sandstone, the Italians have extracted, since prehistoric times, the exceptional variety of materials that formed the basis for a great part of their civilization. Here nature seems to have generously compensated them for the inadequacy of their resources in metal and timber. The genius of Italy found its first durable materialization in stone and marble, as embodied in Sardinia's monumental prehistoric *Nuraghi*. As long as the creative spirit of the Italians was content to defy eternity with the stony riches of their soil, they moved spiritually and, with Roman expansion, even politically toward the conquest of the world.

When they began to imitate the new nations that had based their civilizations on iron and concrete, Italy risked losing her economic independence along with her artistic proficiency.

Today it seems as though a new stone age had begun for this beautiful but unhappy country. The problem of the raw materials, indispensable to a modern nation, is more than· an economic one. For at least two millennia the peoples of the peninsula have regarded stone and marble as the only materials suitable to the dignity of man and the majesty of God. In civic architecture that material represents the stability of Italian life, just as wood and metals express the mutable aspects of Germanic and of American society. To a Latin mind, it is a degradation to live in a wooden house. When writing his *Trésor*, about 1260, Dante's paternal friend Brunetto Latini described the stone towers and tall houses of Italy as something characteristic of his native country. Three centuries later, when traveling in France, Torquato Tasso was shocked by the poor appearance of the wooden houses of Paris, 'built without any architectural discernment' for the uncivilized citizens of a still barbarous nation.

Such feelings were traditional and instinctive. The Italian towns and villages arose as dense and ponderous masses of stone and marble, skillfully cut and fashioned after different styles and patterns. Marble of different colors was used to enliven the gloomy palaces, defiant towers, inhospitable dwellings, and somber churches of medieval cities; but trees and flowers were kept out of their walls as ornaments unsuited to an urban way of life. Suitable ornaments were statues, reliefs, and monuments. Even today what little greenery is admitted to Italian towns languishes in stony enclosures like exiles from a remote world. Petrarca drew his patriotic inspiration from the stones of Rome, and Michelangelo Buonarroti believed that an artist's hand had only to free from its superfluous matter the form that nature had prefigured in a rough block of marble.[1]

---

[1] *Non ha l'ottimo artista alcun concetto*
Che un marmo solo in sé non circoscriva
Col suo soverchio; e solo a questo arriva
La man che obbedisce all'intelletto.

The busy quarries from the Alps to Syracuse were the basis of the unsurpassed architectural achievements that are the pride of every town and region of the country. Yet building with stone on a large scale could be performed only in epochs of regional or national prosperity to which it did not greatly contribute. The erection of the impressive buildings, which are the ornament of Italian towns, implied slave labor through antiquity and the Middle Ages, and starvation wages in more recent time. Immeasurable toil and endurance were needed to build the palaces of Florence, the Canal Grande of Venice, the monuments of Rome, the temples of Paestum and Sicily, the churches, cathedrals, and bridges of all Italy. The oldest known vernacular inscription in Rome (1084) occurs in a mural representing workmen hauling a column. It runs: 'Your dragging of stones is well deserved. Pull, you villains.'

*   *   *

Modern economy is not based on atonement for sin, and modern architecture shuns the obsolete and arduous working of noble and costly materials. The pretentious official buildings erected after 1870, such as the Palazzo di Giustizia, the Monumento Nazionale, the Foro Mussolini in Rome, or the over-ornamented railway station in Milan, clearly show the inability of modern Italian architects to handle stone and marble without losing the traditional sense of proportion and running into ponderous bombast. While almost every kind of building material was always abundant beyond the national requirements, iron and copper were in short supply. The iron mines of Elba and the copper production of Tuscany and Sardinia provided barely enough for local and regional handicrafts, while the country remained self-sufficient and relatively underpopulated.

[Cont. from p. 6.]

(Whate'er conception a great artist fires,.
Its answering semblance latent lies within
A block of marble; but the hand alone,
Swayed by the intellect, can give it form.

Hartford's translation.)

These favorable conditions changed radically with the industrial revolution of the nineteenth century, when iron was needed for railways, industrial production, the navy, and the merchant marine. By a fatal coincidence Italy became economically dependent upon other countries in Europe and overseas at the very moment when national unity was achieved. For the old civilization founded on stone and handicraft she was compelled to substitute an industrial organization based on coal,, metals, oil, rubber, and timber, which are almost nonexistent in Italy. This gave rise to a complex situation involving the whole national life of the country. It would be wrong to consider this development from the economic standpoint alone. At the turning point of her national history Italy had to accept a situation uncongenial to her past and irreconcilable with her natural structure.

No one seriously believed that colonial adventures could alter these unfavorable conditions. Italy's colonial enterprises, inaugurated by Francesco Crispi in 1885, did not result from economic forces. The leading spirits of Italian imperialism were well aware that a country poor in natural resources could not achieve prosperity through the conquest of overseas territories even more impoverished and backward than its own. Modern Italian expansion overseas was closer to pioneering than to exploitation, and had more psychological and moral values than economic. The possession of Rome imposes historic obligations of honor and prestige. Italy is faced with the alternative of dismissing and forgetting her past, which represents her spiritual substance, or of renouncing her position in the modern world, which is indeed inconceivable. Italy is no such idyllic land as dreamers and globe-trotters have imagined. It is a tragic country—with a smiling face.

The ambition to compete with more favored nations, combined with the needs of an increasing population, prompted Italy to develop her metallurgical industries, in which expensive imports and foreign competition made cheap labor indispensable. The essentially national and self-supporting manufactures, such as silk, sugar, canned goods, and dairy products, were all supplied by the natural resources of the country. These industries had developed gradually and organically throughout

Italy over a period of many centuries. Heavy industry, on the other hand, including the metallurgical and chemical branches, was concentrated around Turin and Milan and more or less connected with the international trusts and cartels. These circumstances have developed different regional and occupational types of workers, discordant trends in the labor movement, and an unbalanced labor legislation artificially enforced by bureaucratic control and constant governmental interference. During the last decades all small and large enterprises, as well as the national economy at large, profited immensely from the increasing exploitation of water power drawn from Alpine and Apennine rivers. But the industrial electrification of large sections of the country did not solve the national problem of fuel and did little to create a sound industrial picture. Some leading branches of Italian industry, such as the machine, automobile, and textile industries, have always had a certain artificial character, owing their expansion largely to protective duties and the availability of cheap labor. Industry has never achieved an importance equal to that of agriculture in the general economy and national life of Italy.

Despite the broad variety of tillage and vegetation, Italian agriculture reveals everywhere certain common traits, which are characteristic in both their natural and human aspects. The uninterrupted supremacy of agriculture in Italian life has not created a farming aristocracy. Country life never played a leading part in the cultural and social life of the country. There is, of course, everywhere in Italy a landed gentry and a country nobility, particularly in some of the intensively cultivated areas along the Adriatic coast, in Central Italy and in Sicily. But this rural aristocracy confines itself to the administration of the estate, taking no direct part in its cultivation, which is left entirely to the peasantry, while the business end is handled by middlemen and managers. Never does the owner live all the year round on his property, where he has his summer villa and hunting domain. His residence is in one of the innumerable small country towns, most of which date back to remote antiquity.

It is in these towns that the landed nobility reside in quaint, soberly furnished *palazzi*, while the big landowners of the South

B

live in their more or less sumptuous hereditary residences in the large cities. On the *piazza* of those small and medium-sized towns the managers meet on fixed days for their agricultural transactions, which create a certain occasional contact between townsfolk and peasantry. For the most part these two sections of the population do not mix; there is little migration of the country people into the towns, and urban civilization, has had virtually no influence on the customs and traditions of the countryfolk. For many centuries peace between landowners and peasants has been maintained by the compromise expedient of sharecropping, or *mezzadria.* The produce is equally divided between the two parties; the middleman, or *fattore,* acts at the same time as a representative of the peasants and as the proprietor's agent, drawing his advantage from the weaknesses of both sides.

This system has developed steadily since the late Middle Ages, when the legislation of the Italian city-states abolished rural servitude. In 1256 the preamble to a list of emancipated slaves drawn up at Bologna proclaimed that 'men were brought forth and created free from the very beginning by nature.' The system, it is true, did not solve the problem of rural labor, and eventually transformed the slaves into proletarians. It has, however, withstood all attempts at socialist organization or fascist corporative regulation and has made for rural tranquillity through the centuries. Italy never experienced the bloody and destructive peasant uprisings that occurred in most of the European countries. Nor did Italy ever develop a free and prosperous peasantry of the type created by the French Revolution. The acceptance of sharecropping by the Italian peasantry has historical, psychological, and natural causes which are at the base of the economic circumstances.

There can be no doubt that the system reflects the spirit of compromise, fairness, and mutual understanding that characterizes many aspects of Italian life, past and present. *Mezzadria* imposes hard obligations on the peasant. He is bound to raise a large family for the cultivation of the *podere,* his section of arable land that provides him with a dwelling and at least the means of bare subsistence. On the other hand, he shares with the landowner the natural risks of the seasons as well as the advantages of exceptional crops. The long association with the *podere* and its surroundings creates an emotional bond with the familiar soil. Submissiveness and the typical rural distrust of uncertain changes and untried innovations help the Italian peasant to accept his hopeless poverty with resignation and dignity, more as a destiny than as a burden.

The natural foundations of the system reside in the very character of intensive Italian agriculture. Sharecropping is, indeed, unknown and impossible in the latifundia of the South, where estates are generally exploited by temporary leaseholders with the help of seasonal day laborers living in towns and earning less than a bare subsistence. In other regions, as in Tuscany and Umbria, agriculture takes the form of gardening rather than farming. Grapes, fruit trees, grain, vegetables, flowers, and even olive and citrus trees may be grown on a single piece of land. Here again *mezzadria* is customary, and where the soil is so bountiful the peasants have often attained relative prosperity. Surplus funds were usually invested in gold and jewels until the provincial savings banks succeeded in overcoming the natural—and quite justified—suspicions of the countryfolk. The imperialistic adventures of the twentieth century stripped the Italian peasantry of both jewels and money and decimated their ranks on the battlefields of Europe and Africa.

Yet the rich yield of intensive agriculture in Italy is not attributable only to the benign assistance of the climate and the natural fertility of the soil. Though the country may look like a park and the peasant like a bucolic gardener, most Italian crops are the product of unremitting toil and vigilance. With the exception of *Campania felix*, the most luxuriant and densely populated region of Italy, and of some areas of Tuscany and Sicily, the land is not as generous as it appears to a superficial observer. The whole north-Italian plain from the Ticino to the Adriatic Sea is constantly menaced by floods. Vast areas of Lombardy have to be protected by powerful dams, high-lying dikes, and enforced natural embankments. In the marshy, malaria-ridden, inhospitable lowlands the arable areas stand in permanent danger of reverting to swamp. In the hilly sections all along the peninsula, a system of ascending terraces prevents

the thin stratum of topsoil from being covered or carried away
by landslides. Here no tractors or agricultural machines can
substitute for the efforts of man and beast. The ground has to
be architecturally shaped where fields and meadows rise from
valley bottoms to the edge of forests, pastures, or rocky summits.

The sweat of countless generations has fertilized this generous
but insidious ground. And it is the most typical and basic vegetation of the whole peninsula—the myriad olive trees and the
interminable festoons of hanging grapevines—which claim the
greatest care in every season of the year. Two Biblical animals
share the labor of the peasants: the patient, stubborn, and capricious donkey and the white, ponderous ox, crouched under a
heavy yoke on fields and stony trails. For the Italian countryfolk the horse has remained an aristocratic animal to which only
the owner of the estate is entitled. Nowhere is class distinction
so consistently and almost instinctively preserved as in this tradition. Horses are never used for tilling the soil.

Although country life shows considerable regional variation,
there are certain common features that link the temperate and
subtropical areas of the peninsula with its continental and maritime districts. The tourist who in wintertime enjoys the midday
sun of the fashionable resorts tends to imagine that all Italy is
blessed with the same mild and benign climate. But Italian fields
and towns are bitterly cold in the long winter months and un-
bearably torrid in the dry, exhausting summers. Both these climatic extremes are accepted by the whole population as an
ineluctable fatality against which no precautionary measures
can help. Except in the kitchen, fireplaces are not customary.
Coal and wood have always been expensive, beyond the reach
of the great majority of the Italian people, and elaborate con-
trivances for heating are the privilege of the wealthy. The snow-
fall in the northern plain sometimes exceeds that of Iceland, and
the average temperature is uncomfortably low in churches, classrooms, libraries, museums, shops, factories and, as a rule, also
in the drawing rooms of Italian society. Conversely, from June
to the end of September, the sun shines mercilessly day after
day upon a dry and dusty country in which human life seems to

die out, while the torrid motionless air is filled with the incessant shrill cries of classical cicadas.

There is no escape or relief from this seasonal conflagration. For many hours of the day peasants and beasts abandon the fields and townsfolk go to sleep behind closed shutters. At night the stone pavements and walls radiate the heat stored during the day. Heavy mosquito nets keep the morning breeze from the beds of exhausted sleepers. Hence the paramount importance of the financially ruinous *villeggiatura* for the Italian city dwellers. Yet the weather is not the usual topic of an Italian's conversation. He has come to accept with stoical indifference what the unfathomable decrees of heaven have imposed on the different zones of the earth.

❖   ❖   ❖

Through two and more millennia of human history the varied climate has permitted the acclimatization of the greatest variety of plants and herbs. The indigenous vegetation is represented by evergreen trees and shrubs, which resist the summer droughts and the rigorous winter and are a lasting, dominant note in the flaming but solemn aspects of the Italian landscape. Since time immemorial the dark oak, the glittering box tree, the aromatic laurel, the grayish, knobby olive tree, the lofty pine, the elegant and placid cypress, the dense and somber ivy have provided a classical frame for the deciduous woods of chestnuts, walnuts, elms, and beeches; for the orchards and vineyards, cornfields and gardens; for the tremulous poplars along the rivers. An immense variety of officinal plants, fragrant herbs, and berry bushes completes the picture of Italian fields and hills.

This is the Italian landscape with its infinite shades of green, as described by Roman poets and represented by Italian artists. But many exotic traits have been added to this ancient Virgilian picture. Since remote antiquity the oases, plateaus, and rich valleys of Asia have provided the native Italian flora with many newcomers, which were soon integrated into the landscape. In an almost prehistoric epoch the vine and the fig were introduced from the Near East; at a later period Greek colonists brought the plane tree and the pomegranate, besides many other orna-

mental Mediterranean kitchen plants. In the thirteenth century
the Levant gave Italy the mulberry tree, which covers much of
the North Italian soil and has become the basis of the flourishing
silk industry. In the sixteenth century the citrus fruits imported
from Persia, India, and China began to be grown more and
more extensively, until they became for travelers, poets, and
traders the ever-blossoming symbol of the Italian soil:

> Know ye the land where the cypress and myrtle
> Are emblems of deeds that are done in their clime . . .
> Where the citron and olive are fairest of fruits.
>   (Byron, *The Bride of Abydos,* after Goethe's *Mignon*) .

The final revolution in Italian vegetation began in the sixteenth
century with imports from America. The Venetian plain was
soon covered with cornfields, which added a new variety to
the staple food of the country, consisting of wheat and chestnut
flour. Innumerable parks and gardens from the Alps to Sicily
adopted American magnolia. Italy became the leading tomato
producer, but rejected the potato. Tobacco was accepted and
became a reliable source of internal revenue, and still is, alas!
The stout, spiny-margined Mexican agaves, with their ornate
candelabra-like blossoms, appealed to the traditional Italian
sense of symmetry, while the aggressive, chunky opuntia of
tropical America rapidly spread over the stony heights of
southern Italy and Sicily, where it is frequently used in place
of hedges and fences.

The African palms of various sorts advanced slowly from the
Greek temple districts of Selinunte up to the Alpine border and
the French Riviera. Thus all the continents of the Old and New
World contributed their share to the Italian landscape. Economic
concerns played but little part in its development. Not until
the nineteenth century was any serious attempt made to com-
mercialize agriculture and organize an extensive export trade
with the co-operation of foreign capital. Until that time Italy
was agriculturally self-sufficient. Up to our day the peasantry
of the Upper Country and the central regions have retained
their frugal diet of bread, fruits, corn meal, salad, pork
sausage, bacon, cheese, wine and oil. In the South a starvation

diet has been the rule for centuries among the poverty-stricken rural population.

Italy was never a milk-drinking country. Before the coffee invasion from Central and South America the Italians of all classes and regions drew vigor and hilarity only from the count-less varieties of *nostrano,* or domestic wine, still produced by crushing grapes in large old-fashioned vats. In the South the rural population became desperately impoverished after the First World War, when new barriers to emigration cut off the only possible escape from overpopulated districts and wretched, filthy, and dilapidated villages. The lack of systematic internal colonization and the increasing requirements of the growing urban population made it necessary to import large quantities of cereals from America, adding a new burden to the strained national finances.

For a few prosperous years at the beginning of this century Italy had a balanced economy. It seemed as though an era of social progress and harmonious economic development was at hand. But the First World War and the ensuing social and moral disintegration destroyed the traditional foundations of Italian economic life and made it increasingly dependent upon foreign help and influence. A senseless, misleading policy of economic autarchy during the tense years of the Fascist adventure only spread a cloak of boastful promises over the reality of foreign intervention. Italy became the playground of the conflicting in-terests of the richer European powers, just as her costly colonial enterprise was assuming the air of a shabby imperial revival.

After the Second World War the country had to dig out of its new and inglorious ruins. The towns were blasted to rubble, the fields swept clear of cattle and implements, and much of the landscape was ravaged and polluted. Its fate is poverty, the an-cient heritage of Italy, with the problems of man and soil now harder to solve than ever before. Gifts of money, food, and fer-tilizers will not restore the economic and moral balance of the country. Only a few will profit from its industrial revival. The leaders of all political parties agree that in a modern and vital nation the Franciscan virtues of patience, poverty, and humility cannot be transformed into productive forces of national reconstruction. Everybody knows that Italy can be saved and developed as a free and prosperous country only after a far-reaching agrarian reform that will redeem the soil from adverse conditions and man from social and moral distress. The country's destiny will be shaped in its fields and grounds by that kind of administration which will succeed in mobilizing to that end the practical intelligence, the natural resources, the patriotism, and civic spirit of the nation.

II. *Sociological and Cultural Ethnography*

JUST as the vegetation of many lands contributed to the Italian landscape, so the peoples of the Old World helped to create the *stirps italica*. All had a share in moulding the Italian people, but none was able to impose upon the others the stamp of racial character. Attempts to classify the population of the peninsula and of its islands by racial criteria have always met with failure. The complete Latinization of the country in the imperial era obliterated every trace of the racial origin of the tribes and peoples who settled in the peninsula after the Illyrian, Etruscan, and Celtic incursions. The 'Italian type' is the product of pure speculation and scientific dilettantism, of charlatanism or demagogy. It is a striking paradox, indeed, that the so-called 'myth of the blood' threatened to become a national dogma and a popular faith in the very days when biologists were discovering the classification of blood·and showing that foreign plasma could be injected into an organism without inducing any change in its physical, psychological, or intellectual individuality. Italy, to a much higher degree than any other country, has always been a melting pot. Civilization and climate have collaborated in fusing the most contrasting ethnical elements and the most conflicting tribal groups. The characteristic achievements of the Italian people can be attributed to no one of these groups. All the leading spirits of the Augustan and imperial epoch were provincials, and none of them was of Roman ancestry: Virgil, Catullus, Livy, Pliny, and many more came from the Gallo-Celtic provinces of the North; Propertius and Tacitus from

Umbria; Cicero and Ovid from the mountainous region of the Abruzzi; Horace from Apulia; Juvenal from Campania; Seneca, Lucan, Martial from Spain.

Greek language and customs dominated the South and Sicily long after the Roman conquest. As late as 1017 the Byzantine prefect, Basilius Bujanus, gave the classical name of Troja to a colony he founded on the hills of Apulia. One of the oldest-known Italian poems has been handed down in a Hebrew transcription of the end of the twelfth century. Soon afterwards the first refined Italian poetry flourished at the Sicilian court of a German emperor, Frederick II of Hohenstaufen, and spread rapidly, stimulating the intellectual world of Florence and Bologna to cast off the yoke of scholastics and foreigners. Yet in the fourteenth century, when Dante's poem was transcribed and read throughout the country from Venice to the tip of Calabria, French was the literary language of many courts and of the educated classes in the rich and independent centers of the North.

However, despite foreign influences, the early manifestations of a national literature were Italian in form and spirit; the same is true of the Byzantine-inspired buildings and ornaments of medieval Venice, the Gothic churches of Assisi, Bologna, and Milan, the decoration and architecture of Norman Sicily, with their Greek and Arabic motifs. Foreign styles, arts, and crafts were introduced into Italy from all parts of Europe and the Near East and quickly adapted to the Italian national taste. This assimilation of foreign influences began very early and has always been characteristic of Italian civilization.

Of the indigenous populations of the peninsula we know very little, beyond the names of some of the tribes. Apart from the evidence offered by a few archaeological discoveries, often diversely interpreted by specialists, the origin and development of the early peoples are matters of conjecture. Prehistoric Italian art lacks anything comparable to the representations of primitive animals painted on the walls of the caves of Altamira in Spain or the Dordogne in France. The cultural awakening of Italy was late and slow. The first forms of higher civilization on her territory were of foreign origin and character. Italian history begins with the Etruscans, a people who immigrated in remote antiquity from Asia Minor, and dominated most of northern and central Italy down to the Latin borders until 396 B.C., when the Roman dictator Marius Furius Camillus captured the walled city of Veii. At the same time Greek states and colonies on the coast of Sicily and the lower peninsula expanded, leaving the indigenous tribes only a small portion of land, which was subjugated in the first stages of Roman expansion.

Rome's civilization was thus affected by the influence of the Etruscans in the North and the Greeks in the South, both contributing to the eclectic and syncretistic character of late Latin culture, religion, and customs. But Etruscan art and craftsmanship, whose surviving examples depict religious rites, regional customs, and domestic life, derived from Greek models, while the cultural development of the Hellenic provinces of the South took a direction different from that of Attica and the East. The Etruscan invasion was too far back in time and the invaders had been too few in number to create an effectual national movement.

The conquest of Italy by those Asiatic warriors was not a mass invasion, like that of the Gauls who settled in the vast plain of the Po and occupied, after 600 B.C., the whole of northern Italy. With their higher civilization the Etruscans were able to impose their language (whose affinities are still unknown) upon a population which they organized in a form novel to the Italian aborigines, but that was destined to develop and endure. It was under their influence that the first urban civilization was established in that country of shepherds, peasants, and mountaineers, but it was from the rural stock that the sedentary peoples of Etruria drew their substance and power. The invaders were assimilated so rapidly and thoroughly by the native population that their origins were forgotten and remained unknown even to the historians of the neighboring Greeks and Latins. The cultural impact of the newcomers was, however, so strong and enduring as to keep alive the language they had imposed on the conquered tribes long after the Roman conquest of the Etrurian territories.

Etruscan civilization was consolidated through a defensive union of confederate urban centers dominated by an autochthonous aristocracy, while the Romans, on the other hand, extended their customs, laws, language, and religion over their consular and imperial roads. It took many centuries to subdue the Etruscan strongholds on the fortified hills of Tuscany and to break down their political and military organization, whereas the Latinization of the lowlands of Cisalpine Gaul proceeded rapidly by means of the strategic Roman highways. No trace has been left of the Gauls of northern Italy, who accepted and assimilated Roman customs as swiftly and thoroughly as their kindred tribes beyond the Alps did after Caesar's fateful enterprise. They fought for the right of Roman citizenship, while Roman colonists and veterans settled down as new masters in their fields. A few years before our era, Maecenas, a scion of Etruscan kings, met at the court of Augustus the poet Publius Vergilius Maro, the son of Celtic farmers, who became the prophet of the Roman Empire after having revealed with an unsurpassed delicacy of poetic allusion the tragic aspects of this triumphant Romanization.

By that time the highly differentiated peoples of southern Italy had been almost completely Latinized and absorbed into the Roman community. The policy of internal colonization, carried out through large groups of settlers, had done more than wars and military domination to amalgamate the hostile tribes of the interior, who were already surrounded and pressed by the wealthy and influential Greek centers of Sicily and the continental coast. After the long and bloody Roman conquest of these territories and the final capture of Tarentum (275 B.C.) and Syracuse (212 B.C.), the Greek element of this heterogenous population acted as mediator in the difficult process of mutual adjustment. Little by little the Italic tribes in the mountainous provinces of Bruttium, Samnium, Lucania, and Apulia gave up their regional individuality and were dissolved in the new Greco-Roman commonwealth. Meanwhile the Latinization of the Greeks proceeded simultaneously with the Hellenization of the Romans.

. There is still much evidence of this coexistence and fusion of the three leading races. It cannot be found, it is true, in anthropological measurements or somatic features, but it is clearly shown in the trilingual wall inscriptions and in the buildings and paintings of Pompeii, whose civilization was characterized by a Latin social structure, Hellenistic cultural traditions, and old Italic folklore. And just across the peninsula, on the Adriatic side of lower Italy, Quintus Horatius Flaccus, the son of a freed native slave, grew up in the old military colony of Venusia before becoming a member of the new Hellenized literary aristocracy of the capital, a friend of the Etruscan Maecenas and a favorite of Augustus, the emperor.

For the first time in history Italy was united in customs, language, and political administration. It was a Roman more than a Latin country. 'Roman' at that epoch signified the universal, and betokened political expansion, culture, artistic inspiration, world experience, and human consciousness. Since every Italian town aspired to become a small but complete image of Rome, and since every inhabitant of the regions from the Alps to the southernmost tip of Sicily was or wanted to be a Roman citizen, the whole population of the peninsula began to think, to feel, to live within the vast human dimensions of which every architectural monument and every poem was the spiritual and artistic reflection. From the Black Sea to the Atlantic Ocean, from the Caledonian walls to the African desert, the same buildings, laws, and institutions reminded every Roman functionary, soldier, colonist, trader, teacher, and traveler that he was a citizen of the world. This feeling has been perpetuated by the most representative Roman authors, Virgil, Horace, Lucretius, Cicero, and Seneca, as well as many others. Their poetical and philosophical vision embraced the world and made it omnipresent through geographical allusion and a fusion of foreign memories with the evocation of the native soil.

This long experience banished tribalism and racialism forever from the Italian consciousness, engendered the assimilative power of the Roman Empire, and prepared the Italians to live and feel at home in every corner of the earth. Throughout its history Italian cosmopolitanism has been neither imperial nor

papal, neither political nor religious, but fundamentally human.
It is manifested in Dante's universalism and in Petrarca's humanism, in Marco Polo's tolerant understanding of exotic civilizations, in Columbus' oceanic vision, and, most of all, in the spirit
of Italian science and music. Imperial and Catholic universalism
are the complementary political and religious expressions of that
unique national experience.

In the course of Roman expansion, this universalism found expression in a process of assimilation that implied the extermination of recalcitrant tribes and the continuous shifting of populations from one part of the earth to another. The city of Rome
was not only the center and symbol of this world-embracing
cosmopolitanism, but also its living realization. Its population
comprised all the races of the world: many aspects of its life
and culture were dominated by the Greeks. In the first century
B.C. the civil wars broke down many of the social barriers that
had divided the classes of Roman society in old republican
times. This Roman universalism was consolidated by racial and
social interchange long before it was sanctioned on fiscal and
political grounds by Caracalla's *Constitutio Antoniniana*, which
in A.D. 212 conferred Roman citizenship upon all inhabitants of
the provinces. The juridical sanction merely confirmed an existing
state of affairs.

From the early imperial epoch until the decline of Rome, the
chief foreign colonies in the city and elsewhere on the peninsula
were composed of immigrants from the Near East, Syrians, Jews
from Palestine and Egypt, and various peoples from the Roman
provinces of Asia Minor. These communities, which included
Christians, Mithraists, gnostic sects, Manichaeans, and esoteric
Egyptian cults, played an important part in spreading Oriental
cults, doctrines, and customs throughout Italy and Western
Europe. Indeed the influence of these groups was out of all proportion to their numbers. Among the foreign settlers, the imported Oriental religions found prophets and apostles inspired
by a universal vision of the world and mankind.

The countless Roman legionaries, functionaries, traders, and
scholars who had direct contact with the Oriental peoples and
civilizations contributed as much as the foreign colonies to

superimposing a Greek and Oriental mode of life and thought upon Roman society, with its indigenous Latin and Italic traditions. No particular ethnic group was instrumental in the substitution of Mithraism for the Greco-Roman pantheon when the Emperor Commodus officially embraced that mysterious cult, so popular among soldiers and officials throughout the empire. And it was no racial influence that led Roman soldiers, in A.D. 218, to acclaim Elagabalus, a young Syrian priest of the Sun, as successor to Caracalla. The recognition of Christianity as a Roman state religion by Constantine, in 323, did not result from the influence of any particular group; the religious and social *fait accompli* it sanctioned was of a universal character.

The 'ferments of decomposition' at work in the old Italian society were of many kinds. In the advanced imperial epoch little was left of the indigenous traditions, which were dying out even in remote corners of the peninsula. The population of Italy can at this time be described as a mixed, Latin-speaking, Mediterranean race, more or less interspersed with Eastern elements, which predominated in the provinces and islands of the South. But the immigration of slaves from the eastern provinces of the empire was the chief factor in the enormous increase of the Oriental population of Italy. The mass emancipation of slaves on the peninsula and the increasing prosperity of the upper classes brought about the large-scale importation of serfs and helots who, over a period of time, conspicuously altered the ethnographic character of the population, giving an Oriental cast to men and customs of many provinces and towns, especially south of the old Etrurian borders.

❊   ❊   ❊

A further ethnic element was introduced as Germanic tribes gradually spread across Italy. Mass immigration from Northern and Central Europe into the peninsula was preceded by an influx of barbarians who were attracted by the alluring aspects of Roman civilization and by the interest of the Italians in the strange, handsome newcomers from beyond the Roman borders. Those Romans who were troubled by the ominous changes in Italian public and domestic life after the end of the republic

tended to idealize the sturdy blond men and women who were
beginning to try their fortune in Roman camps and cities, or
were brought as slaves to the capital, or dispersed as colonists
in various parts of the country and the empire. Tacitus' *Germania,* written in A.D. 98, eloquently expresses this mood. The
astute historian contrasts the apparently unspoiled, free, and
high-spirited barbarians with his refined, corrupted, decadent,
and snobbish countrymen.

Germans were admitted in ever-increasing numbers into the
Roman army, first as soldiers, later also as officers, until a regular military aristocracy of so-called *equites singulares* became
highly influential at the court of the Roman emperors. Many of
these men returned home and encouraged a larger influx of
Germans into Italy, while others settled down peacefully and
found friends and protectors among the Senators, politicians, and
influential families of Rome and the provinces. In the third century a large number of Germans were enrolled as mercenaries;
gradually they came to constitute the bulk of the Roman army
and to dominate the military hierarchy. Before the first unsuc-
cessful invasion of northern Italy by the Alemanni, in 254, large
colonies of Germans had settled in the depopulated districts of
the region that was to become, in the early Middle Ages, the
center of Nordic expansion into Italy. The mass invasions of
German tribes were a consequence not only of the migrations of
Asiatic and Northern peoples into Central and Western Europe,
but also of the long collaboration and interpenetration of the
Germanic and Roman worlds. The Romans certainly preferred
these skilled and strong Germanic warriors to the Huns and Slavs
who had plundered and laid waste vast stretches of the country.

The Germanization of Italy was preceded by the Romanization of the Germans. It was favored by leading groups of military 'collaborationists,' as we should call them today. A powerful 'fifth column' operated successfully in Italian territory until
476, when Odoacer became ruler in Italy after the deposition
of the last emperor of the West. It was again at work in 493,
when Theodoric founded the adventurous and short-lived Ostrogothic Kingdom of Italy. Boethius and Symmachus, the last
true representatives of the Greco-Roman culture, paid with their

lives for their illusion that a Latin Mediterranean civilization could exist under Germanic political domination. It is difficult to decide what was more deplorable in this first Italian kingdom, the senseless cruelty of the Ostrogothic ruler or the abject servility of the Roman and Christian senate which gave its *placet* to that shameful double execution.

The history of the frequently revived *Italia Germanica* begins with this historic crime committed after half a millennium of Teutonic penetration from the Alps to Cosenza, where Alaric died in 410. Many of the Latinized Germans were loyal and able defenders of their adopted country. But on the whole the mutual adjustment of Germans and Latins on Italian soil was slow and onesided.

After the triumph of Christianity the Arian Goths broke the religious unity of Catholic Italy by retaining their sectarian faith. In an epoch dominated by the Christian idea of salvation as established by the Councils following Nicaea, the Arian profession of the subordinate nature of Christ divided the nation in the same way that Protestantism, in the sixteenth century, divided Catholic France. An insurmountable religious barrier kept the two peoples apart and prevented their fusion into one Latin nation.

The Langobards, who succeeded the Goths and dominated most of the Italian peninsula from 568 to 774, settled down in powerful armed groups; they had come as Germanic Arians, only to accept, within one generation, the religion of their subjects. They excluded themselves from Italy's spiritual and cultural community and ruled as foreigners and intruders. The Gothic and Langobardic conception of an Italy organized as a kingdom more or less independent of the still influential Byzantine Empire was based on their barbaric heritage and was entirely alien to Roman and Italian traditions. Since the origins of Rome there had never been a king in Italy, and the institution of kingship existed only in the Germanic tribes that had settled down in Roman territories as tributaries, settlers, and allies. Therefore when Charlemagne destroyed the Langobard, or Lombard, power and was crowned Roman Emperor on Christmas day 800, the historic reality of a third barbaric Italian kingdom

ruled by a Frankish dynasty was overshadowed by the revival of
a Roman and Catholic empire. It was this foreign character of
royal power and domination that always caused opposition to
the establishment of an Italian kingdom and made its existence
unpopular and precarious. And it was only in the nineteenth and
twentieth centuries that Italian history was again conceived
under this dynastic aspect.

Like their predecessors, the Franks ruled the peninsula as a
Germanic power, granting no concessions to the Latin section
of the population and making no attempt to reconcile the native
with the foreign elements. The substitution of a new Frankish
aristocracy of counts and marquesses for the old Lombard dukes
and bailiffs, or *gastaldi,* brought little change in the social and
intellectual structure of the country. The weakness and decentralization of the Carolingian power only increased the political
and administrative disintegration of Italy. The decay of feudalism in Frankish Italy was never outweighed by the consolidation
of the central power or the growth of a universal or national
principle as in Carolingian and Capetian France. The Lombard
and Frankish nobility, enlarged by subservient native elements,
never developed a moral code of fealty, justice, protection, devotion, and worship such as that which made French feudalism
so powerful and found immortal expression in the *Chanson de
Roland,* at the turn of the eleventh century.

Consequently feudalism had neither traditional nor spiritual
roots in Italian society. Lacking a historical mission, the Italian
nobility never aspired to leadership or to the organization of a
society based on moral principles and obligations. The German
aristocracy was always more anarchic than monarchic. Its disruptive effect in Italy was increased by the ignorance and illiteracy of its members, who soon forgot their native language without really mastering Latin, and showed little interest in cultural
and artistic achievements.

The complete assimilation of the Germans after a stay of many
generations in the wealthiest regions of Italy was impeded by
their aversion to urban civilization. From antiquity until our own
time, the upper and middle classes of Italian society have
liked to divide their life between town and country, according

to the seasons. For these people, the country has always been the place of rest and pleasure, so often described in classical and modern poems. Italian travelers to England and France during the fifteenth and sixteenth centuries, for example the humanist, Poggio Bracciolini, and the poet, Torquato Tasso, were shocked to find the gentry dwelling in isolated manors where they were unable to acquire courtly manners or lead a cultivated life.

This irreconcilable attitude of the two races divided the Italian population for centuries into a Germanic rural section dominated by its foreign nobility, and an urban class composed of Latin elements racially similar to the peasantry but consisting of traders, artisans, clerics, and officials. While the country nobility preserved Germanic customs, names, and juridical traditions, the townsfolk clung to the language, laws, and urban *mores* of their Latin heritage. Until the end of the twelfth century there were two separate tribunals; cases were tried under Germanic or Roman law, according to the 'nationality' of the parties. Politically this duality was somewhat offset by the fact that the representatives of the Langobard and Frankish central power resided in the same towns as the bishops. Unfortunately the bishops themselves were often Germans or foreigners. It was only after the great revolutions of the eleventh and twelfth centuries that a fusion of the divergent elements was achieved. The complete absorption of the Germanic portion by the Latin, then linguistically Italian, population marked the victory of the cities over the fortified rural castles, of the patriciate over the gentry, and of municipal spirit over the military cast and hierarchy.

While Greeks and Orientals left their mark on Italian civilization, no trace of a Germanic influence can be found in the cultural and artistic life of the peninsula. Even the two most impressive Germanic monuments on Italian soil, the mausoleum of Theodoric in Ravenna and the so-called Langobardic bridge in Spoleto, do not reveal a Nordic architectural style. Since the Germanic peoples did not know how to work stone, masonry, and marble, they employed native craftsmen for the buildings they erected in a country where wood was scarce. Of about 150 Germanic words in the Italian literary language, none relates to the sphere of intellectual life and interests. They all concern practical, military, or juridical matters.

But the effects of German rule on Italian society were immediate and lasting. The Germanic influence was much more disruptive and destructive than in France, where the two races, favored by the similarity of climate and soil, quickly fused to create a strong nation. In Italy, the superimposition of three different Germanic tribes upon the already mixed indigenous population, the continuous shifts in administrative borders and in the ownership of landed property, serfdom, feudal methods of agriculture, high and arbitrary taxation, and the absence of higher cultural aspirations among the leading classes brought about the complete economic exhaustion of the country and the impoverishment of its whole population. For many centuries Italy experienced not even a brief period of prosperity. A lasting and irreparable misery befell especially the towns, where traders and artisans were deprived of the advantages of an organized urban life and compelled to stick to their hereditary professions.

In spite of the magnificent revival of towns throughout the peninsula in the twelfth century, in spite of the subsequent advances in wealth in many regions, the country as a whole never recovered from the total impoverishment of this period. The Ottonian Romano-Germanic Empire (962-1002) and its Salian successors did nothing to improve the general condition of the Italian people. The political interest of the German emperors was largely confined to the feudal and ecclesiastical organizations, which still operated as foreign bodies on Italian soil. The empire was still German and Roman, not Italian, and of this the population little by little became aware. Only the maritime republics—Venice, Amalfi, Pisa, Genoa—escaped the general political enslavement and the universal prostration of the country. But they encountered other foreign invasions that brought new elements into the motley picture of medieval Italian ethnography.

If German rule left a durable heritage of fair-haired mongrels and everlasting poverty, it saved Italy from the incursions of Asiatic hordes, which settled down permanently in Eastern Europe. The Byzantine garrisons in the South were unable to check the Arab invasion of the Low Country, and after 827 they yielded Sicily to the Saracens. Large groups of Arabs and Berbers settled down permanently on the island under the Aghlabite and Fatimite dynasties and transformed the predominantly Greek population into a flourishing Mohammedan community. In the two centuries of Arab domination large numbers of the native islanders were converted to Islam and joined the invaders in bringing cultural and economic revival to a population enervated by Byzantine administration and the long rule of the torpid Greek clergy. The sweeping success of the Mohammedan conquerors was favored by the total absence of Latin competition. The Byzantine contribution to Sicilian civilization had been dull and poor, while Latin traditions had been almost entirely effaced. Consequently the native population did not accept the new rulers passively, but co-operated with them in an economic and intellectual rebirth. The Sicilians of Greek and Latin stock were greatly benefited by an efficient program of land reclamation through a new system of irrigation. The restored commercial routes to Syria, Mesopotamia, and Egypt favored the introduction of exotic plants and fruits, which enlivened Sicilian agriculture. Intellectual life flourished and the Sicilian Fatimite court became a cultural center emulating the glory of Bagdad, Damascus, and Córdoba.

Mohammedan prestige and influence survived the Arab domination of the island and were still active during the Norman and Swabian dynasties. At that time the arts and crafts of the Near East flourished in Sicily. In the epoch of Roger II, Norman king of Sicily, Apulia, and Capua (1105-54), Mohammedan scholarship was still unchecked, while ecclesiastical and civilian architecture were distinctly inspired by Egyptian and Syrian forms. The Arab domination is still remembered with sympathy by the Sicilian population, whose Oriental features are its most lasting relic. Yet, during the Norman rule large groups of Mohammedan Sicilians were forced to emigrate to Calabria and Apulia, where important Jewish communities of African origin had been enjoying a relative prosperity since the fourth century. They still existed in the epoch of Frederick II (1212-50), but gradually dwindled and vanished along with the Mohammedans,

It was the affinity of the peoples belonging to the old Mediterranean commonwealth that contributed to the racial balance existing within those narrow geographical limits. But that commonwealth was exclusively cultural and quite different from the Germanic society of northern Italy and Europe, largely organized in accordance with the traditions of a military hierarchy. It is consequently in the intellectual and artistic field that the lively interplay of different peoples, tribes, and creeds can be followed through the long series of political changes that occurred in lower Italy during the early Middle Ages. This exceptional confluence of so many interests and traditions created certain paradoxical relations characteristic of Italian cultural development. It was, for example, through Arabic mediation that the first direct knowledge of Greek science, philosophy, and medicine was acquired in southern Italy, where the medical faculty of Salerno developed the first professional school of lasting international reputation. Latin culture, on the other hand, was reintroduced into Sicily by the same Norman conquerors who, in 1084, inflicted upon the city of Rome and its inhabitants the most crushing and ferocious punishment recorded in its history.

For the first time in almost five centuries Latin reappeared in Sicilian documents and chronicles as an official language of the state, just as the new conquerors were destroying the last vestiges of the Eastern empire in the southernmost regions of the peninsula. The Normans of the conquering dynasty of Hauteville and their bands of enterprising knights did not come to Italy as Northmen, but as Frenchmen who had completely forgotten their Scandinavian ancestry. They were accompanied by prelates and clerics who had received their modest religious and literary training in the schools of Bayeux, Caen, or Jumièges and spoke French with a Norman accent. They encountered unbroken Latin tradition in the newly subdued continental provinces of the Norman kingdom of Italy, of which Salerno was the political and intellectual capital, Montecassino the leading cultural center, and Bari the easternmost city.

In all these lower provinces of Italy, the Byzantine traditions survived the conquest and the new Latinization of the country.

The cultural link with the Eastern empire was even intensified by the influx of Byzantine artists and craftsmen who helped to build and decorate the magnificent churches and palaces of the continental and insular Norman domain. Never was the Eastern influence upon Italy's cultural and artistic life stronger and richer than at the apex of the Norman rule when, in 1130, King Roger proclaimed himself *Rex Italiae* and became the unopposed master of the whole Italian south. The shining mosaics of Palermo and Venice, the church gates of Pisa and Benevento still remind one of the predominance of the Greek style, taste, and spirit in that age.

❋   ❋   ❋

This Byzantine Italy was not limited to the glorious days of Ravenna, when the Eastern empire still had a political foothold in the country. The Lombards expelled the last exarch in 751, and four years later the town and its Adriatic dominion became a papal territory. It was through direct and lively relations with Constantinople that the Byzantine influence in many fields of Italian life persisted even in those parts of Italy where Greek was never spoken.

A noteworthy phenomenon of this epoch was the Italian reaction against the iconoclastic decree of 726 and the Byzantine trend that was pursued for more than a century. The revolt was unanimous; it gave the Italian people their first opportunity to express sentiments in agreement with those of the Roman pontiff and the Lombard and Frankish rulers. The cult of images was retained throughout Italy as an almost national manifestation of religious tradition. Yet this unanimous attitude inspired no commensurate artistic expression. The *maniera greca* continued to dominate Italian painting and sculpture up to the end of the thirteenth century.

It was as a reaction against this style and tradition, and not against any French or German influence, that the first known Italian painters, from Cimabue to Masaccio, created a new personal and national style. Until that time the sacred images preserved the Greek patterns handed down by workmen unaware of the spiritual background of their rigid, foreign creations. The

Italian people evidently accepted and needed them as one of the few stable and familiar expressions of their spiritual traditions; it is certain that they interpreted these outlandish, wonder-working, unrealistic features as an immutable, ultimate, and perennial mark of supernatural remoteness.

What the workshops did for the preservation of Eastern models in the Italian area, the schools did for Latin letters. In such leading institutions as the Irish monastery of Bobbio, the Langobardic and Frankish court schools of Pavia, the Abbey of Montecassino, the threadbare Latin kept alive by monks and schoolmasters only served ecclesiastical, courtly, practical, and professional purposes, but had no direct connection with the multitudes whose *lingua romana rustica,* or Vulgar Latin, deprived them not only of all culture but even of literacy. Hence the rhetorical and artificial character of a scholarly idiom detached from the classical sources of its vitality and never reanimated by any personal touch or flash of original inspiration. No portion of the writings of Paulus Diaconus, the Langobard historian of the eighth century, or of Luitprand of Cremona, Lanfranc of Pavia, Desiderius of Montecassino, and countless other historians, jurists, and theologians, was ever embodied in the intellectual patrimony of the nation. To the learned Luitprand, who went to Constantinople in 968 as ambassador of Otto the Great, the first Roman emperor of Germanic birth, the Byzantine Emperor Nikephoros Phocas, said: 'You are Lombards, not Romans:' [1] a particularly burning insult two centuries after the end of Langobardic rule over Italy. But the Emperor was substantially right.

In that same year the Neapolitan archpriest Leo translated into Latin prose a late Hellenistic romance about Alexander the Great; he had brought the original text from Constantinople and presented it to Duke John of Campania and his learned Roman wife, Theodora. This was the origin of a secular cycle of heroic legends that spread through Italy and the Western World and became the only literary heritage of those dark ages of Italian history. It preceded in popularity and universal favor the poeti-

[1] Legatio, ch. 12.

cal history of Charlemagne. Except in the monasteries, Scipio and Marius, Caesar and Pompey, Augustus and Hadrian were forgotten, as were all those Roman heroes not mentioned in the stories of martyrs and saints. The fundamental concept of the divine mission of the Roman Empire was powerless to keep alive the memory of the pagan glories of Rome. It was the epics of the Macedonian conqueror of the East and the legend of the Frankish emperor of the West that struck the imagination of the Italian people. For the Italian masses the heroes of Rome went down with the heathen gods.

What were the Italians, i.e. the native population of the peninsula, after more than five hundred years of foreign and mostly barbarous domination, after the absorption of heterogeneous racial groups and immigrants from every corner of the world? Was there any definite ethnical, racial, cultural, spiritual, social physiognomy? Nothing is known about the character, education, experience, feelings, and aspirations of the masses in this period; generations passed without leaving the slightest trace. The documents handed down by literati and politicians are misleading and irrelevant. As for the clerics, they were only a part of this amorphous, mysterious, fluctuating society, whose exceptional, contingent, and unreal aspects they sometimes reveal—but never the normal, human, and natural. It is too often forgotten that even in those dark ages people lived as human beings, feeling love and hate, having beliefs and opinions, founding families and finding friends, liking songs, dances, and jokes, patronizing taverns, appreciating good life, and fearing death and disease.

There is only one early document that reveals in a few poor words the existence of these forgotten multitudes and the vital instrument of their future greatness. In 960 there was a lawsuit in Capua to establish the borders of the territory belonging to the Abbey of Montecassino. Most of the judges, witnesses, and notaries involved had Germanic names, such as Rodelgrim, Garibert, Teodomund, Adenulf, Arechis; a Marcus and a Petrus constituted a Latin minority. The charter is Latin, but the deposition of the witnesses has been handed down in a vernacular form. This is the first document showing the existence of an Italian language independent of Latin, although derived from

it; it showed no Germanic influence.[2] For those who spoke that
vernacular Italian language, Latin was as un-understandable as
any German dialect. Five centuries of common life in homes and
streets, workshops and markets, had developed this still uncouth
language of the masses.

What these anonymous and forgotten masses could do when
left free to develop their vital energies is impressively told by
the early history of the Venetian republic. Since the early mass
invasions of the Huns, Goths, and Langobards, fugitives from
the prosperous Roman towns of the Venetian plain (Padua,
Aquileia, Altinum, Grado, etc.) settled on the squalid little
islands and sandbars of the estuary because they preferred a
free life in dangerous isolation to enslavement by foreign op-
pressors. By the end of the seventh century this group of little
islands had created an independent confederation, of which
Rialto became, in 811, the political and economic center. The
whole story of this first free Italian community is written in
stone in the monuments of Venice. The foundation of its famous
landmark, the campanile, which collapsed in 1902, revealed the
imperial seals of its earliest days. Venice was the only spot in
the whole peninsula that remained free from foreign domination
throughout the fourteen centuries of its existence, from the last
days of the Roman Empire until the Napoleonic peace of
Campoformio, in 1797. Throughout all her dealings with Greeks
and Turks, Saracens and Germans, Venice never ceased to be
an active member of the Italian linguistic and cultural community.

[2] 'Sao co kelle terre per kelle fini que ki contene trenta anni le possette
parte Sancti Benedicti.'

III. *The Italian People Between Papacy*
and Empire

I N the early centuries of the Middle Ages the Italian people
consisted of diverse ethnic and linguistic groups held together by force of arms and the fear of God. Yet the naturally
defined geographical space and a similarity of living conditions
determined by the relative uniformity of the soil and climate
were factors favoring the fusion of all these disparate elements.
Ultimately the invaders were linguistically and culturally assimilated by the indigenous Italian majority. Almost complete religious unity was achieved through the total conversion of the
Langobards to the Catholic faith by the end of the seventh
century and the dissolution, after the Norman Conquest, of the
last substantial Greek and Mohammedan groups in the Low
Country.

During this long process of linguistic, spiritual, and ethnic
equalization several attempts were made by the conquering and
ruling dynasties to achieve complete domination of Italy from
the Alps to the southern shores of Sicily. But the unifying forces
always encountered an insuperable barrier in the historical and
divine right of two universal powers to rule the country in order
to rule the world.

The conflicts between national and universal trends in Italian
history seem to lie far in the past. In reality they have persisted
under different aspects until our day; although often obscured,
they have remained at the core of Italy's political, spiritual, and
cultural destiny. Rome as the center and fountainhead of two
universal institutions has always been the pride but also the

tragedy of Italy. The Italian people has always wanted to be Catholic, but not necessarily papal; it has always felt Roman, but not necessarily imperial. Never since the fall of Rome did the Empire dominate all of Italy, never was apostolic universalism fully accepted. World unity was never attained under papal or imperial auspices—nor even the unity of Italy herself.

The only legitimate claims to Italian rule were those of the Eastern Empire, which found intelligent and heroic leaders to support them. Belisarius and Narses had many brave and successful emulators during the Byzantine domination of the southern provinces. Venice, Amalfi, Naples, and other important centers still recognized the Byzantine suzerainty when the Eastern Empire had lost the Exarchate of Ravenna (A.D. 754) to the Franks and the Adriatic towns of Ancona, Senigallia, Fano, Pesaro, and Rimini to the pope. Throughout the Langobard, Frankish, and Ottonian domination there remained a strong current favorable to the Greeks. We know little about Italian public opinion in those remote epochs, but there can be no doubt that large strata of the population preferred the sovereignty of the corrupt Byzantine court to that of the barbaric German invaders. The rule of a Greek governor in Bari, Taranto, and other places in the south was certainly milder and economically less burdensome than the direct and oppressive domination of the German nobles. At the time of the Norman Conquest, when Pope Nicholas II wilfully invested Robert Guiscard, in 1059, with the imperial territories of Apulia and Calabria, large numbers of the people still favored the Greeks. Later they found temporary support among the native population when the Byzantine emperor Manuel Comnenus made, from 1155 to 1158, the last attempt to reconquer the Empire's lost possessions on the Italian peninsula.

There is evidence of a strong and active anti-German Greek party in Rome during the late Carolingian and the Ottonian period. It was perhaps instrumental in fomenting the popular revolt against Pope Leo III, who had bestowed the imperial crown upon Charlemagne and by that fateful gesture destroyed the Christian unity of the world for all time. Otto III (d. 1002) aspired to restore a universal empire with Byzantine forms and principles, and organized his Roman court and administration accordingly. His imperial dream was destroyed by the Roman populace, which two generations later helped Henry IV to avenge himself for the humiliation of Canossa, inflicted on him in 1077 by Pope Gregory VII. The concept of a universal authority asserted by this great pontiff represented a theocratic Latin version of the Byzantine cosmocracy. Gregory died a prisoner and an exile, not because—as he is said to have proclaimed—he loved justice and hated iniquity, but because of his authoritarian meddling in the secular concerns of his time.

At that time the Roman Church was not a universal but an Italian power, basing its right to territorial and political expansion upon the boldest and most successful forgery in history. This was the 'Donation of Constantine,' concocted by Roman jurists in the eighth century. So skillful was the forgery that for half a millennium it supported the papal claims to temporal domination of Rome, Italy, and the West. A hundred years later another forgery, known as 'Pseudo-Isidorian Decretals,' was added in order to regulate the juridical powers of the pontiff in relation to the ecclesiastical and civil authorities in every part of the Christian world. This voluminous falsification was produced in France in the ninth century, but accepted by the Roman court as a basic legal code. So great was the deference to the spiritual power of the Church that up to the fifteenth century no one dared publicly question the authenticity of these documents. Their juridical and practical justification lay in the fact that the Church could not exert its authority without a legal basis. If the Church, as a political institution, proclaimed itself the heir of Constantine's dominion, it was because at the epoch of the forged 'Donation,' and for many centuries to come, no universal domination, territorial or spiritual, could be conceived except in terms of a Roman empire. The 'Donation' was not invented in order to cheat the world, but out of a political state of mind that conceived of sovereignty only in traditional and consecrated forms. It was only by legal means or by force of arms that the secular powers could counteract the papal claims to Italian territory. When the spiritual authority of the Church made use of excommunications, interdicts, and threats of damnation to support its temporal claims, the secular powers riposted by creating anti-popes and appointing rival bishops.

The story of the war of the investitures has been told by many authors. Here it need merely be recalled that Italy was not only the stage, but also the victim of that unresolved and therefore tragic conflict which embraced the moral as well as the practical foundations of medieval civilization. When the Langobardic kingdom under Desiderius (d. 774) threatened to become an Italian nation, Pope Leo III thwarted this development by urging Frankish intervention and creating the Carolingian Kingdom of Italy. From then on the territorial possessions of the Church cut the peninsula into two sections which were never joined again until the Napoleonic domination and the Italian Risorgimento. Since that time it was the consistent policy of the pontiffs to consolidate and increase these possessions by preventing any secular power—the German conquerors, the Norman invaders, or the Swabian emperors—from extending their domination over the whole country. This destroyed any possibility of a world unity dominated by either of the two powers, or of a unified Italy which might have been achieved under imperial sponsorship or an independent feudal regime. The basic political principle of the Church for the entire duration of its temporal power was to prevent Milan, the center of religious, cultural, commercial, and banking interests in northern Italy, from belonging to the same political unit as Naples, key to the Mediterranean and point of convergence of the West and the East. This simple axiom, calculated to protect its sovereignty and independence, also explains every move of the Church against the national unification of the country from the Langobardic expansion to 1870.

Since the epoch of Gregory the Great (590-604) the papacy had become almost exclusively a political power; its authority rested on its ecclesiastical organization rather than on its spiritual activity or cultural achievements. This accounts for the rigid traditionalism of the sacred arts in Italy during the Middle Ages and the persistence of Greek forms and motifs. Over a period of almost a thousand years, from Ambrosius (d. 397) to Thomas Aquinas (d. 1274), no theological thinker, no philosophical writer, no poet or scientist was active in the Italian community. Even monasticism took on a political stamp, as the ecclesiastical counterpart of Germanic feudalism. Shortly after St. Benedict founded his monastery at Montecassino, in 529, his famous rule of life and devotion lost much of its influence on Italian monasticism, the spiritual authority of which never attained an importance comparable to that of Cluny, Cîteaux, and other French orders. The severe discipline of the learned and passionate Nilus of Rossano, who, in the second half of the tenth century, lived in a Calabrian cave as a hermit possessed by the spirit of earliest Christianity, was an isolated Italian manifestation of a Byzantine trend that found few followers and little understanding in the rest of the country. Even the late revival of the strict Benedictine rule through the founders of the Italian orders of the Camaldolesi, in 1012, and the Vallombrosani, in 1015, was not important as a spiritual or social movement but merely represented an increased tendency toward asceticism and mortification of the flesh.

Early monasticism was an Oriental concept of spiritual existence, totally alien to Latin traditions, habits, and institutions. It offered a haven to those who preferred seclusion to activity and it opposed an orderly life under strict collective rules to the anarchy and insecurity of secular society. The large abbeys of Nonantola and Bobbio, Novalesa and Polirone, Farfa, Montecassino, and several others were the fortified centers of large and wealthy landed estates. Ever since the flight of Cassiodorus from the turbulent, barbarous Rome of the Goths, the libraries of these abbeys had preserved the literary remnants of pagan antiquity. But the laity drew little inspiration from these isolated centers of a poor monastic scholarship.

It seems appropriate at this point to inquire what human reasons may account for the survival of the papacy through a protracted period of conflicts and dangers, when forgeries, intrigues, assassinations, conspiracies, and other factional undertakings seemed to be the only means of preserving this divine institution and safeguarding the very person of the pontiff.

Before becoming the overlord of a large political domain, the Bishop of Rome was one of the richest and most powerful of

Italian landowners. St. Peter's patrimony was an important secular domain, and after Pippin's donation (754), the transfer of
Tuscan territories (1082) and the cession of the principality of
Benevento (1052) to the Holy See, it became one of the leading
sovereign powers of Italy.

This gradual expansion of the Pope's temporal possessions was
accomplished through donations and bequests to the 'Apostle'
or the Church. In the early period the popes had no effective
military organization. Consequently the Roman Church had to
rely more than other religious or secular institutions upon political dealings and juridical expedients. It seems no accident
that Italian intelligence during the high Middle Ages was manifested to a great extent in the field of jurisprudence, a discipline
which, for better or worse, attained its first original development
under imperial, but above all papal, auspices.

In these first centuries of her formation Italy became a country of lawyers and notaries, of officials and judges, not of
theologians and warriors, or of scholars and artists. This characteristic cultural phenomenon was not merely a Roman heritage
but resulted also from the particular structure of early Italian
society, with its inextricable entanglement of legal claims, acquired rights, judiciary customs, juridical competencies, and
diversified concepts of law. The papacy was the true laboratory
of a new empirical and pragmatic jurisprudence based on Roman
traditions and a training in grammar and rhetoric. The coronation of Charlemagne by Leo III gave rise to unprecedented
juridical problems which forced the emperors and their representatives in Italy to multiply their legal counselors and to intensify the study of law. In a rapidly changing society, the very
definition of temporal and spiritual powers required the continuous interpretation and adaptation of juridical concepts and
procedures. Even the sincerest intention to render unto Caesar
that which is Caesar's and unto God that which is God's could
not in itself clarify the theological, political, and juridical implications of this fundamental principle, which was supposed to
regulate the relations between Church and State. It lost its
meaning and became a source of disruptive conflicts when the
ecclesiastical feudalism established under the Frankish sover-

eignty granted the same rights and privileges to the lay and to the ecclesiastical nobility. From this point on, the pope invested his protégés with territorial benefits, just as the emperor distributed ecclesiastical offices and dignities among his henchmen. Both pope and emperor were the chiefs of a clerical nobility and a political hierarchy with overlapping rights and duties.

The forged donation of Constantine was a radical attempt to do away with all controversies over the application of that divine maxim by establishing papal supremacy in the temporal affairs of the old imperial domain. The struggle over investiture had no stronger juridical basis than this falsification. As a temporal power the Church had to elaborate a system of laws defining the principles of its authority, its internal structure, and its foreign relations.

In support of its doctrines and institutions the Roman Church developed, even in its darkest ages, an extensive juridical system, a skilled bureaucracy, and an unsurpassed political organization. The papacy gave the Italian people a continuous political and juridical education, but no direct cultural inspiration or intellectual stimulus comparable to those that emanated from the courts and orders, the convents and brotherhoods of the late Middle Ages. Rome might have been removed from the history of medieval Italian culture without creating any sense of loss. Paradoxically enough, the Church made itself felt in Italian life largely as a pragmatic force. Mainly for these reasons, the political papacy was a failure, ending in disaster after a brief and illusory triumph over the secular powers.

As a mundane institution the Roman Church was protected by its awe-inspiring sacerdotal power and by the deference in which legal rights were then generally held. Even the forgeries perpetrated by its jurists show the great respect of medieval society for the forms of legality. But all the busy notaries and professional legists who worked in the interest of ecclesiastical institutions would never have succeeded in upholding the secular power and enormous wealth of the Church if its hierarchy, offices, and dignities had not been supported by a social organization unique in medieval Italian society. The Church was the only sphere of medieval life open to all classes of the popula-

C

tion. The sacerdotal office was open, under certain conditions,
to everybody, independent of origin and class. Bishops were
elected by the clergy and people of the cathedral town, and the
popes were elected, until 1059, and even later, by the clergy and
the acclamation of the people of Rome.

*   *   *

The importance of this exceptional circumstance becomes evident if the structure of lay medieval society is considered. The
feudal aristocracy, the crafts, and all other occupations in medieval Italian society were based on a hereditary principle. For
an individual to shift from one class to another was impossible
and even inconceivable. The Church alone traversed all social
ranks. The urban communities still preserved some last vestige
of the old Roman republican spirit as a traditional, unconscious
heritage from the days of the early Roman Church. The early
Roman Church did not inherit the Roman Empire but the Roman
republic. The ideas and forms of autocracy, monarchy, despotism, adopted by the pagan and later on by the Christian emperors of the West and the East, were all of Eastern origin and
totally alien to Latin traditions. After the triumph of Oriental
tyranny, the lower classes alone preserved, under Christian auspices, a remnant of the Roman democratic spirit that was able
to manifest itself only in those communities unaffected by the
growing influence of imperial despotism. It may be assumed
that the rapid growth of the early Christian communities was
favored by the concourse of people who found in their free and
democratic organization a spiritual, human, and collective substitute for the Latin liberties lost to the hated imperial autocracy.

The early Roman churches were assembly halls in which something of the old Latin elective system survived in an unpolitical
organization of religious and democratic character. The Germanic invasions and the ultimate dissolution of Roman society
only consolidated these traditions in a form that may appear
shadowy and even degenerate, but was strong enough to make
the Roman people feel that the successor of St. Peter was their
own exponent, a sovereign raised up with their co-operation
and under their control. The popes were invested with sovereign
authority by popular consent, just as the Roman emperors as-

sumed their office and dignity as deputies and trustees of the Roman people. The same procedure prevailed in the election of bishops. The old municipal traditions were preserved in their church assemblies rather than in the civil administration, especially in northern Italy, where the Latin population had for centuries been excluded by its Germanic masters from participation in governmental and political affairs. The Italian communes of the twelfth century did not arise, as political entities, from the markets and courts, but from the cathedrals and the public gatherings within their walls.

After 1059, popes were elected without popular consent, but not the bishops in Italian towns, as the Milanese revolts of 1075 and 1103 impressively show. The refusal of the towns to accept bishops appointed by papal or imperial authority, without the approval of the local congregation, contributed essentially to their communal autonomy. Only in their churches did all classes of society meet as apparent equals. Long years of social upheaval were needed before this republican spirit emerged from the church communities into the secular sphere of local political life.

In the period of feudalism this participation of the lower classes in the election of spiritual leaders provided with temporal powers seems to have been a mere formality. At that time the bishops were frequently feudatories appointed by sovereigns who were not greatly concerned over popular consent. In Rome the popes were the puppets of the local barons, often the protégés of their women. In these cases popular acclamation was little more than a traditional rite, all the more so since the elections were manipulated by bribery and armed intervention. Yet the importance of symbolic acts cannot be underestimated in a society accustomed to accept ceremonial gestures as substantial reality. The popular acclamation of a secular or ecclesiastical ruler, with all the ceremonies, festivals, and rites connected with it, was a constitutive and legal act extended to all the faithful, and consequently implying universal consent. Without this formal public participation an episcopal and papal election was void and arbitrary. When, with Gregory VII, the papacy assumed the forms and ideas of an autocratic power; and when at the same time feudalism attained the apogee of its influence on

Italian life, it was from these traditional expressions of ancient democratic rights that the lower classes regained consciousness of their strength and initiative for political action.

The influence of feudalism confirmed the Roman Church in its role as a political power. The similarity of their hierarchical systems created an interdependence between the ecclesiastical and feudal organizations. The lasting lack of spiritual leadership in the papacy, in Italian monasticism, and in all ranks of the clergy predisposed the Church to the political corruption and social disorder characteristic of Italian feudalism. The vital forces of medieval Catholicism came from France and Germany; in Italy the Church almost ceased to be a bestower of peace and became a mere distributor of benefices. The concept of investiture is also a feudal one and the enforcement of papal decrees or ecclesiastical laws always required the support of lay authorities which the Church could command as feudal subordinates. The power of the bishops, the possessions of the monastic orders, regularly conflicted with the rights and competencies of sovereigns, feudatories, nobles, and municipalities. At that time no dogmatic or spiritual principles were involved in the quarrels between the ecclesiastical and secular authorities, but exclusively questions of power and property. The chief issue consisted in the landed possessions, the revenue, the administration of justice, the military and fiscal obligations of the churches and monasteries.

As the ecclesiastical organization could not function without benefit of earthly goods, and neither arms nor laws were adequate safeguards to Church property, the clergy invoked spiritual sanctions and ecclesiastical threats, much to the detriment of their own prestige. The widespread practice of buying and trading ecclesiastical dignities helped to bring about the rapid moral disintegration of the Italian Church. Since the plague of simony involved the Roman court as much as the sovereigns and the nobility, the measures to combat it suggested by several pontiffs, such as Leo IX and Gregory VII, by German emperors, such as Henry III, or by French reformers, achieved no lasting results. In the end Italy stood discredited throughout the Christian world.

The commercial skill that marks the most characteristic aspect of Italian participation in the Crusades found a vast field of activity in connection with Church properties and dignities which were now traded in a sort of open political market. The phenomenon existed elsewhere in Europe, but nowhere did it assume such proportions. In France simony was kept within bounds by the higher moral level of her feudal nobility, by the influence of a daring intellectual renewal, by the spiritual and monastic reform of Bernard de Clairvaux and his followers. Spain was inspired by the enterprises of the Cid and the national and religious effort of the *reconquista*. In Italy the almost uninterrupted line of Italian and generally Roman-born pontiffs was broken by a series of German popes who attempted a housecleaning. But simony was too deeply rooted in the Italian variety of feudalism, and worldly interests were too dominant in the higher classes of Italian society.

The immediate political consequence of this state of affairs was that the corruption of the Italian clergy gave the German emperors a moral pretext for intervening in the public as well as the ecclesiastical administration of the country and for substituting German bishops for those appointed by the pontiffs. In the social field the outcome was even more portentous: the venality of the clergy destroyed the last remnants of the old corporate spirit of the churches, already reduced to a phantom by the increasing power of the ecclesiastical feudatories. The immense mass of the poor, who could not participate in simoniacal bargains, had to accept with passive resignation what was imposed on them from above. The lower clergy were deprived of all chances to rise in the hierarchy, and had to fulfill all the duties of their ministry under the curse of a proletarian existence.

The reaction against these iniquitous conditions did not come from the clergy but from the lower classes of the Italian laity. This was the source of the desperate revolts and heretical movements that swept the country and ended in rebellions against the ecclesiastical hierarchy as well as the feudal authorities. The great popular movements of the eleventh and twelfth centuries resulted not from a national but from a moral stimulus, although other circumstances contributed to the events from which modern Italy emerged as a country unified in spirit, language, and destiny, if not in government and sovereignty.

The moral impulse in these popular upheavals is revealed by the violent antagonism of the people to marriage among the clergy, a typical ecclesiastical custom of those ages. Although repeatedly condemned by theologians and popes, simony and concubinage were the customary consequences of ecclesiastical feudalism, because both implied worldly property and the privilege of increasing it by feudal intermarriage. These revolts of the common people, called *pataria* after Milan's rag-fair, involved no theological questions such as occurred in later heretical movements. In the eleventh century the ignorance even of the higher clergy was at its nadir; intellectual problems existed only for the very few.

The vast underworld of feudal society became conscious of its power when those popes who were determined to carry out reform of the clergy called on the discontented masses for support. It was only with the help of the lower classes that the papal excommunication and deposition of the ecclesiastical feudatories in the rich North Italian dioceses could be enforced against the resistance of the emperors who sided with the dispossessed dignitaries. Thereby all the classes the feudal system had excluded from participation in political life once again joined in electing or confirming their spiritual and temporal leaders. It was around this first political nucleus of plebeian origin that merchants and artisans, urban landowners, and public officials gathered in a still amorphous and unstable organization intended to protect the decency of public life, the moral principles of their faith, and the interests of their various social classes. This revolutionary state of mind was fostered by the superstitious fear that the sacraments imparted by unworthy priests might be void and prevent salvation. Again the church became a meeting hall for the urban laity, which emerged from darkness and servitude with new emblems, banners, rites, and slogans.

It was solely a critical attitude toward current abuses that brought about these associations of a mixed religious, political, and social character in the eleventh century. The Italian communes were not founded with any clearly defined program. There were no revolutionary doctrines behind the movements that led to the creation of the Italian city-states. Nor was the economic development of the principal urban centers as decisive in this evolution as is generally supposed. Not only the rich and populous city of Milan was seized by this republican whirlwind, but even the small and poor towns in Lombardy, Emilia, Venetia, Tuscany, and Apulia, including many that participated only indirectly in the increasing prosperity of the country. Moreover, the Italian communal revolutions coincided with the vast religious movements inspired by the glorification of poverty and a commonage of goods. When the social reformers of the eleventh and twelfth centuries proclaimed that 'we hold all our possessions in common with all men,'[1] their goal was general participation in a consecrated poverty, not in the wealth and production of their day.

The communes did not begin as a revolutionary movement aiming at the introduction of democratic liberties in the towns. It was only much later, in the second half of the thirteenth century, that democratic institutions were created on a constitutional basis, with the abolition of rural slave labor and the restriction of political life and power to the *arti*, or associations of trades and industries. And even at that advanced period of communal development the word 'liberty,' so frequently employed by statesmen, politicians, chroniclers, and poets of that epoch, had little to do with our modern concepts of freedom. Despite a decided trend toward municipal self-government, the population of the Italian towns accepted their bishops, respected the popes, and recognized the authority of the emperors, provided communal interests were protected, pacts were fulfilled, and no arbitrary interference with established rights was attempted by the representatives of the universal and foreign powers.

Without insisting on details of local history, it can be said that all the Italian communes arose through a voluntary association of the different classes and sections of the urban population for the purpose of participating in the choice of their local offi-

[1] Landulfus, *Historia Mediolanensis, Monumenta Germaniae Historica*, VIII, p. 65.

cials, ecclesiastical as well as secular. There was no violent separation of Church and State, but instead a collaboration of the elected municipal representatives with the episcopal feudatories and officials—the so-called *valvassori* and *capitani*—on the one hand, and with the imperial vicars and envoys on the other. The circumstances did not always make for mutual good will, but this spirit of co-operation was the prevalent mood. At the same time, the townspeople were determined to carry on their civic business when internal troubles or outside interference left the episcopal see vacant or kept out the imperial officials. In any case, associative trends antagonistic to the hierarchical ethos of Church and Empire were predominant and decisive in these civic revolutions. It is in this spirit that the revival of old Roman republican traditions must be interpreted.

There can be no doubt that in conferring the title of 'consul' on the representatives of the people, the communes intended a classical, republican challenge to both forms of autocracy. The title appears in Pisa in 1081, but was current at an earlier date in the maritime republics of the Low Country. Its use soon became general in all Italian towns. The term is no bookish reminiscence; it was appropriately selected because of the similarity of the new authority with the Roman consulate, which also represented and embodied the community of the people and, in the republican period, was shared by a patrician and a plebeian. The procedure of electing the consuls by acclamation in a popular assembly was much the same. During the hundred years' existence of the consular magistracy in Italian communes, it was the policy of the people to transfer more and more administrative and juridical power from the bishops to the consuls, and to confine the episcopal authority to spiritual and ecclesiastical matters.

By the twelfth century the system of popular suffrage had passed entirely into the secular field. The old Roman associative trend came into open conflict with the Germanic spirit of subordination, embodied in the feudal system, and with the form of Oriental despotism assumed by the papal regime under the direct influence of the Byzantine autocracy. The history of the medieval communes reflects the interaction of these three traditional forces and not the emergence of any new ideas or ambitions. In the formation of the Italian people those three elements sometimes worked together and often came to an open and disastrous clash. There is no essential feature of the agitated history of that epoch that cannot be traced back to the effect of one or more of these forces operating in the very depths of the universal, national, regional, and local scene, and involving the social classes, the economic interests, the political objectives, and the general structure of medieval society.

c*

IV. *Republican Democracy—German Feudalism—Papal Autocracy*

THE associative spirit of the Italians was not merely a Latin heritage or a natural gift; it was also the consequence of long subjection to foreign peoples and sovereigns. Local rivalries were certainly as prevalent in Italy as anywhere else; deep-rooted racial and religious grudges made them indeed particularly embittered and lasting. But six or seven centuries of political enslavement and social degradation at the hands of foreign invaders undoubtedly bred in all classes of the population a sense of solidarity and kinship that overcame many of the class barriers prevailing in other medieval societies. The famous German chronicler Otto von Freising (d. 1158), who wrote the history of Barbarossa's Italian expeditions, reported from firsthand experience that the Italians not only preferred to be ruled by their elected consuls rather than by their constitutional sovereigns, but actually forced the most powerful feudatories to submit to the civic authorities of their district. They even went so far 'as to invest with the insignia and dignity of nobility young men of lower ranks and workmen in the mechanical trades, elsewhere banished like a pestilence from all noble and free occupations.'[1]

This is eloquent and reliable evidence of the existence of a civic spirit stronger than class consciousness. Many of the popular leaders were prelates or members of the highest aristocracy, as, for instance, Archbishop Heribert of Antimiano, who organized, in 1037, the first Milanese resistance against the emperor;

[1] *Gesta Friderici Imperatoris*, ii, ch. 13.

or the nobleman Lanzo, whose resolute democratic policy, after 1043, broke the supremacy of the local aristocracy in the administration of municipal affairs. In many other communes the nobility participated actively in popular uprisings and the drafting of republican constitutions. The Italian nobility were not too reluctant to participate in the breaking down of feudal barriers that had been set up in accordance with foreign principles, customs, and laws. This widespread feeling of popular co-operation was not a sudden explosion of democratic enthusiasm, but the result of a long tradition that, in the course of centuries, had attracted and seduced many of the foreign settlers, nobles, and officials.

An expression of this process of mutual adjustment may be found in the peaceful relations between the people of city and country. A good-neighbor policy extended the urban influence into the rural settlements, called *contadi* after the landowning suburban counts. In many cases the rural population gave the townspeople strong support in their struggle for freedom and independence. The rural population generally sided with the insurgent towns in their conflicts with the powerful imperial or ecclesiastical feudatories. In spite of the strong and repeated intervention of Frederick Barbarossa and the scattered resistance of those Italian nobles who were allied by marriage or interest with foreign potentates, this powerful associative undercurrent destroyed the foundations of Italian feudalism in less than a century and opened up the greater part of the country to civic liberties and a powerful organization of the middle classes.

On the other hand, the readiness of the aristocracy to accept plebeians in their ranks gave these military and political upstarts a strong consciousness of their own power and of the intrinsic weakness of feudal institutions. An immediate consequence of the interpenetration of the classes was that many of the great cities, following the example of Milan, organized the neighboring towns into leagues calculated to preserve their liberties against the common enemy. The part played by the Lombard League in the struggle against Barbarossa was one of the most noteworthy achievements of the Italian people.

Almost the whole country was united in this spirit, although
some towns and feudal lords of northern Italy still invoked imperial protection for the preservation of their rights and possessions. In the south the Norman domination, sponsored by the
popes as a bulwark against imperial and Byzantine expansion,
proved no obstacle to this characteristic Italian evolution, which
was transforming the whole structure of the wealthiest and most
active regions. Wherever these associative and federative tendencies prevailed, they contributed to the stabilization of the
medieval social order on a basis of compromise and co-operation.
The balance of political privileges and administrative powers
achieved by the communal insurrections contributed to such
great public enterprises as the construction of fortifications, aqueducts, fountains, bridges, streets, and public buildings; but it
did not prevent factional strife or civic revolts, family feuds, or
religious conflicts. The co-operative trends did however give rise
to a cultural community and a secular mentality that differed
from those of neighboring countries, although remaining within
the framework of the general contemporary civilization.

The most striking manifestations of this renewed associative
and federative trend survived the political consequences of the
communal revolutions. When the principle of co-operation between classes was substituted for the Germanic and feudal system of subordination, the problem arose of giving the new institutions a juridical basis. At first the federative leagues required
only an oath of mutual loyalty that still had a definite feudal
color and savor. But the necessity was felt of defining the power
of the consuls and regulating public life in general. In changing
the structure of the communities and in altering the traditional
conceptions of property, legality, and legitimacy, the civic revolutions created a state of lawlessness. By the middle of the
eleventh century the Germanic laws handed down by Langobardic and Frankish tradition had lost their practical justification in most of Italy, while the foundations for a system of
Roman law had not yet been rebuilt. This juridical vacuum became apparent at an early date. The Salian Emperor Conrad II
said to his German courtiers, before entering the country in
1036: 'If Italy yearns so much for laws, I shall give her plenty

with God's help.' But the Italians wanted laws of their own and
found a new and secular way of rendering unto God that which
is God's and unto Caesar that which is Caesar's.

The revival of Roman law coincides exactly with the establishment of the Italian communes and was first formulated and
put into practice by the famous jurist Irnerius, born in 1055, who
founded the first independent Italian school of law in Bologna
after a long career as juridical counselor to popes, feudatories,
bishops, and towns. There were indeed jurists and lawyers in
Italy before him, working for the papal chancery, for the kings
of Pavia, and for the local authorities in Ravenna, Venice, and
other places. But they were, as far as we can see from their
threadbare and shapeless works, opportunists and hacks. What
remained of the Roman codes was regarded as a sacrosanct and
inviolable authority. In the foreword of his famous *Corpus Juris*
Justinian represented it as a work of divine inspiration. But it
was certainly in the renewed communal spirit that the Roman
law, both in theory and practice, was brought back to its fundamental precept of *suum cuique tribuere*, to give each man his
own. This fundamental maxim of Roman law was applied for
the first time in a fair spirit of compromise and juridical definition when the legal counselors of Frederick Barbarossa and the
Lombard communes met at Roncaglia, in November 1158, a
memorable place and date in the history of Italian law.

The revival of the Roman law presupposed the clarification of
the two principles which again made civic life possible: justice
and authority. The leading legists at the school of Bologna during the era of juridical pioneering in the twelfth and thirteenth
centuries did not content themselves with glossing the *Corpus
Juris* and the other sources of Roman law, but strove hard to
clarify its moral basis, both philosophically and empirically.
They all realized that a secular legislation could not be applied
to the new conditions and attitudes without some generally
accepted theoretical principles. Antagonistic forces prevented
the materialization of these ideals beyond the juridical sphere,
but the trace of this intensive preoccupation with the law still
survives in the theory and practice of Italian jurisprudence, in the
lofty traditions of the Italian magistracy, and in the deferential

attitude of the whole people, including criminals, toward the person and office of a judge. Many centuries of arbitrary and despotic legislation in different epochs of Italian history have, throughout Italy, induced the curious state of mind that respects judges more highly than laws—a circumstance that has always helped to multiply the number of lawyers and lawsuits. A long and hard experience has accustomed the Italian people to regard the judge as the representative of a superior seignorial authority and the laws as arbitrary impositions that can be broken by force, eluded by tricks and eloquence: *fatta la legge, trovato l'inganno.*

In the same period the Italians rediscovered the power of the word and the efficacy of oratorical addresses. They improved so much in their political eloquence that by the middle of the twelfth century Otto von Freising spoke of 'their long-winded sermons after the Italian fashion.' Eloquence is a republican achievement and was practiced in the secular sphere of life where people could speak freely in behalf of their interests and liberties. This kind of eloquence did not come out of books, for not many books were available to laymen. The old Roman orators inspired only those who knew Latin, and their influence was felt mostly in the field of diplomacy. *Oratore* became the current designation of an Italian ambassador.

The masses of the people could be moved only by vernacular eloquence. No example of this early popular oratory has been preserved among the many high-flown Latin speeches handed down in medieval chronicles. But we do know that from the eleventh century on, the people of the Italian towns were continuously harangued by rulers and rebels, who spoke the language of an illiterate population and were able to win them for the most daring and perilous enterprises. There is any amount of evidence to show that Latin was no longer understood by the Italian laymen and very little by the secular clergy. It was at this time that the political speech began to join the sermon as an instrument of popular education. The new forms of political eloquence developed in the *arengo* or *parlamento,* the frequent and tempestuous meetings before or inside the cathedrals, at which town officials were elected by acclamation. Here questions of public administration were discussed and political decisions taken with a sort of plebiscitary consent. This practice was continued until the end of the fifteenth century in the few places that still preserved a vestige of republican institutions.

The popular assemblies also had an almost immediate influence on the structure and architecture of the Italian towns. Toward the end of the eleventh century, first in the northern regions and then in central Italy, all the old cathedrals of the Langobardian and Carolingian epoch were rebuilt in proportions almost unique in the history of Italian architecture. The remains of the old structures, preserved in some of the crypts or in fragmentary parts of the foundations, show the difference between the comparatively insignificant earlier buildings and the monumental new cathedrals of the communal and Romanesque period. In none of the Lombard or Tuscan towns of that time did the population increase enough in one generation to make this sudden reconstruction of old cathedrals necessary for practical reasons alone. This great architectural revival preceded the religious revival by more than a century. Although some of the churches were vastly enlarged, there was no tendency to increase the number of churches. It was the function of the cathedrals as assembly halls that caused them to be rebuilt with spacious aisles capable of holding the greater part of a town's male population.

This characteristic distinguished Italian cathedrals from those of other countries and also determined the later structure and style of Italian church architecture. All the Romanesque and Gothic Italian churches, both in the cities and monasteries, are vast bright halls, with columns and pilasters so arranged as never to disperse an assembly or isolate one of its parts from the whole.

During the feudal period, churches were episcopal or seignorial property and the source of high revenues from tithes, fees, and levies, imposed by authority and enforced at the point of the sword or by the threat of damnation. The Italian people reacted resolutely, sometimes savagely, against those impositions and the habitual abuse of spiritual and legal powers. The religious movements of the twelfth century gained much strength from

the widespread feeling of resentment against this system and
the authorities that kept it alive. In the communal revolution
the cathedrals of the urban centers were erected with public
funds collected from the leading classes or, as in the case of
Ferrara, by donations from wealthy citizens acting in the interest of the community. Thereby, churches became public institutions and ceased to be the sanctimonious investments of
simoniacal benefice hunters. At least they came under the public
control of those sections of the population that contributed to
their construction and maintenance. One of the few contemporary documents preserved in an authentic version shows that the
whole citizenry of Modena, nobles and plebeians alike, participated in deliberations concerning the completion of the town
cathedral. Its construction was begun in 1099 under the direction of the architect Lanfranco. The funds were collected from
the population, probably with contributions by the pious
Countess Mathilda of Canossa, still the feudal sovereign of
the town and region. The architects who built the new cathedrals
came from all over Italy and Europe, and so did the masters
who supervised the decoration. But the manual work was done
by local workmen and artisans.

Only cheap labor and a spirit of civic sacrifice among the
industrious townspeople made these architectural enterprises
possible. It would be wrong to infer from their size and style
that the country was generally prosperous in the period of increasing communal independence. Only a few families enjoyed
a comparatively high income from property and commercial
activity. The overwhelming majority of the population in town
and country was exceedingly poor. The communal revolutions in
most of the Italian cities did not improve general economic conditions. The destruction of property in the upheavals had been
enormous. In 1117, one of the worst earthquakes recorded in
history destroyed many towns in the Lombard plain and interrupted the enthusiastic building activity that had just begun.
The wars between neighboring communes frequently ended with
the demolition of entire towns and the desolation of the suburban
districts. The five military expeditions of Barbarossa, between
1154 and 1175, brought into Italy vast armies that encamped

on the outskirts of the towns, from Milan to Rome, and lived on the land. Long sieges, bloody battles, internal revolts, and finally Barbarossa's destruction of Milan, in 1162, made any normal economic development impossible and obliterated one of the most important centers of Italian commercial and political expansion. Several lesser towns had been sacked, burned, and razed in former expeditions. With the abolition of the consuls and the installation of a *podestà*, or imperial authority, in the cities, their internal structure had to be modified. But for a long time the communal spirit resisted foreign pressure and reactionary trends. The new evolution of public life found a symbolical and practical expression in architecture.

The loss of many republican privileges and the gradual rise of tyrannical regimes under imperial protection did not alter the age-old inclination toward public gatherings and life in the open air. In the course of a few decades the popular assemblies moved from the cathedral to the *piazza,* expressly created as a center of urban life and always showing a strongly secular character. Since the thirteenth century every Italian town has had its main square, which was neither a market place nor a renewed Roman *forum,* but a site characteristic of the new communal life and typical of the Italian town, large or small, old or new. Here ultimately the town hall was erected as a symbol of the wealth, power, and independence of the city. At first, in the early thirteenth century, huge meeting halls, called *palazzi della ragione,* arose in many North Italian towns. Some of these impressive buildings are still landmarks of high historical and architectural interest, as in Milan, Verona, Vicenza, and Padua. As medieval Rome had separate religious and political centers, respectively at St. Peter's and on the Capitoline Hill, so every Italian town marked the separation of Church and State by detaching the episcopal see from the secular center. As can still be observed today, the competition between ecclesiastical and secular authorities was often symbolized in attempts to build the church steeple higher than the town-hall tower, and vice versa. Only in Venice, where a stable form of government preserved a balance between the two powers, did one campanile serve both Church and State. From the beginning most of the *piazze* were equipped with fountains, a useful symbol of devotion to the public welfare.

❦   ❦   ❦

The communal revolutions were not inspired by class hatred, nor did they degenerate into a class struggle for the conquest of political rights. Up to our own day, the social order has been regarded by Italians as something predestined, sacred, and binding, although much earlier than elsewhere it was possible for a man to raise himself to a higher social class. Appointment to a communal dignity entitled one to nobility as well as to military service. When serfdom was eased or abolished, innumerable peasants emigrated to the towns and took over jobs they considered more profitable and dignified. And much earlier the enfranchised serfs had established themselves in increasing numbers as farmers, especially in the vicinity of the cities, which they finally entered as merchants or craftsmen. This phenomenon is much older than Dante's description of the rural influx into the urban population, once 'unsullied down to its lowest workman.'[2]

However, none of these countless upstarts ever contested the legitimacy or privileges of the different classes. It was against abuses and violations of the social and moral order that the popular conscience of all classes reacted and revolted. What opposed the complete development and final success of these vast political and social movements was a strong spirit of subordination, which counteracted republican associative tendencies and nullified most of the accomplishments of two eventful centuries.

Feudalism had dominated in the peninsula for so long that it gradually succeeded in permeating all institutions with the hierarchical concept of human society. The communes had originated as mere private associations of the ruling classes for the protection of their privileges and the administration of public affairs. But as soon as they assumed a predominantly political

[2] *Paradiso*, xvi, 49-57.

character and acquired military power, the forms and spirit of the feudal system supplanted the former democratic trends toward equalization of rights and duties. This intermixture of republican and feudal institutions, of liberty and despotism, was for a long time characteristic of Italian political life and a principal reason for the constant unrest.

There were two feudal hierarchies in Italy. One constituted a social and political bond between the princely feudatories, who depended directly on the kings or emperors, and the vassals of the lower grades: the *capitani*, or district lords, the *valvassori*, or castellans, and finally the knights and squires of the mounted armed forces; the other embraced the *secundi milites*, intermediate rural and urban vassals holding their property in fief from the greater vassals in the country or the bishops in the cities. This lower nobility consisted of native Italians or assimilated foreigners who played a leading part in the communal insurrections and municipal organizations, but at the same time did what they could to protect their caste and maintain class distinctions and restrictions on political liberty.

A new reactionary element entered into urban life when the emancipated rural vassals deprived their overlords of their military support and obliged the great feudatories to move to the cities and accept the rules of the new civic organization. The caste-consciousness of these uprooted and impoverished nobles was stronger than the civic spirit of the insurgents. It soon created those powerful and exclusive associations of kinsmen, called *consorterie*, which erected fortresses and towers around the centers of communal life, and preserved a feudal spirit more harsh and implacable than ever. The narrow space in which old and new feuds were carried on embittered the struggle and perpetuated grudges. A multitude of grim, somber towers began to throw their shadows upon the streets and transformed the towns into fortified wards, the lanes into hollow passages, and the people into armies of civil strife. The town halls of such free cities, as Florence, Siena, Volterra, Todi, and so on, imitated the architecture of baronial castles and their towers expressed the spirit of authority and conquest previously embodied in the strongholds of an aggressive military aristocracy.

It was within this persistent feudal framework that the patricians, commoners, and plebeians organized, after a pact of
mutual understanding, a system of social subordination more
akin to the hierarchic principles of the subdued nobility than to
earlier strivings toward social co-ordination, equality, and co-
operation. Within the new communal constitutions the nobles
as a whole strove to maintain their position by the usual feudal
processes of family alliances, intermarriage, conspiracy, intrigue,
and assassination. This legacy of the Dark Ages remained a
salient feature of life in most Italian city-states as long as they
retained their political independence. As late as 1293 the Florentine *Ordinances of Justice* compelled the nobles to enroll in a
guild if they wished to participate in the political life of the
town, but all efforts toward equality failed to efface the social
superiority and political influence of the wealthy middle class,
composed of merchants and every sort of money-maker, over the
popolo minuto, or artisans and shopkeepers. In all Italian city-
states the latter enjoyed a privileged position in this new order
as compared with the servile classes and the workmen who
could not organize into any association whatsoever or claim any
legal protection. Even the guilds, or 'arts,' reflected this system
and spirit of subordination by maintaining different rights and
prerogatives from the lesser trades and establishing within these
social and political bodies a complicated and strictly differentiated scale of functions and limitations.

It proved impossible to preserve a balance between equality
and subordination, or between republican institutions and despotic trends, and from the very beginning these city-states observed feudal tradition in assaulting, pillaging, and subjugating
their weaker neighbors, and in conducting constant wars inspired
by factional hatred or economic competition. It was the old
warlike spirit of the nobility that stimulated these actions in
which the lower classes took part as foot-soldiers and the traders
as financial supporters and profiteers.

As soon as they were constituted as autonomous collective
bodies, the communes acted like feudal lords. The first undertaking of the Roman popular government, in 1143, was an attempt to destroy the city of Tusculum. Florence inaugurated its

municipal history by subjugating the mother town of Fiesole, in 1125, by force of arms. Milan conquered several suburban places, enforced tribute on some of the cities, erected castles and strongholds, and treated the populations as subjects. All those Italian communes from which the larger city-states developed did likewise. And since legal contracts were devised only in a late stage of this evolution, agreements, liabilities, and mutual obligations were stated in feudal-type oaths of allegiance and fealty, though without the old social and moral implications of such oaths.

Thus, in breaking the old social structure of feudalism, the Italian revolutions destroyed its inner force and logic without abolishing certain of its essential external features. The reason for the incurable confusion in Italian communal history is to be sought in the discrepancy between republican trends and feudal customs, both deeply rooted in the country's social texture and political organism. In consequence of these incongruities in public life, republican institutions remained feeble and inefficient while feudal habits became increasingly strong and uncontrolled. Under these circumstances neither the democratic nor the feudal virtues could thrive. In such an atmosphere of tension and suspicion the democracies became tyrannical, the factions became more and more vindictive, and the barons grew greedy and savage like Ezzelino da Romano in Venetia, or the Azzos in Ferrara. The lack of ideological foundation made these hybrid democracies unstable and restless, while urban Italian feudalism lost the adventurous spirit and the ideals of prowess, devotion, and fealty through which chivalry in France had developed into a superior pattern of life.

Feudal ruthlessness and tyranny were not materially relieved by that elaborate code of honor that mitigated the rough profession of arms. Imprisoned in their towns and castles, the Italian nobles had little opportunity to indulge in the general enthusiasm for armed pilgrimages, venturesome undertakings, and military expeditions that carried the French and German feudatories beyond the seas as crusaders or conquerors. Nor did Italy give birth to such orders of chivalry as were organized from the early twelfth century by the French and Spanish knights who pledged themselves to ennoble their caste and life by protecting the weak, respecting womanhood, serving religion, and observing loyalty to their chief. More than once, to be sure, these noble purposes only cloaked the same concern for power, wealth, and security that stimulated the rise of despots in Italian towns and provinces. But the Spaniards and French did serve a cause, valiantly and against perilous odds. A nation or caste cannot live without a watchword and a battle cry, and Italy had none.

An inscription carved at Nepi near Rome, in 1130, shows that Roland's prowess and Olivier's wisdom were well known in Italy a few decades after the *Chanson de Roland* was composed. The portal of the Cathedral of Verona is flanked by the image of the same two heroes, as conceived by one Nicolaus, a Lombard sculptor who worked in several Italian towns in the middle of the twelfth century. A famous archivolt of the cathedral of Modena shows that King Arthur and his knights were known in that place not long after the time when Chrétien de Troyes was delighting the court of Champagne with the stories of their adventures. Professional storytellers, roaming minstrels, knights-errant, traveling scholars, itinerant traders, always on the roads between France and Italy, carried with them poems and legends exalting the feudal virtues. They created a literary fashion that was to endure for many centuries. But all these poems and tales failed to transmit to the enthusiastic Italian public the epic spirit from which this flowering branch of literature arose in the golden age of French heroic feudalism, courtly chivalry, national resurgence, and religious revival.

The *chansons de geste* reflected the enthusiasm of all French classes for conquests achieved in the name of God, France, and King; the Arthurian epics expanded and embroidered the fabulous legends of Britain and Ireland. In Italy all these 'charming entanglements,' as Dante called them, were accepted merely as fictional tales of romance and adventure, and divested of the courtly casuistry, religious allusions, and ethical implications that transformed the Arthurian legends into vast and complicated allegories. The French code of chivalry did not become authoritative in Italy at the early stage of its evolution. At this period women were mere victims in the feuds of the Italian noble families, and love was mostly a pretext. The ethical code, with its gallantry and pure love, substantiated on a sentimental plane the idea of man's subordination to higher forms of conduct, which the feudal order had imposed in the social and political field. The Italians never took these higher forms of conduct too seriously. In renouncing some of its essential ethical justifications, they transformed feudalism into violence, tyranny, and brigandage.

The internal weakness and external insecurity of both the Italian feudatories and republics prompted them to seek protection either from the emperor, who could rely upon his armed forces, or from the popes, whose spiritual weapons of excommunication and interdict were most redoubtable. Thus, after 1154, the Italian vassals and the small communes appealed to Barbarossa against Milan and the other city-states that had deprived them of their rights and possessions acquired in the course of the communal uprisings. The cities of the Lombard League and of the Veronese March, as well as other isolated places scattered throughout the peninsula, invoked papal assistance at a time when the relations between empire and papacy were particularly tense. In both cases the Italians had to subordinate their policy to that of the superior authorities, which they recognized and strengthened by their very appeal for aid. Thus the Italian communes and feudatories became mere pawns in the great conflict between emperor and pope. By the beginning of the fourteenth century, both had ceased to be decisive factors in Italian history.

Only once in the course of three hundred years were the emperors and popes in complete and sincere agreement: when it came to destroying the Roman popular government, constituted in 1143. In 1154 its intrepid and pious leader, Arnold of Brescia, was executed by joint order of the German Emperor, Frederick I, and an English Pope, Hadrian IV. To be sure, Hadrian's successor, Alexander III, gave his protection to the Lombard League and the Italian communes, but he used them merely as a power to check the determined attempts of Barbarossa and his Italian vassals to reconquer the lost imperial positions in the country.

The communes knew that without papal intervention their cause was lost. But no one went so far as to regard the pope as a protector of republican institutions or as an Italian patriot. Alexander III did his best to strengthen feudalism in his own Roman territory and helped to create the conditions by which, a century later, the papacy became the prisoner and the victim of its own vassals, the turbulent barons of the *Castelli Romani*.

Through the support they gave to the communes in their struggle against the emperor, the pontiffs had become the leaders of a political party called the Guelfi, after the German Welf dynasty that was contending for the imperial crown against the Hohenstaufen princes of Waiblingen in Swabia. So intimately were Italian affairs bound up with foreign interests that German names, Guelf and Ghibelline, were given to the two leading Italian factions. Struggles of all kinds were carried on under these banners, in courts, states, towns, and families. Thereby the Italians acknowledged the overlordship of the emperor or the pontiff, who became irreconcilable enemies in the midst of a divided and demoralized population.

✿   ✿   ✿

At the beginning of the thirteenth century republican opinions and institutions were firmly established in northern and central Italy despite the restoration of imperial authority throughout the peninsula. The emperor had ceded most of his administrative privileges to the cities that had recognized the prestige of the empire and accepted its representatives within their walls. But the imperial officials scattered through the turbulent country remained strangers with little influence and authority as compared with some sovereign vassals in the Upper Country. In 1186, Barbarossa's son Henry married the heiress of the last Norman king of Naples and Sicily, gaining those vast Italian territories for the Swabian dynasty. It was by a marital trick of genuine feudal character, and not by means of a heroic struggle, that the center of the imperial power was shifted from Germany to Italy.

The move was consecrated when, in 1212, Frederick was acclaimed King of the Romans. For this grandson of Barbarossa, brought up in Italy and heir of the Sicilian crown, that dignity was more than a title and represented a program for power and

life. His will and influence, his prestige and ability, released all
the political and spiritual forces in the peninsula and determined
the further destinies of the Italian people. It was in a relentless
contest with that challenging personality that republican democracy, German feudalism, and papal theocracy fought their
decisive battle on Italian soil.

The republican and feudal contests were autonomous achievements of the lay society in which the Church participated and
interfered as a political power provided with mundane possessions and spiritual authority. In order to protect its privileges,
the Church backed the popular movements or the feudal interests according to rapidly changing circumstances. Yet behind
this adaptability of the papal policy there was one steady and
resolute course toward a theocratic absolutism which Gregory
VII had instituted on the basis of canon law and the Donation
of Constantine and the most enterprising of his successors strove
to achieve on a more realistic foundation. In his dealings with
Barbarossa, Alexander III acted on his belief that the papal
authority was superior to that of all temporal sovereigns, a belief
supported by Bernard of Clairvaux, the greatest spiritual leader
of his century. And Innocent III (1198-1216) had even more
theological arguments to support his concept of a theocratic
supremacy involving the absolute sacerdotal and temporal authority of the papacy as an evangelical mandate from the Lord.

Despite its feudal tendency to consider all earthly sovereigns
its vassals, the papal monarchy assumed more and more the
form of an Oriental despotism on the model of the Byzantine
Empire. The Latin concept of the papacy was definitely expressed by Peter Damiani, around the middle of the eleventh
century, as a purely spiritual authority independent of the imperial dignity but co-operating with it for mutual protection and
the benefit of mankind. This concept only confirms the doctrine
set forth by Pope Gelasius I, a Roman, in a letter written in 494
to the Byzantine Emperor Anastasius, and cited by Dante in
his treatise on the Monarchy. The Italian people supported the
German emperors in the belief that the imperial power was of
divine origin; and this implied repudiation of the temporal
powers of the papacy.

The Byzantine idea of universal domination, on the other hand, coupled the *imperium* and *sacerdotium* in the very person of the emperor, who considered himself the Vicar of Christ as King and Saviour. As late as 1200 the Roman pontiff, in emulation of the Eastern theocratic ruler, proclaimed himself Vicar of Christ in addition to his traditional title of Successor of St. Peter. The result of his innovation was a development very similar to that which had turned the Byzantine sovereign power into a complicated bureaucracy without spiritual force or contact with the vital currents of medieval life. The papal bureaucracy was able to co-ordinate ecclesiastical institutions and consolidate its political organization, but it isolated the Holy See from the great intellectual currents and religious movements of the day.

The Italian laity opposed this foreign and obsolete form of autocracy, which ran counter to the revived Roman traditions of civil liberties and the principles of feudal subordination as well. The cities finally deprived the episcopal authority of all its power and influence in secular affairs, and the Roman republic more than once barred the pope from the city or forced him to take refuge in a fortified quarter or in the powerful mausoleum of Hadrian, which long before had been turned into a medieval fortress and renamed Castel Sant' Angelo. By a cunning policy of marriage and succession the Swabian emperors nullified the feudal supremacy over southern Italy that the pontiffs had arrogated to themselves when, in 1059, Nicholas II invested Robert Guiscard and his successors with royal authority over the Low Country and Sicily. In spite of the Guelf allegiance of Milan, Florence, and other lesser towns, and in spite of imperial participation in the struggle against heretical movements, the papacy as a political power was undermined and virtually encircled when Frederick II, King of Sicily and of Germany, was crowned Roman Emperor by Pope Honorius III, in 1220. At that time the religious and secular regeneration of Italy began to gain force against the tumultuous and destructive currents that had engulfed her life and vitality in a turmoil of destructive events.

V. *The Consecration of Poverty and the Rise of a Popular Civilization*

THE communal revolutions represent the persistent and successful effort on the part of the Italian laity to free its privileged classes from feudal domination and ecclesiastical interference. However, through lack of spiritual leadership and organizing principle, the movement degenerated into a tumultuous entanglement of local civil wars. These local contests went on almost continuously in every Italian town, invariably revealing the same factional rage, the same lust for power and gain.

The emptiness of this political agitation was cloaked by evocations of the republican glory of Rome, for every Italian town claimed to be Rome's mythical sister or daughter. Beginning in the ninth century this local patriotism gave rise to a special branch of literature, the pompous, awkward eulogy, either in Latin verse or prose, of the various Italian cities: Milan, Verona, Rome, Modena, Pavia, and so on. The authors of these works never failed to connect the origin of their town with some legendary or historical episodes of Trojan or Roman antiquity.

But these bookish reminiscences of classical authors were rhetorical exercises without intellectual substance or spiritual foundation. Very little of them became a cultural heritage of the laity. The few courtly and clerical authors certainly were highly respected personalities, but their influence hardly extended beyond their own narrow circles, in which Latin was understood and cultivated as the only dignified expression of intellectual concerns.

The writers and schoolmen of the Italian Middle Ages were a

special caste without direct influence on the illiterate laity.
Roman antiquity was known to the general public in the legendary, anecdotal, and distorted form represented by the clerical
and fabulous *Graphia Urbis Romae* of the end of the eleventh
century and its later and more successful version, the *Mirabilia.*
It was a long time before the chivalric French travesties of Virgil,
Statius, Caesar, and other ancient writers became known in Italy.
This sort of literature was appreciated only by the same courtly
audiences that enjoyed the stories of Tristan and Lancelot, Yvain,
and Percival.

It was in this romantic disguise that the upper classes of lay
medieval society became acquainted with the mythical and legendary history of Troy, Greece, and Rome. This literary and
courtly cult of antiquity was limited in scope and had small
scholarly foundation. It was a fashionable and sometimes snobbish compensation for the medieval indifference to the historical
past that transformed history into fable and endowed fiction
with the prestige of history. When Italian mothers told their
children the stories 'of the Trojans, of Faesulae, and of Rome,' as
Dante wrote (*Paradiso,* xv, 126), they conceived their heroes as
types of courtly perfection, martial valor, and chivalrous virtues,
as knights and adventurers embodying all the requisites of chivalry. In the popular view of classical antiquity, certain reminiscences of ancient poetry and history were merely adjusted
to the medieval, feudal, and courtly scene. The Italians did not
go so far as to identify the Romans with the Saracens, as the
French vernacular poets and storytellers had done since the early
twelfth century. But it is certain that hatred of paganism was
everywhere stronger than pride in an illustrious national or local
past.

The question whether it was permissible to read, study, quote,
and appreciate pagan authors in a Christian society was thoroughly debated by medieval theologians and teachers. Most of
them accepted and favored the compromise of an allegorical
interpretation. These very discussions show the persistence of
the Roman cultural heritage. The ancient pagan civilization was
the most complete example in all history of a fundamental and
universal organization based exclusively on human experience.

Consequently, it never disappeared entirely from European consciousness and culture. In a fragmentary, distorted, and latent form the ancient pagan world endured through the ages in monastic thought and in traditional usages. But medieval education granted so little to worldly experience and needs that a purely secular civilization could not be understood even by the most learned and liberal admirers of ancient culture. We know comparatively little of medieval secularism because it was not permitted to develop its own philosophy. But it is certain that of the great body of ancient achievements in every field, it preserved only a few scattered fragments.

Even the few quotations from classical authors, chiefly Cicero and Seneca, and the passages collected in epitomes and excerpts had to agree with the Christian maxims and scriptural texts usually quoted and illustrated in sermons, treatises, letters, and pamphlets. Only schoolmen and clerics were able to participate in these scanty remnants of a great past, whose literary traditions were more intensively cultivated by German emperors or French kings and prelates than by the weak and indigent Italian towns or the rude and restless provincial feudatories. Lay schools existed in many places, it is true, and some of them developed into leading professional institutions during the communal age. But the fundamental study of grammar, rhetoric, and dialectic, which composed the educational trivium, granted very little to personal experience and the swiftly changing realities of life.

There is, in fact, considerable evidence in medieval texts and documents to show that the Italians started very early to rely upon the power of words and rhetorical gestures as a substitute for legal proofs and political power. The elaborate harangues which European potentates were forced to bear more or less patiently in dealing with papal and republican ambassadors were the literary compositions of professional rhetoricians who did not realize the discrepancy between the actual miseries of the country and their pompous evocations of its brilliant past. In the papal chancery, in communal offices, and finally at the court of Frederick II, this oratory became more and more turgid, self-complacent, and formalistic.

The *artes dictandi* and compilations for use in schools and offices helped to conventionalize literary practice and to smother any real sentiment beneath false verbiage and inflated commonplaces. These pretentious treatises on secular eloquence, already influential at the beginning of the twelfth century, developed in the period that followed into the leading branch of Italian literature, and came to determine the style used in all other literary forms, in political speeches, learned discourse, and the writing of letters. The less those eloquent authors in the papal and imperial chanceries of the thirteenth century had to say, the more bombastic they became. Between professional rhetoric and empirical matter-of-factness, the secular Latin literature of the high Middle Ages reveals throughout Italy a spiritual vacuum and a poverty of inspiration sharply contrasting with the intense intellectual life then going on outside the peninsula.

The chief reason for this prevalence of rhetoric over imagination and of routine over originality is that Latin was the language of officials and scholars, not of the people, who were revolting against the authority of Church or State. It was certainly not the language used in the public or municipal assemblies, or by political leaders and ecclesiastical reformers. Latin speeches would not have been understood by the masses, or by the average upper-class layman, to whom literary Latin had been totally unintelligible since the seventh century or earlier. But no more is known of a vernacular oratory before the late thirteenth century than of any other form of original prose or poetry in the vulgar tongue.

The existence of numerous French poems and early Provençal writings allows us to surmise how agitators managed to rouse a whole nation to such daring and fabulous enterprises as the Crusades. But no echo has been preserved of the speeches and disputes that resounded within the walls of the medieval Italian towns. And yet there is no other way in which the lower classes could have been rallied against imperial feudatories, simoniacal and political bishops, or papal absolutism. Literary tinsel and classic frills would have been useless in such agitation, or in the debates and harangues that must have preceded all the innumerable civil wars and military campaigns. The song of a

Modena watchman, recorded in a Latin version dating from *circa* 892, and the bellicose squib of the Milanese lads against the people of Cremona, recorded at the beginning of the twelfth century, confirm the truism that a crude form of vernacular poetry accompanied the great political movements of that agitated epoch. And it was certainly not the only form in existence. Not a word of it was probably ever written down, and consequently this type of eloquence and poetry, spread *per plateas* by professional reciters and enthusiastic amateurs, has vanished without a trace.

Political speeches and street songs do not typify the literary culture and artistic ambitions of a nation, but their importance can be conjectured by the very magnitude of the events of which they are an ingenuous and almost natural expression. The respect that the Latin language inspired as the idiom of religion and authority destroyed all the vestiges of an original vernacular and popular style whose forms and features must have been largely independent of learned rules and the practice of courts and offices. When Italian poetry began to be written during the thirteenth century, it appeared largely as a late and uprooted imitation of foreign models, as if no individual stimulation had been at work. But this is only an appearance. Political eloquence and popular poetry of a special secular character undoubtedly existed in the idiomatic forms of the individual Italian dialects, and also in a basic language understandable to all. This is proved by the vigorous religious movements which began independently in isolated centers, and later became nation-wide.

*   *   *

The popular character of the Italian sects can be seen in the fact that none of them was particularly active in theology or philosophy, while all of them concurred in the praise and glorification of poverty. Consequently, it is impossible to connect these heretical movements with any doctrine taught in the schools and discussed in treatises, from the philosophical revival of theology by Scotus Erigena in the ninth century, up to the flowering of French pre-Scholasticism with Roscellinus, Abelard, the Nominalists, Realists, and Victorins. Those Italians who engaged

in the philosophical clarification of basic Christian dogmas—
such as Anselm of Aosta, Archbishop of Canterbury, Peter Lombard, Bishop of Paris, and finally, more than a century later,
Thomas Aquinas—went to foreign countries which, with their
organized intellectual life, seemed more favorable to speculation
and controversy than the battlefields of Italy.

In Italy the issues were almost exclusively moral, social, and
political, because her religious movements were of a popular
character, supported or inspired by laymen long before the
systematic study of theology was introduced and organized in
Italian universities. Heretical currents and sects, it is true, swept
over many parts of Europe in the high Middle Ages; but apart
from the special nature of Italian heterodoxy, there is no doubt
that these movements started in Italy as a religious revolt against
the ecclesiastical authorities and their political patrons and
partisans. Forty years before 1074, when Gregory VII inaugurated his reform of the Church by outlawing the simoniacal,
married, and adulterous clergy, there was in Milan a dissenting
community so inflexible that many of its adherents preferred to
step 'with hands before their eyes' into the burning pyre rather
than retract their faith and opinions.

This is the first case known to us of mass burning at the stake.
For centuries thereafter European history abounds with the
holocausts of religious martyrs convinced that they were emulating the early Christian victims in their devotion to Christ and
the Gospels. In Italy, however, the persecution of dissidents and
heretics never assumed such proportions as in France, Spain,
and Germany. The Italian municipalities were reluctant to lend
their secular arm for the protection of orthodoxy and the ecclesiastical hierarchy. The extirpation of heresy was the only point
on which the popes always agreed with the Swabian emperors
whom they so bitterly opposed in all other fields of secular and
ecclesiastical policy. For the most divergent religious heresies
and sects consistently opposed the hierarchical systems of the
Church and the Empire and took on a decided republican and
equalitarian trend.

In the beginning the lay believers and the dispossessed lower
clergy refused to accept the sacraments from priests they con-

sidered unworthy of their office and morally unqualified for the care of the soul. This critical attitude did not involve theological problems, but it did question the principle that priests were consecrated once and for all, and it did imply that laymen might judge the validity of the sacraments. The idea that laymen should pass on the worthiness of the clergy was certainly more dangerous than feudal control of episcopal investitures. It might have broken down the whole structure and organization of the Church, and undermined the very theological foundations of its doctrines and dignities, especially since all the sects that arose after the first Milanese holocaust in 1034 concurred in recognizing the Gospel as the sole divine authority and revelation.

As long as this religious enthusiasm represented a state of mind and a longing for spiritual perfection, it might easily have been absorbed and kept under control in the way shown, for instance, by Peter Damiani (d. 1072), who made his hermitage of Fonte Avellana in Umbria a celebrated center of meditative piety. But the popular religious movements aimed at a sanctification of life and activity, at a co-ordination of secular interests and duties with a moral code that was divinely inspired and justly applied. The early Milanese Patarins were still a confused mass of plebeian rebels and visionaries. But soon these inconspicuous flocks organized into communities based on doctrines and maxims they could more consistently oppose to the Catholic orthodoxy and the rules of the Church.

The first and most popular of these heresies were the dualistic Cathars with their syncretistic combination of Christianity and Manichaeanism. They spread over northern and central Italy and had compact groups of adherents in every important center. The success of this movement was due to the impressive, rather candid simplicity of the Manichaean system, which since ancient times had never entirely disappeared in the eastern Mediterranean area; in the twelfth century it spanned the whole Old World from China to southern France. Like Christianity, Manichaeanism was a religion of salvation, but it substituted for the rationally impenetrable mysteries and dogmas of Catholicism the idea of eternal struggle between dual forces of Good and Evil, Light and Darkness, God and Devil. It replaced the

D

hierarchical principle of the Church by a dualistic distinction between the 'perfects' of sacerdotal rank and the secular community members who benefited only indirectly from the priestly redemption from evil.

It was certainly a kind of logic and commonsense that induced so many people to accept the Manichaean system of immanent Good and Evil as a sort of cosmological completion of the Gospels and a road to moral freedom and spiritual life. However, these sectarian groups represented little more than small,, submerged minorities attracting dissidents from other sects and, in general, rebels against the Church of Rome. Those who shrank from radical solutions and the prospect of martyrdom joined the revolutionary reformers who did not attempt to disrupt the dogmatic structure of Catholicism, but merely demanded that the power of the Church should be limited to the spiritual sphere.

The champion of this particular movement was the learned, eloquent, influential, and unfortunate Arnold of Brescia. His followers formed no special communities but claimed to be the true representatives of the Christian spirit. This powerful popular trend was concerned with both the doctrinal and political problems of the Church and aimed at a complete emancipation of secular life from ecclesiastical interference.

In many respects this movement seems more typically Italian in sentiment and scope than the other sects of the time. The Arnoldists constituted a party rather than a community; they spread widely and everywhere sounded the call for political liberty and religious reform. In its essence this movement merely renewed and expanded the early revolt of the Lombard Patarins. With Arnold of Brescia it lost its provincial character and found its fulfillment in the proclamation—in 1143—of the Roman Republic, the first such republic since Caesar. There were no Oriental influences in this development, as in the doctrines of the Cathars and, perhaps, in the ascetic monasticism of Joachim of Fiore, the apocalyptic prophet of Calabria. His doctrines were too heavily burdened with theological subtleties and too much inspired by superhuman ideals of perfection to achieve influence outside the strictly ecclesiastical field.

Other sects then active in northern Italy were the 'Umiliati,'

'The Poor Men of Lombardy,' and the Waldenses, all under the influence of Peter Waldo of Lyon, whose church, founded shortly after 1170, has preserved an independent existence up to the present in some remote sections of the Alps.

The heretical movements of the Middle Ages have been amply dealt with by other historians. What interests us here is not so much the distinctions between the sects as the mere fact of their existence.

The early appearance of organized dissident communities is a symptom of the spiritual isolation and intellectual stagnation that characterized Italian society for so many centuries. But there are other factors to account for it. Italy had never been entirely free from heterodox or frankly heretical doctrines since the Goths introduced Arianism into the country; and, moreover, Byzantine influence had worked consistently as a disintegrating force, especially in the social organization of the lower clergy.

Besides, there is ample evidence that large sections of the Italian people had been only very superficially Christianized; beneath their profession of Christian doctrine they preserved much of their ancient animist superstition. Even today one need not delve very deeply to find evidence of this pagan heritage. The mass of Italians are still very much affected by a pagan superstition, somewhat ennobled, to be sure, by religious education or tempered by a smiling incredulity. Small wonder that with a consistent lack of spiritual guidance the cult of the saints, the adoration of relics, the use of sacred images, the divine service and sacraments lost most of their transcendent significance and degenerated into magic, sorcery, and fraud. On the other hand, this long experience prevented the Italians from becoming religious fanatics. There is no doubt that the never-failing Italian tolerance toward foreign cults and doctrines is due to an instinctive feeling for the immanence of the divine in the universe and the everlasting presence of the numina in the earthly life of man.

All the sects of the high Middle Ages concurred in eliminating every trace of magic from Christian rites and practices. They re-stated the fundamental Christian sacraments in accordance with the letter of the Gospels, and consequently their interpreta-

tions of baptism, transubstantiation, and salvation were unortho-
dox or openly heretical. Only a small minority of believers and
confessors were intellectually and morally prepared to accept
the ultimate consequences of this radical spiritualization and
abstraction of religion. The revolutionary impact of the movement was not determined by doctrines, but rather by a few
principles and practices common to all the sects and arising from
the moral temper and sociological conditions of the day.

In the course of the twelfth century one cult was carried from
the Alps to Calabria by all the sects; it even enjoyed the more
or less tacit approval of many persons within the Roman Church.
This was the cult of poverty and humility, not only as a contrast
to the wealth of the higher clergy but also as resigned acceptance
of the most evident, ubiquitous, and inexorable reality in Italian
life. Enterprising traders and adventurers had made some in-
roads against the general poverty of the country, especially
through the organization of foreign and domestic commerce.
But only the seaports and a few centers such as Milan, Florence,
and some of the Sub-Alpine towns, profited from this commercial activity and the industrial development that followed it.
For the rest of the Italian people famine, toil, and oppression
continued to be the common experience.

From the old Milanese Pataria to the Calabrian hermitage of
Joachim of Fiore, from Arnold of Brescia to St. Francis, all the
reformers and their followers were united in an uninterrupted
effort to break the curse of poverty by spiritual means and to
restore the reign of Christ by proclaiming the supremacy of
indigence over all other virtues. The only possibility of offering
hope to the destitute masses was to transform that curse into a
blessing, to turn humility into spiritual energy, and transmute
the awesome Pantocrator of the Byzantine and papal theocracy
into a King of Mercy and a Redeemer of the Poor. The Roman
Church and the majority of its prelates multiplied the visible
expressions of their power and dignity by encouraging and protecting men and enterprises that added glory and authority to
the City of God. The reformed sects of every denomination did
just the opposite by trying to make the Church share the
indigence of the people.

St. Francis eased the growing tension between these two currents of Italian religious thought by accepting the authority of both. Others contented themselves with skepticism or indifference, occasionally paying lip service to the stronger of the two parties. But everywhere the triumphant cult of poverty made its influence felt. Today it is possible to distinguish between those reactions of the country where resignation toward poverty and suffering meant the passive fatalism of the oppressed, and those where it became the smiling patience of the wise. The serene acceptance of a divine order had a different effect on the Italian character than submissive acceptance of feudal discipline or subservience to a theocratic authority.

*　　*　　*

The sudden rise and great success of the mendicant orders at the beginning of the thirteenth century showed the powerful effect of this glorification of poverty and represented the culmination of a popular movement apparently split by denominational dissensions and weakened by persecution, suspicion, or apathy. When, in 1209, Francis of Assisi renounced all his possessions and became a wandering preacher of poverty and humility, mendicity became for the growing number of his followers and listeners a title of spiritual nobility and a new source of energy. Charity, once a privilege of wealthier people, now became a universal virtue and the counterpart of consecrated begging. The unofficial recognition of the Franciscan doctrine of poverty by Innocent III, in 1210, and the final approval of the order's rule by Honorius III, in 1223, mark the triumph of the Italian pauper movements after two centuries of dramatic vicissitudes and humble, silent, enduring sacrifice. During that time all the sects concluded their mission of bringing about the spiritual renewal and moral education of the Italian people. In adopting the life of a wandering preacher, Francis of Assisi resumed a tradition that had been sanctified by Jesus Christ and the apostles but inaugurated in times closer to his epoch by the founders and missionaries of the new sects.

All the religious movements of the Middle Ages made use

of lay preachers and vernacular church services. Nothing contributed so much to the success of the different sects as their
rejection of Latin as the exclusive language of the Christian
cult. The Gospels were translated into the vulgar tongue in all
the groups and churches that aspired to restore Christianity as
a religion of the people. Sermons in the orthodox Catholic
churches were bilingual and confessions were received in the
vernacular language. But it was only the heterodox and heretical
groups that developed a new religious eloquence in the period
when a popular political oratory was growing up in the public
assemblies. Nothing has been preserved of these early vernacular
sermons, prayers, and translations. But the tradition was well
established and the masters earned public praise for the stirring
power of their words. By the end of the twelfth century Italian
religious eloquence had spread throughout the peninsula and
become pre-eminent in some of its leading centers. But the
suppression of the sects by Pope Innocent III and Frederick II
destroyed every vestige of the preaching style that preceded the
vernacular and popular eloquence of St. Francis and his followers.

Among the scanty remains of early Italian religious literature
there are two documents of different epochs, style, and purpose
that illustrate the evolution of religious sentiments and practice
in the popular sphere. A vernacular confession form written in
Umbria around the year 1100 completely annihilates the personality of the believer. The entire register of sins is recited
mechanically and absolution is given in the correct canonical
way with good works duly taken into account by divine justice
and mercy. Such conventional crumbs of consolation were at
that time about all the illiterate populace received from the
clergy. A century later, in 1224, St. Francis dictated his famous
'Praise of the Creatures' to one of his companions—'a master of
verse and songs.' He intended it to be intoned by his wandering
friars as an inspiration to laymen.

This solemn and jubilant enumeration of all the creatures in
heaven and earth is a hymn of universal brotherhood inspired
by the 148th Psalm and, as such, one of the few Italian poems

directly affected by Biblical spirit and style. It is a three-part song of praise and thankfulness, in which the heavenly luminaries, the four elements, and all mortal creatures join in a simple cosmological vision of love and life. There is in these lines no hint of man's annihilation in the presence of divine justice, but instead an idea of co-operation and solidarity, a cheerful contemplation of peace, harmony, and beauty, a naive wonder at the fitness of all created things. This was, indeed, the fulfillment of the long Italian efforts at moral and religious regeneration. St. Francis only reluctantly accepted the idea of a new religious order. He felt that his doctrine of love, pardon, humility, and brotherhood required no organization but only a free expansion among men of good will. It was with this in mind that Francis added to the early group of his followers the so-called Tertiaries, or lay brethren, who could belong to his religious community without renouncing their active secular life. Consequently, it was not the Church that absorbed the new order, but the order that drew the laity into its sphere of thought and devotion. For the first time the Italian laity obtained an active spiritual guidance and an ethical code embracing rich and poor, nobles and slaves, religious and secular life.

As long as the 'seraphic family' did not become a rigid monkish organization fraught with internal rivalries that belied the intentions of its founder, the Franciscan idea fulfilled Italian aspirations for spiritual freedom and a life embodying the maxims of Christianity. In this form the Franciscan idea of freedom in poverty and exaltation in humility counteracted, at least morally, the growing papal and clerical pretension to world supremacy and domination, as well as the preponderance of worldly concerns in the life of the Italian people. The philosophy of patience and moderation, applied even in the struggle against heretics and unbelievers, became, at least in its beginning, the spiritual appanage of the order, much in contrast to the Dominicans, who inaugurated a more determined and aggressive action against what they called 'heretical wickedness.' Dante expressed the difference between the two methods of religious regeneration by describing the temperament of their founders: the one 'truly

seraphic in his ardor,' and the other 'benign to his own and to
his enemies harsh.' [1]

A psychology of the religious orders has not yet been written
and should be attempted by a scholar capable of dealing dis-
passionately with these matters. Meanwhile, we may sum up the
contrast between the two orders by saying that Francis the Umbrian represents the long Italian effort to rehabilitate the poor
and weak through class brotherhood and universal co-operation,
while Dominic the Spaniard introduced into the religious movements of the late Middle Ages the resolution, defiance, and
fanaticism of the Spanish *reconquista*. The impact of these new
forces upon the medieval mind, life, and society was, of course,
universal; but it was Italy that first and most directly felt their
revolutionary effect. Dominic established his headquarters for
the conquest of souls in Bologna, which for centuries remained
the order's holy site and a center of Spanish influence in Italy.
Florence was soon to fall under the spell of the Franciscan religion of love.

The interaction of the two currents sometimes effaced the differences and the tension between the orders, yet the influence
of each was felt independently in many aspects of Italian intellectual, spiritual, and artistic life. During his apprenticeship as
a religious leader, begun in 1209, Dominic witnessed the massacres of Béziers, Albi, and other places in southern France. He
taught that cogent arguments were much to be desired but that
where they failed, a hard blow would succeed. His order developed in both these directions, producing not only the ablest
logicians and philosophers, but also the most inflexible inquisitors. Francis began his career teaching the love of God through
renunciation of violence and hatred and went on preaching to
men and birds, chasing the demons from Arezzo, arguing with
the Sultan in Egypt, performing all sorts of miracles, and remind-
ing his enraptured listeners of the beauty of the world.

These divergent currents led to the militant theology of
Thomas Aquinas and the contemplative piety of Bonaventure.
Each of the two lines of thought attracted adherents according

---

[1] *Paradiso*, XI, 37 and XII, 57.

to their temperaments. The sensitive and imaginative, the artistic and emotional were attracted to the Franciscan orbit, while embattled natures, rationalists, and casuists rallied to Dominicanism. Both trends appealed to the traditional Italian love of eloquence and spirit of adventure. Black Friars and Minorites soon set out from Italy for the spiritual conquest of the world, extending their influence and organization from Portugal to the heart of Asia, from Sicily to the Baltic Sea. These two far-flung mendicant armies did much to cement the power of the papacy, after the collapse of the Crusades and the failure of its military ventures.

Both of the new religious orders replaced monastic seclusion and ecclesiastical aloofness with direct participation in the secular world and indoctrination of the people. After centuries of chaotic derangement and convulsive anxiety, the Italians achieved a steady course toward an autonomous spiritual existence. One important result of this stirring cultural movement was achieved outside of the churches: the praise of the Lord in the vernacular style inaugurated by Francis. His short poem in rhythmic prose is the first of the innumerable *Laudi* composed and sung especially in central Italy as the most popular expression of the religious enthusiasm of the Italian people. This enthusiasm assumed immoderate forms and even maniacal aspects when ecstatic bands of ragged and half-naked *disciplinati* or *flagellanti* went around singing and psalmodizing to induce public mortification.

These excesses were the result of a mass frenzy inspired by an exaggerated interpretation of the Franciscan ideal of poverty and humility, then the object of tense and subtle discussions within the order itself. The spasmodic fury of this collective religious passion provoked contempt and derision among moderate Italians, but nonetheless brought forth the most original and inspired religious poet of that epoch. This 'minstrel of God,' Jacopone da Todi, an Umbrian lawyer converted to Franciscan ideals in 1279, joined first the lay brethren of the order and then the Minorite Friars, finally devoting his rapturous hymns and rabid satires to the cause of the 'Spiritualists,' the strict followers of St. Francis' rule and doctrine.

D*

In addition to a Franciscan ecclesiastical hymnology in Latin, a popular religious poetry spread over Umbria and Tuscany, paving the way for the poetic consecration and social rehabilitation of the vulgar tongue. The efforts of vernacular poets to purify their native dialects and express the ineffable in a still rude and untamed language made their work more flexible, vigorous, and eloquent than the frigid and impersonal imitations of the Provençal poems of love and courtesy. However, the range and depth of this poetry were still limited to the scope of the common man. Even Jacopone touches our hearts by his fervor and enthusiasm, not by richness of imagination or depth of thought.

These poems were composed for audiences of exalted or scornful throngs and not for the tranquilly devout. In accordance with the early Franciscan idea of human brotherhood every manifestation of piety presupposed companionship and collective effort. For this purpose lay fraternities of singers were created in central Italy that cultivated choral music at regular gatherings of devotees, called *laudesi*, after the traditional form of Franciscan poetry. Florence was the center of this musical revival already under way in the first half of the thirteenth century and then developed with increasing intensity by these associations of spiritual *meistersingers*, which in all probability were never affected by class restrictions. A new trend toward spiritual democracy and a lyrical expression of sentiments governed this popular revival of religious poetry and music outside of the Church, but in harmony with it. In these lay brotherhoods, the legacy of St. Francis was more consistently preserved and developed than within the order itself, soon weakened by bitter quarrels, vitiated by abuses of mendicancy, and widely despised for the discrepancy between its doctrine of poverty and its actual worldly interests, for its exploitation of the poor and unfair competition with the impoverished lower clergy. The intelligent and honest Italian laity were well aware that the order had used a legal trick to safeguard its wealth: vesting its property in the Holy See on condition that the usufruct pass to the friars. Yet the critical attitude of the Italian people toward the worldly aspects of medieval monasticism did not seriously curtail Franciscan influence on the spiritual and artistic life of the country.

* * *

The Franciscan preaching of brotherhood between the classes did much to further the old Italian tendency toward associative forms in spiritual, artistic, and public life. It raised the language of the people to higher levels of expression, and favored the development of choral music. When, in 1223, Francis of Assisi himself constructed the first scenic representation of the nativity for the church of Greccio, he promoted a revolution in the figurative arts no less characteristic and of no less consequence than his literary and musical innovations. For the first time this Biblical scene was reconstructed in a free space, with plastic forms showing the figures of the Holy Family, an ass, an ox and shepherd within the stable where the drama of redemption began. Friar Giovanni Veliti, probably an artisan or one of those artistic-minded persons whom St. Francis often chose as companions, aided him in the completion of this pious and unconventional work. So much was this innovation appreciated by his order and the multitude of his spiritual followers that its eloquent imagery was represented as one of the Saint's most significant accomplishments in the series of biographical frescoes painted at the end of the century by Giotto and his pupils on the walls of the Franciscan basilica at Assisi.

The impulse that prompted St. Francis to erect this first monument to humility arose from his eagerness to give the neglected multitudes full participation in his religious renewal. The three-dimensional realism of his artistic creation achieved a more direct, impressive, and evident evocation of evangelical episodes, and appealed more strongly to the popular imagination than the usual abstract and didactic scenes that adorned the medieval Italian churches. Romanesque sculptors of the twelfth century, such as Wiligelmus, Nicolaus, Benedetto Antelami, and other Lombard masters, had begun to enliven the rigid style of their epoch with a less schematic and a more natural and lively representation of Biblical, allegorical, and historical figures. They were unable, however, to free their statues and

reliefs from the lifeless stiffness and petrified remoteness inherent in pre-Gothic works of sculpture and painting. Moreover,
all those Biblical or allegorical scenes and figures clung to their
supporting walls and columns; reliefs and statues alike disappeared in the height of doorways, gables, parapets, and pinnacles, or retired into their protective niches and recesses.

Instead of the abstract gold ground of medieval painting and
the withering austerity of sculptural attitudes, the new Franciscan realism attempted a naturalistic reproduction of a living
scene with every single figure participating in the represented
occurrence, but having at the same time its individual type,
function, and significance. The single figures in St. Francis'
plastic representation of the Nativity certainly were simple dolls
rather than elaborate sculptural images. But even as such they
were the first plastic works of that kind in Christian iconography.
A holy scene worked out with figures appearing as statues in the
round would have been inconceivable in an earlier time, and
rejected as idolatrous, as they still are today in the Greek Orthodox Church. St. Francis' group not only marks the first step
toward Italian realism in religious art but implicitly expresses
the definitive break between the Latin and Greek concepts, traditions, and rituals that still united the Eastern with the Western
Church. The crib of Greccio is the first symptom of a new Christian attitude that found its expression in art before becoming a
theological system of thought and a moral concept of life. This
plastic group illustrates in a graphic form the inner intention of
the *Praise of the Creatures* in which every element of the world
is treated as a part of an universal organism and also in its individual aspect and function. Although known to us only indirectly, the crib of Greccio marks a new epoch in Italian art, just
as non-conventual Franciscanism represents a new religious,
spiritual, and social trend of Italian life. While Romanesque art
and French Gothic sculpture emphasize the extramundane features of their subjects and drastically limit the worldly traits in
religious figures and scenes, the new Italian realism brings the
divine nearer to human sight and understanding, and substitutes
for the aristocratic aloofness and spiritual abstruseness of the
religious mysteries the tangible reality of God's humanity.

Much time and effort were required before this spiritual realism succeeded in overcoming the contrary currents and the tenacious traditions of the medieval artists and workshops. Yet it was certainly much furthered by the followers of the new doctrine in their direct contact with people of all classes, and particularly with the masters who worked under their influence and authority. The renewal of Italian art was not accomplished through aesthetic doctrines or the desires of a leading class but arose from a vast spiritual experience that taught clerics and laymen to consider the world with eyes open to the beauty of creation.

This discovery of the outward world was so elemental and far-reaching as to baffle all attempts at an adequate theoretical definition of late medieval art by thirteenth-century thinkers and modern sociologists. Niccolò Pisano, who shortly after 1250 inaugurated this new national style of art, reveals in a few famous monuments the source of inspiration and the spiritual direction from which this consecrated realism took the first steps toward an everlasting success. The monumental pulpits of Pisa and Siena, which so eloquently manifest the sovereign importance of popular preaching in Italy's religious life, impressively show the master's attitude toward art and nature. His Biblical scenes and allegorical figures still cling to the traditional sculptural motifs of carved statues and epic reliefs, but with an always evident effort to bring corporeal form and expression nearer to life and reality. It was this sympathetic approach to the tangible and sensible aspects of reality that revealed to Pisano the objective character of classic art and the impressive eloquence of its illusionistic effect. In accordance with the general state of mind created by the spiritual revolution of his time, Niccolò Pisano, his son, pupils, and followers diverted their eyes and inspiration from the abstract realm of symbols and allusions and found that artistic expressiveness consists in fidelity to nature as attained in classic forms.

Remnants of ancient sculpture, sarcophagi, mosaics, and architectural monuments existed at that time throughout the Western World, and their influence on Romanesque and Gothic ornamentation is evident in much French, Provençal, Lombard, and South Italian sculpture and decoration. Yet the medieval imitation of

classic motifs was always limited to workmanship; the creative
inspiration was not stimulated by the essential aspects of classic
art. Even during the reign of the Emperor Frederick II, who
liked to assume the attitudes of an *Augustus redivivus,* the partial revival of Roman reminiscences was only one aspect of an
essentially eclectic culture and of a sovereign will. The spiritual
realism of Niccolò Pisano and his period has little to do with
workshop traditions or courtly luster, nor is his imitation of
classic forms an expression of a national revival of Roman styles
and models.

The pure artistic intentions of the new generation of Italian
masters are shown by the circumstance that their discovery of
classic beauty in corporeal forms coincides with their appreciation of the French Gothic style, which was no less decisive in
the creation of an Italian artistic individuality. Ornaments and
figures of the Romanesque period show many links with French,
Provençal, Catalan, and Spanish models. Italian art was only a
dialect of the universal artistic language of the Middle Ages.
Only the humanization of religion and a new relation between
the outward and the inward world enabled Italian artists to
select from past ages and foreign countries the elements of style
suited to the faith and temper created by a popular spiritual
leader. How much the activity of Niccolò Pisano's workshop was
in harmony with the spirit of his time is shown by the fact that
his masterpieces embodied three leading aspects of contemporary life: pulpits for preaching friars, the public fountain of
Perugia, and the tomb of Saint Dominic in Bologna.

VI. *Guelf Theocracy and Ghibelline Laicism*

THUS, in the course of the thirteenth century the aristocratic, anarchical, and ascetic Italian monasticism was entirely supplanted by a religious activism that affected every
aspect of Italian life. So great and enthusiastic was the popular
response to the ideas and accomplishments of the mendicant
orders that in many Italian towns huge churches were built with
publicly collected funds for the growing audiences of the preaching friars. Franciscans and Dominicans developed a Gothic architecture of a peculiar Italian type that reveals the spirit and
power of the orders, their increasing importance in ecclesiastical
life, and their ability to inspire and direct Italian artists.

The Dominicans, as a learned order, inaugurated this movement, while the Franciscans only joined it in emulation, against
the conviction of their founder, who regarded learning with some
suspicion and never had recourse to it in his preaching. Dominic's love of erudition was another Spanish trait of his personality. It was his native country that had given Europe Latin
translations of Arabic texts that constituted most of the standard
works of the late medieval culture. The Italian Franciscans did
not actively participate in the intellectual development. In their
scholastic activities they represented the Latin and Augustinian
approach to the problems of ethics and theology.

The two competing mendicant orders were not very successful
in their attempts to dominate Italian institutions of higher learning. The leading position they acquired at the Sorbonne was due
to the direct support given the friars by King Louis IX against

the faculty and public opinion. In Italy the lay spirit and the keen competition between sovereigns and republics kept the higher schools comparatively free from the direct influence of the orders and the Church in general. It was only after 1360 that theology was included in the curriculum of the University of Bologna. The municipal authorities, the overlords of the Carrara dynasty, and finally the Venetian republic always guaranteed the University of Padua, founded in 1223, an exemplary autonomy of which professors and students were aggressively jealous. No monkish meddling was tolerated by Frederick II after the foundation of the University of Naples, in 1224. After 1233, when Gregory IX entrusted the Dominicans with the inquisition, the Italian city-states took legislative precautions for the protection of their subjects. Public opinion and an instinctive appreciation of worldly interests safeguarded the religious revival against bigotry and the intellectual interests against ecclesiastical restrictions. In 1244, when Thomas Aquinas, the Dominican, set out to study theology, and after 1250, when Bonaventure, the Franciscan, devoted himself to the mystical search for God, they had to attend the University of Paris. It was only at the Pontifical Curia and the principal episcopal schools that a systematic theological curriculum could be followed on Italian soil. The intellectual level of those institutions did not meet the requirements of exceptional minds.

The Italian universities, though subject to public supervision, were at that time autonomous bodies governed by their students and professors. Most of them specialized in the law, which assumed more and more importance because of the increasing administrative complexity of the ecclesiastical administration. This discipline attracted numerous talented men and gained the interest of the papal curia. In 1234 Gregory IX sent the University of Bologna the ponderous *Decretals* of Raimund of Pennaforte as a standard code for use *in iudiciis et scholis*. Less than a century later Dante heaped scorn on popes and cardinals who neglected the Gospels and the 'great doctors' in favor of the study of these juridical compilations.[1] The secular states reacted

[1] *Paradiso*, ix, 135-8; *Convivio*, iv, xii, 9; *Monarchia*, iii, iii, 9; *Epistolae*, xi, 16.

against canonical interference in their affairs and put their own jurists to work compiling 'statutes' or constitutions. The decline of the imperial power in Italy after the death of Frederick II, in 1250, diminished the importance of Roman law in favor of canon and communal forms. After that date Italy became even more a country of jurists and notaries.

All branches of university education emphasized preparation for practical careers, although the methods of teaching were purely theoretical and scientific procedure was essentially speculative. The leading schools were still organized on the traditional international patterns that linked together all the centers of scholastic culture. The role of the teachers was to comment skillfully and eloquently on the standard authors and texts on the liberal arts. The specialization of some Italian universities attracted an increasing number of students from all over Europe, a trend that persisted for centuries and contributed to the unification of European culture. Salerno produced generations of medical authors and practitioners, Bologna educated the leading jurists of Italy and Europe, Naples provided southern Italy with learned functionaries, and Padua rapidly developed into a European center of practical and philosophical studies.

The Italian universities took just pride in men like the learned Florentine jurist Francesco Accursio, who taught at Bologna with many other famed authorities *utriusque juris;* medical men like Maurus and Ursus of Salerno; masters of style and rhetorics like Guido Faba or the Florentine Boncompagno. Yet the essentially laical and professional character of these institutions deprived them of the intellectual background and spiritual ferment that gave Paris the leadership over all other medieval schools.

In consequence of this trend toward specialization, the old medieval curriculum of liberal arts (the *Trivium*) and sciences (the *Quadrivium*) was losing importance and prestige. Yet, though various branches of learning made rapid advances, it is hard to establish a connection between any intellectual trend or spiritual movement of medieval Italy and any particular university or professor. Italian translators working in Spain and Sicily, such as Gerard of Cremona or Bartholomew of Messina, contributed greatly to the diffusion of Aristotle and Plato, Avicenna and Ptolemy, Euclid and Galen, and other Greek and Arabic authors. But the Italian universities played no part in drawing the newly revived doctrines and sciences into the culture and educational system of the times.

Their leading masters participated in the general advancement of learning, it is true, and composed valuable manuals, compendia, treatises, and commentaries. But it was not this didactic literature that formed the living culture of the epoch, any more than the leading ideas of our day are molded by routine college textbooks. The methods of teaching and thinking were conservative and impersonal, interpretative and doctrinal. This educational system was not based upon a scientific organon or a body of philosophical doctrine. It was outside of the classrooms, and especially in the public disputations of theses, that teachers and students were able to show their mettle in the discussion of living ideas.

Despite their secular character and comparative independence, the university faculties never inaugurated intellectual movements of a specifically Italian trend. None of the great men who set the stamp of their genius on Italian poetry, art, science, politics, and technology was the products of scholastic or academic institutions. The universities sometimes caught up and absorbed the intellectual currents developed outside of their classrooms, but never promoted a spiritual innovation or ventured an independent approach to practical or scientific problems. They are completely absent in the masterpieces and currents of Italian literature.

This intellectual passivity on the part of the Italian schools can be attributed to their emphasis on the professional career and to the interference of the preaching orders and ecclesiastical authorities, especially after the recognition of the inquisition and the growing power of Minorites and Dominicans in educational affairs. The personal protection granted by the states to doctors and professors was powerless to undo the resolution of the Council of Siena (1210) forbidding the use of Aristotle's book on natural science. Subsequently the writings of Thomas Aquinas,

Siger of Brabant, Duns Scotus, and William of Ockham were condemned by the University of Paris, while the Inquisition destroyed the life and works of the Paduan physician Petrus de Abano. This remained for a long time a warning to timorous faculty members and a source of intellectual uneasiness for conscientious teachers and unconventional minds.

It is characteristic that the greatest revolution in the mathematical sciences since antiquity was promoted, shortly after 1200, by Leonardo Fibonacci of Pisa, a man who never received regular training in university arithmetic and geometry but organized with his natural talent whatever was handed down of Greek and Oriental mathematics. After the appearance of his algebra and geometry the masters of the *Quadrivium* were forced to adopt the new mathematical methods and concepts that affected the whole course of Western civilization. But it was at the Sicilian court of Frederick II that Leonardo Pisano's system found the first appreciation of its theoretical and practical interest.

Although they represented timeworn traditions, official doctrines, and intellectual isolation from active spiritual forces, the Italian universities soon became important centers of cultural life because of the concourse of students from every part of the country. The continuous influx of students into the leading centers and the foundation of branch schools in several minor Italian towns promoted a cultural homogeneity and a mutual stimulation that raised the general intellectual level and spread ideas throughout the peninsula. This cultural mission was carried out mainly by the turbulent student bodies that appointed the teachers, elected officials, and fought for the privileges obtained from emperors, communes, and bishops. Intellectual interchange was favored by the custom of boarding students with the professors, who gave those guests private instruction in addition to the regular curriculum.

This arrangement persisted for centuries and somewhat attenuated the rigidity of the university routine. In stimulating a free exchange of ideas, in expanding new intellectual interests and currents, the taverns contributed more than the classrooms, and the wandering students and bachelors more than the ap-

pointed professors. It was through these unofficial channels that
the Italian youth of the late Middle Ages participated in cultural movements and contributed to the intellectual development of their country.

*   *   *

The decentralization of Italian life throughout the Middle
Ages led to an intellectual variety and an eclecticism of artistic
styles, unparalleled in other countries. The particularism of the
city-states stimulated the compilation of local chronicles, which
recount local events in the general framework of medieval history and in connection with the glory of Rome. These narratives
reveal no sense of intellectual or political solidarity with the
rest of the country. The only cultural link between the cities
was the Latin language, used in all branches of public life, in
schools and offices, and, of course, in international intellectual
and political relations. That artificial language was dissociated
by traditions and conventions from the natural sources of practical, psychological, and spiritual experience. With its dry style
or rhetorical bombast it gives a false picture of Italian life and
culture. This literary mannerism did not prevent some authors
from creating a lively, lucid, and personal style, as, for instance,
the Minorite Salimbene of Parma in his entertaining chronicle
(1168-1287), Jacopo de Varagine in his delightful *Golden Legend*,
and several other writers in historical, religious, and theological
fields. But the stylistic originality of these authors derives rather
from the influence of the spoken vernacular upon their Latin
wording than from any virtuosity in the handling of the classical
tongue.

At the same time, the particularism of the communes strengthened the vitality of the local dialects, which lacked the dignity
and prestige of a literary idiom, and isolated the vulgar tongue
from the ennobling and corrective influence of the Latin language. That is why, beginning in the twelfth century, the Provençal and French literary languages found a place between
scholarly Latin and the popular Italian dialects, creating a new
element of cultural confusion. Professional troubadours, flocking in from southern France, carried the taste for courtly love,

political invective, and graceful melody throughout Italy. French became so popular that Brunetto Latini, the Florentine, preferred it for the compilation of his famous *Trésor* (1260) and Dante confessed that 'everything easy and pleasant written or composed in a vernacular tongue belonged to that language, as, for instance, the Biblical tales compiled with those of the Trojans and Romans, the beautiful adventures of King Arthur, and many other narratives and teachings.' [2] When the Pisan Rustichello met Marco Polo, the Venetian, in the prison at Genoa, in 1298, he wrote down the traveler's report in a mixed Franco-Italian language developed in the northern provinces as a literary idiom for romances, tales, and poems.

There is adequate evidence to show that the educated young men of Milan, Bologna, Florence, Naples, Palermo, or any other leading city, were familiar with the Latin, French, and Provençal languages, beside their native dialects, which they strove to enrich and raise to the level of the literary idioms. Businessmen, bankers, and traders had to know some Latin for their legal affairs and at least French for commercial transactions. Greek was spoken in Venice, Apulia, along the Adriatic and Ionic coasts, and in Sicily; and in Sicily, moreover, a Mohammedan minority had kept alive, at least until 1250, the literary and spoken Arabic language. This cultural eclecticism compensated for Italian particularism and opened the minds of the more active and enterprising element to general trends and a knowledge of the world. The universalism unsuccessfully pursued by papal diplomacy and the Empire was realized by the Italian people through the secular pursuits of commerce and maritime exploration. Dante created in the legendary Ulysses the poetic symbol of the roving and inquisitive spirit that prompted the Vivaldi brothers of Genoa to venture, in 1294, on the first navigation *per mare oceanum ad partes Indiae*.[3] Marco Polo is the most popular representative of this type of universal-minded explorers.

While the Italians did not take part in the first Crusades, they

---

[2] *De vulgari eloquentia*, I, x.
[3] *Inferno*, XXVI.

had no share in the heroic experiences or in the cowardly brutality of the French and German nobles and prelates who perpetrated the most cruel and senseless massacres from the Rhine
to Jerusalem. There is nothing in Italian national experience that
can be compared with those barbarous explosions of fanaticism.
Although Italian factional passions were no less ferocious, they
represented an aspect of a political struggle fought among
equals.

Most of the medieval missionaries in Asia were Italians, as
were the Franciscan monks who went to China in the fourteenth
century and became the bishops of the first Catholic communities in the Far East. The roving spirit was characteristic of the
Middle Ages, and Italian wanderers only followed the general
trend. In their expansion over the whole eastern Mediterranean
area, the French transplanted their feudal institutions and customs. The conquered territories, particularly those of Greece,
Cyprus, Syria, and the Levant, became a colonial appendage of
the mother country. Unlike the French aristocracy, the Italian
nobility was essentially sedentary. The Italian expansion was
carried out almost exclusively by members of the middle classes
and was mercantile both in character and purpose.

Consequently there was competition only between the Italian
maritime republics, not with foreign powers and their possessions
overseas. The history of the Fourth Crusade, which started as
a joint enterprise of the French nobility and the Venetian merchants and ended, in 1204, with the conquest and plundering of
Constantinople, is a typical expression of the different types of
political expansion. The French organized the Latin eastern empire after feudal patterns, while the Venetians secured for their
traders and shipowners privileges and advantages that survived
the French territorial conquests by many centuries. In Italy itself maritime expansion was balanced by the continental trade
and financial operations, initiated and developed by the joint
efforts of Florentine manufacturers and bankers, Lombard middlemen, and Alpine carriers. From the middle of the thirteenth
century on, the urban nobility was thoroughly involved in these
economic enterprises, and such participation in the experience

of the middle classes drew them, more or less reluctantly, into the Italian cultural community.

*　　*　　*

The development of this cosmopolitan civilization in the thirteenth century shows the coexistence of two cultural currents that affected the whole spiritual life of the country. One of the two currents was independent of school authority, thoroughly secular, and closely related with the Ghibelline concepts of government, faith, and education. The court of Palermo was the center of this spiritual trend, which spread among all classes throughout Italy. The other current, which might be called the Guelf, had its center in Bologna, the headquarters of the Dominican order, and represented the cultural interests dominated or influenced by ecclesiastical concepts, methods, and traditions.

The first of the two currents was empirical and secular, the second speculative and Catholic. The leading expressions of the Ghibelline culture reveal a strong trend toward ancient and Islamic philosophy, while the rival movement stood for the strict observance of Biblical doctrines as interpreted by the Latin fathers of the Church. The Guelf movement subordinated secular life and knowledge to Christian maxims and ecclesiastical judgment. The Ghibellines more or less explicitly proclaimed the moral and metaphysical equivalence of all religions. The famous parable of the three identical rings representing the three Biblical religions is first told in the vernacular *Novellino,* a collection of popular stories deeply pervaded by the Ghibelline spirit and secular interests of the thirteenth century.

This laical, critical, and sometimes skeptical tendency favored a more tolerant attitude toward non-Christian doctrines, methods of thought, and ways of life. In choosing between these two cultural spheres, the individual was motivated more by temperament and intellectual considerations than by social bonds, party interests, or practical concerns.

The cosmopolitan and secular aspects of Italian culture in the late Middle Ages are embodied in Frederick II, King of Sicily and Emperor of Germany, a sovereign, a foreigner, and, as his

admirers called him, 'the wonder of the world.' Born in Jesi, he
was the first and last emperor after the fall of Rome to grow up
and reside on Italian soil. He was brought up under papal tutelage at the Norman court of Palermo, then dominated by Greek
influence, Oriental customs, French culture, and German or
papal interests. In this eclectic environment he strove to surround himself with the best men in every field of human activity. He lived like a caliph, ruled like a Caesar, and considered
himself an Italian sovereign destined to reconquer Rome and
make it the center of a renewed Christian and Roman Empire.

These far-reaching ambitions, which were justified rather by
his exceptional personality than by the real conditions of the
world or the extent of his political authority, brought him into
relentless conflicts with the leading powers and political groups
of Italy and Europe. The German supporters of the Swabian
dynasty resented the Emperor's absence from their country as
well as his adoption of a despised foreign culture. The Norman,
German, and indigenous nobility of southern Italy resisted the
imperial policy that deprived them of their feudal rights and any
active political role by transforming the central power into an
Oriental despotism served by a bureaucratic body of learned upstarts and cunning diplomats. The Italian city-states feared the
growing prestige and personal power of a resolute potentate
situated dangerously close to them and supported by Italian
feudatories in Piedmont, Venetia, Tuscany, and a number of
free republics with Genoa at their head. Finally, the popes, and
especially Gregory IX, had the most reason of all for antagonism to the Emperor; Gregory and his successors made common
cause with Frederick's other enemies until they had achieved
the total destruction of the first Italian dynasty and the political
ruin of the country. The dramatic contest between the Pope and
the Emperor marks the vanishing of the imperial authority, the
final decline of papal supremacy, and the end of the medieval
history of Italy.

Political unification of Italy would have destroyed the privileges and advantages so hard won by the papacy after Gregory

VII, and would have definitely diminished its power and prestige both in the religious and temporal fields.

*   *   *

The growth of an independent secular autocracy in a territory where the popes represented the highest political and spiritual authority would have been fatal to the papacy, and this fact accounts for the unrelenting energy with which the pontiffs pursued the struggle. The battle was not restricted to the political field, as in the days of Frederick I and Henry VI. In the meantime the papacy had organized the mendicant orders as a sort of militia and vanguard whose task it was to disrupt and destroy the subtle and powerful influence the Sicilian court was gaining over the Italian people. The conflict between the Guelf and Ghibelline civilizations was no less dramatic in the cultural than in the political sphere.

For the first time a secular system of thought and conception of life had dared to enter into open competition with the Christian tenets concerning nature, the world, and God. The popes were able to nullify the Italian ambitions of the Emperor; they destroyed the imperial power itself and put an end to the Swabian dynasty. In the religious sphere they succeeded in suppressing every overt trace of heresy. But the effort failed to check the spreading influence of a pagan philosopher whose learned translators and commentators had enjoyed the protection of Frederick II.

Various circumstances contributed to the reappearance of Aristotle in the Christian world, which had hitherto all but ignored him. There is little trace of his influence in the works of the Latin Fathers of the Church. A few treatises translated in the twelfth century remained confined to scattered groups of specialists. The familiarity of Arabic philosophers and Jewish theologians with Aristotle cannot account for the central position he rapidly acquired in Italian culture. There is a fundamental difference between the Arabic or Jewish appreciation of Aristotle and the enthusiastic interest he aroused in Italy beginning with the Sicilian court.

In the Semitic Orient and in Arab-Jewish Spain the Aristotelian philosophy served, as later in Thomas Aquinas' works, to complete a religious system and to support its methodical and rational foundation. Nothing of this kind had been undertaken in the Christian world, not even by the Parisian school of philosophy. These schoolmen, from Abelard to Albert the Great, had employed much dialectical skill in clarifying special questions pertaining to the relation between reason and faith, but they made no attempt to co-ordinate into a rational system of thought the empirical world of phenomena with Christian dogmas and tenets. In the twelfth century Peter Lombard created the type of all further theological *Summae* and Bernard of Clairvaux initiated his active mysticism as a substitute for all worldly knowledge and curiosity.

The generations that had experienced the feudal and communal revolutions, expansion of trade by land and by sea, an era of social change, and religious controversy could not be satisfied with trends and doctrines that granted so little to the secular aspects of life. The popular maxims of conduct and salvation collected by Gregory the Great in the sixth century no longer sufficed for the moral guidance of busy and enterprising laymen. Even St. Francis knew that poverty and renunciation did not solve all the problems of his time.

For these generations with a broadened experience of the world, the doctrines of Aristotle were a secular revelation, disclosing the truth in every aspect of the universe. It was not Aristotle the logician that interested these alert and enterprising spirits, but rather the inquirer and empiricist who granted so much importance to common-sense evidence and ordinary human activities. The first works of Aristotle to achieve a restricted but lasting popularity were his writings on natural science; they were also the first to be condemned by ecclesiastical authorities. When men inspired by a desire for learning became acquainted with the *History of the Animals,* the writings on physics, on cosmology and meteorology, the poor stock of scientific knowledge purveyed for centuries in the *Quadrivium,* or compiled in the encyclopaedias, compendia, and treatises of late antiquity, appeared hopelessly obsolete and dull.

Besides offering an insight into the essence of things within a systematic frame that reflects the order of the world, Aristotle called attention to the significance of concrete phenomena. He directed the human intellect and the curiosity of experienced laymen to seek truth through knowledge of the forms and aspects of the outward or material world. His system was not based on abstract ideas, but was organized according to scientific categories; it was intended as a guide for living, an introduction to empirical culture, learning, and education. In revealing to man all things in nature and all beings on earth, in teaching him the structure of the universe through its material forms, Aristotle stirred up an intellectual enthusiasm for the same heavenly and earthly appearances that Francis of Assisi had taught his contemporaries to praise as manifestations of God's wisdom and love. In that way Aristotle became for the generation of Dante 'the master of all who know.'

To these generations that had learned to value the things of this world the ascetic ideals of renunciation appeared to have lost all bearing on normal secular life. The great success of Aristotle's *Ethics,* already known in excerpts before the translation of the complete works by Robert Grosseteste, Bishop of Lincoln, is explained by its conception of active virtues and the pre-eminent position it accords to the theory and practice of human justice. In this system of ethics justice is conceived as the substantiation of moral life and the fulfillment of human perfection, independently of any transcendent or religious consideration. It is also a civic virtue, the highest aim of political organization directed toward the common good, the condition for the happiness of the citizens of an ideal city-state.

In these fundamental maxims, so typically Greek in character, the great philosopher had anticipated and expressed the latent aspirations of secular medieval society, which had not yet developed a moral system of its own for its laws, and an ethical code for its life. Chivalry represents the first attempt at a secular code of morality, but it never attained in Italy an exclusive pre-eminence or a leading importance. The true or legendary exploits of knights in protecting the weak, liberating women, honoring hermits, and serving kings and ladies always amused and thrilled the Italian people, but solely as literary motifs, never as models for life. Quixotism is nonexistent in medieval life and literature.

Hence the general acceptance of the Aristotelian ethics in late Middle Ages does not, at least in Italy, represent a middle-class substitute for the moral code of the nobility, or a revolutionary step toward the secularization of life and culture. Aristotelianism meant so much for the cultural evolution of Italy because it was in harmony with the experience and the spiritual needs of the most active groups and individuals, a way out of almost total ignorance and a guide to knowledge and understanding of the things of the world. In that form it fascinated clerics and laymen alike.

It was in Italy, as a student in Padua, that Albert the Great, a German, became acquainted with the Arabic revival of the philosophical system that was to be transformed into a Christian philosophy in the thought and works of Thomas Aquinas. The ethical system and natural science of Aristotle pervaded and directed the inspiration of the first original Italian poets, from Guittone d'Arezzo to Dante Alighieri. Aristotle's ethics, and above all his concept of justice, gave the *Divine Comedy* its philosophical support and rational structure.[4] That very system substantiated the passionate desire for justice that inspired so many Italians in their inexorable political struggles.

In these efforts justice was not achieved by feudal ordeals, pious charity, or divine intervention. It is a human aim and virtue embodied in political institutions and in the persons of righteous men. In France justice was embodied in the person of the king. In its imperial disguise in Italy it appeared as a mere phantom. The republican constitutions emphasized the concept of justice as a moral aim and reality represented in institutions and offices. But in order to avoid partiality and venality these constitutions had to take into account human weakness and the prevailing factional spirit. With governments changing every two months and the highest magistrates appointed for six months

[4] *Inferno*, XI.

or a year, justice did not appear as an overwhelming moral force, but rather as an abstraction realized by political expedients and compromises.

*   *   *

We do not know exactly how this predominantly ethical and scientific Aristotelianism spread from the Sicilian court over the rest of Italy during the first decades of the thirteenth century. Its chief carriers were probably wandering university students. It prevailed as a spiritual Ghibellinism in the provincial courts of the imperial vicars in central and northern Italy, who imitated the Emperor in their style of life and cultural aspirations. Be that as it may, the Aristotelian ethics emerged in the poetry of the early Tuscans, of Dante and his friends, as a familiar philosophy and an intellectual background of lyrical inspiration, as a rational scaffold for the spiritual ascent of the soul.

Before Thomas Aquinas and Giles of Rome [5] nobody in Italy seems to have systematically objected to the philosophical, scientific, and religious shortcomings of a system that ignored the fundamental Christian doctrines of creation, free will, personal immortality, resurrection, and divine revelation. Discussions of its inconsistencies, multiplied and magnified by Arabic translations and adaptions, were left to ecclesiastical authorities or to the sagacity of Parisian professors who specialized in the matter. Even after Thomas Aquinas the Italians insisted on the theoretical pursuit of the common good as taught by Aristotle's ethics and in the practical realization of basic civic virtues.[6] In his politics the state is conceived as a civic community, in contrast to St. Augustine's 'City of God,' which served as a basis for papal universalism.

The Florentine republican constitution of 1293 was called 'Ordinances of Justice' in accordance with a secular doctrine that conceived the state as a protector of human justice. Papal universalism aimed at the realization of divine justice for mankind as a whole. The Italian Ghibellines, however, were convinced that the Emperor, residing on Italian soil, would create what

---

[5] *On the Errors of the Philosophers,* around 1270.
[6] See below, ch. x.

Dante called the *humana civilitas*,[7] an autonomous, universal community based on the principles of the Aristotelian ethics. These three conceptions of the nature and motives of political power show more clearly than any social or economic analysis how the Italian communes were driven into a position between the two universal powers and compelled to choose between their doctrines and trends.

Yet it was not in the city-states but at the imperial court of Palermo that the principles laid down in Aristotle's treatise on *Ethics* were most fully understood. Frederick II had given Italian feudalism a death blow by transforming his authority into a personal despotism and establishing a secular, hierarchical bureaucracy in his domains. While most of his predecessor's counselors and chancellors had been high church dignitaries, Frederick's court was composed mainly of scholars and literati.

The Emperor was certainly far from wanting to have his state ruled by philosophers; but he was an enlightened and highly civilized sovereign who knew that knowledge is might and that his authority required a moral support and a spiritual foundation other than those inherent in the feudal system. As he intended to realize an autocratic realm of order and justice by secular methods of government alone, he turned to a philosophy that had spread over Western Europe during his childhood but had never found its center and forum. It is because of these internal circumstances and not because of any personal ambitions that the court of Palermo promoted and, to some extent, co-ordinated all the advanced ideas and intellectual ferments of Europe.

In this entirely secular environment, dominated by Mohammedan philosophers, Jewish scholars, and Christian freethinkers, the spirit of inquiry fostered by the Emperor was able to develop freely through courtly discussions of the great problems arising from the different interpretations of the Aristotelian, Platonic, Arabic, Christian, and Jewish doctrines. The Emperor, who took harsh measures in exterminating the heretics because he wanted to keep order in his domains and save his soul, never associated himself with the papal repression of the secular philos-

[7] *Monarchia*, I, iii, 1.

ophy that was shaking the very foundations of Christianity. He believed that religion and philosophy should each be sovereign in its own domain and accordingly rejected papal intervention in temporal affairs.

It was at Palermo that for the first time the rational interpretation of the universe by Aristotle and his Arabic commentators was accepted, theoretically at least, as the equivalent of the theological system elaborated by the early fathers from Origen to St. Augustine. This idea of theoretical equivalence did not imply the substitution of a secular philosophy for the religious conceptions of Christianity, but it favored the growth of certain ideas incompatible with the Christian doctrines. The Aristotelian ignorance of creation and providence led to the Averroistic negation of the personal immortality of the soul in favor of the concept of the universal unity of the human intellect. These conclusions drawn from the Aristotelian system of the world were as un-Christian as the principle of the eternity of the world or the repudiation of divine sanctions in a life to come.

Italy produced no philosopher who dared to complete the Averroistic scheme of the world, as was done in Paris by Siger of Brabant. On the contrary, the two great antagonists of this natural and rational interpretation of the universe were Italians by birth and education: Thomas Aquinas, the Dominican, who conceived the synthesis of faith and reason in the most comprehensive system of thought ever achieved; and St. Bonaventura, the Franciscan, who first warned of the incompatibility between the revived Aristotelian and the Christian doctrines, and then strove to restore the authority of the Platonic-Augustinian theology, supported by the self-evidence of the existence of God.

The very zeal of these two great champions of the faith and the unrelenting efforts of the Black and Minor friars in combating a damnable un-Christian philosophy prove that its influence was not limited to a courtly circle of freethinkers or a few scattered philosophers, but, on the contrary, that doubts, criticism, and skepticism were spreading like an epidemic among the Italian laity. The violence of the reaction is a symptom of the popularity of those doctrines. The repression of their influence was more difficult than the suppression of the heretical sects, because the new philosophical attitude was not concentrated in communities and conventicles of dissenters, but was rather a general frame of mind. At the most, the Aristotelian approach to nature, science, and life seems to have subjugated two of the Italian cultural centers: the University of Naples, where Thomas Aquinas studied philosophy, after 1239, under an Averroistic professor of the arts; and the University of Padua, whose international body of students enjoyed the liberal protection of the Ghibelline party even under the tyrannical and cruel regime of Ezzelino da Romano, the Emperor's most powerful Italian vassal.

It was at this time that the objectionable mental evasion of the 'double truth' began to trouble and undermine the conscience of many Italians who wanted to preserve their faith in God and their trust in human reason. The intellectual poison of Averroes' materialistic and pantheistic dualism continued to work on Italian minds long after the canonization of Thomas Aquinas. Dante, like many of his contemporaries, went through the crisis of decision between science and revelation. Every thinking being was in some way involved in this crisis, because centuries of Christian education had accustomed men to justify their acts and thoughts before God and His vicar on earth.

It is against this cultural background that the great drama of that agitated epoch reveals its deep historical significance. To attribute the civil strife of the thirteenth century to a special factional spirit of the Italians is to explain a historical problem by a psychological absurdity. A factional spirit cannot feed on itself. At a time when the fear of God troubled even the hardest sinners, when an unbelieving emperor felt impelled to do penance and destroy the heretics, civil strife cannot be explained by political and economic forces alone. In medieval Italy the pursuit of politics was not principally directed toward the management of public affairs but was generally conceived as a means for acquiring power and wealth. The prominent role played by economic interests in certain Italian centers, such as Venice, Genoa, and Florence, is evident and must be taken into account as a decisive factor in historical as well as cultural developments. But any attempt to reduce the most characteristic achievements of Italian civilization to economic terms is historically and phil-

osophically untenable, because it is human intelligence and
ingenuity that create economic needs and inspire material progress, and definitely not the other way around. For an adequate
historical interpretation of men and events the essential thing is
to know the substance and direction of that creative intelligence
and to understand its manifestations in all the fields of human
activity.

It is obvious that during the thirteenth century the policies of
the Italian states were not determined solely by the quest for
markets, but equally by a desire to realize some rather utopian
ideals that inspired the ecclesiastical authorities no less than the
secular leaders, a monkish prophet like Joachim of Fiore no less
than a skeptical emperor or a communal revolutionary leader.
The frantic efforts of the popes to achieve world unity are explained by the apparently favorable conditions for the fulfillment
of this Christian aim while a Catholic and Latin sovereign ruled
over the former Byzantine Empire. Frederick considered himself, and was indeed, an Italian potentate by birth and culture,
if not by race, which in princes counts even less than in others.
He drew the natural and logical consequences from these exceptional circumstances and frustrated all attempts at papal expansion. The city-states were not torn by commercial competition or class struggles alone, but also by political disagreements.
In all these cases spiritual motives played a decisive role.

Gregory IX and Innocent IV, the popes who planned to bring
the Berbers of Morocco as well as the Tartars of Eastern Asia
into the fold of the Church, first had to free Italy from the dis-
rupting influence of a militant secular culture. By all the means
at their disposal, they mobilized Italian public opinion for an
internal crusade against the Emperor, his court, and his family.
By repeated excommunications, by absolving Frederick's subjects from their oath of fealty, by laying an interdict on his
residences, by organizing coalitions of the free republics against
him and his followers, and finally by depriving him at the
Council of Lyons, in 1245, of all his dignities, the two popes
believed, each in his turn, that they had broken the power of
the supposed Antichrist.

The success of this relentless spiritual and political mobiliza-

E

tion of the Italian people against the Swabian dynasty did not
come up to expectations. Although Innocent IV insistently proclaimed the subordination of the temporal to the spiritual power,
the cause of the dynasty had supporters enough to maintain
itself throughout Italy, even after the Emperor's death (13
December 1250). His popularity grew in legend, and a widespread sympathy, reflected in Dante's pious apotheosis, favored
his unfortunate son Manfred during his brief career as a regent
and king.[8] But all these friendly feelings were not inspired by a
political enthusiasm for the already declining imperial idea and
its incomplete constitutional realization. The personal prestige of
these sovereigns, considered as Italian leaders, was stronger than
any obsolete and abstract utopianism.

It was through the influence of Frederick's court that Italian
poetry acquired for the first time artistic forms and a literary
style. The Emperor, his natural son Enzo, Manfred, his chancellor Pier delle Vigne, knights like Rinaldo d'Aquino, judges like
Guido delle Colonne, high functionaries like Giacomo da Morra,
the notary Giacomo da Lentino, the governor Ruggeri d'Amici, and
several other imperial officials all wrote pleasant verses on the
usual courtly topics. This poetry was not very original and perhaps was intended only to provide texts for songs, but every
section of Italy was involved in this poetical and musical competition. The officials and knights participating in it were men
born or residing in different provinces of the peninsula. All of
them held court after the imperial pattern and thus contributed
to the creation of a literary language common to all educated
men, who now strove to merge their vernacular provincialism
with the more elevated and harmonious idiom.

This artistic and linguistic community, supported by a common
philosophy, is the first consistent symptom of an Italian cultural
unity. The Swabian dynasty also came near to transforming it
into a political consciousness. Manfred almost succeeded in
rallying the powerful Ghibelline forces of the country to this
idea. But at last he was deserted by his followers and comrades
in arms, whose morale had been undermined by Guelf propa-

[8] *Purgatorio*, III, 103-45.

ganda and the hopelessness of the political and military situation. However, the twelve popes from Innocent IV until the election of Boniface VIII, in 1294, could not have succeeded in their attempts to keep Italy divided and subservient to the interest of the papacy without the support of a foreign power. Just as Hadrian I had called on the Franks for help against the Langobards, and the Normans had protected Gregory VII against the German emperors, Urban IV, a French pope, offered the Sicilian crown to a French prince, Charles of Anjou, who destroyed the last remnants of the Swabian power by defeating Manfred at Benevento, in February 1266, and beheading Conradin, Frederick's last descendant, in 1268, in a public square in Naples. By political intelligence and military skill, the Frenchman was able, little by little, to take over all the privileges of the extinct imperial dynasty, and at the same time to place himself at the head of the Guelf party.

❋   ❋   ❋

This papal move was fatal to all parties. Despite the efforts of the most energetic political popes, such as Gregory X and Boniface VIII, to stem the tide of French imperialism and to restore the theocratic hegemony of the Holy See, the papacy was unable to free itself from French tutelage and the influence of the Angevin dynasty. The imprisonment of Boniface VIII, 7 September 1303, by William of Nogaret, chancellor of Philip the Fair, and some Roman nobles, appeared *urbi et orbi* as a ludicrous and ominous event, coming as it did after the great success of the first jubilee, in 1300, and the publication of the bull *Unam Sanctam*, which embodied the most pretentious spiritual and temporal claims for the papacy. The merely symbolic existence of the Holy Roman Empire could not prevent the establishment of the Holy See in Avignon, in 1309, on Angevin territory guarded by the mighty castles of the King of France. With that the papacy ceased to be free and ceased to be Italian. For nearly seventy years the popes were French provincial sovereigns, most of them holding court like ostentatious temporal potentates.

The revolting cruelty displayed by Charles of Anjou in killing and maiming the faithful followers of the last Hohenstaufen, the

oppressive fiscal policy imposed on a population already exhausted by unbearable taxation, and the transfer of French
feudal families and customs into the newly acquired territories of
Sicily and the Italian Low Country provoked for many years
scattered revolts and a unanimous feeling of resentment and
hatred that finally exploded in the famous Sicilian Vespers
(1282), the first national revolution in Italian history. The Angevin
dynasty lost Sicily to the Spanish house of Aragon and established its seat in the gloomy and powerful Angevin castle at
Naples. From that time until 1860, French and Spanish dynasties
kept these vast and glorious parts of Italy detached from the
rest of the country and perpetuated the methods of a voracious
foreign feudalism in a country already impoverished by fiscal
exploitation, dynastic wars, social disintegration, illiteracy, and
the hopeless revolts of a people in despair. The decline was so
rapid that by the end of the century the total revenue of the
Angevin Kingdom of Naples from fiscal sources amounted to
less than the income of a Florentine bank from its investments in
that part of the country. The petty nobility in Sicily and the
continental Low Country resorted to banditry and an organized
system of robbery in order to survive. Six centuries of oppressive
and chaotic mismanagement by corrupt royal functionaries, ruthless landed nobility, Spanish governors, and mercenary armies
completed a process of moral and national destruction from
which the country never recovered.

The Angevins advanced into central and northern Italy as a
conquering political power after the popes had proclaimed King
Charles as imperial vicar and the Guelf party had accepted his
leadership and protection. With that the political and cultural
center of Italy rapidly shifted to the High Country and especially to Florence and Bologna, which had an overwhelming
Guelf majority after the banishment of the Ghibelline notables
and leaders. Both towns developed rapidly under particularly
favorable conditions. The residence of the Angevins was far
away and the popes had no need to exert much pressure on a
population almost entirely devoted to the Guelf cause. During
this epoch of uncontested French supremacy over Italy, the
Florentines were able to increase their banking business and

trade connections with France, Flanders, England, and Spain. Bologna was a college town of international character but strongly in the power of the Guelfs, who kept King Enzo in confinement for twenty-three years within its walls and made the town the spiritual center of the anti-imperial league.

Like the Ghibellinism of the first half of the thirteenth century, the Guelfism of the following epoch was not merely a political faction but a philosophy, a concept of life, and a moral attitude toward the questions of power and right. While Ghibellinism represented the secular autonomy in thought and life, Guelfism stood for the supremacy of religion in every manifestation of human activity, cultural and practical as well as spiritual. While Aristotelianism and the Averroistic doctrines were the intellectual expression of Ghibelline secularism, the system of Thomas Aquinas represented the Guelf approach to life and science. Its inner structure and ultimate goal were determined by the idea of the hierarchical gradation of all beings. This philosophical and theological system gave to the ecclesiastical and feudal order a prestige hitherto realized in the organization of the Church mainly by juridical means and the power of tradition. The two *Summae* were conceived and completed in the decisive years of the Guelf triumph, between 1258 and 1273. From 1261 to 1264, when papal supremacy over every other temporal and spiritual authority was firmly established, Thomas resided at the pontifical curia. In considering the universe as a hierarchy descending from God to material forms, embracing first the angels as pure intelligences and then human beings in their intermediate rank between a creative divinity and passive matter, Aquinas completed a metaphysical paradigm of the ecclesiastical order of dignities. His mode of thought and the scheme of his doctrine reflect the two hierarchical systems to which he belonged as a nobleman of royal descent and as an ecclesiastic of the highest spiritual rank.

Every section of this stupendous system of thought is dominated by the hierarchical principle that creates a harmonious dialectical and imaginative co-ordination of all things and beings in a metaphysical society centered in God. Accordingly, the order of the heavenly bodies, the aspects of the natural world, the ethical system and political organization of mankind are conceived in a hierarchical sequence of degrees that logically establishes, throughout every detail of this universal chain of beings, the subordination of the physical world to the metaphysical rules of creation and existence. On the practical plane, the system culminates in the statement of the supremacy of the papacy over all temporal sovereigns. This supremacy is justified by the higher rank possessed in the order of the universe by heaven over earth, the soul over the body, the sun over the moon, the spiritual over the material world.

This great system of thought represented a more powerful basis for papal domination over Italian territories and public affairs than the spurious *Donation of Constantine* or the false and authentic *Decretals*. It gave the Dominican order the philosophical foundation for its political endeavors and its organization of an educational system. The Guelf faction received an ideological support that appeared more consistent and suitable to a Christian civilization than the Aristotelian system and the Averroistic conclusions had ever been for the Ghibelline theories of the autonomy of the state and the merely spiritual authority of the Church. In this sense, Thomism, energetically disseminated by the Dominicans, was soon accepted by many thinkers throughout Italy. Even the tepid spirits, the indifferent, and the open adversaries of that philosophy and its political conclusions could not resist its doctrinal efficacy and intellectual authority. With this universal explanation of the sensible and transcendental world, scholasticism was soon transformed from a method of thinking into a method of teaching, embracing every possible field of knowledge and inaugurating an epoch of scholarly rather than creative thought.

But the Italian mind had not been educated to accept without opposition a hierarchical concept of life, religion, and society. Even in the Guelf intellectual strongholds of Florence and Bologna there was little enthusiasm for a philosophical system culminating in the theoretical subordination of the civil power to ecclesiastical authority. Moreover, there were everywhere in Italy strong forces that reacted against a dogmatic philosophy developed with a logical formalism of exceptional flexibility. In working against its influence, the traditions of republican laicism were as strong as the mystical efforts of Franciscan seers who, adopting Neoplatonic and Augustinian patterns, taught the contemplative union of the human mind with God. Furthermore, an outspoken practical realism and a widespread philosophical indifference worked together against the new trend of thought. The reaction of the laity to the new doctrinal buttress of total Guelfism is known by the attitudes of some of its most conspicuous representatives.

Dante, for instance, accepted the Thomist theology as a *scientia divina*, but the ethical system of the *Divina Commedia* is Aristotelian. His political doctrines are a passionate and rational confutation of the Saint's consecrated Guelfism. The explanation of this preference is to be sought in the fact that Aristotle argued most convincingly for the pre-eminence of human activity and earthly well-being. For the same reason Dante's master and friend, Brunetto Latini, had condensed, in the vernacular *Trésor*, the *Ethics* of Aristotle as the only system of moral rules based on a secular and rational concept of human life and experience. For Dante this system presupposes a secular authority to make it effective, hence it constitutes a theoretical basis for regarding the imperial power as the God-given guardian and dispenser of human justice. 'There is no philosophical authority connected with your government,' he warned his fellow-countrymen,[9] and then gave them his own conclusions in proclaiming the pope's mission to be the guidance of mankind to eternal life, and the emperor's task to direct it *'secundum philosophica documenta'* to mundane happiness.[10] To render unto Caesar that which is Caesar's is not a concession of the spiritual to the temporal, but divine sanction of the equal rights granted to the authorities by God himself.

Nowhere is Dante so far removed from Thomist concepts and Guelf principles as in his political ideas, for which he suffered exile and persecution. These ideas were also condemned by the Church, and the treatise on the Monarchy was publicly burned as a heretical work. This was not a practicable theory of the state, but a symptom of the nonconformist attitude of the lead-

[9] *Convivio*, IV, vii.
[10] Ibid. IV, ix; *Monarchia*, IV, xvi.

ing spirits of the Guelf epoch and an expression of the lay intelligence seeking to understand the ethical foundation and spiritual substance of the essential forces in human life: love, faith, justice, community, nobility, and humanity. In consigning to celestial beatitude the condemned representative of Latin Averroism, Siger of Brabant,[11] Dante did not canonize his rationalism and the speculative materialism of St. Thomas' adversaries, but he certainly did want to express his devotion to a philosopher who fell victim to doctrinal fanaticism when he was assassinated at Orvieto in the very midst of the papal court.

In this critical attitude and inquisitive pursuit of enlightenment and truth, Dante's friends were no less determined and active than he. A spirit of rebellion linked those young insurgents together against Guelf radicalism in politics, culture, and intellectual life. Guido Cavalcanti, an intelligent nobleman, a sensitive poet, and an outstanding citizen of Florence, frankly professed dissenting and skeptical convictions. In his day that attitude implied a predilection for the Averroistic distinction between the material and the spiritual forms of existence. His love poetry strives to become a revelation of truth, and his contemptuous attitude toward the lower classes of the Florentine people arose from intellectual snobbery rather than patrician pride. His bitter 'Song against Poverty' is a challenge to the mendicant orders after the paroxysms of ascetic pauperism that had shaken the country and wrapped the soul, as he says, 'with hate, with envy, gloom and doubt.'

A similar attitude linked his friends and followers with many other educated laymen who created a young intellectual aristocracy in the two leading centers of Italian culture. The doctrine of nobility, love, and wisdom that inspired their *dolce stil nuovo* was revealed in a famous poem by Guido Guinizelli.[12] He was a learned nobleman of Bologna and a political exile, as were most of the members of this spiritual community moved by a youthful enthusiasm for feminine beauty, moral aspirations, secular learning, and political ideas. His fundamental maxim of the necessary

[11] *Paradiso*, x, 133-8.
[12] A cor gentil ripara sempre Amore
Come l'uccello in selva alla verdura.

interdependence of love and nobility created a metaphysical hypostasis of courtly love: the enamored soul in its worship of beauty and perfection presupposed an intellectual nobility as a condition for its spiritual union with the beloved creature. Each of these fundamental concepts of a new secular philosophy has many doctrinal, religious, mystical, moral, and sociological implications. A divine breath pervades the poetic effusions of this group. The mind of these poets is moved and stimulated by a philosophical unrest. Love, beauty, perfection, nobility, death have a double significance in the vocabulary of the 'sweet new style,' and the spiritual union of the lover with the beloved is a sort of mystical tie that acquires cosmic proportions in the metaphysical framework of that vague and visionary doctrine. The Platonic background of these sentiments is evident, although the philosophical substance of the poems is largely Aristotelian.

From this spiritual impulse a new literary culture developed toward the end of the thirteenth century, still as a regional manifestation of a profound intellectual and moral renewal. Dante emphasized the provincial character of the new style of life and poetry inaugurated and represented by his fellow-countrymen, Guido Cavalcanti, Cino da Pistoia, Lapo Gianni and many others.[13] But his superior genius made it Italian and universal.

[13] *De vulgari eloquentia,* I, xiii.

E*

D ANTE was born into an epoch of didacticism. In early
Italian poetry there is hardly an example of an intimate,
unaffected, lyrical inspiration. The dead and monotonous forms
of a displaced courtly poetry as well as the timid and awkward
efforts at popular verse were filled with a more or less ponderous
intellectualism. Italian poetry did nòt arise from an outburst of
national and epic sentiments, as in France, or as an expression
of particular social conditions, as in the Provençal courts, but
from a spiritual anxiety groping for suitable expression in a
language not yet fully formed. None of the many Tuscan writers
prior to Dante ever dared to give poetic form to the fancies of
his heart or the insights of his mind. This early literary florescence
is characterized neither by strength of emotion nor by a serenity
of countenance, but rather by a cold didacticism manipulating
fixed motifs and formal devices.

The master of this early poetry, Guittone d'Arezzo—who spent
his life between his native Florence and Bologna—was respected
by Dante and his contemporaries for the determination with
which he championed the Italian style and manner. His verses
are uncouth, his diction stiff and unadorned, his mood splenetic
in love and patronizing in friendship. He played with words and
indulged in rhetorical devices. But this half-enamored, half-
ascetic wiseacre always reveals the peculiar concept of poetry
that moved him to write his poems of love, faith, politics, and
admonition. He was obsessed by moral uneasiness. It shaped
his style, which is consequently more petulant than vigorous and
more eloquent than impassioned.

His common-sense wisdom and moral generalizations sounded obsolete, empty, and plebeian to the learned dilettanti and provincial dandies of the new generation caught in the cultural and political whirlwind of the eventful years after 1250. When the towers and houses of the Florentine nobility were reduced to an equal level, when slaves were freed in town and country, and all noblemen obliged to enroll in the craftsmen's guilds, the new social order and way of life remolded the traditional concepts of medieval civilization. The democratic regime of the wealthy commoners—the *popolo grasso*—tolerated no dissenting minorities but obliged every citizen to participate in the tumultuous political life of his town.

We see all the poets of Dante's circle involved in family feuds and party struggles, yet striving to remain themselves. There were among them, of course, some skeptical and reckless outsiders like Cecco Angiolieri from Siena, whose cynical, frolicsome sonnets are still popular in Italy. Another man of the same type was Forese Donati, with whom Dante exchanged verses of lively and scurrilous invective. Corresponding to these outsiders there was the audience that enjoyed the crude Italian imitations of the *Roman de la Rose,* or admired the ludicrous poems of Folgore da San Gimignano or Cene della Chitarra. They were loafing gluttons who gathered in clubs to make merry and enjoy life despite the ascetic, moralizing atmosphere that surrounded them. Within the narrow limits of their busy provincial towns they made a noise far in excess of their importance and are still noticed because of their unconventional behavior. But those fools count little in the development of the new local and national culture.

It was the more composed expressions of mundane feelings and profane customs that revealed a spiritual anxiety arising from the conflicts between sentimental inspiration and moral constraint, between human fatality and divine order, individual desires and social conventions. The whole secular life of those generations, even if strongly autonomous and decidedly lax, was nevertheless embedded in a transcendental spiritualism that made such conflicts inevitable. The professionals and amateurs who imitated the 'gay science' of the troubadours treated poetry as music, with little concern for the bygone motifs of courtly woman-worship; but true poetical inspiration lay elsewhere for a man who could say in Dante's words:

> I am one who, when
> Love inspires me, take note, and go setting it forth
> After the manner which he dictates within me.[1]

Similarly, there were many painters prior to Giotto who adorned churches and chapels with mosaics and pictures .after the traditional Byzantine patterns, until a new attitude toward God and nature, world and eternity, altered the background of religious art. The intellectual impact on the inner life was so powerful that poetic imagination was never dissociated from philosophical meditation. The world of reality assumed the aspect and function of a spiritual symbolism. The eternal lyrical motifs of love, desire, death, and sorrow became objects of philosophical discourse. Love in Dante's poetry is the creative Eros of Neo-platonic and Scholastic conceptions rather than the romantic emotion of his youthful passion. And since for the medieval mind philosophy was the intellectual quest for God, these lyrical effusions take on a mystical aura of profane devotion and ecstatic contemplation in which emotional realities dissolve and vanish like visions and dreams.

Yet this world of poetic phantoms has a certain doctrinal consistency and various common features that distinguish Italian lyricism from the offshoots of courtly poetry elsewhere in Europe. The leading idea in this new philosophy is the interdependence of love and spiritual nobility, of feminine beauty and heavenly perfection. The basic symbol of this lyrical imagery is the beloved woman conceived as the embodiment of a celestial intelligence and as an angelic intermediary between God and man. On the whole, this half-sentimental, half-intellectual frame of mind. corresponds very closely to the general cultural currents and social influences of the time. Spiritual nobility is substituted for chivalric aristocracy. The concept of the celestial intelligence belongs to the Ptolemaic cosmology theologized by Thomas Aquinas. The idea of perfection suggests the mystical approach

---

[1] *Purgatorio*, XXIV, 52 ff.

of the human soul to the divine essence, as taught by Dionysius Areopagite and his followers, while the notion of love is interpreted, according to the Aristotelian system and its Arabic and Christian commentators, as the natural inclination of everything to join its elements and to mingle with it in an essential union. Hence the corporeal death of the beloved is also a mystical act of such a transcendental necessity that such idealized women as Beatrice, Selvaggia, and later Petrarca's Laura die in the prime of life in order to live in eternity as divine and poetic symbols.

These half-religious, half-philosophical doctrines so consistently dominated the sentimental experiences of the major group of Italian poets that the reality of their inner life and the dreams of their poetic imagination mingle in a speculative transfiguration, esoteric both in tone and character. It was in this spiritual climate that the poets developed their own ideas expressed in lyrical symbols, learned allusions, moral maxims, and doctrinal reflections. The continuous meditation on the nature of love developed within this circle a rudimentary psychology that borrowed its principles and conclusions from Aristotle and his commentators, from Platonic tradition or Averroistic conceptions. The cult of feminine beauty stimulated lucubrations on the relation between the pleasure of the eyes and its transcendental significance. The application of metaphysical conceptions to this aesthetic contemplation led to the speculative cosmology that constitutes the background of this visionary poetical world. The shadow of death that casts a sentimental gloom upon the eternal triumph of this spiritualized love also inspires reveries on the essence of life and the question whether things were created for an earthly contingency or an eternal existence.

All these lyrical motifs interwoven with psychological, moral, natural, metaphysical, and mystical reflections are well known from Dante's *Vita Nuova*, in which the tenuous love story of a sentimental adolescent is transformed by the poet's sacred awe and elegiac temper into a lyrical and scholastic initiation into the secrets of the human heart and the beatitude of a better world. Scholars and critics have thoroughly investigated the philosophical elements and trends that constitute the subject matter of all these poets who called themselves the *fedeli d'amore* believing themselves to be the priests of a new secular religion.

After Guinizelli, in his famous *canzone*, represented the enamored soul as ascending to the throne of God, the *fedeli d'amore*, fascinated by the idea, committed themselves to the mystical influence of the contemporary Franciscan philosophy, which preserved the essential concepts and procedures of late Platonism and Augustinian intuitive idealism. This was the source of their lyrical pantheism and the background of the profane ecstasies in which it was manifested. Its positive content and rational support were determined, for the empiricists of the group, by the Aristotelian system, for the intellectualists by the Averroistic conclusions, and by the Thomistic synthesis for whoever, like Dante, aspired to a fusion of reason and faith in God.

There is evidence enough that this lyricism did not remain confined to the narrow sphere of a few connoisseurs and enthusiasts. Dante himself hints at the speed with which his early poems became known throughout his native Florence and the eagerness with which the educated public of his day welcomed the new vernacular poetry. The notaries of Bologna filled the margins and empty spaces of their parchments with quotations from the most popular poems. Cavalcanti, Dante, Cino da Pistoia, Guido Orlandi, and many others liked to challenge their friends and the public to discussions of love casuistry. The poets of this mundane but spiritualized cult of love entered upon the strife-torn scene and disclosed the purifying, ennobling, and edifying power of a poetic symbolism that transformed the petty events of private, municipal, or provincial life into significant adventures and portentous phenomena. The 'sweet new style' of that poetry became the expression of a communal court of love and a purely intellectual nobility.

The prettiest women of each town, whom Dante numbered at sixty in Florence, were represented as a sort of celestial court centered around the elect—Beatrice, Selvaggia, Monna Lagia, Monna Vanna, and all the others. The multiple appearances, dress, acts, friends, and families of these ladies participated in the glorification, while the town itself was conceived as the stage of this visionary drama of transfiguration through the torments and beatitude of love. The usually reserved and modest behavior of a well-bred Italian lady assumed the character of a ritual, with a look, a salutation, or a smile as the only manifestations of a sympathetic or critical reaction. In this poetical sublimation of human life, the external world becomes an assemblage of symbols and symptoms, of marks and vestiges of a higher reality, the understanding of which is made possible by poetic imagination.

This lyrical state of mind of the *fedeli d'amore,* transformed by Dante into a coherent doctrinal symbolism, gave to the limited experience and emotional life of a circumscribed provincial world a cosmic amplitude. Poetry was no more than an agreeable game, a pleasant fiction, or an allegorical travesty of doctrines and maxims. It became the revelation of eternal truth, the source of profane ecstasies, the way to enlightenment and contemplation, the lyrical counterpart, and the fulfillment of the philosophical attempts to understand the spiritual structure of the world. Poetry no longer followed the precepts of an *Ars amandi* or an *Ars dictandi,* but appeared for the first time since antiquity as a transubstantiation of reality, as a hypostasis of human experiences, in which facts and things were nullified by the superior reality they were called to represent. Consequently it is almost impossible to prove the existence of those transfigured persons and to believe the events related or simply mentioned in this fictional sphere of a poetical symbolism. Yet through its personal or material embodiment the doctrinal mysticism of this spiritualized poetry takes on the human and realistic appearance that transforms a visionary inspiration into a living image of thought. Every lover of poetry who was affected by that sublimation of earthly reality felt himself connected with the divine order of the world and participated in the mystical love that rules and moves the universe.

❋   ❋   ❋

Poetry consequently acquired a new function and the poet a new mission. In an ingenious language of symbols and allusions, the poet made a higher wisdom accessible to the understanding of the common people. The vernacular idiom was ennobled by the

subject and refined by the poet's skill and imagination. For the
first time the Italian language dared to compete in higher forms
of art with the Latin of the philosophers and theologians. But
the *volgare illustre* had still to be created. The vague feeling of
an Italian linguistic unity had to be raised to the level of general
consciousness.

To that end Dante proclaimed his intention to create a dignified literary language endowed with the prestige of Latin and the
intelligibility of the vulgar tongue, an ideal and stable Italian
adequate to higher forms of style and to lofty topics of thought
and poetry. The delusion that a literary idiom could be set up
artificially revealed only the handicaps under which he labored
and the anxiety of a creative spirit in search of the material in
which to shape his world. After scrutinizing, one by one, fourteen of the leading Italian dialects, Dante concluded that they
were unfit to express any dignified idea. This systematic elimination of the spoken tongue in his incomplete treatise *De Vulgari
Eloquentia* is based on sensibility and insistence upon logical
consistency. Despite the negative attitude toward the Italian
dialects, Dante grew aware of the linguistic unity of the country
from the Alps to Sicily; for him the geographical concept of Italy
became a linguistic and cultural reality that lacked only spiritual
cohesion and a purified language. Dante felt it was his mission
to supply his country with these requirements. In the face of
the political corruption of his country and of the demoralization
of empire and papacy, he determined to rally the disintegrating
Italian people around a poet. He would make the vulgar tongue
an instrument of national regeneration by ennobling it with
spiritual substance.

Dante's speculations concerning an imaginary language belonging to everyone and no one led the poet to underrate his own
Florentine dialect. Yet in his own work it became the noble and
expressive idiom he had been seeking. Since the early years of
an Italian literature, the Sicilian court poets had assimilated the
uncouth native idiom to the morphology and phonetics of the
Tuscan dialect in an effort to purify and enrich their diction.
Tuscan had become the potential Italian language even before
Tuscany achieved its cultural pre-eminence. The political and

social factors that determined the development of a literary and national language in France and Spain were entirely absent in Italy, a decentralized nation, divided by stubborn particularism.

The persistence of Latin in all the higher fields of medieval life and culture favored the disintegration and diffusion of the vernacular idioms, since the language of the Church, of the schools, and offices represented the superior spiritual and cultural authority that unified the *disjecta membra* of Italian society. But secular poets in search of a language almost instinctively chose the dialect closest to Latin. The relative affinity of the Tuscan dialect to the literary Latin did not reside in grammar and syntax. In grammatical structure, the Italian dialects were all alike; they differed mostly in phonetics, vocabulary, and idiomatic expressions. In the Gallo-Italic group of the Upper Country, and in the dialects south of a line roughly connecting Orbetello with Ascoli Piceno, the shifts from the Latin phonetic system are so profound and varied that the original words are scarcely discernible. Dante was horrified by the harshness and vulgarity of all these dialects, when compared to the monumental nobility of Latin.

Only Tuscan preserved almost intact the old Latin vocalism, while adding a number of new sounds that made for increased sonority, fluidity, and variety of intonation. The Tuscan Italian dialects retain Latin consonants unaltered at the beginning of the words and dropped them at the end; they tend to soften certain harsh consonantal groups characteristic of the Latin, thus achieving increased flexibility of vocal timbre. In Tuscan all sounds have their full value, with no slurring or contraction, and the result is a fullness and expressiveness superior to that of any other language. The complete absence of nasals, the expressive ring of the lingual *r*, and the vibrant double consonants give the Tuscan dialects an incomparable mobility and clarity of articulation, a clear, natural emphasis, and a tonality that is supple but not mellow, energetic but not harsh.

The peculiarities of the Tuscan dialect predisposed it to become the literary language of Italy. Its fluidity, rhythmic refinement, and grace make it particularly suitable for singing. With its sonority, variety, and intense clarity it could compete favorably with the Provençal, which, despite a long process of literary refinement, still retained a certain asperity and inflexibility of sound, resulting largely from its frequent consonantal endings.

The phonetic advantages of the Tuscan dialect caused the first group of Italian poets at the Sicilian court to take over many of its natural sounds, which proved so suitable for singing. Soon, however, the intrinsic sonority of the language led these poets to abandon the traditional musical accompaniment and allow the natural accents of the poetic tongue to speak for themselves. By Petrarca's time only the *canzone* and other minor lyrical forms were still composed for musical recitation. The musical accompaniment for the sonnet, the most characteristic and successful form of Italian poetry, was dropped at an early date.

This first separation of music from poetry brought many changes in poetic style and language. For the first time in literary history, words, verses, and rhymes existed for their own sake, independent of tones and modes. Consequently the greatest possible expression had to be brought forth from words, sounds, rhythms, and rhymes. Because of the musical virtuosity required by sung poetry, minstrelsy had been a profession since the middle of the twelfth century in Provence, France, and Italy; poets and singers wandered from one petty court to another, participating in banquets, receptions, weddings, and public festivals. Poets usually composed their love poems for others; such works were regarded as mere artistic performances that did not engage the feelings of the authors. It was only when musical accompaniments ceased to be the fashion that lyric poetry achieved a quality of intimacy and sincerity. It was at the end of the thirteenth century, in Dante's day, that this development occurred in Italy; the poet and the musician became distinct personalities and a poem no longer required the mediation of a singer and lute-player.

The poets of Dante's circle left to professional composers the task of setting to music their *canzoni, ballate, madrigali.* Occasionally they introduced the recitation of their sonnets with a short instrumental prelude intended to give the keynote of the poem. But this could be dispensed with. The rendition of those higher lyrical forms assumed the character of a melodic recitative.

Under these circumstances a more substantial poetry was developed in the two new centers of Italian culture where the penchant for making verses spread to all classes and developed into a literary infatuation. The appearance of a *canzone* by Guinizelli, Guido Cavalcanti, or Dante was a sensational event; it became the talk of the town and was recorded in chronicles. Poetry ceased to be a game for courtly idlers or a trade for professional literati; it became the substance of life for a resurgent laity. It was through this lyric poetry, rather than by the vernacular encyclopaedias in verse and prose, that Dante's contemporaries participated in the higher spiritual aspirations of their day. It was through this lyricism that he conceived of a more substantial and edifying type of poetry, in which the sentimental spiritualization of love was associated with the figurative indoctrination and intellectual refinement of a new secular aristocracy.

Dante first realized this very personal idea of poetry in his *Banquet,* an incomplete treatise in verse and prose written in the early years of his political exile, when he was forced to wander 'as a pilgrim, almost as a beggar,' from one Italian court to another. It was during this desperate search for a home that he became fully aware of the misery, ignorance, and confusion of his countrymen in a world dominated by the rapacity and venality of its masters. The idea of becoming the spiritual and moral redeemer of his country came to him after the failure of his attempts to bring peace, dignity, and order to his native town of Florence, 'fairest and most illustrious daughter of Rome.' For the fulfillment of his national mission there was no other instrument than his countrymen's common language, to the praise of which he dedicated the first book of his *Banquet.* The audience he had in mind was not composed of 'people who are friends of knowledge for utilitarian reasons, as are jurists, physicians, and almost all the ecclesiastics, i.e. people who do not study for the sake of wisdom, but for the acquisition of money and dignities.' [2] Dante set out to fulfill the vague old longing of the Italian laity for free expansion of the secular personality. And ultimately he

[2] *Convivio,* III, xi.

was able to rescue from a paralyzing impasse those sections of Italian society that had always been deprived of the spiritual advantages of the professional scholars and of their ecclesiastical or feudal protectors. He felt himself to be the representative, master, and leader of a new nobility that did not reside—as he said—in birth, wealth, or power, but was an individual privilege of the moral personality distinguished by the practice of intellectual and social virtues.

Poetry was for Dante the school of this nobility, and the poet its herald and leader. In the *Banquet* he strove to be for his country what the Virgil of the *Divine Comedy* was for mankind: a mentor on the way to human knowledge, wisdom, and perfection, conceived in a secular spirit. Dante intended his scientific and moral encyclopaedia to be read as the Latin classics were read in the schools of the learned, with the poetical text interpreted allegorically, and the heroes, myths, and figures conceived as the embodiment of philosophical ideas and moral concepts. Under the veil of his amorous poems he developed a substantial, comprehensive philosophy. And science—astronomy and physics —is introduced into this parabolic system of knowledge and art in the double function of a scholastic discipline and of a cosmic symbology.

This intentional and consistent dualism of indoctrination and fantasy, of positive knowledge and allegorical intrepretation, transforms the wonders of nature, the experiences of life, the artistic emotions, and the human passions into intellectual phantoms and subtle allusions. A 'noble lady' is both the beloved woman and philosophy; the heavens first appear in the scientific order of Ptolemy and then as images of the different sciences; love is represented as an erotic transport and as the 'zeal that leads a man in his practice of art and science.' It is clear that this web of fantasy and science could neither create an art nor produce a philosophy. This visionary, contradictory, indeterminate attitude toward art and nature, life and philosophy, reality and ideas did not belong to the Italian spiritual traditions and was consequently abandoned by the poet himself, who evidently never felt at ease in this labyrinth of facts and dreams. How little convinced he was of the efficacy of this poetic style is shown by

the first *canzone* of the book, which is also the first allegorical
poem either in the vernacular or Latin literature of Italy. Dante
turns to this poem—directed to the Intelligences of the third
heaven—and asks it, if the readers find it too difficult to understand, to show them at least how beautiful it is.[3] He rightly
felt that the formal elegance of his work would appeal more
directly and convincingly to his countrymen than all the occult
science buried in the strophes of his poem. If the attempt to
introduce allegories into Italian mind and art failed, these ingenious poems still possessed an outward beauty that justified
them and caused them to survive.

This primacy of the aesthetic, however, did not mean that the
poet and his public renounced the immanent symbolism of art.
For Dante and for Italians of all times, beauty is never merely
extrinsic, but an absolute moral category, independent of specific
doctrines, maxims, and educational intentions. If the ascetic
morality of medieval times supported Seneca's contention that
virtue in itself, regardless of external features, is beauty, the
secular feeling was that, on the contrary, beauty is virtue, or at
least its expression and condition. Beauty remained for the
Italians a privilege with metaphysical rather than intellectual
and ethical implications. It is for the sake of beauty that the
Italian artists and artisans tend to disregard the practical, moral,
functional, pragmatic, and empirical aspects of their work. This
tendency is more manifest in the further development of Italian
art and poetry. In the doctrinal fervor of his day and in the
consciousness of his national and universal mission, Dante combined the intrinsic virtue of his poetic intuitions with the moral
purpose of his work—until he recognized the futility of this attempt and turned to a more personal, sound, and impressive
poetical conception.

His philosophy did not change essentially in this development
of his artistic personality. The fundamental concepts that determine the structure of his *Banquet* are the same as those attributed
by Virgil to the expected secular redeemer of the world: namely,
wisdom, love, and virtue.[4] To each one of these concepts a sec-

[3] *Ponete mente almen com'io son bella.*
[4] *Inferno,* I, 104.

tion of Dante's treatise is devoted, revealing in the whole, despite
the fragmentary character of the book and its scholastic texture,
a unique spiritual intensity and an independent approach to the
moral reintegration of his country. Love, in this context, is the
spiritual union of the soul with the beloved thing according to
the degree of its perfection, which is at its height in the human
mind in quest of truth and virtue. This quest is the origin of
philosophy, which emanates from the divine wisdom and is the
goal of the human intellect. Nobility is the origin of the intellectual and moral virtues, which are the conditions for the attainment of wisdom through love and of spiritual happiness through
science. Every single virtue of the eleven that constitute, according to Aristotle, the code of human perfection was to be discussed
in the treatise to the end of 'leading back the people to the right
path toward the knowledge of the true nobility.' The substantial fragment of this last book reveals the symptomatic importance of the whole work in the growth of a moral consciousness
suited to the peculiar conditions of the Italian society of the
time.

Although deeply religious and animated by Biblical pathos,
Dante was never directed by ascetic ideals or mystical aims in
this quest for an ethical foundation and organization of human
life. To him it was self-evident that the realization of his ethical
ideals would be pleasing to God and therefore he had no need
to stress it. His main concern is with human activity within the
framework of an organized and stable society. It is this moral
approach to the problems of general well-being and individual
responsibility that leads him to consider the political conditions
for the establishment of a human community. First of these conditions is universal peace, necessary for the realization of human
happiness and guaranteed by the moral power of an imperial
world ruler whose authority rests on a philosophical foundation.
However important theological considerations may have been,
Aristotle's *Ethics* provided the real substance of the new moral
code. In this context there is no question of the theological virtues—faith, hope, and charity—which lead to eternal beatitude in
the celestial Paradise. Nor are the intellectual virtues particularly
stressed, because, as Dante says, intelligence, knowledge, and

wisdom intervene only in contemplative life, while here he is concerned with guiding his ideal layman toward an active life that will be both happy and worthy.[5]

He enumerates not only the four cardinal virtues of the Christian ethic as conditions for the attainment of this goal, but also the eleven discussed by Aristotle, which Dante classifies according to the four ages of man. The ethical concepts taken from the Greek philosopher are illustrated with topics from classical and Arabic authors, and the symbols of this moral nobility are borrowed from Virgil, Ovid, Statius, and Lucan. Ethical perfection is never considered from the point of view of sin and penitence or illustrated by stories from Scripture or the lives of the saints as in the usual didactic literature of the day. It is 'not only those who follow Saint Benedict, Saint Augustine, Saint Francis, and Saint Dominic in dress and life, who may live up to a right and true religion.' [6]

Dante declares himself to be 'the experienced and obedient servant' of all those laymen who did not wish to make a profession of learning but to achieve wisdom for its own sake. His political career and private life had shown that there was no escape for a victim of adverse fortune and human malignance, who wished to preserve his dignity, individuality, and human rights in the active community of men, and not to vanish into monastic seclusion or the twilight of professional scholarship. His philosophy is conceived as a living being, to be worshiped as a 'noble lady,' because his moral regeneration of the world is intended in a pragmatic and not in a contemplative spirit. Christian morality, which looked on secular activity as a road to damnation rather than salvation, offered little scope for such virtues as liberality, magnanimity, munificence, and tolerance, when applied in the common practice of life.

Some of these virtues were the prerogatives of the feudal aristocracy that had developed the rules for their practice in court and public life. But a fluctuating, unstable society composed of a disrupted nobility, an industrious and turbulent middle class, and destitute plebeian multitudes held little room for the

[5] *Convivio*, IV, xvii.
[6] Ibid. IV, xxviii.

theory and practice of the courtly virtues. Dante's intention was
to do away with the demoralizing, pharisaical conflicts between
the intellectual and moral virtues, in order to make earthly happiness possible without a renunciation of God's gifts to man.
He wanted human redemption to begin on earth through active
justice and not only through renunciation and contempt of the
world. And that justice he conceived as embodied in the imperial power as a secular institution working under divine protection and consequently independent of the papal power and
the clerical hierarchy.

These conceptions imply a more or less overt profession of
the equivalence of contemplative and active life, of ecclesiastical and secular dignity, of theological and philosophical conclusions. Dante is thoroughly orthodox in all dogmatic and institutional questions, but he consistently asserts the autonomous
essence of active life and morals. This conviction justifies and
supports his belief in the autonomy of the two groups of virtues,
with the Pope, inspired by revealed doctrine, as a guide to
celestial beatitude, and the Emperor, directed by philosophical
enlightenment, as the secular leader of mankind. Dante elaborated this thought with greater vehemence, consistency, and
scholarship in his treatise on the *Monarchy*, written for the representatives of the two universal authorities and consequently
composed in the pretentious Latin of the papal and imperial
courts. In the more popular and theoretical *Banquet*, the political
aspects of morality are considered only in allusions and parables;
the Emperor is represented as the embodiment of the new nobility of the righteous and likened to a rider of the human will.

It is in this context that his 'wretched Italy' appears to him in
its lawlessness and moral disorder that no theological and intellectual virtues, no ecclesiastical authority and influence can remedy. From this point of view Rome had not even accomplished
her mission as the predestined center of human redemption. As
the seat of both authorities for all time, Rome was still the center of the two independent divine institutions created for the
celestial beatitude and worldly happiness of all mankind. Only
in a framework of universal peace and monarchy could Dante's
native country and town be restored to a state of well-being.

Only a reversion of the Church to her original spiritual mission would preserve her power of salvation. In this utopian vision of two equal and independent authoritarian powers ruling over the whole world, expressed with impassioned dialectic in the treatise on the *Monarchy* and with almost frenetic eloquence in the epistles, we see a great soul in despair and anger transcending the limits of national concerns and municipal strife in search of a total, radical, revolutionary solution of the problems arising from general ignorance, political wickedness, and moral obtuseness.

All the extended scholarship and dialectic ability displayed in these writings could not make that lofty vision more realistic and definite. However, the medieval web of abstractions, deductions, and subtleties in which those political ideals are entangled should not lead us to discard them as mere dreams of a visionary poet. Their utopian substance is no more utopian than the ideal of Plato's republic, the liberty, equality, and fraternity of the French Revolution, the hopes embodied in political manifestos, in Wilson's League of Nations, and in the Atlantic Charter. Dante believed that a total solution of the political problems was, in the last analysis, a moral and not a practical task. Yet he was realistic in reckoning with empire and papacy as with two indestructible institutions. The Holy Roman Empire survived until 1806 and was succeeded by many unholy empires which still subsist in name or fact. And as to the Roman pontiff, he remains a potential and actual political power, still resisting the age-old pressure of the laical world for the separation of Church and State.

*   *   *

Contrary to superficial impressions, Dante's theories represent the first daring and consistent attempt to overcome the characteristic forces of medieval politics and society. Neither the empire nor the papacy was of purely medieval character; both were stable institutions handed down from antiquity. It makes little difference whether they are considered as divine institutions or simply as human accomplishments. What counts is their existence and survival even under adverse conditions. It would have been utopian and even absurd to ignore or repudiate them.

What Dante assailed was the medieval idea of supremacy and hierarchy, which he replaced by the concept of the balance of the leading powers, inspired by Averroistic dualism and the imperial policy of Frederick the Second. Dante was neither a Guelf nor a Ghibelline and was well aware of the emptiness of those factional designations. Although a nobleman himself, speaking—as he said—to princes, barons, knights, and the whole Italian nobility, he rejected the privileges of the medieval aristocracy, which he wanted to transform from within into a spiritual and cultural élite. Feudalism counted so little in Italy that it could be neglected in these discussions without prejudice to political reality. For Dante, only spiritual reality was decisive in human destinies; he was consequently able to transcend the contingencies of his contemporary world and to discover the vital forces of Italy's intellectual and cultural renewal.

Dante is the first representative of an intellectual interest that studied the ancients not as models of Latin eloquence, but rather as the living sources of human wisdom and symbols of human accomplishment. He knew only indirectly the Greek authors mentioned in the *Banquet,* but all the Latin poets and writers quoted in his works were familiar to every educated man of his day, in Italy and abroad. He became acquainted with the classics not through any school curriculum, but by his own efforts when the death of Beatrice Portinari, in 1292, led him to seek consolation for the anguish of his heart. He wanted to remain in the world, whose attractions and evils he experienced as a gentleman, a politician, a state official, a husband, a *paterfamilias.*

The ascetic and didactic literature of ecclesiastical character had little to offer such men. Only the books of pagan antiquity dealt with the common problems of practical morality and the things of life, such as love and friendship, youth and age, laws and liberty, adversity and fortune, affliction and rejoicing, and all such aspects of human existence that cannot be judged from the standpoint of sin and redemption alone. Divine providence, for example, never entirely absorbed the ancient concept of fortune which continued to live as a deity throughout the Middle

Ages because there was no substitute for it in the Christian system.

Dante found pertinent answers to all these questions in the works of Boethius and Cicero, which aroused his interest in philosophical solutions to the moral problems raised by the secular and practical way of life. He confessed to having been initiated into philosophy by Cicero's treatise on friendship, and there is no doubt that the *Banquet* was inspired by a passage in Cicero's *De Officiis*,[7] which teaches the science of virtue in accordance with Socrates' fundamental principle that ignorance is the cause of all human wickedness. Whether by emulation or unconscious affinity, Dante felt aware of a mission akin to that of Cicero, who was the first preceptor of Rome, while Dante, with his treatise, aspired to become the first mentor of Italian laymen, the mediator between professional philosophy and practical wisdom, the intellectual leader of an enlightened people. He followed the Roman orator in his effort to construct a code of practical morality for the élite whom he designated to revive the universal monarchy in the Stoic sense of a secular *patrocinium orbis terrarum,* a moral guardian of mankind,[8] rather than in the Guelf and Thomistic spirit of a universal papal theocracy.

Thus Dante's attitude toward Cicero is essentially different from the exclusive and scholarly humanism of Petrarca, who a generation later aroused the enthusiasm of his countrymen for the formal and moral qualities of the same dialogues and treatises. Petrarca and his followers intended to create upon the ruins of medieval society an aristocratic republic of letters that might live and flourish as a self-sufficient intellectual community protected from vulgar influences by the refined aesthetic sense and literary enthusiasm of its adherents. While Petrarca learned from Cicero the polished Latin that guarded him from the distressing reality of the world, Dante drew from Cicero the substance of his vulgar eloquence and set himself the task of creating a philosophical language that might compete with classical Latin in purity and clarity, and of divulging to the laity the noble doctrines of the Greek and Roman world.

[7] II, 2.
[8] *Monarchia,* II, v.

These conflicting aspects of Italian humanism will be considered in connection with its further development. Significant here is the circumstance that Dante became acquainted with the leading Latin classics before he embarked on the philosophical curriculum of the medieval schools. It was, as he said, the reading of Cicero's *Laelius* that prompted him to join both the schools of the friars and the debates of the *filosofanti* in Florence.[9] This famous passage of the *Banquet* shows that besides the theological schools organized by the mendicant orders, there were in Florence, as in several other towns of Italy, free disputations of laymen on current topics of culture and philosophy. Dante called these amateurs *filosofanti*, to distinguish them from professional scholars. The provincial nobility and bourgeoisie were, in their own way, carrying on the tradition of free disputations inaugurated as a courtly custom by Frederick II and spread throughout Italy by his vicars and officials, and this custom was to survive for several centuries. These informal groups, meeting in palaces and country houses, were later designated as 'academies' by way of emphasizing their secular, classical, and independent character.

In the schools of the friars Dante became familiar with the great systems of theology and the standard ecclesiastical literature of his day. In the disputes of the *filosofanti* he learned the intellectual needs of his contemporaries. It was under the influence of these groups that Dante's poetic inspiration became more and more enmeshed in scholastic intricacies and scholarly habits of thought and expression. He was prompted to arrange his youthful romantic verses in a cycle tied together by a prose commentary; this was the *Vita Nuova,* in which some scattered flowers of erudition adorn the grave of the glorified Beatrice. For years the creative imagination of this incomparable artist was thwarted by philosophical preoccupations that transformed his penetrating intuitions and perceptions into complex allegories and cryptic ambiguities.

The eclecticism of Dante's philosophy—though it can hardly be called philosophy in a scientific, systematic sense—not only

[9] *Convivio,* ii, xii.

reflects his irregular and polemical approach to the subject, but reveals the progressive disintegration of medieval philosophy as a whole. The deeper one penetrates into its labyrinth, the more evident and disturbing become the contradictions and dissensions between the different trends and schools. As can be seen by his treatises and poems, Dante seized on any doctrines that appealed to him, and did not follow the *filosofanti* in their efforts to conciliate all the many heterogeneous elements of current thought. Dante accepted the theology of Thomas Aquinas, the metaphysics of Bonaventura, the ethical system of Aristotle, Augustinian mysticism, Averroistic dualism, and the political vision of the Stoics, with many more concepts, maxims, and implications of Greek and Christian philosophy mixed in. He made no attempt to weave all these disparate elements into a coherent system. Not even the most resourceful dialectician of medieval Scholasticism was ever able to reconcile convincingly such basic and conflicting concepts as grace and nature, eternity and creation, matter and form, faith and reason, free will and Christian liberty, physical and ecstatic love, soul and intellect, et cetera. Inspired by his ardent love for personified philosophy, Dante transposed these concepts into a universal poetic imagery in which they live and act as figures and symbols, intimately bound up with the reality of human life.

This transfiguration of philosophy into poetry did not follow any didactic and practical purpose, but emanated from Dante's spiritual temperament, which induced him to experience, consider, and judge everything human and divine in universal, cosmic terms. This he had done since his adolescence, when the poets of his circle tried to overcome the narrow limits of courtly, literary, and occasional inspiration to broaden and spiritualize their sentiments. All his works were conceived in these catholic dimensions and in a transcendent mood; in the end he did give shape and consistency to the vague, discordant image of the universe created by myths, visions, and science. His poetic reality was always a universal harmony that prompted him to consecrate and deify the earthly and human aspects of the world and to bring divinity as close as possible to the experience and destiny of man. These cosmic relations were mere suggestions and

allusions in the *Vita Nuova,* written in or after 1293; they became scientific and moral links in the rational system of the
Banquet, a work of the early years of Dante's exile; and finally
they determined the structure of the *Divina Commedia,* the
poem of revelation and redemption,

'To which both heaven and earth have set a hand.' [10]

All these works have an autobiographical stimulus. Dante first
told the story of his love (*Vita Nuova*), then of his intellectual
enlightenment (*Convivio*), and finally the epic of his way to God
(*Divina Commedia*). In each case his personality is the focus
and center of a poetical world extending from the local and national stage of his life up to the heavenly spheres and the mystery of infinity and eternity. The *Divina Commedia* is the poetic
tale of the visionary journey that brought the poet 'from bond-
age to liberty' [11] without ever losing sight of this earth, his country, and the wants and troubles of mankind. For the attainment
of that metaphysical liberty through which his will coincided
with the divine, Dante created a poetical hypostasis of the universe embracing the contingent aspects of earthly existence, the
eternal phenomena of the natural world, and the mythical scenery of heaven, hell, and purgatory. His imagination was directed by the Aristotelian ethical system into giving shape to
hell, by the Catholic system of salvation in building his purgatory, and by the theological spiritualization of cosmology in
describing the realm of the blessed.

There is in this eschatological structure a perfect symmetry
determined by the idea of the Trinity, which is reflected, with
its multiples, in all the basic formal elements of this imaginary
world and even in the strophe of the poem. In this way Dante
transformed into a congruent architectural order the vague, confused, traditional, and primitive representations of the supernatural realms of damnation, hope, and glory, which never were
organized and regulated by ecclesiastical precepts or a theological norm. The old chaotic images of damnation and salvation,
as well as the contradictory assumptions of seers and philoso-

[10] *Paradiso,* xxv, 1.
[11] *Paradiso,* xxxi, 85.

phers, are replaced by an architectural symmetry supported by theological reasoning. His architectural genius was not inspired by a geometrical idea of the universe, but by the vision of an ideal order of all things. Although eminently personal and without precedent in art or literature, this artistic harmonization of the divine, human, and natural aspects of the world carried a force of conviction superior to all comprehensive systems of philosophy, because the poem appealed with equal vigor to intellect and imagination, to rational objectivity and mythical fancy, to realistic temperaments and visionary spirits.

By these means Dante imposed on faith and reason a universal order of his own creation so stringent and exhaustive that no substitute for his other world is conceivable in terms of poetry or theology. This poetic mythology is substantiated by every human experience known to Dante through his own life or the study of history, and by the most complete knowledge of science and learning accessible in his day. But neither his orthodox theological scheme nor that vanished historical substance determined the vitality of the poem and its survival. It is the artistic mastery of structure and detail, of forms and tones, of motifs and ornaments, of words, rhythms, and rhymes that perpetually rejuvenate the obsolete substance, the episodic elements, the scholarly ballast, the remote allusions to a world long dead. In fact, Dante's Catholicism is pre-Tridentine and his culture thoroughly medieval in scope and sense. His lofty Christianity never materialized nor did his imperial patriotism ever become a vital aspiration of the Italian nation. There was nothing in his philosophy to enlighten even the generations close to his own, and his political theories appeared utopian even to his contemporaries, who hunted Henry VII to his death in Buonconvento, in 1313, and drove Louis the Bavarian from Italy, in 1329. Nor did those bits of medieval science included in the poem or its cosmology contribute essentially to its perfection.

What animates all these antiques and oddities is Dante's vigorous poetic flow. It was his poetic genius that made it possible to realize the didactic and practical aims of his work, but in a way very different from that intended by the poet. He wanted it to be read for its literal, allegorical, moral, and anagogic sense,[12] and some of his commentators, both early and modern, have tried to do this by burying Dante's creative inspiration under a mass of irrelevant erudition. In reality it is the power of Dante's imagination that keeps alive the heterogeneous bulk of medieval lore enshrined in his poem. Dante gave heed to every aspect of his world, the religious, the moral, and the political, the passions and dreams, the glories and horrors. And if all these still inspire the modern mind, it is because of the artistic transfiguration they received through Dante. His poetry kept alive through the ages all the varied components of his writings, which became inalienable elements of the Italian cultural substance, just as the facts and myths of antiquity survived, in different intellectual climates, through the genius of classic poetry.

*   *   *

The secret of this vitality is to be found in Dante's style. Without the magic touch of his language much of the substance of his poem would be dead information, of purely academic interest. In Dante's case style is not only the man but everything. And although its dynamics is determined by imponderable elements that cannot be logically formulated, certain of its essential traits are accessible to precise investigation.

Its most characteristic feature is the richness of its figures. Dante's poetical reality rests on the abundance and precision of the similes that substantiate his imaginary world. It was the natural and human aspects of empirical reality that most contributed to the construction and description of his supernatural cosmic system. His vision reflects the realities of his earthly life in innumerable images, scenes, personalities, events, and sentiments. While the structural design of his *Inferno* is inspired by Aristotle's moral system, the Mountain of Purgatory suggested by an ideological geography, and the *Paradiso* conceived after the spiritualized late classical and Christian cosmology, the body of this rational, fictional, and supernatural organism is determined by the reality of our earthly existence. His *Inferno* is the

---

[12] Epistle to Can Grande della Scala, par. 7.

realm of human passions, his *Purgatorio* reflects the human yearning for perfection, and his *Paradiso* fulfills the human aspiration to divine knowledge and final salvation.

The intimate and ultimate connection between the transcendent and the empirical world, the interdependence of metaphysics and physics, of the realms of eternity and of earthly contingency, are all expressed through a poetical dialectic of similes: the divine is described in terms of human experience and the human permeated with the light and essence of divinity. And the spheres from which the terms of comparison are taken embrace heaven and earth, the phenomena of nature, the life and works of man, the arts and trades, myth, legend, history, and every other aspect of reality. With this chain of images and allusions all things and aspects of the world appear linked together in a poetic pantheism; all participate in the cosmic harmony of Dante's universe. The perfect correspondence of the single elements with the whole system of the world—an effect which no philosophy had ever fully achieved—here appeared in the grandeur and symmetry of a vision. Thus Dante the poet outdid the philosopher, dissolving the contradictions of a discordant intellectual eclecticism in a living, intuitive synthesis.

Naive admirers of the poet in his day and ours seem to have been fascinated by the amount of doctrine collected in the poem and displayed in the harmonious sequel of its hundred cantos. We know now that this immense store of erudition subsists by virtue of Dante's poetic language and artistic design. The poet did not leave behind an encyclopaedia of medieval knowledge, but a body of living symbols, a galaxy of similes in which truth and fiction appear thoughtfully intertwined. In this way poetry achieved such proportions and dimensions as never before. Classic metaphor had been limited in scope to a determined number of motifs and spheres. The medieval Latin poetry is almost entirely bare of imagination and realistic detail alike. Only a few conventional comparisons constitute the poetic imagery of the troubadours. Dante was able to infuse poetic life into the most ordinary, familiar, and even prosaic occurrences in natural and human reality, into the theological abstractions and the doctrines of science and philosophy.

F

In the *Divina Commedia* the divine unity of the world is not demonstrated by logical disquisitions or perceived in a mystical rapture. It is represented through the interaction of the elements of reality, by their conformity and harmony as revealed in poetic comparisons. It is this poetic communion that made it possible for the divine and human mind to meet in an intimate synthesis never attained in any mystical philosophy, natural science, or theological system. Hence it is arbitrary and unsuitable to encircle Dante within any single school of thought. Because of its poetic essence Dante's mind and work transcend the limit of creeds and systems, and reveal themselves only to those who are susceptible to the charm of poetry and the magic of art. The poem is truly universal, beyond the interest and validity of its intellectual and factual content, because of its consistent figurative interchange between the two spheres of abstraction and corporeality. Dante disclosed to his contemporaries the whole world of God and man; future generations learned to discover and contemplate these things through his eyes, in his spirit, and in terms of poetry, not of science and scholarship. In this way he became the master and leader of a nation that did not yet exist as a political or cultural unit. Into that nation Dante transfused his passions and ideals, his resentments and his magnanimity, his criticism and optimism, his religious devotion and homely feelings, his transfiguring love and his destroying hatred; and, more than anything else, a sense of justice, measure, equity, and moral nobility.

Dante's command of his native language, his aptness and versatility in the use of metaphor, was unequaled. He once said that no rhyme ever induced him to express anything contrary to his purpose, 'but that often he made words in his poetry express meanings differing from those of other people.' His awkward dialect with its brief and poor literary tradition became, in Dante's hand, an instrument equal to the graphic representation of a universal vision. The relative affinity of the Tuscan dialect to the Latin language favored the unobtrusive absorption of learned words. But what gave his language its incomparable force of expression, its personal touch and breadth of meaning, was the poet's skill and audacity in discovering in words the unexpected relations between all things and beings of the physical and spiritual world.

Dante seldom indulged, however, in the etymological puns so frequently used in the scholastic writings of his day. The expressiveness of his words is derived from the accommodation of their original and literal significance to the specific function determined by the will and imagination of the poet who lifted the entire bulk of his native language into the dimensions of his world-embracing poetical vision. Furthermore, he enhanced the intensity of his expression by stressing the intrinsic musicality of the language through a delicate distribution of accents and sounds. Internal assonances, shifts of intonation, retarding pauses, and animated rhythms give his triplets an inimitable fluidity, equally expressive of lyric tenderness, epigrammatic sharpness, and monumental composure. Dante's poetic mastery penetrates even the duller and more prosaic passages of the poem, which participate in the general counterpoint of the work.

The importance of the language and prosody for appreciation of the poem has limited its diffusion and influence. Foreign translations of the *Divina Commedia* destroy its poetic essence and emphasize its learned and historical aspects. Only a few episodes of the *Inferno* have acquired a certain popularity in other countries. The French have ignored the poem completely; the Spaniards toward the end of the medieval era were attracted by the gruesome and pathetic scenes of Dante's Hell; while the Germans and the English-speaking peoples have long considered the poem as a book with seven seals, in spite of many attempts to translate it and numerous learned commentaries. In Italy, from Dante's lifetime up to our day, the *Commedia* represents the substance and foundation of national culture, literature, and education. Dante's treatise on the *Monarchy* could be publicly burned as heretical by the order of the papal legate, Cardinal Bertrand du Pouget; the vernacular poems could be prohibited by the Dominicans of Florence, in 1335; but such was public enthusiasm for the *Commedia* that no ecclesiastical authority would have dared to suppress it or condemn it as dangerous. The poet was granted the satisfaction of hearing his verses publicly sung in the streets and squares of Italian towns.

The poem was transcribed in all parts of Italy and soon became the country's most famous and cherished book. The oldest preserved manuscript was written a few years after Dante's death by a man from Fermo in the Marches, for the order of a Genoese patrician; and the last fourteenth-century copy was transcribed, in 1399, in the small town of Tropea on the southernmost tip of Calabria. Giovanni Boccaccio inaugurated, in 1373, the public explanation of the poem from the pulpit of a small church in Florence. At that time the cultural unity of Italy had already been achieved in the name of Dante.

What this poet gave to his countrymen is at the same time evident and incommensurable. His political and religious universalism had no practical consequences and met with little understanding, but it was part and parcel of a transcendent, moral aspiration that his consummate art and communicable enthusiasm have preserved for all time. His inspiring vision of justice and moral brotherhood became the measure and test of human and national reality. After centuries of spiritual conflict and moral laxity, Dante conceived Christianity in the spirit of Italian religious secularism. In this mood and conviction he carried his wrath from the depths of Hell to the threshold of the Empyrean, castigating the clerical and monkish contamination of the divine truth. The whole theological and scientific structure of the poem is permeated with a Biblical spirit derived directly from the Scriptures by a layman, deeply religious yet filled with the love of life. Here Dante fulfilled an old aspiration of the Italian people, who frequently risked the snares of heresy in order to hear the unadulterated word of God.

Along with the Holy Books, the pagan literature of antiquity emerged from the schools and chronicles and became the support of a poetical world that reflected the history of human vicissitudes. In his appreciation of antiquity Dante accepted the traditional medieval opinion that respected and praised the ancient civilization as an instrument of divine providence and as a secular prelude to human salvation. But what distinguishes his attitude from that of all philosophers, theologians, and historians of the Middle Ages is his conviction of the actual and perennial value, significance, and authority of pre-Christian achievements.

For Dante only 'the false Gods of lying fame' [13] were gone forever; but all those who contributed to the greatness and glory
of that world 'with skill and art,' [14] i.e. by human means, still
lived as a necessary element of human happiness and perfection.
In Dante's opinion, antiquity is a substantial part of the modern
world and not only a historical episode in the predestined development toward the final triumph of Christianity. The primary
importance of antiquity in his moral consciousness and system
of thought, involving even the salvation of unbaptized heroes
like Cato, Trajan, and Ripheus the Trojan, manifests his belief
in the essential unity of enlightened secularism and divine revelation, both of which he finds indispensable for the establishment of a perfect human society and the individual emancipation of man from sin and error.

Dante owes his salvation to divine intercession, it is true, but
it is only in the last stage of his ascent toward God that a saint
and mystical seer, Bernard 'of Clairvaux, guides his purified
mortal eyes to the contemplation of the divine mystery. Up to
that final episode of his visionary journey, a glorified Roman
poet and a consecrated Florentine woman, Virgil and Beatrice,
lead his steps from error to perfection. In this ascent from the
material world to the mystical union with God, human reason
precedes the sacred doctrine as its necessary condition, just as
in the history of mankind the epoch of secular knowledge anticipated the final revelation of divine truth. As a layman, a believer,
and an Italian, Dante felt the vitality of that historical past embodied in Virgil's figure and mission. Virgil, in Dante's vision,
is the perfect representative of the secular, Roman, and imperial
civilization whose Christian renewal the poet proclaimed as the
special task of the Italian people.[15] In Dante's mystical humanism, antiquity is ubiquitous as a spiritual reality, with its myths
and doctrines, its glories and fallacies, its wisdom and blindness,
its accomplishments and delusions.

But antiquity is also a great national and universal reality,
expressing with Ulysses the tragic zeal to know the world and

[13] *Inferno*, I, 72.
[14] *Purgatorio*, xxvii, 130.
[15] *Monarchia*, iii, vi, etc.; *Epistolae*, vi, xi.

man's evil and virtue; or with Cato the uncompromising love of
civic liberty; or with Trajan the triumph of justice even over
the dogmatic order of the universe. The poetic co-ordination of
antiquity and Christianity is extended over the entire vision as
an intimate structural element of the poem, appearing in the
mythological figures of Hell, in the classical examples of human
virtues represented, or whispered by mysterious voices, in Purgatory, and, finally, in innumerable reminiscences and allusions in
the *Paradiso,* where St. Peter's terrible invective against his
iniquitous successors culminates in the praise of Scipio, the
defender of the Roman 'glory of the world.' [16]

Thus pagan antiquity is inseparably intertwined with Christian actuality, just as reverence for the Roman virtues is coupled
with devotion· to the Biblical rules of life and the evangelical
maxims of redemption. Dante's vision of antiquity is not a bookish one. The myths, ideas, and facts of ancient times contribute
as a historical reality to the representation of his imaginary world,
in which they live as symbolic figures in innumerable episodes
and descriptions, along with the expressions of human passion
and personal experience, along with the geographical location, the
meteorological, physical, and astronomical aspects of nature, the
political events and local anecdotes, the great and petty figures
of history, and all the elements of life and art that constituted the
personality of the poet and the originality of his work.

[16] *Paradiso,* xxvii, 62.

VIII. *The Early Development of Italian Art*

D ANTE'S influence on Italian culture is ubiquitous, although in some aspects imponderable. Never did the poet attain a definite spiritual leadership in the political, religious, or even literary field. His popularity was never able to revive the idea of a universal empire, centered in Rome, or to break the power and tradition of a political papacy transformed in his day into an instrument of French expansion, and later into an Italian principality and military power. The embittered Italian particularism was not affected by the patriotism of a man who combined a devotion to his native town with love of his country, and proudly proclaimed the world to be his home 'as the ocean is to the fish.'

The intellectual interests of the country soon moved away from the basic scholasticism of his thought and culture. The loftiness of his inspiration, the vigorous mark of his personality impressed upon every nuance of his style, and the intense conciseness of his verses made his poetry inimitable, unique, and inaccessible to those rhymesters who tried to profit by his popularity. Nor can the great success of his work be measured by the vast commentaries it inspired, beginning with that of his sons and developed by others to encyclopaedic proportions.

It is one of the most paradoxical expressions of literary fame that the *terza rima* of the *Divina Commedia*, created by Dante as the form suited to his poetical inspiration, soon came to be used for frivolous, satirical doggerel. And while some Tuscan painters were inspired by the poem, only Michelangelo Buonar-

roti was really congenial to his great countryman, whose monumental solidity and transcendent vision he shared.

Dante's influence is felt not in special fields of literary and
artistic activity, but in the whole Italian atmosphere, in the
reverence and familiarity that surround the poet's memory, in
the popular legends and jocose anecdotes that have grown up
around him, in the Italian language molded by his genius. For
more than six centuries the Italian people have found in the
Commedia an inexhaustible source of instruction and inspiration, of consolation and delight; the whole life of the nation has
become identified with it. In the course of so many generations
it has gathered vitality, luster, and grandeur from countless individual and national experiences reflected in Dante's work as
if in a sacred book embracing the sum of human accomplishments and wisdom. A generation after Dante's death, Giovanni
Boccaccio expressed this thought in an inscription for a portrait
of the poet:

> Dante Alighieri, a dark oracle
> Of wisdom and of art I am; whose mind
> Has to my country such great gifts assigned
> That men account my powers a miracle.[1]

To his contemporaries Dante disclosed the reality of the external world with its natural features, its intrinsic beauty, the
infinite variety of its aspects and spectacles, the inspiring power
of its phenomena. In his poem nature and history appear not
only as divine allegories and designs, but also for their own sake.
In a more elaborate and significant form the *Commedia* teaches
the same community of the creation with the Creator disclosed
by Francis of Assisi to a less critical generation. In Dante's poem,
human achievements and the outward world belong to a universal
reality reflecting the divine wisdom. It is from the contemplation
of this reality in its multifarious evidence that a new religious
sense developed, embracing a scientific curiosity and a joyful
appreciation of life's appearances.

This is the spirit and mood that led Dante's contemporary,
Giotto di Bondone, a simple man from the country around Flor-

[1] Translated by D. G. Rossetti.

ence, to introduce his inspired realism of form and color into the pictorial representation of sacred scenes. Trained in the workshop of Cimabue, he was a craftsman, not a philosopher or scholar. Even in his maturity Giotto never burdened his natural genius with theological doctrines or intellectual ambitions, and never deflected from his determination to project upon the walls of churches and sanctuaries living images of Biblical episodes and the miracles of the saints. Though he was deeply imbued with the spirit of St. Francis, scenes from whose life he often represented, the only poem by Giotto that has come to us in reliable manuscripts is a humorous protest against poverty:

> For us discernment, nor integrity,
> Nor love of life, nor plea
> Or virtue, can her cold regard instil.
> I call it shame and ill
> To name as virtue that which stifles good.

It was not the Franciscan doctrine and philosophy, the mystical trend of the Spirituals or the Joachimite apocalyptic visions, but the seraphic love of the creature that gave shape, body, and life to Giotto's artistic genius. It found its freest and keenest expression in the great cycles of Biblical narratives and lives of the saints painted, with the collaboration of his pupils, in the early years of the fourteenth century in the Arena Chapel at Padua, in Santa Croce at Florence shortly after 1317, and finally in the basilica of St. Francis at Assisi. In these lively, colorful scenes the mystery of redemption and its revival in St. Francis are represented as contemporary events, with features, types, and gestures as close as possible to those of the public for whom they were intended. Only a few unobtrusive symbols of divinity persisted in these lifelike images of the metaphysical drama of salvation and sanctification. The majestic rigidity of Byzantine models, the ecstatic aloofness of Romanesque sculpture, and the frail, elegant, expressive spiritualism of Gothic types were transformed into a familiar, natural style, whose keynote was human in gestures, in emotion, aspects, and traits.

The whole past of Christian art persists as reminiscence in Giotto's style. But the theological abstractions, the iconographical

F*

motifs, the hieratical attitudes and didactic intentions vanished
in the dramatic lyricism of his inspiration. Supernatural happenings were imbued with a contemporary, even local, reality, and
seemed to unfold under the very eyes of the spectators. Such a
consistent humanization of religion and art had never been undertaken since antiquity. The figures in Giotto's sacred scenes
are men, women, children, animals directly observed by the
artist. In the life of Christ only the golden halos mark the supernatural character of the figures and gestures, while a discreet
orientalism, a Negro hangman, a typical Roman official such as
Pilate, emphasize the geographical and historic remoteness of
the events.

This first attempt at a realistic representation of religious
scenes on the flat surface of a wall required space and dimensions, background and scenery, all the elements of a naturalistic
painting that had to be created out of the very vision and intention of the artist. This conception of artistic perfection and illusive three-dimensional representation marks the origin of Italian
art as an autonomous, national expression of a characteristic
attitude toward religion and the outward world. For this pictorial expression of sentiments and living appearances Giotto
had no models or traditions in classical or medieval, western or
oriental art. Nor is there any artistic theory in medieval philosophy, in the doctrines of Bonaventura, Aquinas, or their contemporaries, to account for the new trend in the figurative arts.
All these artistic theories were far behind the needs and experience of the new generations of masters and craftsmen. Giotto's
efforts to give his scenes and images depth and relief were certainly favored by the increasing naturalism of the sculptural
masterpieces of his contemporaries: Niccolò, Giovanni, Andrea
Pisano, who learned so much from French and North-Italian
craftsmen, and from the Roman monuments all over Italy. But
the plastic effect of Giotto's painting, the surprising variety of
his subjects and details presupposes a new technique, a new
relation between spirit and matter, a different conception of
art and nature. Much thought was devoted by later generations
of Italian artists to the aesthetic, technical, and general problems surrounding Giotto's innovations. But the master himself

spent little thought on the intellectual and spiritual justification of his style and skill. His natural genius was guided and inspired by the same exalted sense of bodily kinship with the external world, the same physical enjoyment of its aspect, as Dante had experienced.

This humanization of the arts was not inspired by any new theory, but fostered by a general revival of broad spiritual and artistic interests coinciding with the economic expansion, political consolidation, and urban development of Florence at the turn of the century. The artistic competition among the mendicant orders and the many artisan's guilds; the renewed architectural activity, leading to the construction of the towering town hall and the imposing cathedral amid unprecedented popular enthusiasm; the increasing number of talented craftsmen and masters; all were circumstances favorable to a more concrete and positive conception of the arts and a more daring expression of the creative imagination. Giotto was a true representative of the Florentine bourgeoisie, so little appreciated and understood by Dante, but ambitious and enterprising in its own way. Like the majority of his fellow-countrymen the master was not burdened by higher problems of science, philosophy, and religion; he took no part in the political strife and intellectual contests of his contemporaries. Their appreciation and his indefatigable activity endowed him with riches and honors, enabling him to lead a quiet, dignified life. This freedom and security made it possible for him to live entirely for his art. The traditions of medieval craftsmanship, which never was entirely specialized, helped him to master relief, sculpture, architecture, and certainly some of the minor arts, so that, in 1334, the Florentine municipal authorities appointed him chief architect and engineer of the state whose outstanding and most popular citizen he had become.

Giotto saw the world with the eyes of a free artist who was not, like most of his predecessors, obliged to take orders from a bishop, a prince, or a public authority. He had the daring and self-confidence of a sovereign spirit who conceived artistic activity as invention through imitation—we would say creation. He was still a painter of sacred stories devoted to the glorifica-

tion of God, the saints, and the celestial hierarchies, with all the
moral implications of medieval art. But Giotto's aim was to
create a holy reality with the elements of earthly experience,
and not merely a 'beautiful fiction' after the consecrated pattern
of the older church decoration. He turned away from the spectacular, hieratical, decorative mosaics and frescoes of the Roman
churches in which he worked in the last decade of the thirteenth
century, when the old theological symbolism sought to express
its abstract meanings through more animated gestures and imposing figures and scenes than before, but without any concession to the new generations that had learned to see the
world with new eyes. This, in its essential features, was the
so-called *maniera Greca*, which later generations of painters and
art historians praised Giotto for having overcome and replaced
by a 'modern,' Italian style. It was certainly not in that stiff,
solemn, and remote manner kept alive by tenacious traditions
that Dante liked to draw figures of angels in memory of his beloved Beatrice.[2] Giotto's angels and sacred figures were human
beings surrounded by a divine aura and ennobled by a superhuman perfection of feature and demeanor.

In contemplating the familiar episodes of the Passion or the
life of the Virgin on the walls of the Paduan chapel, erected,
in 1304, for the peace of the soul of a notorious usurer, or the
frescoes in the churches of Florence and Assisi still brightened by
the radiance of his most mature masterpieces, Giotto's contemporaries learned to recognize themselves in the harmonious, eloquent, and never cryptic representations of the divine immanence
in the human scene. The natural and architectural elements of
dramatic stagecraft assume a prominence and function never
before experienced in Christian art. The artistic problem of composition supplanted the old concatenation of symbols, and the
nothingness of golden infinity is replaced by exuberant life and
nature. But Giotto's effort to create a harmonious proportion between his human figures and their natural, architectural, spatial
environment was still purely personal. His perspective lies more
in his feeling than in any exact proportion. His anatomy is

[2] *Vita nuova*, xxxiv.

intuitive and not yet based on any systematic study. With his natural genius and artistic instinct, he inaugurated the long struggle of his countrymen for an illusive art that would bring together the divine and earthly aspects of the world in a perfect cosmic and objective harmony. Giotto was not concerned with determining the philosophical and mathematical canon of that harmony, but only with making the supernatural accessible to the simple devotion of the common folk.

The old Christian symbols of Oriental and Greek origin disappeared. The crushing mystery, the awe-inspiring twilight, the portentous suggestions and latent meaning of the Byzantine, Romanesque, and Gothic church decoration gave way to a clear and communicative imagery within the range of general and direct understanding. Giotto's style marks, in the field of the arts, the triumph of the vernacular over the learned idiom, the substitution of the popular and exoteric for the aristocratic and remote, the frank and decisive elimination of asceticism, mysticism, and spiritual abstraction from the general practice and cult of religion. Art was no more, as in the earlier medieval centuries, a 'literature for the layman,' a mere concession of the seers, thinkers, and spiritual leaders to the vulgar and uncouth intellect of the illiterate masses. It now became an essential element and function of religion, the final fulfillment of an age-old aspiration of the Italian people for an adequate manifestation of their metaphysical instincts, anxieties, and beliefs. Giotto freed his countrymen from all the hesitations, contradictions, perplexities, and dialectical expedients that had provoked the spiritual restlessness, the fluctuations of religious sentiment, the heretical temptations, the tumultuous upheavals, and latent skepticism of the Italian Middle Ages.

In the few panel pictures that have come down to us the master does not appear to be very daring in supplanting traditions by individual conceptions. In the famous Madonna of Ognissanti, the Mother of God appears in the severe majesty of her former representations, but a pair of kneeling angels offering symbolical flowers add a touch of humanity always present in Giotto's work. And the enthroned Virgin with the Holy Child has lost the rigidity of traits and countenance that still clings to similar images, even those of Cimabue so much appreciated at the end of the thirteenth century by the Florentine people, who are said to have carried one of his enthroned Madonnas jubilantly through the streets of the town. This popular enthusiasm was assuredly an elemental reaction to the more flexible, tender, and vital style of that first individual master as compared with the gloomy stiffness of his Byzantine models and forerunners. But those images were still icons, and much of that excitement was inspired by the miraculous power believed to be inherent in such consecrated objects of public worship. However, the more realistic and human the supernatural beings became, the less likely it grew that a sculpture or painting would be regarded as a wonder-working image. After Giotto hardly any Italian painting was endowed with the power attributed to so many works of art of an earlier period.

What was lost in iconographic tradition, didactic values, and magic power was compensated by fervency of conviction, clarity of vision, and richness of invention. Giotto created a pure art that reveals the kindness, dignity, and nobility of a mind intent on finding in the reality of life and nature an intelligible reflection of the divine. These broad, luminous, animated frescoes fitted beautifully into the architectural frame of the newly built, spacious, bright, and sober churches, whose Gothic structure expressed a more temperate and composed striving toward heavenly heights than was usual in the North. The Italian type of church architecture, formerly determined by ancient craft traditions, now embraced new structural conceptions, such as those materialized by the Florentine Arnolfo di Cambio in dissolving the lofty heavenward drive of the pointed arch into a series of simple but spacious and sunlit vaults. The cathedral and the most conspicuous churches of Florence arose in this style in the last years of the thirteenth century, emulated in an extraordinary contest of craftsmanship and popular enthusiasm in most Italian towns.

*   *   *

How greatly Giotto's style appealed to the artistic and spiritual sentiments of the country is shown by the fervor with which it was quickly accepted. The master himself worked in all the leading centers, in Milan, Padua, and Naples, and numerous pupils redecorated the churches and chapels of many small places after the new pattern. Even Venice, which clung so long to Byzantine and Romanesque models, felt the impact of the new enthusiasm. It certainly contributed to bringing the town nearer to the West in the decades of her early territorial expansion. Among those pupils, collaborators, and followers of Giotto many were so gifted that it was often impossible to distinguish their share of the frescoes executed in common from that of the master.

Several excellent followers carried on Giotto's tradition for almost a century, with sufficient marks of individual talent to make them easily identifiable among the lesser artists and craftsmen who worked in northern and central Italy, and even in regions still dominated by the southern and Byzantine tradition. In Florence, where the people had acquired a remarkable refinement of taste through influence of the master, only a few, like Orcagna, the Gaddis, and some others, could really claim to have perpetuated Giotto's spirit and creative skill. But there is a certain perplexity, a slight awkwardness and rigidity, even in the masterpieces of the best of those painters, who were probably embarrassed by the authoritative influence of their master. This is apparent when, for instance, the daring originality and monumental grandeur of Orcagna's architectural works are compared with his pictorial masterpieces. In spite of his outstanding achievements that make of him the best painter of that transition period, there is an imitative quality that mars our enjoyment of so fine and exuberant an art. The artists of the school of Giotto were led toward an overemphasis of the decorative, colorful, and spectacular, and transformed the thoughtful intimacy of the new pictorial style into a showy pageantry.

While Giotto's own work found enthusiasts throughout Italy, his pupils and followers had to compete with provincial and even local masters evidently representing a conservative reaction to the realistic virtuosity of the young Florentine tradition. The painters of Siena, Duccio, Simone Martini, the Lorenzettis, and other prolific masters were the first able to contend with the

neighboring Florentines for leadership in the arts. Toward the
end of the century Umbria distilled a special artistic genius from
the eclecticism of its native Franciscan traditions, and produced
in Gentile da Fabriano an artist of such high qualities of invention, brilliancy, and charm as to acquire prestige and lasting influence in Florence, Siena, and cosmopolitan Venice. In the
neighboring towns of Padua and Verona a few capable and
enterprising painters developed a style of their own. Altichiero's
lively frescoes in the principal churches of both towns inaugurated a regional school of art whose influence still overshadows
the epigones of the early Florentine and Sienese masters.

Each of these and several other centers of late medieval art
represented a nucleus of the thriving artistic growth that made
the following two centuries the Golden Age of Italian painting.
The history of the fine arts has outlined with the refined methods
of modern criticism and research all the individual, regional, and
traditional traits of their early flowering, stressing the slight and
sometimes almost inappreciable differences between the styles,
schools, and workshops of these 'primitives,' as they are called
by amateurs. But taking a broader view of this extraordinary era
of artistic enthusiasm, it is the general addiction to exuberant,
colorful, decorative manifestations of religious feeling that gives
the Italian art and civilization of that epoch their mark of
national originality. There is nothing anywhere else in Europe
to be compared with this extraordinary display of artistic interest,
revealing the special Italian attitude toward the things of the
world coupled with the transcendent aspects of religion.

This extrinsic evidence of religious and spiritual feeling marks
the supremacy of the fine arts over every other popular manifestation of cultural life and renewal. Only the Low Country
did not participate in this characteristic evolution and never
joined the rest of Italy in this national artistic competition. As
compared with the exceptional number of original artists in the
northern sections of the country, the south contributed only one
outstanding genius to Italian art. This great painter, Antonello
da Messina, who lived in Naples and flourished in Venice toward
the end of the fifteenth century, adopted the technique and
theories of the Flemish masters and finally became the founder

of the Venetian school of painting; he represented an artistic 'freedom of the seas,' implying an international exchange of suggestions and influences and an eclecticism of taste and style.

But all this happened late in the development of Italian art. Tuscany was the uncontested cradle of Italian painting, and the schools of Florence and Siena contended for primacy in prestige and influence until the vigorous, realistic, and secular spirit of the Florentine masters carried off final victory over the mystical, conservative, and provincial tradition of the rival neighbors. Yet it would be misleading to insist upon the differences and to overlook the common traits and mutual influences that link the two leading towns despite the raging political rancor and the bitter economic contests that filled the contending republics with mutual hatred. As a matter of fact, even the most thoroughgoing critical investigations have failed to show conclusively whether certain Tuscan masterpieces of the *trecento* should be attributed to Florentine or to Sienese masters. From the time of Giotto and Duccio there was a stimulating interchange between the two cities. It is evident in Lorenzetti's frescoes of a 'narrative' character, and continued up to the culmination of Florentine devotional painting in the famous works of Fra Angelico.

The antagonism between 'mystical' Siena and 'realistic' Florence has been greatly exaggerated. The collective mysticism frequently attributed to the Sienese population is a fable contradicted by the turbulent, enterprising, bellicose character of its factional and social life. Siena remained the stronghold of the Ghibelline imperial party and only reluctantly bowed to the Guelf influence of Charles of Anjou after the destruction of the Swabian dynasty. A strong republican feeling caused it to cling even more tenaciously than its neighbors to the popular municipal institutions. Antagonism against Florence and its aggressive policy of political expansion and conquest encouraged the conservative trends of the Sienese people. The most popular ascetic authors of the fourteenth century came from Florence, as in the case of Friar Jacopo Passavanti, or from Pisa, as Giordano da Rivalto, Domenico Cavalca, and Bartolomeo da San Concordio. And if Siena could boast of a leading saint, such as St. Bernardino, Florence had its popular archbishop, St. Antonino, whose influence was much felt in the public and religious life of the town.

The saga of Sienese mysticism reposes largely on the memory of the ecstatic St. Catherine, one of the outstanding women in Italian history and a charming, sagacious writer. But it ought to be remembered that her almost fanatical asceticism did not imply renunciation of the world. Most of her activity and influence were felt in the social field, in public life, and in political affairs, not only in her native town, but in Rome, Florence, and Avignon, where she incited Pope Gregory XI, in 1376, to return to Rome. Her letters to statesmen, politicians, warriors, sovereigns, pontiffs, and ecclesiastics reveal the active, militant devotion of the Italian religious leaders of the late Middle Ages, especially of those belonging, like St. Catherine, to the Dominican order. Her mysticism was only a fervent concentration of spiritual forces that exploded in active energy. Her fight for the social redemption of the destitute was in line with the old Italian revolutionary tradition directed against the power and wealth of the higher clergy, the ecclesiastical class privileges, and the political captivity of the Church.

There is, indeed, little reason to insist too much on the pure symbolism, asceticism, and idealism of Sienese art when Ambrogio Lorenzetti, for instance, outdid Giotto and all his own contemporaries in the display of color when representing the Oriental scene of the martyrdom of some Franciscan missionaries in Ceuta. His addiction to secular pageantry and ornamental splendor is shown by his allegoric frescoes in the Siena town hall. Almost at the same time Simone Martini, in his religious and secular pictures, showed a realism of feature, a delight in landscape, costumes, and ornaments far exceeding those of any contemporary painter. Giotto was still alive and famous when the influence of this excellent and versatile Sienese artist spread from his native town as far as Naples and Avignon, where he died, in 1344, after Petrarca had expressed in two grateful sonnets his admiration for Simone's lifelike portrait of Laura.[8]

[8] *Rime*, LXXVII, LXXVIII.

Thus the famous conservatism and abstract symbolism of Sienese art appear restricted to a particular section of the religious field and essentially to altarpieces and panels representing the image of the *Madonna in Majesty* or other traditional and canonical motifs. Here the influence of the first master of Sienese painting, Duccio di Buoninsegna, was as decisive and instrumental as Giotto's models had been for the Florentine school.

It was the temperament of the leading artists that created a pictorial reality in harmony with the spiritual and practical experiences of their environment. These artists of the *trecento* brought the whole world into the pictorial scene, just as Dante had brought the universe into his poetical vision. Siena was no exception in this general development. The persistence of the icon-type in images of the Blessed Virgin and the conspicuous number of Sienese Madonnas certainly arose from the local cult of the Mother of God. The Byzantine tradition of the wonder-working Virgin was favored by this particular circumstance. The Sienese painters intensified the supernatural character of their Madonna by adding to the remote sanctity of the traditional type the frail grace, the incorporeal air, the spiritualizing charm, and nobility of an idealized image. This artistic aim was attained by a harmonious combination of pictorial elements that mitigated the rigidity of the Byzantine figure through mildness of colors, gentleness of traits, and balance of detail. In these aspects the Sienese style is a variation of the Gothic art of France. More than any other Italian center, Siena was particularly attached to Gothic forms of art, which gave the architecture and general pattern of the town the character it still preserves. This style was European, and its Italian variants appear as the dialects of a common artistic language. It represents a transitory stage in the evolution from an international expression of artistic ideals to the *character indelebilis* of a national style.

❖ ❖ ❖

In this early epoch of Italian art religious considerations were almost entirely predominant, and only timid attempts were made to overcome the age-old mistrust of any autonomous secular expression. As elsewhere, it was the minor arts that offered free scope to imagination and technical skill. The first known decorative murals with literary motifs appear comparatively late, in the last years of the *trecento*. Examples are the fine episodes of the French poem *La Châtelaine de Vergy* in a bedroom of the Davanzati Palace in Florence, the game of chess in the castle of Poppi in Tuscany, the bold, anecdotal frescoes in a typical medieval building of San Gimignano near Siena. These are only poor remnants of what must have been an appreciable variety of home decoration. But the symptoms of a general passion for ornament, pomp, and splendor are many and widespread. It is apparent in the rapid development of all the crafts and minor arts, in book illustration, textiles, ivories, and furniture.

That this increasing enthusiasm for the embellishment of life and the enjoyment of the external world is connected with the prosperous development of the bourgeoisie (at that time still the leading class) is a mere truism, explaining nothing. Economic prosperity does not necessarily imply a flowering of the arts or sciences—as the history of ancient Rome and modern America proves—and moreover the *trecento* experienced one economic calamity after another. It is perhaps more nearly correct to consider the artistic enthusiasm of the period as just one manifestation of a growing Italian vitality. Be that as it may, new forces became active even under most adverse conditions. It seems reasonable to assume that the acquisition of republican liberties in a considerable section of the country during the second half of the thirteenth century released and favored creative energies in every field of human activity. Only the two remaining feudal regions of Piedmont and the foreign-dominated South did not participate in this spiritual and social revolution. The republican institutions and the spirit that made them possible gave opportunity to every talent, will, and enterprise. The same spirit that made possible the free expansion of the human personality stimulated every talent, interest, and intelligence to join in the renewed activities of a commonwealth regulated by the power and prestige of the arts and trades.

Under these circumstances the Italians were able to develop their characteristic decorative sense with its predilection for lively color. In the early eleventh century, Florentine architects began to ornament their most representative churches with horizontal, parallel, or interlaced strips of colored marble. This typically Florentine decoration soon came to be used in numerous private and public buildings. It spread to many towns of western Italy, from Genoa to Amalfi, and was more and more enlivened by sculptural reliefs, statues, and shining bronze doors. The five hundred vari-colored columns framing the magnificent mosaics and resplendent Byzantine vaults of St. Mark's in Venice are one more aspect of the exuberant use of color in the religious architecture of medieval Italy, surpassed only by the sumptuous monuments of Palermo, Cefalù, and Monreale. In the twelfth century Roman craftsmanship created the colorful, elegant style of inlaid ornamentation for floors, altars, pulpits, columns, door frames, chairs, and tombs, which became identified with the Cosmati and spread rapidly through southern Italy.

The industrial development of central Italy in the fourteenth century, the improvement of the dyeing technique, the substitution of mural painting for the costly, rigid, and pretentious mosaics, the introduction of Oriental and Asiatic patterns, and the importation of various kinds of textiles and embroideries immensely increased the production and distribution of ornamental luxuries and helped to create a gaudy, iridescent, variegated setting for religious and profane life. Because of this general revival of artistic and decorative enthusiasm in late medieval Italy, the prestige of the leading painters, of skilled sculptors, and ingenious architects, like Giotto, the Pisanos, Arnolfo di Cambio, and the Sienese masters, rose to an almost sovereign position in public life, although the popular participation in artistic enterprises and competitions kept the masters in permanent contact with voters, taxpayers, guilds, and municipal authorities.

Public recognition of outstanding artists was introduced in Italy as early as the first half of the twelfth century, when inscriptions honoring Masters Nicolaus and Wiligelmus were fixed

to the cathedrals of Modena, Ferrara, and Verona. The most
striking expression of this popularity is certainly the vernacular
quatrain composed in 1135 in honor of the master who decorated
the cathedral of Ferrara. In later epochs great artists became
leading citizens and princes did not lag behind republics and
democracies in expressing their esteem for the men who, by
talent and skill, added luster to the royal residences and perpetuated their glory. In this way the old separation of the
'liberal' from the 'mechanical' arts, which condemned the latter
to a state of humiliating inferiority, was effaced in Italy, and
especially in Florence, where the painters, sculptors, and architects, that is, the creative artists, belonged to the same constitutional group as the physicians, apothecaries, and learned men. In
feudal countries like France, Spain, and Germany, the artists
were for a long time merely servants of sovereigns or bishops,
and their social assignment to the class of 'mechanics' drove even
the best of them back into the anonymous mass of ordinary
craftsmen and subordinate employees. Only the Italian influence
in those countries provoked a change in favor of the artists, but
in the order of courtly dignities they remained ignoble 'mechanics.' In Italy continuous triumphal progress of the fine arts can
be discerned from the early day when the anonymity of the
masters was abolished by popular favor and official praise, up to
the moment when Emperor Charles V stooped to pick up the
pencil that had slipped from Titian's hand. Shortly before that
event, brigands showed their respect for the painter Antonio
Allegri from Correggio, whom they had captured in a wilderness
and set free unharmed with their humble apologies.

*   *   *

This extensive renewal of the arts in the century after 1250
was still limited to the religious sphere of inspiration, although
after Thomas Aquinas and Dante there were fewer symptoms
of intensified devotion and spiritual fervor. There were still outbreaks of religious infatuation and ascetic fanaticism, masses of
penitents still wandered from one sanctuary to another; but after
the paroxysms of the flagellants toward the end of the thirteenth

century, and the destruction of the last Italian heretical sect of
the desperate Fra Dolcino in Lombardy, a general appeasement
seems to have occurred. The great masses of Italian society seem
to have found peace, satisfaction, and consolation in the contemplation of the extrinsic expressions of religious devotion.

Yet that joyous nation did not yet dare to express its secular
experience in an autonomous art. The humanity, the enjoyment
of life and nature, the new impressions of the world still appear
indirectly as accessory aspects of a religious scene or a pious
tale. The characteristic exceptions are those connected with
public life, when sculptors and painters were charged with por-
traying the political and military leaders of a town. But when
Simone Martini was commissioned in 1328 by the local authorities of Siena to immortalize the *condottiere* Guidoriccio in a fresco
in the town hall, the artist composed this earliest of his secular
works in the old Italian sculptural tradition, of which Antelami's
equestrial relief of Oldrado da Tresséno in Milan is an outstanding example. This tradition of politically inspired glorification of
great soldiers can be followed from this early date, in different
styles and places, up to the equestrian portraits of military leaders painted on the walls of the Cathedral of Florence, or to the
monumental statues of Gattamelata in Padua, by Donatello,
and the Colleoni of Verrocchio in Venice.

Despite the increasing naturalism in religious painting, portraits of outstanding laymen appear but seldom in the religious
frescoes of the *trecento*. The youthful portrait of Dante attributed
to Giotto is only a fragment of a representation of the Paradise
intended to adorn the chapel in the Florentine residence of the
former *podestà*, the highest executive authority of the town. The
famous men painted among the throngs of worshipers in the
teeming frescoes of Santa Maria Novella in Florence hardly stand
out from the general type of the crowd. The predilection for mass
representations in these vast paintings certainly reflects the
democratization of the arts and the participation of the multitudes in their development. Not only political and economic
undertakings but higher education and even artistic life had
assumed a popular character in the stable constitutional order

that followed centuries of civil strife and revolutionary movement.

It was only after a profound and lasting change in the spiritual
structure and intellectual substance of the country that the individual portrait appeared as a vivid expression of the deeper
understanding of the human personality. Individual characters
never disappeared from the scene of the world and the religious
or social conformism of the Middle Ages did not alter human
nature to the point of wiping out the human personality or lessen-
ing its influence in public affairs, intellectual life, and spiritual
currents. The outstanding achievements of the Middle Ages in
every field of human activity were inspired and carried out by
exceptional individuals who found their followers or antagonists,
as in every other epoch of human history. But willingness to
subordinate the individual to the idea, to religious or lay authority, and to the fatality of a providential order of things weakened
the interest in human personality and the belief in its particular
merits.

Consequently, the Middle Ages created and preserved the
type rather than the portrait, and a general symbolism rather
than any realistic reproduction of features and gestures. A universal feeling against the profane practice of the figurative arts
destroyed as thoroughly as possible the Greco-Roman traditions
of the sculptural or pictorial portrait. The Christian world joined
the Oriental peoples in the dislike and proscription of realistic
imagery, even in the representation of ruling sovereigns in
mosaics, miniatures, and ivories. Yet it seems doubtful whether
that aversion really lasted throughout the Middle Ages until the
first true-to-life secular portraits were painted in the fourth
decade of the fourteenth century by Simone Martini in Avignon.
Most probably Giotto also practiced this neglected branch of
art. French masters of the Gothic era were already drawing
animal pictures *sur le vif* instead of using model books or copy-
ing and varying old patterns handed down in the workshops.

But the first evidence of portrait painting is given by one of the
earliest Italian poets, the notary Giacomo da Lentino, a Sicilian
living in Tuscany at the epoch of Frederick II and praised by
Dante as one of the outstanding troubadours of the old courtly

style.[4] In one of his most famous songs, mentioned in every important history of early Italian poetry, the inspired and enamored notary tells his lady how he finds consolation in his solitude when looking at her faithful portrait.[5] This strange mixture of pictorial realism and blind faith in salvation is not a commonplace of medieval poetry or a sentimental reminiscence of classical literary motifs, but is the personal fancy of a poet whose words reveal the ideal and practice of contemporary portraiture, rather than the intensity of his own feelings. Actually the song is based on the conventional topics of courtly love and service characteristic of those last offshoots of the old Provençal lyricism. But this one original touch demonstrates the existence of a 'portraiture' intended for secular purposes and profane devotion. No example of an early portrait has been handed down. The degree of objective likeness actually achieved in those works is difficult to imagine. It is even probable that there was no likeness at all and that only the imagination of the spectator found a resemblance in a more or less conventional image.

This portraiture no doubt was only a form of refined craftsmanship and very far from the unsurpassed pictorial mastery achieved in the further development of Italian art. Professional artisans who made miniatures or coins probably turned also to portrait painting. The allusions and expressions of our poet seem to indicate his belief in a certain magic virtue inherent in such portraits. The secret spell of those figures was the secular counterpart of the wonder-working power attributed to the religious images painted by the same masters. A profound spiritual, intellectual, and social revolution was required before the function and conception of the figurative arts could undergo a radical

[4] *Purgatorio,* xxiv, 56.
[5] 'Because desire was strong,
  I made a portraiture
  In thine own likeness, love;
  When absence has grown long,
  I gaze, till I am sure
  That I behold thee move;
  As one who purposeth
  To save himself by faith,
  Yet sees not, nor can prove.' (Translated by D. G. Rossetti)

change. In the early period of secular sculpture and painting a type was individualized by names and symbols, that is, by indirect marks of an unartistic character; just as in a leading trend of medieval philosophy, the true artistic realism consisted in the type, and not in the individual. It was only after a long process of development that an artistic image could speak for itself.

IX. *The Rise of Tyranny and the Commercialization of Power*

THE renewal of Italian art and poetry, the appeasement of religious passions, and the rise of regional prosperity took place in the most tumultuous epoch of the country's political history. In the course of a century, from the final fall of the Swabian dynasty in 1268 to the restoration of the papal dominion in Italy a hundred years later, the whole political structure changed radically with the successive disappearance of democratic republican institutions and the consolidation of innumerable regional principalities of a dynastic and tyrannical character. It is one of the many paradoxes of Italian history that this political dismemberment of the country took place when the cultural unification of the people had been almost entirely achieved. Dante and Giotto were already famous men throughout the country when the poet wrote that 'the cities of Italy are full of tyrants and every clown that comes to play the partisan becomes a Marcellus.' [1]

Since Sismondi's classical work on the history of the medieval revolutions,[2] the development of the democracies into tyrannies has been frequently described as a typically Italian phenomenon. The external facts are almost everywhere the same. In the course of a few decades, the civic liberties acquired at the cost of inestimable sacrifices were surrendered to local political leaders who endeavored to maintain their power by every possible means, by currying popular favor, by manipulating factional

[1] *Purgatorio,* VI, 125-6.
[2] Published between 1807 and 1818.

163

groups, by the use of military force, foreign support, ecclesiastical protection, conspiracy, bribery, treachery, and assassination. In spite of the great variety of personalities and interests involved, the procedure is everywhere the same and the culmination so true to form as to be almost monotonous. The history of every Italian city, however dramatic, shows, when compared with similar events in antiquity and modern times, how narrow the scope of political practice and possibilities has always been.

In the face of this ultimate monotony and dullness of political imagination, one must conclude that political ability ranks very low in the scale of human intelligence. The 'dirty business' of politics as practiced in that era, and perhaps in any country at any time, could be transcended only by the visions of great men in other fields of human thought, such as philosophy, poetry, and science. The new political ideas that arose out of experience and despair were expressed in Dante's *Monarchia*, in Petrarca's famous *Song to Italy*, in the *Defensor Pacis* of Marsilius of Padua, and in the 'mirror of princes' literature that followed the treatise *De regimine Principum* by Thomas Aquinas and Giles of Rome. But none of these late medieval monuments of political thought is of any use as a guide to the political practice of the time. The various ideals of imperial, national, popular, theocratic, and autocratic government discussed in this literature arose from wishful thinking and moral indignation, or from a merely speculative approach to the problems of public life.

Italian despotism of the late Middle Ages was pure power politics in the form of individual tyranny or factional coercion. The vicissitudes of the small states and petty princes were determined by power interests with none of the higher aims that inspired the communal revolutions of the preceding era. The political tension that brought unrest, civil strife, and foreign intervention in internal Italian affairs was no longer provoked by the resistance of communal particularism to the claims' of the two universal powers, but by the implacable political dialectic of liberty and authority fought out within the walls of the free towns or in the rural domains of feudal overlords. In the development from republican rule to individual despotism, the old system was typified in the ruthless suppression of communal liberties through mass executions, wholesale extermination, and devastation carried out before 1259 by Ezzelino III in the towns and domains of the Venetian mainland around Treviso, Padua, and Verona, with the help of his German henchmen. Scion of a German feudal dynasty, vassal and kinsman of Frederick II, he subjugated free cities by the same brutal methods as the Teutonic Knights were employing to conquer the Slavic borderlands of the empire. So ghastly were the deeds of this sanguinary tyrant that he became the dreaded protagonist of many popular legends and, shortly after 1300, of the first regular tragedy of Italian literature, Albertino Mussato's Latin *Eccerinis*.

After a coalition of Italian cities supported by Pope Innocent IV ended this reign of terror, despotism in Italy assumed milder forms. Although political violence still remained a customary feature of Italian public life, no regime of such extensive and protracted cruelty was ever seen again. Almost all the petty local and regional rulers acquired their power through constitutional forms, and with popular favor and consent. The founders of most of these provincial dynasties, the so-called *Signorie*, were men of prestige and influence who held high offices in the civic magistrature. In those administrative positions they exercised a power superior to local factions and class interests and acted, at least nominally, as representatives of a higher principle or authority. This higher authority was the dominant party, radical or moderate, Ghibelline or Guelf, in accordance with local interests, divisions, and traditions.

The usual trick of those public officials consisted in transforming a temporary appointment into a life position and finally into a hereditary privilege. These changes could not take place without some personal merit and political ability, but they also required favorable circumstances, popular acquiescence, and a higher sanction. In many cases despotic powers were acquired by the violent elimination of political competitors. In Florence, in 1302, all the leaders of the Guelf opposition, to which Dante, already a fugitive, belonged, were executed by order of the *podestà* Cante dei Gabrielli, who had introduced a regime of terror to keep order in the turbulent city. But in few cases could a successful ruler keep his power, even temporarily, by a simple *coup de main* or by force of arms. The popular acquiescence to despotic rule was not unlimited, and after a mutual agreement the people persisted in their watchful control of public administration.

As always, the new despotism was accepted in the name of peace and liberty. Peace and liberty, at least, were the two pledges a new ruler never failed to give in exchange for popular recognition of his power. In most cases these men had been the favorites of the people or of the leading classes before acquiring full authority over them. The two municipal offices that generally led to local despotism were those of the *podestà*, who acted as a chief executive, and of the 'captain of the people,' who was the military chief of the community. Both authorities were elected by the representatives of those citizens entitled to political activity. They were both supposed to exercise their power with the utmost impartiality, and in complete disregard of conflicting parties, families, classes, or interests. As a means of achieving such impartiality, both magistrates were frequently called from other Italian towns and appointed for a year, along with a staff of jurists and petty officials also not involved in local affairs. Generally those high functionaries were Guelf or Ghibelline noblemen, according to the dominant local party. Thus every Italian democratic republic ruled by the mercantile upper classes and the guilds of the 'arts' had at least one high official of aristocratic and usually 'foreign' descent, who preserved in his new environment some of the characteristic traits and ambitions of his class.

The interest of an official of this rank and prestige was to keep his position or, as they used to say, *mantenere lo stato*. The term *stato* (status or state), which began its career so humbly in the usage of medieval Italian politicians and chroniclers, was later to take on a new and revolutionary significance. The aim of these *podestà* and 'captains of the people' was to keep as long as possible their profitable and honorable office, their *status* as public functionaries. In that first acceptance the term 'state' simply designated the position occupied by the principal executive of a city, who did not like to be dismissed after a short time in office. In their minds *stato* was the administration to which they had been appointed and the bureaucratic position they had acquired. To put it simply, their *stato* was their political job, with the power, income, and dignity implied in it. It was only in the further development of the Italian autocracies and in the political literature of later epochs that this typical vernacular expression came to designate the whole administrative and sovereign power exercised by the political institutions of an independent community. In its early acceptance among Italian authors of the fourteenth century the term still indicates the personal situation of a public official, but it implies at the same time an idea of stability much in contrast with the restless mobility of all medieval political bodies.

The 'state' was not conceived by those men as an organized political body or as an abstract collective personality provided with sovereign rights and supreme internal power. The term designating such a political organism was *il comune;* this adjective transformed into a substantive by the new political consciousness was, in medieval art, sometimes personified as an allegory. The Italian overlords who anticipated Louis XIV in declaring—as the legend has it—'I am the state' were expressing the static idea of conservative authority, remote from the political practice of their day, but characteristic of a widespread new trend. There is much evidence of a changing popular attitude toward communal and republican institutions during the critical decades of the age of Dante. Exhaustion of the civic spirit, political weariness, and military laxity become evident as two new types emerge in Italian public and cultural life: petty tyrants and influential literati. The shrewd, able, ambitious, and educated men among the executives of the city-states took advantage of the changing political mood and truly became an aristocratic caste, quite different from the feudal nobility whose forms of life and dynastic interests they took over, but in a new spirit and way. These executives, indispensable in the public administration, acted as the trustees of the democratic institutions and represented an aristocratic superstructure supported by popular acknowledgment.

The consent given by the population to the officials in transforming a temporary appointment into a permanent post never

was intended as a return to the feudal system that had always
been alien to Italian traditions and conditions. But it is evident
that the old disenfranchised nobility recognized in those administrative ranks a way to regain power and prestige without
necessarily returning to violence and hazardous adventures. For
the dispossessed nobles the offices of *podestà, capitano del
popolo,* and *condottiere,* or army chief, represented a career with
infinite possibilities. And as numerous cities needed public
officials, opportunities were open to many young scions of noble
families, who were educated accordingly. In these circles politics
became a profession. The popular favor enjoyed by the professional political aristocracy is evidence of the increasing conservatism of Italian society at the close of a long and turbulent
revolutionary epoch.

*   *   *

Symptomatic of this nation-wide tendency is the Venetian
constitution of 1297, which restricted the political privileges of
the nobility to a fixed number of aristocratic families and established an oligarchy that ruled the republic for exactly five hundred years until its end, in 1797. Although Venice, like the two
other maritime republics of Pisa and Genoa, had a political development of her own, she nevertheless participated in the most
characteristic trends of Italian public and cultural life. This
Venetian constitution was no isolated phenomenon. Florence at
that time was practically, if not constitutionally, ruled by an
oligarchy, after a few wealthy and influential families succeeded
in undermining the 'Ordinances of Justice,' which had excluded
the nobility from political leadership. The subservience of these
politically privileged classes became evident when the majority
agreed to recognize Charles of Valois, brother of the King of
France, as papal satrap, and a few months later, in February
1302, assented to the banishment of Dante Alighieri and all the
citizens who opposed the intervention of Boniface VIII in Florentine public affairs. For love of peace and business the town's
Guelf majority would have finally consented to the unconstitu-
tional rule of Corso Donati and his kinsmen and followers, had
not his stupid arrogance and bullying ambition provoked the

popular reaction that put a bloody end to him and his political group.

While the Venetians had protected themselves against either popular rule or the personal rule of their *doge*, the Florentines wavered constantly between the two forms of government, and by that attitude, which Dante attacked,[3] they strengthened the unofficial rule of old and new oligarchic groups. In 1342, for example, the successful military leader Walter of Brienne, a French feudatory and Duke of Athens, became uncontested overlord of the whole Florentine jurisdiction after a popular election amounting almost to a plebiscite. He was noisily ousted ten months later because of the psychological and political blunders he had committed. He misunderstood his subjects, clumsily abused his power and office, and irritated the industrial entrepreneurs of the major guilds by granting political concessions to the workers.

From then on the Florentines were always suspicious of personal rule and favored the political supremacy of small family groups belonging to the mercantile aristocracy of the town. Until the consolidation of the Medici dynasty, in the second half of the fifteenth century, a *de facto* oligarchy of the chiefs of a few enterprising families—the Albizzi, Pazzi, Strozzi, and their circles—controlled the affairs of the republic, whose democratic constitution remained formally unaltered. In Florence the *Signoria* was always the impersonal government of the republic, never the rule of a despot. When, in 1463, Cosimo de'Medici was granted a title, it was 'father of the fatherland,' while in 1529 Jesus Christ was elected 'King of the Florentine people.' The Florentines naively believed that no potentate would ever dare to contest the power of the Saviour. But a few years later Cosimo I, who had become Duke of Florence through papal protection and intervention, publicly abrogated that last futile manifestation of Florentine republican sentiment.

The characteristic forms of Italian despotism were largely developed within the Ghibelline sphere of the rich and active Upper Country, where the republican regimes and disenfran-

---

[3] *Purgatorio,* vi, 127-51.

G

chised rural population had made notable progress toward agricultural and urban prosperity. All the great historical dynasties of this transition period originated in the republican communities of Lombardy and Venetia. The Visconti of Milan, the Scaligeri of Verona, the Bonaccolsi of Mantua, the Estes of Ferrara, the Polentani of Ravenna, the Carraresi of Padua, all belonged to the Ghibelline nobility, although they were unanimously opposed to any revival of imperial domination. All the founders of these dynasties rose to power from one of those executive municipal offices which placed the armed forces of the state in the hands of energetic and supposedly impartial noblemen. The first political ancestor of the house of Este, Azzo IV (died in 1212) was *podestà* of Verona, Padua, and finally Ferrara, which became the cradle and residence of this famous dynasty. Likewise, the Polentani of Ravenna, who gave hospitality to Dante Alighieri in the last years of his life, descended from the first Ghibelline *podestà* of that municipality. In the other leading centers of Lombardy the first despots established their power as 'captains of the people': Matteo Visconti in Milan, who in the last decade of the thirteenth century extended his territories from the Alps to the Po River and definitely consolidated the rule of his family; Alberto della Scala, lord of Verona from 1277 to 1301, the most refined and human of these founders of provincial dynasties and an example to his brilliant and gallant successors; Luigi Gonzaga who, in 1328, succeeded the last of the Bonaccolsi as overlord of Mantua and inaugurated one of the most illustrious princely families in Europe.

A number of short-lived dynasties and single rulers came up in the same way, as for instance, the Guelf Correggios of Parma after 1303, the Malatestas of Rimini, the Ordelaffis of Forlí, and other families, later absorbed by mighty neighbors, or rapidly declining after a promising start. Of the outstanding men who climbed high in the favor of their contemporaries and became legendary figures in Italian political and literary history, none attained the success and reputation of Castruccio Castracani of Lucca, then a powerful Ghibelline stronghold and until the Napoleonic era always a political outsider in the history of Tuscan regionalism. It was as a 'captain of the people' that

Castruccio, a typical medieval adventurer, half soldier and half businessman, managed, in the course of only five years, to conquer a large territory with Pisa and Pistoia as key positions. His conquests were so impressive that he was made a duke by Emperor Louis the Bavarian. This crafty and ruthless political gambler so impressed the imagination of his countrymen that two centuries later Machiavelli made him the hero of a fictional biography.

In reality all these political leaders, warriors, and adventurers owed their position to a popularity acquired through some personal merit, particularly through a knack of making themselves indispensable in internal or external affairs. The many popular revolts and threats of revolt reveal that the new despots could not maintain their positions by mere political trickery. For practical purposes the short appointment granted those potential leaders by the municipal authorities only meant a time of probation in which the magistrates might be put to the test. It was not in the general interest to dismiss a chief executive or commander of an army who had demonstrated his ability. None of these popular heroes dared to establish his power solely by force, terror, or treachery. In creating the typically Italian forms of regional despotism, the people of central and northern Italy were co-operative rather than passive and subservient; with characteristic political instinct they sacrificed legal principle to expediency. It was for the sake of expediency that they gave away a substantial part of their sovereignty and finally lost even the right of co-operation.

In these circumstances it was easy for men of political ability to gain power and popularity. Soon the perpetuation of this authority based on popular consent became customary. The mechanics of consolidating such authority varied but little from place to place. Usually the potential overlord of a town or district found his strongest support in the wealthy middle classes, which represented the element of stability in the social structure. He was able to mobilize, when necessary, the unorganized mass of the plebeians, the so-called *popolo minuto*, but he could never count on the support of the nobility, to which he most often belonged by birth and education. This lack of class solidarity contributed decisively to the extreme individualism characteristic of Italian despotism, putting the emphasis of political life on personal power, ability, and prestige.

The development of this new Italian nobility is unique in late medieval Europe, where the traditions and institutions of feudalism were still very much alive. The Italian despots emerged as self-made rulers from the democratic institutions of the numerous particularistic city-states and consequently were never bound by the obligations of their social rank. Once aware of the public favor, they proceeded to abolish the privileges of the urban and landed aristocracy to which they originally belonged. They all knew that effective competitors could arise only from among the dispossessed and disenfranchised nobles. Thus these despots joined with the democratic middle classes in their attitude of suspicion toward the nobles, while the plebeians who had nothing to lose and everything to gain usually persisted in the hopeful political indifference of leaderless masses.

This lack of obligations, personal convictions, ethical principles, and higher ideals accounts for the unscrupulous methods employed by these professional power-politicians in establishing and consolidating their power. Murder, treachery, and torture were the rule. Yet it would not be correct to assume that the Italian despots were mere criminals and corrupt adventurers. And it would be equally wrong to attribute these almost routine excesses and crimes to the 'times.' It is men who make the 'times' and not, as so often supposed, the other way around. There can be no doubt that the era of Italian despotism received its characteristic features from the attitude of the men who made it and tolerated it. It was the specifically Italian species of headless feudalism, the individualistic development of dynastic and personal power, the moral indifference of the men invested with public authority by popular consent, that led to the political disintegration of the country.

Dante deeply despised all those provincial tyrants whom he called hangmen, defrauders, and robbers.[4] He attempted to imbue them with a political creed that would replace their moral

---

[4] *De vulgari eloquentia,* I, xii.

nihilism and cynicism. Petrarca tried to do the same in an inflammatory poem [5] and in a polished treatise on a good administration.[6] But the political reality could not be altered by lofty utopian visions or friendly exhortations. And there was nothing about the private wars of Boniface VIII or the political papacy of Avignon to inspire the despots with more virtuous and God-fearing ways. Italian despotism developed in a moral vacuum.

The despots themselves, however, always came to some arrangement with the powers above. Educated to have faith in divine mercy and confident in the power of human intercession, they knew that timely repentance, formal observance of religion, and largess to the churches would finally secure their souls a place in Purgatory, where indeed Dante gathered so many contemporary potentates. Papal excommunications of the most aggressive Ghibelline lords could always be revoked through a political deal, or eluded with the help of friendly prelates. At the end of their careers these despots who had lived in luxury and splendor prepared to die in humility, with the comforts of the Church. To be buried in a monk's frock became almost a rule. And the monumental tombs erected in cathedrals and memorial chapels gave promise, with their noble artistry and impressive Latin inscriptions, of lasting earthly fame. Every traveler to Italy knows the ornate and impressive tombs of the early Visconti in the Milan cathedral, the statues of the Scaligers in Verona, and similar monuments throughout the country. No crime was too bestial to exclude a single one of these princely upstarts from divine pardon and posthumous glory. They always took timely precaution to redeem themselves from their sins against God and man.

The political legitimation of these self-styled autocrats was not such an easy matter. Internally, they could do without it. No foreign recognition could have prevented the people from ousting an unpopular leader. But imperial or papal legitimation was indispensable in external relations and sometimes implied the armed support of those sovereign authorities. And since outward

[5] *Italia mia.*
[6] *Epistolae seniles,* xiv, 1.

prestige was often needed to cloak the weakness of such hybrid regimes, the new rulers were always eager to exchange their juridically vague title of *Signore* for a more definite and substantial dignity. The end of the direct and actual sovereignty of the empire and papacy over Italian territories favored the bestowal of vicariates to local overlords. The Ghibelline despots aspired to become imperial vicars and dukes; the Guelfs obtained the papal vicariate implying pontifical sanction and protection. This dignity was granted especially when the popes contested the legality of the imperial authority and sought temporal power for themselves.

In the fourteenth century, owing to the political and military weakness of both empire and papacy, the vicariate was little more than a title granted to men who had already acquired actual power and popular prestige from other and more substantial sources. But the international value of that dignity immediately raised the despots and their families to the rank of recognized reigning dynasties with the rights and privileges of the higher feudal nobility. One of the first consequences of this development was that ambitious Italian rulers intermarried with foreign potentates, creating further openings for foreign intervention. Furthermore, all these dynasties proved disastrous to the political development of Italy as a nation by supporting a particularism that remained unchallenged until the nineteenth century, when the *risorgimento* put an end to both the dynasties and the situation they had perpetuated.

In the course of three generations the Viscontis became closely related to the kings of England, France, and Cyprus, the dukes of Bavaria and the markgraves of Thuringia; they were emulated by the Gonzagas, Estes, Medicis, and other families. Within Italy these political newcomers created a neo-feudalism which, despite certain new forms, preserved a whole body of the old rights and customs. While the Italian communes had created new ordinances and statutes, and the papacy had elaborated a new juridical system in canons and decretals, the new despots simply revived the old feudal regulations in support of their power, regardless of their subjects' republican traditions. This new political aristocracy was modeled after foreign and particularly French patterns, although it obtained its authority through popular consent and its legitimation through the German emperors and the Roman pontiffs in exile. Feudal rights over territories acquired by marriage or succession became a further instrument of power in the hands of the new despots. The continuous changes of sovereignty experienced by Italian towns during the fourteenth century, though usually consummated by force, treachery, and bribery, were often legitimized on the basis of authentic or faked family rights based on old feudal usages.

The cultural consequence of this paradoxical evolution was the revival of French chivalrous literature in Italy on an unprecedented and almost nation-wide scale. While a French dynasty closely allied with Paris and Avignon ruled in the Lower Country, the whole new political nobility of the Upper Country turned to French customs, language, poetry, and fashions. It was during this revival of feudalism that a Franco-Italian literature, full of the paladins of Charlemagne and the Knights of the Round Table, developed at the large and small courts of Piedmont, Lombardy, Emilia, Venetia, and Romagna. The Italians revived the dwindling French traditions of chivalry as literary motifs and ideals of life. While Petrarca was discovering the true nobility of the Ancients in the classical elegance of the Latin language, the libraries of the castles and palaces all over the country were filled with old and new fictional compilations of French origin and style. In the age of Pulci, Bojardo, Ariosto, and Tasso, long after the medieval traditions of poetry and life seemed to have vanished forever, these works still had power to stir the imagination.

The basis of this phenomenon was the cultural poverty of the Italian nobility. But it also shows that the adventurous and sentimental chivalric romances, both old and new, were willingly accepted by the Italian people along with the rule of the despots who had destroyed, or at least deeply altered, the political, cultural, and moral structure of the country. Princes and commoners joined in the enthusiasm. Italian nobles imitated the heroes of chivalry, borrowing their dress and attitudes. In reality all this pageantry was nothing but a show, because the rude and cruel rise to power of the most successful rulers had no relation

to the old idea of vassalage, fealty, homage, and service that
still survived in other European countries. Since the power of
the Italian despots was established mainly at the expense of the
petty nobility, the relation between the overlords and their gentry
was one of complete subjection, with no suggestion of an organized hierarchy or reciprocity of service. When the lords of Milan,
Verona, Padua, Mantua, Parma, and Ferrara appeared in public
like princes out of fairy tales, resplendent in their costly attire,
riding fine harnessed stallions and followed by a colorful attendance of Oriental archers, servants, and heralds, it was not
the dispossessed and disenfranchised nobility that took pleasure
and pride in those spectacles of power and wealth, but rather
the burghers who were inspired to loyalty and confidence. Without this display of colorful romanticism, the provincial potentates
would not have been so infatuated with the heroes of French
chivalry and the legendary personalities of the Carolingian cycle.

*   *   *

How unrelated these jousts, tournaments, and literary recrea-
tions were to the adventurous spirit of early chivalry is shown
by the methods followed by the new generations of conquering
knights in extending and consolidating their authority and possessions. The dominant role of money in the political and ecclesiastical affairs of the fourteenth century is one of the most striking aspects of that epoch. The alliance of the dynasties and the
middle classes against the urban and landed aristocracy was not
only the result of expediency. What is more significant, it reflected a *rapprochement* in spirit. The aristocracy of most Italian
city-states was being quickly commercialized. Wealth had become the most common way to political power, and money played
a decisive part in the consolidation of autocratic authority acquired by personal prestige and popular support. Wealth and
money were virtually sanctified by the 'perpetual edict' of Pope
John XXII, who in 1323 proclaimed as heretical the opinion held
by many Italians that Christ and the Apostles possessed no personal or common property.

The sale of charges and dignities, which in the era of the
communal revolutions had been habitual with the higher clergy,

now became a characteristic aspect of the new feudalism, from the lower grades of the hierarchy up to the emperors and kings. The republican administration of the Italian city-states continued, by and large, to be as honest as humanly possible; a close system of supervision and public controls still prevailed. But in the autocratic spheres of the new society, bribery and corruption were practiced on a scale scarcely equaled before or since. The vicariates and all manner of dignities implying political power were most frequently the object of financial deals between the emperors and the Italian magistrates or overlords. These transactions became a matter of course after Matteo Visconti purchased, in 1294, from Adolph of Nassau, King of Germany, the title of imperial vicar and the juridical recognition of his authority. In spite of his excellent intentions and good character, Henry VII, Dante's last hope for the political redemption of mankind, had to adjust himself to the new political methods: he invested his representatives and vassals in Italy with rights and dignities for which they paid ready money. The weakness of the empire in arms, men, and prestige had to be compensated by material wealth, and it was for financial advantages rather than for political objectives that Louis of Bavaria, John of Luxemburg, and Charles IV of Bohemia undertook—respectively in 1329, 1331, and 1355—their predatory incursions into Italy, which contributed far more to the dismemberment of the country than to the strengthening of the empire. In 1338 Louis the Bavarian, on one of these Italian jaunts, proclaimed in high-sounding words the divine right and origin of his imperial authority and eloquently upheld the claim of the Minorites to integral poverty, meanwhile marching from town to town selling privileges, offices, and dignities for cash and tribute.

The popes who thwarted Louis' almost entirely nominal rule over Italy and mobilized the whole Guelf hierarchy and party against him had recourse to the same measures when excommunication, interdicts, and political intrigues did not yield satisfactory results. Although it was only after 1389, with Boniface IX, that the sale of political and administrative offices became a matter of routine, papal vicariates were sold for cash at all times, and sovereign rights were granted in the same way to

G*

overlords in Lombardy, Venetia, Romagna, and elsewhere in the sphere of actual or pretended papal jurisdiction. Receipts from the sale of titles and temporal dignities have remained since that time one of the principal sources of papal revenue, and the consequence has been the almost infinite proliferation of a petty and not always picturesque Italian nobility.

The methods of financial war were inaugurated on a vast scale by Boniface VIII, who, in 1296, forbade the taxation of the clergy, provoking the expulsion of the Italian bankers from France by Philip the Fair. The Pope had to withdraw this order under pressure of his direct financial supporters, mostly Florentines, who were highly influential in French financial life. Both sides recouped their losses in that financial war when the great jubilee of 1300 became a spectacular financial operation. Money poured into Italy from all over Europe and the Florentine bankers monopolized the business transactions. Half a century later, when the Spanish Cardinal Albornoz restored the papal authority in the central Italian territories from Bologna to Urbino, Perugia, and Rome, money was instrumental in reducing the power of the petty tyrants and adventurers who had established a reign of terror and disorder in the extended dominions of the absent pontiffs. It was not long before pontifical governors came to regard the extortion of money from their subjects as the principal goal of their administrative activity.

Public opinion reacted violently against this commercialization of power by the consecrated authorities. Strangely enough, the resentment of the Italians against this particular aspect of political life was much stronger than that produced by the innumerable crimes of the great and small despots. The reasons for this moral indifference concerning the despots were manifold. The Italians were not moved by their political crimes because they considered them as family affairs of the 'Signori,' who were entitled to kill, betray, imprison, and dispossess each other provided the peace of the town and the administrative order were not affected. The Italian people as a whole seem to have tacitly accepted the existence of a nobility enjoying special rights and privileges, and this no doubt is why they were not unduly outraged at the horrible family crimes by which the rule of the

Visconti, the Scaligers, and many other dynasties was established and consolidated. None of the ruling families lost popularity through such iniquities. Even Francesco Petrarca, who spent his life in moral meditation and was deeply concerned with political events, never condemned the family crimes of the Italian despots. As a guest of the Correggios in Parma, of Bernabò Visconti in Milan, and of other Italian and foreign potentates, he witnessed with calm resignation the sinister crimes of their private life and their persecution of political rivals.

Yet when heavy taxation or an extraordinary levy was introduced in order to pay for an imperial or papal vicariate or other dignity, the relations between the ruler and his subjects became tense, often leading to conspiracy or open revolt. Heavy taxes and levies have always been unpopular. But the Italian people seem to have been less sensitive to fiscal burdens when their money was turned to the advantage of the community. When, shortly after 1380, Gian Galeazzo Visconti projected the construction of a new cathedral in Milan, which he wished to be the largest in the world, he obtained the enthusiastic support of his subjects, although they were well aware of the heavy financial obligations that the undertaking would entail. Such was the particularistic pride of the Milanese that, despite the risks and costs involved, they supported their enterprising rulers in the campaigns by which they extended their dominion over nearly all of Lombardy and large sections of central Italy. A crew of vernacular poets in the service of every despot took pains to encourage such feelings of local and dynastic pride which made the people willing to part with their money.

But resentment against the financial policy of the emperors and popes was general and bitter. This reaction was provoked not only by the tributes the towns were constantly paying to get rid of some blackmailing foreigner with an army and a fanciful claim to sovereignty, but also by the overbearing demeanor of those sovereigns in whose divine authority the people still believed. This feeling is best expressed by one of the most remarkable among the minor poets of that epoch, Fazio degli Uberti, in an invective against the 'ignominious' emperor, Charles of Luxemburg, who traversed Italy 'grabbing money and then went home with it.'[7] The poet belonged to a conspicuous group of convinced Ghibellines who still clung to the idea that a Roman and Christian emperor might bring peace and happiness to the Italian people and perhaps to the whole world. Petrarca was also inspired for some time by this vision, and an emperor elected in Germany seemed to possess the requirements for its fulfillment. He had seen Charles IV in Prague and was encouraged by his majesty's good manners and excellent education; keen was his disappointment when money turned out to be of greater interest to the Emperor than the political and moral redemption of Italy. Petrarca joined the general chorus of protest and indignation, writing, it is true, in a polished Latin accessible only to a small élite. The last dreams and illusions binding his generation with the distant past vanished in the face of the haggling and bargaining that were now the customary adjuncts of political life.

All the conscientious observers of public life perceived the significance of these symptoms of moral disintegration. The three allegorical wild beasts representing pride, envy, and avarice in the prelude to Dante's *Commedia* were still up to their mischief.[8] Judicious observers were brought to despair by the scandalous financial policy of the pontiffs in Avignon and of their representatives and agents in Italy. The papal curia had become one of the richest and most magnificent European courts, representing an enormous financial enterprise utterly lacking in spiritual power and cultural influence. Money had to substitute for the loss of moral prestige and of territorial sovereignty suffered by the Church during its 'Babylonian captivity.'

This was resented by the Italians much more than the occasional ransom and blackmail extorted by the emperors. The Church had become an autonomous body without inner organization or leadership. The mendicant orders still acted as a papal militia, but these organizations of poverty also followed the general trends and habits, gradually taking their place as one more financial power. And since the papacy and the mendicant orders were closer than any other institutions to Italian traditions and sentiments, the animosity of the people was great when

---

[7] *Canzone a Carlo di Lussemburgo.*
[8] *Inferno*, I, 44-60; VI, 73; Fazio degli Uberti, *Dittamondo*, I, xxix.

it was felt that they were selling away their spiritual authority and betraying their mission of guidance and salvation. A particular source of chagrin to Italians was that most of the funds raised in the country during the pontificates of John XXII, Benedict XII, Clement VI, and Innocent VI served to finance Italian wars, to support the policy of the French kings, and to stabilize and develop the unpopular papal court at Avignon.

The spreading trade in indulgences fits perfectly into the vast framework of the mercantile transactions of that epoch. The commercialization of Purgatory was the most daring and ingenious of all the tricks ever invented by the human mind for the sake of financial benefits. It was during the fourteenth century that it became customary to release a soul from Purgatory for money and to accelerate salvation according to fixed agreements and bargains. This extension of the credit system to the supernatural was a boon to the wealthy who could count on their survivors to settle their accounts with heaven.

In the religious field the reaction against these abuses was expressed by the more or less underground movement of the *Fraticelli*, the persecuted and fanatical observers of strict Franciscan poverty. But these scattered conventicles of messianic prophets, visionaries, and ascetics could not rally the active forces of a secularized society deprived of common ideals and dominated by a frantic quest for money. The creative spirits of an epoch deeply agitated by passions, ferments, and struggles showed little inclination to solve the great problems of public and religious life by renunciation and apocalyptic hopes. The most significant protests against the rapacious policy of the papacy were of secular inspiration.

Petrarca, the most admired man of his century, became the authoritative interpreter of contemporary public opinion. The many years he spent at the papal court made him thoroughly aware of the general resentment, which he expressed in a cycle of famous sonnets damning that 'covetous Babylon, fountain of sorrows, centre of mad ire, school of errors, and temple of heresy.' [9] This invective against Avignon preserved its striking

[9] *Rime*, cxxxvii.

power for so long a time that it was deleted, by ecclesiastical order, from the editions of his poems published two hundred years later in the epoch of the Counter-Reformation. Petrarca also gave vent to his anger in nineteen Latin letters, so vehement in tone and fierce in wording that he had to protect the addressees from inquisitorial procedures by suppressing their names and preparing a special collection of his epistles *sine nomine*. In a sixteenth-century German translation these letters became one of the most effective instruments of anti-papal propaganda and Petrarca the crown-witness to the secularization of the Roman court.

Yet the most direct and courageous ambassador of the Italian people at that court was St. Catherine of Siena, a woman ignorant of Latin and without interest in refinement of form. When, with her interpreter and first biographer, Raimondo 'Capuano, O.P., she was presented to Pope Gregory XI, she first bowed to the pontiff, then raised her head and exclaimed: 'To the honor of Almighty God I am not afraid to say that I smelled the stench of the sins committed in the Roman See more strongly in my native town than do the people in this very place who commit them here daily.' Whereupon the Pope remained silent.

These open protests and other expressions of dissatisfaction did not imply a repudiation of secular interests or any desire for radical alteration of existing institutions. The main source of discontent was the complete lack of spiritual guidance and the overwhelming power of material wealth. All this is illustrated by the famous episode of Cola di Rienzo, the son of a tavern-keeper and a laundress, who inflamed his countrymen with the idea of a Roman regeneration of the world. The initial success of this buoyant visionary, who proclaimed the Roman Republic in 1347, was favored by the absence of the pontiffs. His adventurous career has been repeatedly represented as symptomatic of the intellectual renewal of the Italian people through the memory of the glory that was Rome. And, indeed, this eloquent man of good faith and daring soon had behind him the best minds of Italy and several powerful friends who expected a national regeneration through the realization of his half-classical, half-theocratic ideals. But closer scrutiny of his deeds shows the violence and treachery characteristic of his epoch.

This Roman tribune who claimed to rule over the city and the world 'by the authority of our Lord Jesus Christ,' rose to power from an administrative office very much as every other Italian leader and tyrant had done. With all his classical solemnity, he acquired his authority through a typical medieval parliament; he was supported by the middle classes and opposed by the restless nobility of the town and surrounding *campagna*. He organized his private life just like any other Italian *Signore*, accumulating wealth and ostentatiously displaying his power in public appearances and courtly splendor. At the end of his turbulent life, all the classical reminiscences and messianic attitudes he had half-naively employed to consecrate his leadership and inspire his supporters fell away from him like a shell and his spectacular career stood revealed as little more than a characteristic episode of political brigandage. When Cola re-entered Rome, in 1354, under the dubious protection of Cardinal Albornoz, the papal legate, and again became senatorial head of the local government, he initiated the customary deceitful and spoliative policy of extorting money from his friends and subjects. He arrested and executed his financial supporter, the French military adventurer Fra Moriale, in order to keep the money he had borrowed from him shortly before resuming his senatorial office. The Roman people refused to be ruled any longer by a treacherous fool. Cola was killed by an inflamed mob at the foot of the Capitoline Hill, and Rome became once more a provincial republic, ruled by representatives of the middle classes and supervised by papal functionaries who showed no interest in transforming the popular city-state into a despotic regime. After the tribune's death Cardinal Albornoz, in the name of Fra Moriale's victims, seized the rest of his fortune, which had been deposited in different Italian banks.

*   *   *

In an epoch of general misgovernment and turmoil an orderly financial administration was next to impossible. It was achieved only in Florence and Venice, the two Italian states having a remarkable public spirit, a high standard of political education, and the basic gold coins of international value: florins and sequins. Both centers were out for the conquest of markets, Venice overseas, Florence on the European continent. While the popes were acquiring money in the name of God, the emperors in the name of justice, and Cola di Rienzo in the name of Rome, Florence did business in the name of liberty, a word much abused in the proclamations, statutes, and official literature of that period. And for the Florentine wool, silk, wheat, and money magnates, liberty meant the rule of the Guelf party, then well organized under the influence of a commercial oligarchy of wealthy families. Through their financial transactions and commercial monopolies these magnates controlled the court of King Robert II in Naples, then the Guelf stronghold of Italy, and were the basis of the intimate relations of Florence with the Angevin dynasty and its French ramifications. King Robert, poor and ambitious, was little more than a tool in the hands of the Acciaiuoli, Scala, Bonaccorsi, Bardi, and Peruzzi, whose commercial interests dominated the Kingdom of Naples and the papal economy, both deprived of their normal and direct resources by burdensome concessions, military weakness, and misgovernment. The Florentine policy was to support the Angevin dynasty and its Guelf adherents throughout Italy as a bulwark against the expansion of the Viscontis. The bankruptcy of the Bardi and Peruzzi after the English crown and the King of Naples suspended payments, in 1345, was a shock to the Florentine economy, and had immediate political repercussions affecting all Italy.

For almost a century the Venetian and Genoese fleets had been battling one another for the domination of eastern markets. After the disastrous defeat of Pisa at Meloria, in 1284, and her loss of Corsica and Sardinia, Venice and Genoa remained the only Italian seagoing powers, only to become implacable enemies and ruthless competitors involved in the incessant struggles and foreign entanglements of the continental city-states. Petrarca eloquently intervened, recalling to the two rivals the higher ideals of human and national brotherhood that would end the senseless strife over foreign markets.[10] The final peace of 1381 concerned the eastern trade rather than the Italian relations between the two republics. But from then on Genoa developed as a prevalently mercantile power, with increased banking interests and little political importance. In Venice the extension of its political dominion on the mainland was a prelude to the extraordinary cultural development that transformed the Adriatic city into a leading center of Italian civilization.

The general acceptance of power politics as the only determining factor in public affairs deprived all agreements, treaties, oaths, contracts, and arbitrations of their moral basis. Political power acquired by the customary legal tricks could not count on durable popular support. Only money could insure the safety and aggrandizement of the state. It became customary for potentates to purchase new territories. The establishment of mercenary armies on an unprecedented scale made military affairs a purely financial matter. Where ready cash was not forthcoming, defection and pillage might always bring the state to ruin and the dynasty to its end. Material wealth, powerful military bands under the leadership of professional soldiers, and skillful diplomacy exploiting the endemic state of fear and unrest were the chief instruments of political expansion.

By these means the most successful, intelligent, brutal, and wealthy among the innumerable Italian despots were able to absorb the petty provincial overlords and establish a durable regime. Their subjects felt no moral obligation to give military support to their ruler; and he in turn did not trust the people enough to accept their military co-operation. Under these circumstances the Italian people who had valiantly fought for their independence were morally and physically disarmed. Armed bands of foreign mercenaries, homeless desperadoes, and impoverished noblemen, all ready to enter the service of the highest bidder, became the only military power in Italy. The effect of these 'companies of fortune' on public life was disastrous, not only because of the material damage and moral corruption they created, but also because of the popularity sometimes acquired

[10] *Epistolae familiares*, xi, 8 (1351).

by their ruthless *condottieri* through success, skill, gallantry, and imperial gestures. While Petrarca, in his famous ode to Italy, deprecated the shame and scandal of mercenary service that 'sells souls for money,' painters began to glorify the most successful soldiers of fortune. In spite of the ravages they created, such *condottieri* as the Italians Uguccione della Faggiuola, Luchino Visconti, Facino Cane, and Carlo Malatesta, as the Germans Werner of Urslingen and the Count of Landau, or the French Moriale and the Englishman John Hawkwood, acquired enormous popularity. The cynical ruthlessness of these early *condottieri* is exemplified by the motto with which the Prince of Taranto harangued his motley army: 'Beware of loss! We'll survive the shame.' [11]

The military and political adventurers who dominated public life in this epoch were maniacal in their thirst for popularity; it not only satisfied their vanity but also brought them followers. Their self-glorification sometimes assumed eccentric and farcical forms that reveal the blind and morbid lust for power and earthly glory that determined their acts and thoughts. The megalomaniac excesses of Cola di Rienzo are well known. The worthiest and most popular of the Veronese Scaligers—Can Grande I—took his name from the Great Khans of Asia, and often appeared before his court and subjects in sumptuous Oriental garb, as if to symbolize the universal destiny of his dynasty.

A fanciful orientalism was a characteristic trait of the Italian courts of the fourteenth century which perpetuated some striking aspects of the court of Frederick II, with its astrologers and magicians, poets and philosophers, artisans and musicians, Asiatic and African servants, dwarfs, jesters, hunters, and tamers of wild beasts. The Italian despots vied with one another in these costly and showy extravaganzas, which became almost a normal feature of courtly life and served to conceal from the eyes of the masses the emptiness and ugliness of power acquired by money, force, and treachery. In that commercial-minded epoch the display of pomp implied great wealth, and wealth signified credit, power, and authority. It was against the spiritual hollow-

[11] *Guardiamoci dal danno, ché della vergogna camperemo.*

ness of power that Italy's best minds, from Dante and Petrarca
to Machiavelli, warned the potentates of their time.

*   *   *

With all their rivalries and petty particularism the leading
sovereigns of Italy did take certain steps toward the unification
of the country. The idea of national unity was still vague and
confused even in the mind of a spiritual leader like Petrarca,
who felt more than anyone else the intellectual and sentimental
lure of a national home. The rulers and conquerors who, in his
day, attempted to overcome Italian particularism were led by
political instinct and considerations of power rather than by any
clear national vision. But it was the King of Naples who had the
greatest opportunity, and actually planned to extend his power
over the whole country. By one of those paradoxical reversals
characteristic of Italian history, Robert II, the recognized chief
of the Guelf party, succeeded, temporarily at least, in establishing his hegemony over a large part of Italy in line with the policy
of the Swabian emperors. Through papal support and party
affiliation the Angevin sovereignty was extended to some important strongholds in Tuscany, including Florence, to Genoa and
Piedmont, laying the foundations for incorporation of the whole
country into the Neapolitan sphere. But King Robert was a foreigner and his proper dominion in the Lower Country was threatened by the Aragonese kings of Sicily and weakened by internal
misgovernment, dissension, and debt. Through their henchmen
and agents, popes and emperors worked against the political
unification of the country; and King Robert, the protector of
Petrarca and Boccaccio, was rather an amateur of the arts than
a political or military leader.

His aspiration to Italian supremacy passed to the Visconti,
who had annexed the territories of the Scaligers and absorbed
many of the petty dynasties of the Upper Country, extending
their power south of the Apennines in a push toward the papal
territories and the Guelf strongholds of central Italy. At the
apogee of his diplomatic and military successes, Gian Galeazzo
Visconti, already invested with the title of duke, made prepara-
tions for his coronation as King of Italy, to his mind a dignity

as vague as it was grandiose. When that great sovereign died on 3 September 1402, the idea of an Italian kingdom virtually disappeared from the political scene. The consolidation of the Italian principalities in the fifteenth century, the revival of papal authority after the return of the papacy to Rome, in 1377, the rise of the Medici in Florence, and the final detachment of Naples and Sicily from the rest of the country led to an Italian balance of power, in which dynastic particularism was the decisive factor.. It was under these conditions that Italy became the land of poets, artists, scholars, musicians, and scientists, military adventurers, merchants, travelers, and industrialists. All intellectual energies were diverted from the political to the cultural field. The republican spirit and republican institutions dwindled and vanished; the Italians ceased to be a political people. In surrendering their political initiative to selfish autocrats and international dynasties, they recovered the peace of mind that favored material prosperity and intellectual conquest. It was during that long era of political self-renunciation that the Italian people created a national civilization that spiritually unified the country and made a name for itself in every corner of the Western World.

By surrendering their political power to a leader or an oligarchy, the middle classes that accepted or supported them did not lose their influence or privilege in the city-states. This partial abdication permitted those citizens who enjoyed political rights to concentrate on the guilds, or 'arts,' to which they belonged as artisans, professional men, traders, and shopkeepers. They were all organized in a strict hierarchy; judiciary power, for example, was the prerogative of the top-ranking guilds. The relations of the guilds with the despots or ruling oligarchy rested, as a rule, on agreement and mutual consent. The statutes of the guilds themselves embodied strict regulations concerning relations with workers and hired laborers, to whom the right of association was constitutionally denied. The individual emancipation of plebeians was always possible in Italy, where personal merit always prevailed over considerations of rank. But the masses of the *popolo minuto,* who had played so important a role in the epoch of the Lombard *pataria,* were no longer active in political life and only a potential force, maneuvered by the ruling classes and despots as circumstances required.

Unrest and attempted revolts are mentioned in the local chronicles, but they were easily checked by the armed forces of the state and the internal police of the guilds. In Florence, and no doubt elsewhere, the priests admonished the workers to stick to their jobs, lest they be deprived of religious consolation. In Guelf centers, like Bologna and Perugia, the insurrections of the common people were crushed by the direct intervention of the ecclesiastical authorities. In Florence, however, the working classes, for a time at least, obtained certain economic and political advantages through the famous revolt of the carders, or *Tumulto dei Ciompi*, in 1378. For the first time in history the 'proletarians' were united in an association of a marked syndicalist character. The movement, which had begun in 1342 and had been temporarily halted by the execution of its leader, Ciuto Brandini, a humble worker, flared up again after the terrible plague of 1348, which depopulated and impoverished vast regions of Italy and Europe. The workers' revolution of 1378 ended in bloody repression after a brief period of proletarian domination.

Labor history has thoroughly investigated that first example of proletarian organization. Unlike the popular revolts of the time in England, Flanders, eastern France, Spain, and somewhat later in Germany, the revolt of the *Ciompi* seems to anticipate the general struggle of hired labor to improve its economic, moral, and political conditions. While the proletarian revolts north of the Alps included the rural population and had a marked religious character with strong communistic tendencies, the Italian *Ciompi* projected a strictly secular, urban, and class revolution inspired not only by claims for higher wages and better working conditions, but by the idea of social emancipation as well. The proletarian mass movements in the feudal countries were still of the medieval type, headed by fanatical visionaries and inspired by evangelical precepts. The Florentine upheaval was a rehearsal of modern class movements, characterized by public meetings, strikes, walkouts, and disputes over wages and the right to organize. When the statutes of the guilds spoke, as they did, of the fraternal charity that bound together the members of the association, they meant the social brotherhood of the privileged citizens to the exclusion of the disenfranchised workers. The *Ciompi* wanted to create a brotherhood of their own, emphasizing trade organization rather than fraternal charity. This is what chiefly distinguishes the social movements of the North from those of the South.

Neither these outbreaks of the popular fury, nor natural cataclysms, nor financial disasters succeeded in changing the peculiar economic structure of Italy. Venice was still the busiest and richest seaport of Europe, led by a powerful and well-organized aristocracy of merchants. Mercantile activity absorbed the chief intellectual energies of the population who participated in the general prosperity. Florence maintained her leading position in the European markets organized by her merchants and bankers. The old monopolies of industry and trade established in the thirteenth century withstood every adversity, because their products, especially woolens, were irreplaceable in foreign markets, while internally the monopolies were protected by the whole political and judicial organization of the state.

The population was, on the whole, unpretentious, sober, and old-fashioned. Savings and surplus earnings became the foundation of Florentine banking capital, while money lending and changing were universely practiced as a private sport. The laws granted full protection to creditors, all manner of tricks were used to cloak the exorbitant rates of interest that became prevalent, and Florentine or Lombard usury became a byword everywhere in Europe. Yet the Italian banking and business system served as a model for the whole commercial and financial organization of Europe, which took over the Florentine technicalities of bookkeeping and the phraseology of Italian traders and agents.

X. Sources and Origin of a National Culture

IN the 1360's an ingenious second-rank Florentine painter, Andrea da Firenze, was entrusted with the decoration of the chapterhouse of Santa Maria Novella, the leading Dominican church of Florence. Among the large frescoes on the chapel walls, one of the most conspicuous represents the triumph of Thomas Aquinas seated on a throne like a conqueror, with Arius, Sabellius, and Averroes at his feet as his subdued adversaries. The subject of the painting was one of the most favored in the decoration of Dominican churches of that epoch; it expresses the objective of St. Thomas' *Summa contra Gentiles,* the militant spirit of the order, and the dominant position of the Saint in the contemporary orthodox philosophy.

The import of this pictorial apotheosis was largely prophetic. The supremacy of the doctrines and methods of Thomism was not yet uncontested, and the influence of the *doctor angelicus* was less universal than the painting made it appear. At that time, it is true, the Dominican order was capturing many chairs in the leading Italian universities and almost monopolized the teaching of theology and philosophy in the schools of the Catholic world. The general trend in Italian culture, however, was largely unaffected by the authority of Thomist scholasticism. The philosophical indifference of Italian intellectuals and the strong influence of the Franciscan spiritual leaders combined to remove the cultural life of the laity from the absolute mastery of one system of thought.

Dante's attitude toward intellectual leadership is character-

191

istic. Although his thinking was permeated by Thomist scholasticism, he expressed in poetic symbols and plain words his belief
in the ultimate equivalence of the leading philosophical systems.
For him Thomas Aquinas is not *the* universal philosophical authority, but simply the 'good friar.' [1] In reserving his greatest
enthusiasm for Aristotle, Dante shows his awareness that the
true originality of Aquinas lay in interpreting more correctly the
Aristotelian system and in adapting its methods and conclusions
to the Christian dogma. But all the .Christian philosophers share
equally in the eternal beatitude of Dante's Heaven of the Sun,
where Thomas Aquinas praises 'the holy light' of a condemned
Averroistic thinker along with other spiritual leaders of the
Christian world. [2] For Dante the essential religious truth is self-
evident and its 'physical and metaphysical proofs' a matter of
discussion and criticism. [3]

Thus Thomism did not then possess the dogmatic authority it
enjoys in the Catholic world today. In the fourteenth century
Averroism had developed in Padua an intellectual stronghold
that even the condemnation by the Inquisition of Peter de Abano,
its most versatile representative, was not able to shake. Averroistic
influence remained strong, particularly in this cultural center
where the chief citizens of Venice received their higher education. Its impact on the secular mind corresponded very closely
with that of Positivism or Darwinism in modern civilization. It
was in the name of a simple faith unspoiled by scholastic entanglements that Petrarca passionately opposed the materialistic
libertinism of those Venetian noblemen infected by Averroistic
doctrines. [4] The burning at the stake of Dante's adversary, the
poet and astrologer Cecco d'Ascoli, proves that, in 1327, men
were prepared to risk their lives for a scientific system based on
concepts developed by Arabic philosophers and expressly rejected by Thomas Aquinas and other leading theologians. Those
Averroistic doctrines concerning the influence of the stars on
individuals and communities had been elaborated and system-

[1] *Convivio*, IV, xxx.
[2] *Paradiso*, x, 64-138.
[3] *Paradiso*, xxiv, 130-38, etc.
[4] *De sui ipsius et multorum ignorantia,* written between 1367 and 1370.

atized by Guido Bonatti of Forlì, the master of all astrology for almost three centuries.

Scholasticism remained in Italy mainly a method of intellectual training for churchmen. Its influence on the laity was superficial and had little effect on the body of Italian achievement in the arts and sciences. Thomism contributed almost nothing to the elemental expression of religious feelings embodied in painting and sculpture. The abstract rationalism of that system was not compatible with the realistic interests and positive spirit of a predominantly secular age. The crude determinism of astrological conceptions and the profitable aspects of magic and science appealed far more than dialectical subtleties to a society of capitalists, traders, and tyrants.

The Italians took little interest in the philosophical controversies waged in Paris and Oxford, mainly by Franciscans and Englishmen, after the canonization of Thomas Aquinas in 1323. Few Italian thinkers were involved in the controversies of Scotists and Ockhamites against Dominican emphasis on the power of human reason in the quest for evidence and truth. The Italian universities continued to be professional institutions, and their teachers appear to have been more interested in practical disciplines such as medicine, astrology, or mathematics, than in quarrels about whether knowledge is acquired by divine illumination or rational thought. Dante transcended scholastic didacticism by his world-embracing imagination. He substituted symbols for concepts, images for reasoning, and intuitive evidence for dialectical abstractions.

It is because of this characteristic attitude that the intelligent and even the meditative Italians of that epoch were not disturbed by the contradictions and paradoxes that disintegrated their intellectual and moral life, and made the fourteenth century an era of confusion and spiritual derangement. Naive piety frequently appears conjointly with frank heresy, while unimpeachable orthodoxy often went hand in hand with moral insensibility and spiritual unconcern. The double truth was for a long time more a mental habit than a doctrine. The Averroistic opinion that theological truth may subsist side by side with philosophical truth without giving rise to insoluble conflicts was

more than an expedient and became a characteristic Italian state
of mind. Free from dogmatic fanaticism, the Italians were able
to accept and absorb the most contradictory ideas. This sort of
intellectual neutrality has hardly an equivalent among other
Western peoples. The expressions of this Italian state of mind
are numerous and varied. It accounts for the poverty of philosophical interests in the fourteenth century, the moral unconcern of the most popular writers, such as Boccaccio and Sacchetti, and the peaceful coexistence of a severe asceticism (as
expressed by the mystical writers of Siena) and an almost un-
bounded enjoyment of life. It enabled Petrarca to combine his
pious devotion to the Christian faith with a passionate enthusiasm for pagan civilization, and permitted even the most orthodox writers of his century to dabble in astrology and magic.
Humanism became the national Italian philosophy, and astrology the popular Italian 'science.' This clearly distinguishes the
Italian culture of the period from that of any other European
nation.

Although not confined to Italy, it was in that country that
astrology found its greatest theoretical and practical development. For more than two centuries innumerable rulers and leaders, traders and entrepreneurs, physicians and magistrates, ecclesiastics and laymen resorted to the 'science' of the astrologer
or geomancer in order to know the future and to determine 'con-
stellations' favorable to the performance of important acts. Resistance to the fashion was negligible, and even learned members of the mendicant orders succumbed to the lure. Many were
aware of the blasphemous character of a discipline that pretended to compete with the divine prescience, limited free will,
subverted individual responsibility, and claimed power to alter
the predetermined course of events. But, apart from the cheap
escape offered by the double truth, astrology had a sound theoretical foundation in the prevalent doctrines of natural philosophy. Both the secular clergy and the preaching orders finally
had to tolerate and even accept astrology because of its scientific background, just as confessors and educators today have
come to terms with the theory and practice of psychoanalysis.

That exact pseudo-science was derived from the metaphysical

principles of the Aristotelian cosmology. Once it was admitted that the motion of the celestial spheres was caused by the 'unmoved mover,' and that the heavenly bodies acted upon the inferior, sublunar world for the benefit of man, it was theoretically difficult to limit the influence of the stars to particular sections or aspects of the universe. And since Thomism, like every other contemporary system of natural philosophy, accepted those principles of the Aristotelian cosmology, astrology could be criticized from a moral or theological standpoint, but not on the basis of the metaphysical arguments then considered objective, irrefutable, and orthodox. Its chief opponents were moralists who claimed that the power to know and manipulate the future was disruptive to faith and morality. In the public opinion of that epoch opposition to astrology was not a progressive struggle against superstition, but rather a reactionary attack on science.

Thus, from the thirteenth to the seventeenth century, astrology became a leading discipline on a par with medicine and law. The number of outstanding men in this particular field is surprisingly high; every Italian province contributed to its development, while every university endeavored to secure the most famous, skilled, and learned theorists and practitioners. As long as their writings and teachings did not slip into the domain of lower occult arts, as long as they respected the monopoly of the Church in the exorcising of demons and the curing of bewitched souls, these professional astrologers enjoyed ecclesiastical protection. Famous scholars like Bartolomeo da Parma, Andalô di Negro of Genoa, Paolo Dagomari, and many others were less concerned with penetrating the secrets of nature than with perfecting and extending the traditional methods of juridical and medical astrology handed down from antiquity and organized by the Arabs into a workable system of doctrine and procedure. Consequently these learned masters did little for the advancement of science and a great deal for its teaching and practical application. With their thorough training in mathematics and their vast erudition, they enjoyed a leading position in all the institutions of secular learning.

But it was in public life that the domination of astrology was almost universal. Since the days of Michael Scotus, chief astrologer at the court of Frederick II, every Italian potentate, despot, or republic, and even bishops and popes appointed 'mathematicians' (as they were often officially called), who became highly influential in political affairs. Astrology became an instrument of power, determining the decisions of politicians, generals, and tyrants, and affecting the destinies of the Italian states. Astrology became a weapon in the struggle for wealth and hegemony in a country dominated by power politics. The general belief that human fate and natural cataclysms were written in the stars made astrologers indispensable to despots and *condottieri,* just as today scientists have become indispensable to the state and its machine.

The intimate relation between astrology and political practice is reflected in Giovanni Villani's famous chronicle of Florence, the masterpiece of fourteenth-century Italian historiography. In narrating the history of his native town with a dispassionate objectivity and a strong sense of positive reality, the learned Florentine merchant and official showed a remarkable sense of universal historical continuity from the creation of the world up to his own time. Villani, who died of the Black Death in 1348, was an orthodox believer and a faithful adherent of the ruling Guelf party. But he was evidently unable to see the divine hand and a providential design in the atrocious series of calamities that befell his town and country in that most unfortunate epoch of Italian and European history. More by instinct than by reflection, he interpreted the course of events from an astrological point of view.

Strangely enough, neither Villani nor any other author showing an equally consistent belief in planetary influences seems to have been troubled by the contradiction between naive piety and astrological science. Both religion and science concurred in condemning as impious and foolish the black magic of divination, conjuring tricks, and diabolic arts. The general belief in natural 'virtues,' on which the whole of medieval science was based, and the most popular and authoritative treatises on occult science made it very difficult for the average mind, or even the subtlest intellects, to trace clearly the boundaries between divine miracles and wonders wrought by magic, between approved doctrines and traditional superstitions, or between scientific procedures and occult practices. That is why, in a later cultural environment, the astrological interpretation of natural and human history could provoke strong opposition both for philosophical reasons, as in Pico della Mirandola's famous book against astrology (1494), and for religious motives, as (exactly at the same time) in Savonarola's pamphlets and sermons. But, in general, the divine mysteries of the faith and the scientific secrets of nature did not arouse conflicting opinions or burden the conscience of believers and skeptics. For the average Italian the authority of religion and the authority of science were not irreconcilable. He accepted both, just as he simultaneously accepted autocratic despotism and republican institutions. In writing for the educated middle class to which he belonged, Villani showed a keen curiosity for the things of the world, much local pride, a sharp interest in facts and figures, but no opinion other than that of an honest and experienced businessman. With the rest of his countrymen he simply ignored the spiritual conflicts that Boccaccio evaded with an accommodating smile and Petrarca bemoaned as a tragic burden. In meditating on life and history, those generations faced the alternative of resignation to the will of God or to the whims of fortune. In their spiritual neutrality they accepted both, and that remained for a long time the typical Italian attitude.

*   *   *

Although triumphant in schools and Dominican convents, Thomism had little effect on Italian life and culture. The Italian people were not moved by theological questions and soon became tired of philosophical controversies. From the day of Giovanni Campano, who, toward the end of the thirteenth century, reintroduced Euclid's *Elements* into science and practice, up to Biagio Pelacani and Prosdocimo de' Beldomandi, leading mathematicians a hundred years later, innumerable algebraists and abacists developed and propagated a branch of knowledge suited to the pragmatic needs and interests of their contemporaries. Bookkeeping, banking, navigation, medicine, and architecture were the leading spheres of Italian activity. Unlike their contemporaries among French and English scholars, the Italians were less concerned with purely scientific developments than with their practical application.

Thomism remained more than ever a Guelf philosophy, with strong political implications. The opposing Franciscan doctrine became the official Ghibelline philosophy, but for political rather than doctrinal reasons. It has already been pointed out that Italy did not participate in the theoretical controversies that were fought out mainly in Paris and its scholastic colonies in Central Europe. The Italian universities remained cosmopolitan, and exchanged professors and students with other countries. But the foreign scholars who came to Italy had little influence on general intellectual trends. There is not the slightest trace of Scotism in the works and thoughts of the leading Italian thinkers, although one of its ablest adherents, the French Pierre d'Auriole, taught at Bologna in 1312. Nor did William of Ockham's forced stay in Pisa, in 1332, occasion any noticeable propagation of his doctrines in Italy. Conversely, we see several Italian opponents of Thomism working, teaching, and agitating abroad, especially attracted by the political implications of the Franciscan philosophy embodied in the schools of Duns Scotus and William of Ockham. The meeting place of those adversaries of the Guelf and papal philosophy was the court of Louis of Bavaria, who availed himself of these intellectual exiles in his merciless fight against the French Pope, John XXII, who canonized Thomas Aquinas and excommunicated William of Ockham.

An outstanding member of this group of political-minded opponents of the Thomist doctrines was the famous Marsilius of Padua, whose extended treatise *Defensor Pacis*, published in 1324, was compiled in collaboration with the Parisian Jean de Jandun, a Franciscan schoolman of Ockham's circle. While this joint literary effort documents the intellectual solidarity of the Franciscan movement, the theory it embodies developed entirely from Italian experience, both in the religious and temporal fields. It grows out of the spiritual and political evolution of the Italian people since the earliest communal revolutions, and reflects their bitter opposition to papal absolutism and every kind of spiritual or political autocracy. For the unlimited theocratic authority of the popes, Marsilius demanded the 'general council of believers,' acting through a majority vote. To power obtained by divine right he opposed the sovereignty of the people as a collective legislator ruling through their elected representatives. What Marsilius meant by the sovereign people is still a matter of debate. And even his definition of the people as the *universitas civium* [5] leaves his concept of citizenship in doubt. But in a marked republican spirit, he makes peace, wisdom, and human happiness dependent upon the will of a popular majority and condemns the feudal principles of hierarchy and hereditary power as un-Christian and pernicious and the temporal power of the Church as heretical and arbitrary.

It was outside of Italy, however, that these daring ideas operated as revolutionary ferments. In Italy, to be sure, the old ideals of democratic liberty and republican administration were still alive, as is shown by the conspiracy of the Venetian Doge Marino Faliero, who in 1355 made the last attempt to break the power of the aristocratic oligarchy, or by the revolt of Genoa's local hero Simone Boccanegra, leader of the popular party against the ruling nobility and the domination of the Visconti. But these and other lesser revolts were hardly more than spasmodic outbreaks of the dispossessed groups that, like everyone else, abused the word liberty and the idea of the common good. All this strife for political power and material advantages took place in a spiritual vacuum and in an atmosphere of mutual suspicion and unbridled ambition. The disintegration of medieval Italy is evident in every aspect of life. The country was tired of politics, disappointed in theology, and indifferent to philosophy; it wavered between resignation and despair, bigotry and skepticism, commercial cosmopolitanism and political particularism.

It is against this somber background of disillusionment and demoralization that the momentous significance of humanism can be fully appreciated. It is this background that gives the powerful personality of Francesco Petrarca its appropriate historical setting. Without a philosophy or even a fixed place of residence,

[5] *Pars,* III, ch. 5.

he became Italy's preceptor and bard. Humanism as a new and
consistent spiritual attitude, equally personal, national, and universal, was his indestructible accomplishment. Poetry as a perfectly polished, highly stylized manifestation of human sentiments was his imperishable artistic conquest. He never faltered
in his purpose of keeping his own Christian faith free from the
dialectical subtleties in which religious beliefs had been en-
trapped by logicians and casuists. Throughout his life he remained consistently critical of the Aristotelian system and
method that dominated the science and thought of his time. He
dared to question the validity of a philosophy that endeavors
'to investigate the nature of beasts, birds, fishes, and snakes but
ignores or neglects the nature and destiny of man.' [6] It was because of this theoretical hostility to scholasticism and intellectual
dogmatism that he bitterly opposed and satirized the theory and
practice of medicine, for in that field traditional ignorance and
blind faith in authority appeared most evident and disastrous.

Thus, Petrarca consciously broke with the most characteristic
trends and habits of his time. Only by isolating his mind from
his intellectual environment could he become what he remained
throughout his life: the principal object of his own human curiosity. He discovered man by searching his ego, and unveiled the
essential values of humanity by ignoring the practices and doctrines of his day. From his youth he avoided the attraction of
Dante that might have made him, as he said, a poet 'applauded
by innkeepers, dyers, and wool-weavers.' [7] Petrarca was not en-
vious of Dante's fame. A sane and honest instinct taught him
that he would never perfect his poetical and moral personality
by letting the overwhelming power of Dante's art and doctrines
work upon his own style, opinions, and ideals. Aloofness from
Dante's world was for Petrarca a sort of self-protection; it implied his complete estrangement from the most vital sources of
Italian culture and the highest expression of the medieval mind.
But through this attitude he succeeded in laying the foundations
of a new civilization without destroying the old one.

The son of a Florentine exile, Francesco Petrarca was raised

---

[6] *De ignorantia sua et aliorum*, ch. 1.
[7] *Epistolae familiares*, xxv, 15 (to Giovanni Boccaccio).

in the international papal territory of Avignon. Thus he never became involved in the feuds into which every native Italian was born. Four years as a law student in Montpellier revealed to him the intrinsic vitality and universal prestige of the Latin language in the secular field of culture and literature, while three more years of studies in Bologna disclosed to him the poetic flexibility and inherent expressiveness of his native tongue. As he took little interest in law and even less in public life and the questions of the day, he seems to have concentrated all his intellectual passion on purifying and enriching the two idioms that became the main concern of his life. All his life Petrarca had had only one determined ambition: to be a poet.[8] Yet in the light of Dante's glory this was the most ambitious vocation to which a man could aspire. Like Dante he associated poetry with the idea of a moral mission, both national and universal. Poetry, for him, was the epitome of glory, the expression of a supreme human dignity. The crown of laurel bestowed upon him in 1341 by the Roman Senate at the suggestion of King Robert II of Naples, fulfilled the poet's lofty aspiration and became the insignia of a new universal sovereignty.

Petrarca's coronation consecrated a new spiritual leadership centered in Rome, then a ghost town of ruins and misery, deserted by emperors and popes alike. In the course of many years spent in the frivolous atmosphere of Avignon, or traveling through France, Italy, and Germany in the train of various high prelates, the young poet established a cosmopolitan republic of letters independent of the international universities and the political trends of his era. In one decade Petrarca succeeded in superimposing on schools and courts the prestige of the new intellectual sodality and directing the cultural interests of his generation toward an ideal and lasting center of universal civilization. The instrument of this spiritual renewal was the Latin language, reduced to the substantial purity and dignified elegance of the classics. The substance of the new culture consisted in the practical philosophy of the ancients as taught chiefly by Cicero and Seneca and as represented in the attitudes of

[8] 'Mihi sufficit esse poeta.' (*Epistolae metricae*, i, 6, 20.)

H

Virgil and the exemplary virtues of Roman heroes and sages. The objective of his aesthetic and moral approach to life and antiquity was to create a new universal aristocracy whose learned, virtuous, and active members might contribute to redeeming humanity from moral degradation, cultural vulgarity, and the fallacies of scholastic rationalism. The vehicle of this spiritual regeneration was Petrarca's extended correspondence with friends and adherents, begun in 1325, at the age of twenty-one years, and continued without interruption until the end of his life.

His role of *praeceptor Italiae* induced the poet to intervene in the country's public life with no fixed political program but with a vague vision of glory and grandeur, which he eloquently proclaimed. Of the social forces and political interests that had shaken the foundations of medieval society, he had only the vaguest and most general understanding, but he clearly sensed the vacuity, mendacity, and general demoralization of the society around him. In his environment he found no remedy or escape. He was no political leader, theorist, or conspirator. His aspiration was to become the spiritual counselor, the good genius, the inspiring guide of the potentates 'in whose hands fortune has put the bridle of this beautiful country.'[9] He never dreamed of changing the political and social structure of Italy, yet he did provoke a spiritual revolution that brought his country through the moral and cultural crisis of the time.

Unlike Dante, Petrarca accepted every political happening as a *fait accompli* and only intervened as a poet and monitor, disclosing evils and errors, and exhorting the princes and leaders of his country to a more human rule and a worthier life. He was more eloquent than active. He enthusiastically embraced the cause of Cola di Rienzo, but he also tenaciously urged the German Emperor, Charles IV, to be a true Caesar and a new Augustus. He dedicated to King Robert of Naples his poem *Africa*, with its apotheosis of the republican virtues of Rome embodied in Scipio the conqueror of Carthage. His raging invectives against the papacy of Avignon did not prevent him from so-

[9] *Song to Italy*, Strophe 2.

liciting and accepting from the popes the rich prebends that
secured his life in ease and independence; and ordination as a
priest was no hindrance to the amorous escapades that made
him the father of at least two illegitimate children. For years
he enjoyed the hospitality and protection of the same Italian
despots—the Viscontis, Correggios, and Carraras—whose misgovernment, greed, and violence he stigmatized both in prose and
in some of the most moving passages of his vernacular poetry.

These inconsistencies reflect the confusion of his environment.
With his refined sensibility and alert worldly curiosity he participated in all the laxity and error of his time, but in full consciousness of his weakness, guilt, and deviation from rectitude
and faith. Petrarca shared the vices and libertinism of his age
but not its callousness, apathy, and cynical complaisance. Much
of his work is confession and contrition, and much of his life is
devoted to the scrutiny and emendation of his faults. He was
incessantly molding and perfecting his personality with the same
care he devoted to the smoothing and polishing of his verses.
His amorous sighs and tears resolved in the melodious music of
his vernacular poems. His intellectual anxieties dissolved in the
harmonious flow of his Latin style.

*   *   *

These two spheres of Petrarca's inner life and literary expression remained strictly separate. Laura, beloved in life and death,
hardly inspired a line of all his voluminous Latin works. And
there is no definite vernacular expression of his philosophical
and scholarly interests. Only his love for his native country is
expressed with equal intensity and perfection in both languages,
whether he exalts its glories or bewails its afflictions. There were
no linguistic limitations to his patriotism. And there is no doubt
that of all the passions and interests that agitated and inspired
him, none was as spontaneous, consistent, and sincere as patriotism. Despite her human reality Laura became a poetic phantom. Hence the stilted mannerisms intermingled with the most
genuine fervor. Similarly, his Latin eloquence combines sincere
moral indignation with complacent rhetorical bombast. But there

is no false note or forced accent in any of his invocations and
salutations to Italy, because his patriotic enthusiasm is a genuine
sentiment, uncontaminated by factional interests, unaffected by
traditional trends, free from political commonplaces and personal
commitments.

By putting himself above sovereigns, tyrants, and parties,
Petrarca raised the idea of Italian spiritual unity to the level of
the general consciousness. Italy ceased to be merely a geographical expression and a vague political concept as it had been since
antiquity. The poetical exaltation of the country in verse and
prose, the incessant evocation of its memories, the passionate
praise of its beauties in letters and songs infused that indeterminate concept with a lyrical sentiment and spiritual substance
strongly contrasting with the rabid particularism of the Italian
city-states, despots, and republics.

In his praise of Italy, Petrarca did not confine himself to the
obvious recollection of her ancient glories and the admiration of
her natural beauties, but also paid an unusual tribute to the
human qualities of the Italian people.[10] This is a new contribution to the intricate texture of Italian national sentiment. This
feeling of sympathy and solidarity with all his countrymen, this
recognition of a distinctive national character, is especially striking in a man who professed utter contempt for the common herd,
the *profanum vulgus,* and he always affected to despise its praise.
Apparently his intellectual snobbery did not destroy his natural
sensibility. He admonished the princes of Italy to mend their
ways for the sake of the 'sorrowful people' ruined by their lust
for power and money.[11]

The poet did not elaborate the concept of the 'Italian people'
politically; it remained vague and ambiguous for many years to
come. But through this wise limitation of his patriotism to merely
sentimental and moral values he avoided a theoretical utopianism such as that of Dante's *Monarchy,* and remained within the
sphere of the possible and historically auspicious. He never abandoned the traditional Italian idea of a double universalism. He

[10] *Epistolae familiares,* xxiii, 2 (to Emperor Charles IV, 21 March 1361),
and elsewhere.
[11] Cf. the canzone *Italia mia,* Strophe 6.

revered the papacy as a divine institution, but wanted it to be first Italian and then ecumenical.

Petrarca discovered the Italian people as a human community endowed with a peculiar nature independent of political contingencies and institutions, regional or dynastic interests. He gave body to this vague idea of national brotherhood by identifying the Italian people as a whole with the Romans of old, disregarding, however, the theological and political implications of this view. Although no less pious and orthodox than Dante, Petrarca for the first time formulated the national identity of Rome and Italy without the traditional reference to their divine mission.

This attitude underlies Petrarca's implicit acceptance of Italy's new secularized political structure. He considered the 'Babylonian captivity' of the popes a national disgrace rather than a religious handicap. In his repeated warnings to the Emperor he did not stress Italy's need for personal guidance, but blamed him as a usurper of the imperial title as long as he resided in a remote and barbarous country.

This national approach to such basic medieval conceptions was a momentous occurrence in the history of Italian and Western civilization. It affected the whole spiritual situation of Petrarca's time and brought about a new turn in the development of Italian culture and life. His view of the autonomous distinction of the Italian people led the poet to consider the national predestination of his country from the cultural and moral, rather than from the theological or political angle. He contemplated the country's past and present in a human conciliatory mood without the apocalyptic and prophetic pathos of Dante. Convinced of the general depravity of his environment, Petrarca took refuge in the idealized world of the ancients, from whom he expected the moral regeneration of his country and age.

This idea, eloquently expressed in his imaginary letter to Livy,[12] prompted him to engulf himself in the classic world with greater enthusiasm, system, and understanding than anyone before him. He did not greatly add to the contemporary knowledge

[12] *Epistolae familiares*, xxiv, 8.

of ancient authors. His Greek was less than elementary. His distinction lay in the soundness of his opinions, the novelty of his approach, and the relevance of his literary endeavors to the needs of his country and his epoch.

Petrarca never pretended to have discovered the ancient world. Pagan antiquity was more or less present in almost every aspect of medieval life and culture. The imperial dignity, the papal sovereignty, and the republican movements all invoked their real or legendary ancient antecedents. The cyclic concept of human history, the Augustinian vision of human destiny, and the very weight of literary traditions kept alive the ancient heritage, though in a distorted fragmentary form.

The passionate opposition to pagan thought and customs, led by Augustine, Lactantius, and Orosius, reanimated from generation to generation the doctrines and attitudes of the ancients. The medieval Church was powerless to halt the revival of pagan science and philosophy that prompted Thomas Aquinas to renew the debate *contra gentiles* and to impose Aristotle on Catholicism as a Christian philosopher. And in Dante's poetical transfiguration of Aristotle's moral system the Biblical and classical examples of good and evil actions appear side by side, in a symmetry implying equal validity.[13]

Likewise, every judge and lawyer of Italy—and there were many—was perfectly aware of the ancient origin of the standard legal compendium, kept up to date through the centuries by a multitude of commentators until it was systematically revised by the leading jurists of Bologna. The authority of ancient medicine and science rested upon a traditional veneration of classical antiquity and not on clerical conservatism. Virgil, Cicero, and other Latin authors were revered for their mastery of style and not merely for the wisdom supposedly concealed beneath their imagery. And numerous medieval authors imitated the Latin classics and attempted to realize the literary precepts of Quintilian.

This sense of continuity with the classical era was not limited to Italy. The Carolingian and Ottonian revival of Latin and

---

[13] Especially in *Purgatorio*, x and ff.

Greek culture was accomplished entirely without Italian participation, while the Swabian restoration of pagan philosophy and science developed essentially through Arabic mediation. The popular revival of ancient authors, heroes, and legends in French poems and tales affected the Italian imagination only indirectly. Such was the general veneration for antiquity that even the most typical motifs of medieval history and lore were fancifully connected with the ancient world in numerous works composed *en romance et en latin* at the courts of England and France.

The Norman historians of the conquest of Britain began their narratives with the Argonauts or legends of Brutus. Chrestien de Troyes proclaimed in one of his poems that chivalry was the early glory of ancient Greece, first transmitted to Rome, whence the French finally received it with the whole sum of ancient wisdom.[14] In the same period the French writer Pierre of Blois, who lived at the Norman courts of Sicily and England, confessed 'we are like dwarfs on the shoulders of giants, by whose grace we see farther than they,' and that 'our study of the works of the ancients enables us to give fresh life to their final ideas.'[15] There is no doubt that the legacy of the ancient world was much more alive in the Middle Ages than it is today.

A general familiarity with the Latin language throughout the Middle Ages helped to preserve this universal sense of continuity. Petrarca's achievement did not consist in carrying this tradition to its culmination. In reality he revolted against the current adulteration and falsification of antiquity, which kept alive a deceptive image and reduced the ancient glory of Latin civilization to barbarism and vulgarity. He broke this deceptive cultural and intellectual continuity by conjuring up a new and personal vision of antiquity and its significance in a Christian world. Of this he was perfectly aware.

Modern scholarship seems to have reduced Petrarca's accomplishments to a largely formal revival of classical elegance. And, indeed, classical purity, ease, grace, and distinction certainly were Petrarca's unchanging aspiration from his early school years to the day of his death. Yet the new refinements of taste and

14 Cligès, 1 ff.
15 Epistle 92 in Migne's *Patrologia Latina,* ccvii, col. 290.

increasing familiarity with classical authors led Petrarca's successors to criticize the awkwardness and irregularity of his Latin style, which is not always free from blunders and solecisms. Those critics as well as his friends and followers knew only too well that—much as they admired the poet's efforts and accomplishments—the true classical Latin was that of the Augustan era. It follows that the success of his works cannot be attributed to their formal qualities alone. Erasmus praised his erudition and eloquence, and in the same breath criticized his awkward, old-fashioned style. Petrarca's lasting influence and prestige were not founded solely upon his literary elegance. What impressed his contemporaries and attracted his followers was the originality and relevance of his attitude toward antiquity and the society of his day.

In many letters and poetic allusions Petrarca elaborated the contrast rather than the affinity between his age and the ancient world. He ignored whatever had happened between the end of the Roman empire and his own time. In that development he saw only abuses, barbarism, and errors in every field of culture, politics, and religion. Of the recent achievements and currents of Christian theology he took no notice and restricted his religious meditations to the inner circle of the Latin fathers, chiefly to St. Augustine. There is not the slightest trace of scholasticism in his extended and many-sided works; neither Thomas Aquinas nor any other of the contemporary thinkers, masters, and spiritual leaders is ever mentioned in them. He regarded the whole of medieval Latin literature as a perversion, a hollow and nauseous gibberish. And as for the influence of Greek thought in the Aristotelian revival of his day, he considered it harmful to the faith and disastrous to the mind.[16]

The reason for this antagonism is that the poet, like many of his contemporaries, considered the tenets of Christianity self-evident and consequently found a Christianized Aristotelianism useless, misleading, and heretical. Without embracing the doctrines of St. Bonaventure, Duns Scotus, or Ockham, he realized that Aristotle's principle of the eternal self-sufficiency of the nat-

[16] *De ignorantia; Epistolae seniles,* xv, 6, etc.

ural order and the consequent dominance of natural science in his system estranged the human mind not only from God but also from man. A generation earlier Dante overcame the dangers of spiritual isolation by dissolving abstract reasoning and logical constructions in intuitive knowledge and poetical revelation. From the imaginary mountain top in Purgatory, Dante plunged his mind into the divine light of the heavenly spheres and aimed at a complete dissociation from human worldliness. Atop Mount Ventoux in the Provence, which he had toilsomely climbed on a spring morning in 1336, Petrarca meditated the passage of the Confessions in which St. Augustine deplores that 'human beings go around admiring the mountain heights, the mighty tides of the seas, the broad streams of the rivers, the circle of the ocean and the orbits of the stars, but do not care to look more deeply into themselves.' [17]

It was with these feelings and convictions that Petrarca—who never was troubled by religious doubts or controversies—substituted for the scientific scrutiny of nature the exploration of the human heart and the contemplation of the outward world. Through this very personal attitude he became aware of his kinship with the ancient mind, both as a poet and a philosopher. And, indeed, the medieval tradition had little to offer a man of learning and letters who thought the search for God superfluous for a believer and the quest for man indispensable. For the spiritual regeneration that he wanted to inspire and direct, the Christian virtues of humility, patience, poverty, and renunciation did not seem suitable. He never praised them as public virtues, not even when disappointment, boredom, and lassitude led him to preach contempt of the world and withdraw to the wilderness of Vaucluse.

Hell and Purgatory have no more place in Petrarca's works than the current controversies with pagan and Arabian philosophers about the principles of knowledge. It was the Roman virtues which he believed essential for the regeneration of Italy and the world, and that is why he never wearied of evoking the heroes of pagan times. He did not read Livy for his rhetoric but

[17] *Epistolae familiares,* IV, 1.

H*

because, like the Roman historian, he felt that the recollection of past Latin glories would, 'in the face of the miseries of his age,' help to restore public and private virtue.

This new function of ancient history is often mentioned in his extensive correspondence and in didactic works such as his long treatise *On Famous Men* (*De Viris Illustribus*), in which past and present, men and the world, are represented according to the testimony of the ancients, without recourse to the Bible or the lives of the saints. Christian concepts of charity and humility are replaced by more practical human and civic virtues, such as the *probitas* on which Livy insisted, and the *honestas* which in the pragmatic Roman ethics became almost synonymous with virtue itself. His moral principles, as developed in letters, treatises, and poems, may be reduced to those which epitomize the whole of Roman law: *neminem ledere: suum cuique tribuere; honeste vivere.*[18] A reflection of this moral code is to be found in the most inspired and popular of his patriotic poems, the *Song to Italy*, in which the barbarians appear as lawless hordes and their 'furor' as the counterpart of the disciplined valor of the Romans. In violating those basic precepts of civil life with the help of foreign mercenaries, the Italian princes were betraying their country, crippling their people, wrecking morality, and damning their own souls.

Petrarca's nostalgic vision of ancient rectitude and nobility found its most ambitious expression in the poetic glorification of Scipio Africanus in a Latin poem of vast proportions conceived as the Italian *Aeneid*. The content of Petrarca's *Africa* is drawn from Livy's history, of which it is a metrical paraphrase much in the manner recommended by Quintilian and practiced, with less eloquence and literary polish, in the medieval schools.[19] The poet's own attitudes and enthusiasm break through the rhetorical mist whenever Scipio appears as an embodiment of the Roman virtues struggling against African malice.

In this medieval maze of allegories and parables, the Roman hero is no longer a historical prefiguration of chivalry or an in-

[18] To harm no one; to give each his own; to live honestly. Cf. *Epistolae seniles*, XIV, 1, etc.

[19] Quintilian, *Institutiones Oratoriae*, x, 5.

strument of Divine Providence. He is rather the poetical reincarnation of the old Roman *virtutes,* the names of which were preserved by Christian ethics but with quite altered meanings. With Petrarca, for the first time since the classical age, *fides* no longer has the sense of belief in God but expresses the synthesis of fairness, loyalty, and mutual confidence for which modern languages have no equivalent word. Scipio's *pietas* is not compassion or devout belief, but rather the devotion to parents, family, race, and country glorified in Virgil's 'pius Aeneas.' *Honor* is never feudal fealty as in the romances of chivalry, but—as in classical times—personal glory and the fame of illustrious deeds.

Besides these general human and pagan virtues the poem exalts those pertinent to sovereigns and leaders, such as magnanimity, justice, and clemency, all replacing the feudal and chivalric virtues of courtesy and liberality, obedience and fidelity, piety, and respect for womanhood. The same classical topics recur in the long letter to Francesco di Carrara, overlord of Padua, later published as a treatise on government and the perfect ruler.[20] For the first time in the extensive literature on the 'good prince,' the office and duties of a sovereign are not deduced from religious precepts or developed according to a system of Christian ethics as in the widely known treatise of Giles of Rome.[21] Petrarca derives his image of the perfect prince from the maxims of classical writers and examples drawn from Greek and Roman history. Despite the moral generalities characteristic of this kind of work, the treatise cannot be dismissed as an eloquent reverie, for it also has its practical side: the poet appeals to the Paduan despot to mobilize the civic spirit of his subjects for urgent public undertakings, such as the drainage of marshlands, the repair of highways, and, last but not least, the removal of pigs from the streets of such an old and venerable college town.

All these moral and practical obligations of sovereigns and subjects are conceived by Petrarca in an ancient spirit, as is evident from the most diversified of his writings. He was determined to connect his personality and environment with the

---

[20] *De republica bene administranda liber (Epistolae seniles,* xiv, 1).
[21] Aegidius Columna Romanus, *De regimine principum* (1285).

ancient world as if a thousand years of human experience, with all its profound intellectual and social convulsions, could be effaced from the memory of man. Here Petrarca was deluding himself above all; his own personality and ideas were closely bound up with medieval traditions of culture and literature. Yet in half a century of passionate endeavor he succeeded in presenting every intellectual achievement of the past and every problem of his day in the double light of late antiquity and early Christianity. If Scipio embodied the heroic aspects of pagan humanity and Livy represented the culmination of its historical development, Cicero embraced its philosophical, literary, and cultural totality. Like every other medieval writer Petrarca drew much of his worldly wisdom from the works of Seneca. It was Cicero, however, who most deeply inspired him, not merely for the musical charm and elegance of his style, but because of the incomparable variety of his ethical themes and his comprehensive insight into Greek thought.

*   *   *

Long before Petrarca, Cicero's works had enjoyed high favor among medieval intellectuals. This widespread enthusiasm for the great orator was based on respect for his republicanism and admiration for his literary skill and philosophical ability. St. Augustine had praised Cicero almost as if he had been a Christian author, and it seems probable that all those who shared Petrarca's aversion to what he called theological sophisms joined in appreciation of Cicero's literary legacy. Translations of his main treatises greatly extended the popularity and influence of his work. Cicero became an Italian author and Ciceronianism not only a literary style but a state of mind and to a certain extent a national calamity. His revival and popularity in the fourteenth century are one symptom and expression of an increasing tendency to argue, dissert, and moralize upon all subjects, sacred and profane, grave or trivial, factual or fabulous.

No author could compete with Cicero in variety of moral themes, extent of practical knowledge and human experience, and in the eclectic appreciation of intellectual accomplishments. His mild and elegant skepticism appealed to many free spirits like Boccaccio, who kept aloof from bigotry, penance, and mortification as well as metaphysical controversies and scholastic subtleties. Dante absorbed into his vision of salvation the ethical system and political cosmopolitanism that Cicero had elaborated according to the doctrines and practice of the Greco-Roman Stoicism. Petrarca learned, as he taught, to appreciate the wisdom of the ancients as an independent achievement of the human mind. In his extensive correspondence with men of every rank and age, he accustomed his countrymen and a few outstanding foreigners to view the eternal problems of life and the world from that classical, profane, and eclectic angle.

For the medieval sense of continuity Petrarca substituted the idea of a renewal of intellectual and moral virtues through the inspiration of the ancients. This is the significance of early Italian humanism as initiated by Petrarca. By making the past a part of the present and a goal for the future, he replaced tradition and habit by a sense of renascence; the ancients would come to the rescue of his disrupted country and disillusioned world. He convinced his contemporaries that the medieval dream of a *renovatio imperii* could be achieved only on a new moral basis. If Dante expected the moral redemption of mankind from the divine power and wise administration of a Roman emperor, Petrarca believed that the spiritual regeneration of human society must precede the final triumph of peace and justice.

The moral and erudite content of Petrarca's Latin works assured their reception as something more than skillful pieces of literary composition. His convictions and aspirations gave body to his resuscitation of classical Latin. Petrarca's return to the style of the Augustan writers was only the literary aspect of his determination to dissociate his mind and age from the barbarism and vulgarity of his day. He wished to make the idiom of Rome the personal, national, and universal expression of a spiritual revival and of a new cultural ideal.

The consequences of this rebirth were as profound and far-reaching as the discovery of the external world by the painters and sculptors of the age of Giotto. These literary and artistic expressions of a new spirit are connected and concurrent. The new style in art and literature manifests the determination of creative minds to find truth and beauty in the reality of life and not in the abstractions of thought. By educating their contemporaries to appreciate the noble rhythm and formal purity of the authentic Roman language, Petrarca, his friends and followers, succeeded in turning men's minds away from medieval cultural traditions. And in opposing the Latin of Rome to that of Paris, these early humanists expressed also the reaction of their patriotic pride against the French intellectual hegemony. The conviction grew that the formal qualities of the old and new classicism implied a higher degree of truth and nobility than the uncouth, amorphous, and cursory Latin of the medieval philosophers, jurists, and chroniclers.

This development provided Italian intellectual life with a national cultural substance but isolated the country from the great spiritual currents of the late Middle Ages. Petrarca's belief that all wisdom and morality were contained in the works of the ancients inspired many gifted men to explore the classical world more widely. But their antiquarian fervor led them to ignore and evade the great problems and conflicts that were raging in the rest of Europe. Under the constraint of his more critical than co-operative and creative attitude, Petrarca turned to a philosophy of misanthropic, egotistic, and weary contempt for the world. He never committed himself personally and entirely to the ideals he was so eloquently proclaiming. He substituted for Christian zeal and contrition a Stoic ideal of tranquillity and aloofness suitable only to a man who lives from benefices or annuities, shunning family obligations and the responsibilities of public life.

His contempt for the world did not induce him to retire to a monastery, like so many less religious men of letters before and after him. He wistfully praised the leisure, dignity, and holy life of the monks and hermits,[22] but he avoided every form of associative tie, and never sought refuge in the mystical search for God. The charming wilderness of Vaucluse, the simple country life of Selvapiana, the Arcadian tranquillity of Arquà and the various other places where he spent years of his life in seclusion

[22] *De vita solitaria; De ocio religiosorum.*

and meditation, appear from our historical perspective as the secular counterpart of the mystical refuge where the great saints of the high Middle Ages—Bruno, Bernard, Joachim of Fiore—found light and peace in God. For Petrarca, who felt the presence of God in the radiance and beauty of nature, a life in solitude meant the contemplation of his ego in the ideal setting of a restored antiquity. Estrangement from men and the world became essential to his lyricism and the literary realization of his moral and patriotic dreams.

His incessant self-contemplation is not always a symptom of a new attitude concerned with the perfection of the individual. It is sometimes an expression of the disdainful, asocial, conceited character of a man of letters who imparted lessons to rulers and advice to authorities, but showed complete contempt for the common man. His polished Latin was, in part, conceived as a barrier to keep the general public out of the holy precinct of the renascent Muses and create an exclusive literary aristocracy. And, indeed, the new classicism soon disrupted the spiritual unity that Dante had initiated in consecrating and dignifying the native tongue as a *volgare illustre*.[23] The Italian courts, always in quest of a solemn style of diplomatic interchange and official phraseology, rapidly adopted the elevated and sonorous classicistic diction introduced by Petrarca. His friends and followers became diplomats, chancellors, secretaries to sovereigns, overlords, and republics. The forms and manner of antiquity soon became a mark of official and courtly dignity. The collaboration between princes and humanists was one of the most characteristic features of the new Italian civilization.

The large sections of the middle classes that had already accepted the political tutelage of local and regional despots acknowledged the new turn of courtly civilization and adopted the revived classical taste and culture with enthusiasm, although there is no indication that the constant praise of ancient wisdom and valor produced the slightest change in the brutal conduct of princes, soldiers, bankers, and traders.

Those conspicuous sections of Italian society that did not join

---

[23] *De vulgari eloquentia*, I, xvi.

in this new courtly and literary movement clung to the medieval traditions of language, thought, and taste and constituted a separate, conservative community, in part antagonistic and in part indifferent to humanistic trends. For generations this community preserved the inherited habits of life, the consecrated methods of thinking, and the medieval approach to art, science, and poetry. The two currents sometimes merged both in individual minds and in collective moods, but finally came to a revolutionary clash, typified by Savonarola, that revealed the power of tradition and the lasting resistance of vast groups to the classicistic, profane, and individualistic trends of Italian civilization. The orders and their schools were the centers of this conservative opposition that clung to the cursory, unadorned, and corrupt medieval Latin, condemned the perverting influence of the courts and their literati, and perpetuated in vernacular treatises and sermons the cult of the saints, respect for the ecclesiastical hierarchy, and the practice of the Christian virtues of charity, penitence, and devotion.

The historical importance of these strong undercurrents has been frequently underestimated, if not ignored, because of the lack of a creative power in this enduring and provincial conservatism. But the tension produced by its existence is evident in every aspect of life, art, and literature. Modern Italy developed out of these conflicting spiritual forces. The individual efforts to free men's minds from obsolete, exhausted traditions were as strong as the general desire to create a new civilization within the framework of consecrated and basic traditions. Petrarca, with his refined Latin and his cult of pagan virtues in a Christian spiritual environment, produced a cultural and social duality. His impassioned criticism of astrology, scholastic theology, and medical science brought no result; they remained a powerful influence in the courts and schools. To a certain extent, he even consolidated the typical medieval situation of two conflicting forms of culture: a higher one represented by his exclusive, ornate Latin, and an inferior one restricted to the domain of his mother tongue.

Petrarca's scholarly legacy to his age and followers was not a doctrine but a state of mind, an aspiration, a spiritual guidance that reached far beyond the medieval horizons of thought and art without ever losing sight of them. Along with his glory as a poet, he transmitted to posterity a cultural task and some human problems that have never vanished from the consciousness of educators, philosophers, and spiritual leaders. Those problems, relating to the incorporation of pagan and secular civilization into the modern Christian world, are still very much alive.

Petrarca drove out the counterfeit heroes of the Homeric saga, as represented in popular medieval tales, in order that they might be replaced by the original poems, first translated into Latin prose under his auspices, if not with his approval, by a learned adventurer from Calabria, Leonzio Pilato. To future generations Petrarca transmitted the task of resuscitating the Greek authors from long oblivion, and to this end he aroused the enthusiasm of many well-intentioned but not always successful pioneers. Although unable to read the Greek poets in their own language, he collected their works and took delight in their manuscripts as a blind man does in the sunshine. Finally he had a clear presentiment that the shallow, abstruse, and fallacious intricacies of the current philosophy could be overcome, for the glory of God and the salvation and dignity of man, by Plato's intuitive dialectics, by his repudiation of empiricism and rational deductions, and finally by the power of his inspired eloquence. Guided by St. Augustine and Cicero, Petrarca pointed to Plato as the 'divine' mind that would free the intellects of his age from the perverting influence of the hated and despised Arabic mediator of Greek philosophy and science.[24]

[24] *Epistolae seniles*, xii, 2.

I N a famous letter mentioned by all his biographers Petrarca reported that when as a child he listened to the reading of Cicero's works (evidently a custom in his father's home), he was fascinated by the mere sound of words and sentences although still unable to understand their meaning.[1] This confession reveals the underlying significance of his appreciation of an author whom in his mature years he praised for the loftiness of his mind as well as the eloquence of his style. From that early experience the poet developed the conviction that formal perfection is a value in itself. He believed that no truth, knowledge, or insight could be dissociated from the artistic perfection of its expression. A generation before him the same idea had inspired Dante and his friends to dissolve philosophy into poetry and substitute artistic intuition for dogmatic schematization. It led Petrarca back to the Latin classics, to which he accorded an exclusive and universal supremacy.

Yet it was this tyrannical Latinity that tied his mind and inspiration to the medieval literary traditions and to the old moral, didactic, and rhetorical concept of poetry. His Latin writings assumed the allegorical, visionary, and parabolic forms that had dominated the poetic style of the Middle Ages. Petrarca's accomplishment consisted in directing those medieval traditions toward new ideals and in transferring intellectual enthusiasms from schools and convents to courts and homes. The poet's immense popularity was attested by the eagerness of sovereigns and

[1] *Epistolae seniles*, XVI, 4.

republics to honor him with high dignities and important appointments. And even more significant is the touching devotion expressed by that Lombard artisan who received the poet in his rustic home with the deference due to a saint or a hero.[2]

Petrarca realized only in his declining years that the glory he had expected from his Latin works would in reality be built upon his *rerum vulgarium fragmenta,* his vernacular lyrics in praise of the living and dead Laura. He invented no new forms for his poetry; he preserved the motifs and attitudes of the poetic cult of love characteristic of the Provençal courtly lyrics that had died out with the disintegration of medieval society. The *Canzoniere* is full of the ecstatic music and ethereal subtilization of the 'new style.' But the substance and function of that poetry is entirely different. Love and death are again the fundamental motifs of Petrarca's lyricism, but without the scholastic and metaphysical implications of Dante's short poems. Laura still has the vague and shadowy features of Beatrice, but she has greater corporeal reality and her allegorical meaning is not transcendental. Her name hints at Petrarca's highest earthly aspiration—the laurel wreath of the poet. His *amor* has no supernatural implications and it is not a chivalric virtue such as courtesy, gallantry, or the spirit of adventure. His love is a human passion that obtains nourishment from its own substance and hence survives its object in a search for eternity in art and not in God. This kind of love is no longer the contemplation of the divine order as practiced by the *fedeli d'amore* of the older generation. The self-sufficiency and self-justification of Petrarca's concept of love explain the poverty of his metaphoric language. His poetic imagination does not, like Dante's, plunge into the mysteries of theology and nature or disclose through symbols and similes the secret links between things human and divine. In Petrarca's poems there is no other drama than that of his mind and no other problem than that of his heart. His amorous experiences never crystallize in objective statements or in maxims for the practice of life. He never speculates on the essence of love, whose yoke he accepted reluctantly and thankfully as a sweet martyrdom

---

[2] *Epistolae familiares,* xxi, 11 (1359).

and a blissful torment. All his interest is directed toward the minute scrutiny of his reactions to the seductive and distressing power of love, whose blind impact on his soul is stronger and firmer than the shining beauty of the beloved woman. She dies and disappears, but love persists as a source of grief and inspiration, of nostalgic yearning and unresigned remembrance.

Thus, only love—and not a woman or an idea—lives in those poems as an unshakable reality and an invincible power. Laura is eternal for the sake of art. She has no other function and mission than that of provoking sentiments, of evoking memories, and of inspiring a hopeless passion, in life and death. God's mercy, the beauty of the outward world, pagan mythology, Biblical phrases, and classical reminiscences are drawn into the sphere of this earthly love that drives the poet 'from thought to thought, from hill to hill,' into a solitude populated only by dreams and recollections, tender accents and melodious rhythms. For the first time in the Christian era Petrarca reveals without moral purpose or courtly conventions the lover's enchantment and despair, transports and torments, whims and vagaries, visions and derangements.

From him Italy, a country of resourceful lovers, truly learned to love. Petrarca replaced the courtly casuistry of the Provençal and French fashion with the reality of the human heart, which he had dissected in lifelong contemplation of his own amorous exaltation. He replaced allegories and rational entanglements with real psychological situations and emotional predicaments. In his poems sensual seduction is not concealed under spiritual veils or monkish garments, nor is it displayed with the gentle libertinism of Ovid's *Ars Amatoria* or the French *Roman de la Rose;* it is accepted and ennobled as a fount of rapturous emotions, a refined stimulus of life and art, and a human problem of abysmal depth.

Petrarca dwells upon every mood, experience, and intimate adventure of love. His unobtrusive psychological precision and poetic clarity extend over the whole gamut of sentimental tones and topics, and dissolve into a charming, troubling, and winged musicality. The whole of Italy was subjugated by this poetic wonder, and has ever since conceived of love and love poetry in the forms laid down by these sonnets and *canzoni*. They became an essential factor in the formation of the Italian mind and the national literary style.

Petrarca's inspiration is purely secular but permeated by a religious spirit. It is aristocratic but not exclusive in sense and expression. And although he never acquiesced in the pagan philosophy of *carpe diem*, his poetry is full of sensuous charm and erotic implication.

The solemn dignity of this poetry, its warm eloquence, cultural substance, and penetrating human insight rapidly conquered the Italian people. For centuries lyric poetry was conceived in this form and spirit; 'Petrarchism' became an ingrained habit. The influence of Petrarca's poetry was by no means limited to literature or to a restricted group of connoisseurs and enthusiasts. But there is no doubt that its lasting success depended upon its formal qualities and artistic refinements, quite aside from its intrinsic human substance.

The fascination of this poetry proceeds from artifices both subtle and transparent, woven into a delicate texture of sounds, rhythms, and accents. Petrarca's poems fully exploit the music and expressiveness of the Italian language. His style never has the austere rigidity, the impetuosity, the cramped concentration of Dante. Petrarca's formal ideal is a balance between intensity and delicacy of expression, a perfect proportion between epigrammatic terseness and natural fluency, a studied alternation between declamatory gravity and easy levity. He learned the secret of this varied style from the classics, which he studied and recited unremittingly. At the same time he retained certain artifices of medieval poetry, which played so much with words because of the substantial significance believed to be inherent in verbal roots and sounds: 'Words are the consequence of things.' [3]

Petrarca's lyric poems are 366 in number—one for every day of the year. In every single one, the opening words carry a special quality of inducement. In these exordiums the tonality and tension of the poem are set forth with concentrated vigor and charm. Those striking introductory lines supplanted the instru-

[3] Dante, *Vita nuova*, XIII.

mental prelude. With their magic they detached the listener
from his original mood and drew him into the sphere of a lyrical
harmony. The poet does not always succeed in maintaining the
pitch of his initial inspiration. But when he does, when his elegance of detail is developed into a perfect harmony, the effect is
overwhelming and lasting.

No Italian of his day escaped the influence of this art. Dante
was read, interpreted, revered, and discussed; Petrarca was imitated in all epochs of Italian literature. This fact is attested by
innumerable poetic compositions of which, fortunately, relatively
few—though still running into the thousands—have been preserved. Aside from their intrinsic merits, his poems were loved
for their absence of abstruse learning and doctrine.

The imitation began shortly after his death. It became increasingly dominant in the Italian courts of the fifteenth century. The professional poets and courtly amateurs who charmed
the gentlemen and ladies in the entourage of Lionello d'Este in
Ferrara, Sigismondo Malatesta in Rimini, the Gonzagas at
Mantua, the last Viscontis in Milan followed by Francesco Sforza
and Lodovico il Moro—resumed the traditions of the old troubadours, roving from court to court in search of acclaim, protection, and money. It was especially at the brilliant Aragonese
court of Naples that the most skilled, versatile, and prolific poets
of this style met with the greatest success.[4] There the medieval
traditions, revived in the conservative spirit of the Spanish rulers,
were transformed to the pattern of Italian taste.

Literary history has listed these amateurish potentates and
princelets as well as their minstrels whose individual inspiration
remained confined within Petrarca's lyrical sphere and phraseology. The Florentines did not join in this vogue of stilted and
languorous court poetry. Courtly manners and poetic juggling
did not thrive in Florence, with its higher cultural level and
enlarged experience of the world. It is not by pure chance that
the first, if not the only, satirist to ridicule and parody that style
should have been Francesco Berni, the Florentine.[5] Meanwhile,

---

[4] Especially Benedetto Gareth, called Cariteo (d. 1514), and Serafino
Aquilano (d. 1500).
[5] d. 1535.

the modish lyric had attained its most personal expression in the songs and sonnets of Matteo Mario Boiardo, the learned count of Scandiano, who devoted all his time to the Muses and first infused into the literary hobbies of the upper classes as much humanity and natural emotion as could dwell in the mind of a nobleman of his rank and line.

For Boiardo's great Florentine contemporary, Lorenzo de'Medici, poetry was less absorbing but still important. Although Lorenzo's poetry of love was only one aspect of his intense and varied life, it has again the philosophical pretension that stirred the generation of Dante. Seeking the embodiment of divine harmony and perfection in the image of the beloved, this extraordinary man wrote tortuous, abstract poems of a distinctly medieval cast. Yet whenever a poetic fancy leads Lorenzo away from this covert platonic symbolism to the color and beauty of the external world, then again Petrarca phraseology resounds through the harmonious lines of his amorous poems.

Until modern times neither the changes in cultural substance nor the individual experiences of talented poets were able to emancipate the Italian poetical consciousness from the mastery of Petrarca. The sixteenth century conceived of no love poetry that was not a mere variation on his basic themes. New spiritual experiences, changing intellectual aspirations, infinite human experience were all cast into the old molds.

The reasons for this tenacious conservatism in an epoch of free expansion of the personality in life and art are manifold and closely connected with the whole structure of Italian civilization. But the intrinsic artistic worth of that style, with its perfect balance between intense passion and literary polish, certainly had more to do with its survival and influence than any such external circumstances as the static structure of Italian society. What made the *Canzoniere* the school of Italian poetry and the source of general inspiration was its immense variety of lyrical themes and the perfect proportion between lyric inspiration and literary artistry. This explains why the greatest poem of maddening love and amorous conquests in world literature—Ariosto's *Orlando Furioso*—abounds in reminiscences drawn from Petrarca's lyrical store, as do Michelangelo's elderly transports of

Platonic love. Many poets and innumerable men and women of his era grasped and developed the latent philosophical nucleus of Petrarca's poetry: that is, the Christian and eternal problem of reconciling the enjoyment of life and nature with the salvation of the soul.

Yet the poet's artistic mastery survived this lyrical conflict of 'sacred and mundane love.' The revival of courtly gallantry prompted its most gifted interpreter, Torquato Tasso, to intensify the languid accents, the declamatory flourish, the antithetical repartee, and ornamental tinsel that adorn Laura's poetic image. Many of the Arcadian pictures that enchanted frivolous enthusiasts of art, music, and courtly gallantry in the successive era grew out of the same literary climate in which Petrarca's idyllic sceneries took shape and color in praise of the beloved woman.

The intensity of his influence and the power of this tradition of taste and inspiration are evident in the thoroughgoing study, minute analysis, and unconscious imitation of his poems by the most original, admired, and versatile Italian poets of modern times—Alfieri, Leopardi, Carducci—each one of whom composed a line-for-line commentary on the *Canzoniere* as a sort of *gradus ad Parnassum* and guide to artistic perfection. These highly influential authors are the classics of Italy's more recent poetic past. In shaping the national spirit of their period they never broke their ties with the Petrarcan tradition, despite the changes in intellectual experience, literary trends, and social environment. These poets, supported by the spiritual affinity of five centuries of national life, carried Petrarca's influence to the threshold of our contemporary world, in which poetry counts for so little and formal elegance for even less.

The great ascendancy of poetry in the early stages of Italian culture is not satisfactorily explained on the basis of any 'national disposition' of the Italian people. It was no less dominant in medieval France, which provided the rest of Europe with every kind of literature. Poetry was only one aspect of French intellectual and artistic leadership. In Italy poetry was instrumental and unique in shaping the spiritual physiognomy of the country. The three masterpieces of its early literature—Dante's

Commedia, Petrarca's *Canzoniere,* and Boccaccio's *Decameron*—grew out of the laical Italian genius at a time, 1300 to 1360, when every other source of spiritual life seemed to be exhausted or submerged in material concerns.

In a country of political upstarts, military opportunists, ruthless money-makers, and intellectual skeptics, poetry was the only ideal reality that could satisfy higher human aspirations and unite that nation in common appreciation of a superior existence. In this unique fraternity of letters Dante's poetry was addressed to the intellect, Petrarca's lyrics to sentiment, Boccaccio's prose to a broad and illuminating experience of life. These exceptional men grew up outside of the universities and the centers of the professional culture of their day. Their intellectual leadership grew strong with the consciousness and recognition of the new nobility which they represented both in the cultural sphere and in active life.

❖   ❖   ❖

One of the most fallacious commonplaces in literary history is the designation of Boccaccio as the spokesman of the mercantile middle classes of Florence. The light-minded carelessness, the joyous hilarity, and tolerant skepticism that seem to run through his writings are generally interpreted as the literary expression of a class essentially intent on the enjoyment of life. Yet life in an Italian town of the fourteenth century was not very cheerful, and the great majority of its inhabitants were not much bent on enjoyment. 'Many customs were uncouth and rough,' says the chronicler Giovanni Villani. The same institutions that protected money-making and voted enormous expenditures for municipal and ecclesiastical purposes controlled very closely the private life of the citizens and limited their expenditures by strict sumptuary laws. While usury was a sort of popular sport practiced on a large scale with the help of legal trickery, every display of luxury was forbidden and heavily fined; the possession of jewels, the fashions in dress, even the number of buttons that might be worn were strictly regulated. This was the Florentine conception of democracy, but these regulations were adopted also in other parts of Italy where the traditions of democracy were not so consistent.

Only a few patrician families that dominated economic activities and influenced the political institutions of the republic succeeded in eluding these limitations on personal liberty and in developing a more brilliant style of life. The palaces of this new aristocracy of wealth and business arose where formerly the gloomy towers of the old feudal nobility had darkened the narrow, noisy, and unclean lanes of the town. Even these palaces, with their spacious rooms, high ceilings, sober furniture, and chilly parlors, still bear witness to the severe customs, the disregard of comfort, and the austere life characteristic even of the higher classes of medieval society. These patrician residences with their vast cellars and storerooms for wool and wheat were landmarks in the long rows of poor, thatched, overcrowded plebeian dwellings. Disastrous fires and epidemics, such as that described in the introduction to the *Decameron,* were a familiar occurrence. In Florence and Rome frequent floods caused heavy loss of life and property damage. The rate of infant mortality was devastating.

The chronicles and documents of the day allow us to extend this gloomy picture to all Italian towns. In Florence a quarter of the population lived from alms, and large numbers earned hardly enough to afford the slightest recreation. In the crowded slums of Genoa and Venice, in turbulent Rome, in tumultuous Naples, and industrious Milan, in the stagnant provincial towns, conditions were even worse. For the average people life was dangerous, austere, and dull, relieved only by a few public festivals at fixed intervals. Hardships were accepted with resignation, and the praise of God was never omitted either in good or evil luck.

The ruling classes of Florentine bankers, merchants, and industrial entrepreneurs were intellectually conservative, opportunistic in politics, and bigoted in matters of religion. In the rest of Italy, where democratic institutions had disappeared, a spirit of submissiveness to the rule of local despots or an organized oligarchy limited the interests of these same classes to business, home, and church. The fortunes accumulated through trade and banking transactions or by the exploitation of cheap labor were modestly spent and invested in stable values. The building of town houses lent prestige to the owners and their families. It became a widespread custom to possess a country house with some landed property—a first step towards the 'villa' which later played such a characteristic role in the life of higher Italian society. It was customary to give children a sound and costly education, to wear decent clothes; large sums were spent on food, spices, and wine. But the most considerable expenditures of these well-to-do people were for the construction and decoration of churches, chapels, and sanctuaries, the organization of pious confraternities, or for the endowment of hospitals, convents, and ecclesiastical institutions.

The relationship of the bourgeoisie to the clergy was as close as that of the feudal nobles had formerly been, with the difference that the ruling middle classes were much more subservient to the ecclesiastical authorities and generous toward friars and nuns. This attitude was not dictated by any profound devotion or religious zeal, but rather by practical and social considerations. The mystical, ascetic enthusiasms of the preceding era had vanished along with doubts, heresies, and religious discussions. The bourgeoisie and the mendicant orders clung together in a spirit of mutual protection and defense. With their rich legacies and donations, their formal but regular observance of religious rites, the middle classes had become the strongest and most reliable support of the Church and its institutions.

In return, these mercantile benefactors could count on the protection of the only organized institution that had emerged intact from the political and social revolutions of the late Middle Ages. No one seemed particularly perturbed by the widespread corruption of the clergy and the equivocal policy of the orders, which, while preaching poverty, became the wealthiest and most influential possessors of the good things of the earth. It was a long time since the faithful had refused to accept the sacraments from the hands of unworthy priests. Most illuminating is the story told by Boccaccio of the Jew who found the triumph of Christianity even more evident, convincing, and miraculous after having observed the debauchery, greed, and gluttony of 'the Shepherd and all the others' at the Roman court.[6] In an era in

[6] *Decameron*, I, 2.

which money bought everything, regular donations to the Church helped to silence many timorous consciences and to placate the superstitious terror of death and damnation.

The countless churches and shrines built in that period reveal this attitude of the Italian middle classes. Their ranks included innumerable hardened sinners. Blasphemy and obscene language were as customary then as now, but practiced on a wider scale and with greater emphasis. Adultery was a common practice with little consequence to a man's career and little trouble to a woman's conscience. But all this moral laxity did not imply intellectual skepticism, or indifference to religion. Clerical leniency and generous gifts washed away both the customary and exceptional offenses. The humanity of the Blessed Virgin and the Saints brought them nearer to the people than Christ and God the Father. God was regarded as an inexorable creditor, who could be cursed, appeased, and cheated, but never ignored. Devotion was a sort of bookkeeping in which assets and liabilities must be balanced. It was more than a simple joke when the liturgical words 'you will get a hundred for one and gain eternal life' were interpreted after the usurious practice of those days.[7]

Skepticism and frivolity had already become a privilege of the aristocracy, although noblemen were bound to the same external obligations and were no less superstitious churchgoers than other Italians. The difference was mainly that the noblemen were accustomed to settling their affairs with armed might and to concealing their superstitious fears beneath the delusive rationality of astrological science. Much of the old philosophical Ghibellinism still ruled the minds of these privileged classes, although the term had lost its political implications and was forbidden, along with its Guelf antithesis, by the cruel and powerful Bernabò Visconti, Lord of Milan until 1385. In fourteenth-century Florence, when the *capitani di parte guelfa* dominated the public life of the republic, there was no other means of escaping the oppressive atmosphere of bigotry and mediocrity than to become a knight or a poet. Merely by paying a sum of money to the pope, the emperor, or a recognized Italian potentate, the

[7] Poggio Bracciolini, *Facetiae*, IV.

scion of an enriched commercial family could become a patrician and enter the lists for or against the oligarchic wire-pullers of the Florentine democracy. Inherited wealth was, after the Aristotelian definition, officially accepted by all political powers, an essential condition of nobility. The intellectual aristocracy made common cause with the old and new patriciate in a more or less disinterested aspiration for free expansion and unrestricted self-assertion.

* * *

Giovanni Boccaccio, the Paris-born illegitimate son of a Florentine commercial agent, inherited almost nothing of the middle-class spirit and interests represented by his father and by so many of the types he ridiculed in his tales. But even before the writing of the tales, Boccaccio had expressed his contempt for 'mean, factious, and rapacious Florentine democracy,' [8] ruled by men he considered 'dishonest, ignorant, hypocritical, and thievish,' unworthy of the popular favor that gave them power and prestige.[9] Although these authorities entrusted him with several honorable political commissions and sent him as an ambassador to the Emperor, in 1351, and to the Pope, in 1353 and in 1365, he never liked to live in Florence. He even preferred poverty and rustic solitude in his dreary village of Certaldo when public charges, family affairs, and lack of opportunity kept him far from the courts. Since his youth a royal or princely residence had become his favored domain and the focus of his nostalgic remembrance.

His poetic genius enabled him to fulfill this aspiration without ever becoming a snob or incurring humiliations. Dante, whom he religiously revered, had proclaimed the nobility of poetry, Petrarca had raised it to a sovereignty. It was Boccaccio's natural poetical enthusiasm and lively intelligence that opened the doors of the court of Naples to him as a young man, when he was still employed as a clerk in a shop and studying law in the famous university. Naples was at that time the residence of Robert of Anjou, the 'sermonizing king,' [10] whose court was dominated by French influence and customs and whose kingdom was a colony

---

[8] *Fiammetta*, Book III.   [10] Dante, *Paradiso*, VIII, 147.
[9] Letter to Pino de' Rossi.

of Florentine finance. For more than two centuries Florentine traders, bankers, jurists, scholars, and teachers flocked into the town, which had become the goal of countless adventurers from all over Italy. Some people liked it, although few of those new-comers settled down permanently. But many found the place detestable and left in anger and disgust, as did Dante's friend Cino de Pistoia, famous as a jurist and poet, who was appointed as a teacher at the university. Petrarca was attracted to the court by the personality and fame of the learned king, but he complained of the disorder and corruption of the state and the town's gloomy, unsafe streets.[11]

In those days life in Naples was no less turbulent than today, and the social contrasts were even more tense, appalling, and demoralizing than in more recent times. But the court exerted an irresistible fascination upon those susceptible to pomp, elegance, merriment, and adventure. After Robert's death, in 1343, the court of Queen Joan the First rivaled those of Semiramis and Theodora in luxury and dissipation. It stood in striking contrast to the harsh old-fashioned provincialism of Florence and most other Italian cities or petty courts. Small wonder that an adventurous and imaginative young poet should have been captivated by that alluring atmosphere of gallantry and refinement. From that time on Boccaccio glorified courtly dignity and elegance, which became the source of his poetic inspiration.

He was less than twenty when he first ogled Maria d'Aquino, King Robert's spurious daughter, who granted him temporary favors before throwing herself into more gratifying adventures. For a year or two the son of the Florentine merchant lived like a troubadour at his lady's attendance. The courtship began in a church in Naples, after the exact poetic pattern of the day, and developed into a light and gay vassalage of love in a setting of garden parties and picnics, festivities and recitals, jousts and entertainments. It was in the spirit of this licentious and cultivated society that the young poet molded his celebrated literary style. With his versatility, flexible talent, learning, and broad experience of life, Boccaccio was able to draw a harmonious

[11] Petrarca, *Epistolae familiares*, Lib. v, 3 and 6; *Epistolae seniles*, x, 2.

literary picture of this exuberant courtly society. And in so doing, he exerted a polishing, cultivating influence on the coarse minds and provincial manners of his Tuscan countrymen.

This was the double mission of that amiable and industrious poet, who never forgot the agreeable stimulation and encouraging success that made his Neapolitan years decisive for his life and for Italian literature and civilization. In many of his best lyrical poems the evocation of the Neapolitan landscape with its luminous water, delightful islands, colorful gardens, verdant hills, and sylvan recesses transforms the old conventional literary scenery of courtly poetry into a vivid, real panorama of natural beauty and human delight. We certainly know too much of Maria d'Aquino to be fooled into a celestial idealization of the women of the Neapolitan court; yet all the golden-haired 'angels' of modish lyricism appear now in the classical landscape of the Bay of Naples, in the shadow of Virgil's tomb, amid the landmarks of the Homeric saga, the splendors of Baiae, the marvels of Pozzuoli, the sibylline mysteries of Cumae, the legendary ruins of Roman baths, villas, and temples. The whole mythological apparatus that drags along in pallid allegory through the didactic literature of the Middle Ages here reappears for the first time in a congenial environment and spirit; all the idyllic, sensual, genial, and provocative aspects of the minor pagan deities are restored to life, divested only of their religious significance and superstitious charm.

The power of Boccaccio's lyrical imagination was not brilliant or free enough to revive or create a mythical world of pure poetry and free invention. But all the nymphs and dryads, all the figures of Ovid's metamorphoses that emerged from an obsolete literature in the train of the lean medieval Venus and her sexless Cupid find at last their natural ground and atmosphere in the Neapolitan framework of Boccaccio's literary fancy. He displays his mythical microcosm in the poems of love and adventure inspired by his beloved princess, who certainly admired but hardly understood the French tales of Troy and Thebes, or the Byzantine love stories of Hellenistic and Oriental origin. The Italian poet was able to revive these phantoms amid the sentimental reality of his courtly love, because he felt the congeniality of that mythical imagery with his own environment. The fabulous story of Theseus; the vicissitudes of Troilus and the 'golden' Chryseida (Shakespeare's Cressida); the mythical allusions that adorn his measured and harmonious lyrics all seemed more convincing and alive in Boccaccio's poems than in the old-fashioned and awkward lucubrations of the professional French storytellers.

From then on the old mythological fables never left the Italian poetic landscape; they appear in the ingenious literary artifices of humanistic Latin verse and in the elegant vernacular vagaries of Poliziano and his friends; in Lorenzo de' Medici's carnival songs and in the public festivals of Italian princes; in innumerable paintings, frescoes, tapestries, sculptures, and reliefs. They developed through the centuries in endless variations, up to the classicistic revival of the Napoleonic era, to Foscolo's *Sepolcri* and *Grazie,* to the poems of Vincenzo Monti, and the sculptures of Antonio Canova.

Yet this semi-millenarian vogue inaugurated by the son of a Florentine trader amid the classical Neapolitan landscape always remained a literary and courtly phenomenon that never affected the popular imagination, not even when Bacchus and Ariadne, Cupid and Silenus, paraded through the streets of Florence in a magnificent masquerade of satyrs and nymphs singing the joy of life and the triumph of love. The majority of the devout and illiterate populace that loved religious processions in honor of the Holy Virgin and the patron saints of their parishes detested these blasphemous displays of pagan divinities and gladly made bonfires of those fashionable fetishes when Bernardino of Siena or Girolamo Savonarola incited them to do so. It was no *sancta simplicitas,* but a true instinct for the realities of contemporary cultural life when the writings of Petrarca and Boccaccio were placed on the pyre that destroyed the artistic images of those literary idols. Those iconoclastic outbreaks of an organized popular furor brought to the surface republican undercurrents consistently hostile to any form of courtly or secular culture.

Boccaccio was the initiator of this culture, which he propagated throughout Italy. In two widely read idyllic poems [12] he transferred to his native Tuscan environment an atmosphere inspired by the Neapolitan landscape and totally alien to a hardworking, businesslike people 'that smacks still of the mountain and the rock.' [13] With the magic of an exquisite art and simple, human accents, he populated the hills and plains around Florence with lovesick shepherds and soft-hearted nymphs, transforming the rough ground of sweating plowmen and stone-workers into a Hellenistic scene of Arcadian adventures.

Some bucolic motifs had been carried through the Middle Ages in a Virgilian, and consequently consecrated, type of literature full of enigmatic allegories and cryptic allusions. The tradition survived in Petrarca's eclogues, the driest and most obscure of all his writings. Rustic scenes are the principal element in the descriptive, narrative, and lyrical *pastourelles* from France and Provence, which represented the most refined type of medieval courtly poetry.

Boccaccio suffused these musty bucolic phantoms with the poetic vision of his Neapolitan experience, and transplanted into the Florentine landscape the pastoral and mythological mummeries of his early poems and novels. In all those chimeric reveries the poet is present with his love and disillusionments, his nostalgic recollections of the Neapolitan scene where his heart and mind opened to the reality of life and dreams of love. Unlike most Florentines of his class, he remained indifferent to the great spiritual and practical problems of his era, and concentrated even more than his friend Petrarca on the emotions of the human heart.

For his contemporaries, troubled by harsh, perplexing reality, he created an imaginary Arcadian world substantiated by personal experience and refined by courtly artifice. Through his use of popular stanzas and vernacular terms he infused a fresh poetic life into bookish traditions and courtly conventions. For the first time in the history of his country he united the whole nation in the contemplation of a purely poetic landscape trans-

[12] *Il Ninfale d'Ameto* (shortly after 1340); *Il Ninfale Fiesolano* (around 1346).
[13] Dante, *Inferno,* xv, 63.

I

formed into an ideal reality by sincerity of sentimental detail and accuracy in external features.

Boccaccio popularized the hobbies and habits of a restricted, refined society. After him Arcadian elements became ubiquitous in Italian literature and art. By the second half of his century, those idyllic, rustic, and pastoral motifs had become the chief theme of poetry and song. All Italy resounded with 'madrigals,' ballads, and hunting songs, as if a new Arcady had arisen among the tumults and convulsions of an agitated epoch. The vogue became so general that, a generation after Boccaccio, his Florentine countryman and emulator, Franco Sacchetti, composed the most delightful little poems on 'ye graceful peasant girls and mountain maids,' although he knew very well from firsthand experience as a merchant, state official, and provincial governor the hard reality and poor conditions of Italian country life.

The courtly character and artificial rusticity of this type of literature created a fanciful world that persisted for centuries in the imagination of poets and the public favor. This idyllic landscape of Arcadian and mythological character was ordinarily evoked whenever nature had to be brought into sympathy with human sentiments and amorous adventures. More than a hundred years later these sceneries and types were revived, along with medieval fables of Charlemagne and King Arthur, in the classicistic environment of the Italian courts. It was to the mythological pastorals of Boccaccio rather than to the rediscovered Greek models that the learned Angelo Poliziano and Lorenzo the Magnificent turned for inspiration.[14]

The same was true at the height of this new Arcadian vogue when Jacopo Sannazaro wrote his famous pastoral romance *L'Arcadia* (1489) in the same Neapolitan environment that had inspired his Tuscan forerunner and master. Since that time the Italians have never ceased to be enraptured by the adventures of enamored shepherds, mischievous satyrs, jealous nymphs, and wise old villagers living in a fanciful natural society of free and simple folk, menaced only by boorish ruffians and wild beasts,

[14] Poliziano's *Orfeo*, 1471; Lorenzo's *Selve d'amore* and other mythological poems.

a society in which love always triumphs over hate and innocence over iniquity.

This is the spirit that inspired the 'rustic fables' and pastoral dramas, and kindled the idyllic imagination of Tasso and Guarini. Up to the time of Goethe, Byron, and Lamartine, Italy remained a new Arcadia in the eyes of poets and educated people beyond the Alps. In the nineteenth and twentieth centuries, however, the poetic horizon was so immeasurably extended that the Arcadian tradition finally dried up, its products relegated to learned treatises, school anthologies, and the hobbies of a few literary gourmets. Today all those labyrinths of love appear rigid, stilted, frivolous, and dull.

Nevertheless, that kind of literature helped to shape the cultural personality of Italy, with its penchant for romantic fiction and literary refinement. For half a millennium poetry was conceived by the Italians as a revealing fiction that realized their dreams of beauty and perfection, either in the moral and religious domain as in Dante's vision, or in the psychological and secular field of Petrarca's lyricism and Boccaccio's narratives. The Italian poets transferred to the classical, epic, and bucolic sphere the elaborate casuistry of love that the French had developed long before in a courtly, chivalric spirit and in allegoric reveries. For the wondrous equipment of magic sorceries and Nordic enchantments Boccaccio substituted pagan mythology as a sort of poetic transfiguration of human whims and passions displayed in the superior reality of an artistic creation.

He succeeded in these original literary attempts because he attuned his bucolic and mythological poetry to popular and human accents. As a matter of fact, only a few of the lyrical and epic forms of that early Italian literature are reproductions of French or Provençal models. But it was Boccaccio who raised to courtly and literary dignity some old popular forms and accents of Italian poetry of which little is known and nothing preserved. In doing so he became the creative mediator who fused all Italy into an integral community of taste and culture.

A symptom of this synthesis of popular style and aristocratic sophistication is the adaptation of the popular stanza, called *ottava rima,* for bucolic and mythological poetry. The eight-line

stanza was used in all subsequent Italian epic poetry. Like other
Italian verse forms the *ottava rima* had existed in popular songs,
but because of its rustic character it had not been accepted at
court or set down on costly parchment. Boccaccio might have
picked it up in Naples or elsewhere. Similar schemes were invented and developed in central and southern Italy.

Be that as it may, the stanza in Boccaccio's early use of it
retains a simplicity of accent and uniformity of structure very
much in contrast with his highly ornamented prose and ex-
quisitely elaborate lyrics. In its later evolution it became as
characteristic of the country's poetic feeling as the Alexandrine
in France and the *copla* in Spain. After having delighted the
Neapolitan circle of Maria d'Aquino in Boccaccio's *Teseide*, it
startled the Florentines in his *Ninfale Fiesolano*, and was developed to a balanced literary perfection in Poliziano's *Giostra*.
In Pulci's *Morgante*, composed for the entertainment of the
entourage of Lorenzo the Magnificent, the same *ottava rima*
maintains the old popular tone, with a peculiar drollery rising
from the alternating gravity and scurrility of the discourse.
Subsequently the elegance of Boiardo, the mastery of Ariosto,
and the ornamental chromatism of Tasso gave the form its full
sonority, sharpness, and balance. From its earliest days to the
end of the eighteenth century it remained the most popular
stanza of the Italian street-singers, who went from place to place
intoning their innumerable *cantàri* of the Arthurian knights,
Scipio and Caesar, Alexander and Charlemagne, the lives of
the saints, the historical vicissitudes of their country, the discovery of America, and the news of the day. It was these street-
singers who completed the poetical unification of a country
divided by a diversity of interests and traditions. Through these
professional storytellers the Italian people from Sicily to Piedmont participated in the same rudimentary culture and poetic
education. During his stay in Venice, in 1786, Goethe listened to
the last gondoliers able to sing in alternating duets the stanzas
of Tasso, the sense of which they hardly understood.

It seems worth while to consider the secret of the poetic form
that united all classes of Italians in the same enthusiastic literary

response. It consists of six lines in alternating rhyme, followed by a rhymed couplet. When skillfully used, it is highly varied in accent, with a fluid rhythm brought to a sharp close by the epigrammatic couplet, then resumed and again broken.[15] A story told in this form tends to break down into a dynamic series of separate pictures and episodes; the stanza has a sharp, light resonance and lends itself to the melodious, well-balanced phrases so dear to Italian ears. The typical Italian verse forms, such as the sonnet, the stanza, the madrigal, and several others developed in the fourteenth century, combine a strong structural symmetry with a great variety of rhythms and an antithetical, pointed conclusion.

*   *   *

This characteristic mixture of vivacity and poise corresponds very closely to the Italian musical style of the time, which, though many of its features are derived from French models, preserves an unmistakable national temper and vein. A lover of old music can easily discern the Italian manner in a madrigal, ballade, or song composed by Jacopo da Bologna or Francesco Landini, the Florentine. The characteristic of Italian music was a 'suave and sweet melody' within the harmonious structure of a traditional and already popular scheme, in sharp contrast to the contrapuntal complexities, the bold flourish, and the excited accents of the French *ars nova*.

The fourteenth century reveals a definite trend toward overemphasis of musical values in every branch of eloquence and poetry. Petrarca initiated this tendency with the same sense of artistic perfection and courtly dignity that molded his whole career as a writer and scholar. Boccaccio attuned his vernacular prose to the new musical sensitivity of his contemporaries. The poverty of creative imagination, of moral substance, speculative originality, and cultural resources in that era of calamities and social fluctuations favored the cult of purely formal values and external elegance. Inventiveness and originality found their expression in the realm of pure form, in the variation, refine-

---

[15] Examples in every anthology of Italian poetry.

ment and brilliance of detail, never in the substance and basic structure of a poetic composition.

The tenacious conservatism of a culturally amorphous epoch gave rise to the practice and theory of imitation. Even the most daring and fanciful poets clung to medieval and classical models, traditional motifs and styles. From Boccaccio to Ariosto the vernacular poets of Italy sought to create higher forms of art and inspiration from the popular motifs of a time-honored medieval literature. This realm of *belles lettres* was inaugurated when the flirtatious daughter of King Robert of Naples asked her lover and minstrel to give courtly refinement and literary dignity to the widely known story of Floire and Blancheflor, a near-Eastern romance handed down in Byzantine tales and elaborated first in an aristocratic, then in a popular, French version in the last decades of the twelfth century.[16] In the hands of these Italian authors the extravagant adventures and rhapsodic mummeries of the old French vernacular poetry were given artistic form and inner motivation. In the monumental poems of Pulci, Boiardo, and Ariosto, little remains of the old French legends except for a few historical names, traditional details, and extrinsic features.

What Boccaccio tried to do was to intensify by artistic means and psychological rationality the human substance of the narratives as conceived and understood in the courtly environment in which he lived as a poet and entertainer. The learned and declamatory style of his prose is for the first time forged after the Ciceronian pattern, although the Italian language bowed only reluctantly to the turgid grandiloquence, inversions, sinuosities, and metaphors of the Latin model. Italian grammar is totally different in structure from Latin. Consequently it is only through artifices and expedients that the vernacular can reproduce the accents, tone, and measure of the classical prose.

This was the beginning of a trend toward artistic elaboration of the natural parlance of the common people. When this tendency corresponds to an artistic ideal, it is perfectly legitimate, because it is an artist's or a poet's sovereign right to impose his

---

[16] *Il Filòcolo* (1338).

vision and style on his public. But Boccaccio's first efforts in that elaborate prose were intended for a small group of frivolous courtiers to whose narrow interests and fashionable requirements he adjusted his talent. Consequently there is no proportion between his solemn, scholarly, and inflated prose and the fatuous or childish story it conveys. The display of erudition and casuistry seems utterly incongruous. And despite many fascinating details and truly poetical pictures, this disproportion makes Boccaccio's autobiographical novel unpalatable to modern readers.[17] Since very few authors found themes equal to this grandiloquent style, the increasing vogue of pretentious and vacuous prose proved more harmful to the Italian national character than all natural, political, and economic disasters put together.

It was only in the *Decameron* that Boccaccio succeeded in achieving that perfect balance between content and form which comprises the main charm of its hundred short stories and made it the masterpiece of Italian narrative prose. Most of the stories were derived from the tales, anecdotes, witty and instructive sayings that circulated everywhere in the Old World and served for the entertainment of merry-makers in courts and taverns. Some others were inspired by local gossip in the many places where the poet lived in the course of his travels—Naples, Florence, Ravenna, Padua. Clerical and profane French, Byzantine, and Oriental literature contributed their share of the material collected from so many and diversified sources.

The *Decameron* is often quite erroneously designated as a typical expression of bourgeois society of Boccaccio's time. In reality most of its comical, lewd, grotesque, or pathetic stories had, in a crude form, been current for many generations. The same type of framework had been used by earlier authors and compilers of the East and West. Those *fabellae ignobilium,* or plebeian tales about cuckolds and harlots, cheated merchants and dissolute priests, insolent squires and foolish peasants; about monks, shrews, villains or louts; about strange happenings, foolhardy undertakings, pranks, and severe trials had for a long time been the delight of French noblemen, Italian merchants,

[17] *La Fiammetta,* probably written in 1346.

high prelates, rough adventurers, and unprejudiced ladies of the ruling aristocracy.

The earliest collection of these tales was the laconic, dry, and simple *Novellino,* compiled shortly before 1300. The *novella* was a report before it became a literary type. In medieval Italian, *nuovo* served to designate a wondrous thing, a strange man, a stupendous story: *cosa nuova; uomo nuovo; vita nuova.* Marco Polo, who set out for the East with his mind full of the popular tales then circulating all over Europe, reported the wonders of Asia in the form of stories heard (between 1270 and 1295) from travelers and residents encountered during his peregrinations from Venice to Peking and back through India and Armenia. The reports of pilgrims to the Holy Land and various Italian chronicles provided further material for *novelle.*

In the age of hermits and cenobites, storytelling and other forms of sociability were very much alive. The loneliness of modern man was unknown to medieval society. It was this sociable spirit that underlay the three great fourteenth-century collections of tales: the Spanish *Conde Lucanor* (1337), Boccaccio's *Decameron* (1353), and Chaucer's *Canterbury Tales.*

In his *Decameron* Boccaccio gave literary dignity and artistic veracity to those ubiquitous or local tales, making them into a universal mirror of human folly and wisdom, deceit and honesty, cowardice and bravery. The seven young ladies and three dandies who tell the stories and discuss them as typical human cases are Florentine patricians who have fled from the horrors of the plague-ridden town. With this project of entertainment against a background of death and disaster, the poet has transferred to the Florentine scene the habits of the Neapolitan court described in his *Filòcolo.* Here ladies and gentlemen are assembled for merriment and conversation at a picturesque spot on the Bay of Naples. There are dances, music, poetry, storytelling, and other entertainments, all carried on with an aristocratic unconcern for the misery of the common people.

Behind this social unconcern lies the general tendency of that age to accept one's lot as an inevitable and irrevocable fatality, depending on God's will or on astral influences according to faith or science. Much of that attitude has survived in Italy. The symptoms of that nation-wide fatalism and resignation are still evident in large sections of the Italian population in our day. It is historically incorrect to extend Boccaccio's smiling aloofness and moral neutrality to the townspeople of his day or to interpret the fancy of a poet as a typical expression of a new and general attitude toward life, religion, and reality.

Skepticism, frivolity, and profane intellectual refinement were habitual with the Italian aristocracy, especially in Naples, since the days of Frederick II. They continued in vogue among the Florentine and Venetian nobility. The prosperous middle classes, on the other hand, were characterized by the devout, sharp-witted common sense expressed in the tales of Franco Sacchetti or the rhymed reports of Antonio Pucci, Florence's most notable streetsinger, town-crier, and official trumpeter. For these representative but not influential men the writing of poetry and telling of stories were a spiritual necessity like going to church, singing religious *laudi*, reading edifying books, or listening to the sermons of famous preachers. Their simple, realistic pictures of local life reveal a serene but uncompromising moral strictness very much in contrast to the mundane levity of the higher classes as reflected in the *Decameron*. When Boccaccio's remembrance of bright days at the regal southern court began to fade, when the first shadows of old age descended on him, the provincial austerity and bigotry of his native Florentine environment began to curb his natural joviality. When a monk warned him, in 1362, to think of his soul and of its impending damnation, he repudiated the works that had already assured his immortality on earth. Grown devout, irritable, and acrimonious, he plunged into the impersonal and amorphous erudition of the rising humanistic studies.

The consummate mastery of Boccaccio's style, his unbiased, realistic vision of human life and nature, worked as a revelation upon the Italian mind. In the *Decameron* the Italians had a monument of art that was also a document of life. Its influence was universal. Yet the assumption that it contributed to the religious and moral disintegration of Italian society is unjustified. To scoff at unworthy priests and greedy monks was a traditional habit of the most devout and intelligent believers and never

I*

shook the fundamental principles of Christian morals. Everyday life offered infinitely more examples of human errors, vice, extravagance, and guile than are to be found in the *Decameron*.

It was in the literary field that its influence became ubiquitous. The short story developed as the most specific type of Italian narrative literature. Boccaccio's style, if not his freshness and ingenuity, is found in numerous collections of more or less successful imitators.[18] While Dante's *Commedia* almost disappeared from the cultural scene during the seventeenth and eighteenth centuries, and while Petrarca's prestige diminished during Italy's short romantic diversion, Boccaccio never vanished from the literary foreground as a source of delight, enlightenment, and inspiration. To a keen stylistic sensibility the symptoms of that influence are perceptible even in the 'sundry items' of modern Italian newspapers, not to mention Pirandello's surrealistic reincarnation of some of Boccaccio's most significant attitudes.[19]

The extraordinary and continued flowering of the *novella* in Italy becomes more striking when the Italian novel is compared to those of France, Spain, England, or Russia. The Italian penchant for the tale must indeed be regarded as symptomatic of Italian interests, tastes, and preferences. It certainly cannot be attributed solely to the influence of Boccaccio. The narrative inspiration of the Italians has always tended toward fragmentary, rather than integrated, elaborate, and conclusive compositions. Apparently they have always preferred the frame to the plot and clear-cut solutions to involved and troubling conflicts. Their narrative literature seldom discloses a perplexing situation, a perturbing problem, an equivocal dilemma elaborated into a profound picture of the forces and influences, paradoxes and enigmas, demons, and fatalities that dominate human thoughts, passions, and destinies. The authors of Italian tales were not conscious of the implications that Shakespeare found in them. Their tragic and comic situations are individual accidents without any relation to the cosmic unity and the moral order of the human and divine world. Therefore they dissolve into myriads

[18] E.g. *Il Pecorone* by Ser Giovanni Fiorentino (1378), Giovanni da Prato, Masuccio Salernitano (1476), Gentile Sermini, etc.

[19] *Novelle per un anno.*

of luminous meteors that grant no insight into the conflicts and abysmal mysteries of human life.

A faith without spiritual anxiety and a wisdom without philosophy withheld from the Italians the tragic sense of life. There is no tragedy in the shrewd or naive common sense of those innumerable storytellers. A vague instinctive sense of normality and fitness determined the attitude of the best Italian *novellieri* toward human passions, foolishness, and crimes. They are depicted with sharpness of relief, intensity of colors, crudity of tone, and scurrility of language, softened by the artifices of an ornate, florid, eloquent, and frequently verbose rhetoric. This is the narrative style of the later masters of the type: Anton Francesco Grazzini, Straparola, Cinzio Giraldi, Agnolo Firenzuola, and, most famous of all, Matteo Maria Bandello.

These loquacious authors never resorted to a stylistic *mezzotinto* that allows a gradual and balanced distribution of light and shades in the picture of human destinies and adventures. The rhetorical style inaugurated by Boccaccio was cultivated by a long line of imitators; it still inspired the Italian *puristi* of the early nineteenth century and the custodians of national academic traditions.

XII. *Divinities and Humanities in Italian Civilization*

D URING the four decades of the Great Schism (1378-1417), three decisive events completely changed the internal structure of Italy and the course of her political and cultural development. Leaving Avignon to the French and their schismatic pontiffs, the popes elected by Italian cardinals returned to Rome, a town fallen into squalor and provincial isolation since Cola di Rienzo's stupendous adventure. The Venetians, ceasing to be a purely maritime power, extended their sway to the mainland, where, in a sweeping push to the west and north, they acquired such important centers as Vicenza, Belluno, Rovigo, Verona, followed by Udine and Brescia in the foothills of the Alps. And in Florence, with the rise of Giovanni de' Medici to wealth and political power, the democracy of that city-state turned toward a veiled and finally an overt autocracy.

The impact of these three new political forces was so profound that the powers they created survived political changes for more than three centuries and became nuclei for the constructive and creative energies of the nation. The papal state, reorganized after the end of the Great Schism, lasted until 1870. The Venetian republic retained most of its mainland territory until its demise in 1797. The Medici dynasty died out in 1737 only to be succeeded by the house of Lorraine, which preserved the territorial heritage of its predecessors until the plebiscite of 1860 united Tuscany with the new Kingdom of Italy.

Meanwhile, the Anjous of Naples were on the decline, surrendering to Alfonso of Aragon in 1442, after a period of grim dynastic strife, of crime, intrigue, depravity, and utter administrative disorder. In the Upper Country the Visconti dynasty was succeeded by the short-lived Ambrosian republic, with its latent democratic trends and communal traditions; and, after 1450, by Francesco Sforza, a successful military leader and shrewd politician who conquered Milan by force of arms and set himself up as a 'duke' in opposition to the Emperor and to the King of France.

The dynastic and hierarchical connections of the ruling houses of Naples and Milan with foreign powers caused the final severance of vast territories in the south and north from the rest of Italy. In 1522, Milan with the rest of Lombardy became like Naples a Spanish province, which in 1714 finally passed into the hands of the Austrian Hapsburgs. A branch of the Spanish Bourbons reigned over southern Italy with brief interruptions from 1735 to 1860, while Austria ruled the Lombard plain until 1859.

Throughout this development the whole of Italy was more or less subject to foreign interests and encroachments. Paradoxically enough, only the universal power of the papacy and the cosmopolitan Venetian republic became more and more Italian, successfully resisting Spanish, French, and German pressure. From Urban VI, the first pontiff elected in Rome (1378) after the 'Babylonian captivity' up to our day, only four foreigners ever ascended the papal throne, among them the two Italianized Borgias in the fifteenth century and Hadrian VI, who died in 1523, the last non-Italian pope. At this time, the advisers of Emperor Charles V seriously considered moving the Holy See to a place beyond the Alps. They believed that the Church had become more Italian than Catholic, and were opposed to this development in an empire on which the sun never set. Nevertheless, the Roman pontificate remained an Italian institution from then on.

The means by which the papacy was converted from a universal power to an Italian principality were very much the same as those employed by secular conquerors. Territorial rivals were crushed by mercenary armies under the command of able *condottieri;* the various petty Italian despots were played off against one another; the moral and political assistance of foreign sovereigns was enlisted through territorial deals. Funds were amassed through the sale of indulgences, ecclesiastical dignities, prebends, privileges, and everything else. Finally, since the clergy could not marry, ecclesiastical rights and territories were bestowed on 'nephews,' that is, sons or other relatives, who, raised to wealth and influence, supported the pontiff's authority and prestige and his secular and political interests.

All this, however, would never have created a national pontificate, except for favorable circumstances and the ecclesiastical prestige of Rome. Unlike the schismatic popes of Avignon, the Roman pontiff had a fundamental advantage in the eyes of the whole Christian world. As the Vicar of Christ, a pope could reside anywhere. In this sense a Roman and an Avignonese pontiff were theoretically equal. But the Vicar of Christ is also, or primarily, the successor of St. Peter, and in this original quality and dignity he is bound to the Roman see—the *cathedra Sancti Petri*—which cannot be transferred elsewhere without breaking the continuity of Western Christianity and making apostolic Roman Catholicism a term as empty and obsolete as the Holy Roman Empire. This was a stronger argument in favor of the Roman pontiffs than all the legal opinions given to their Avignonese competitors by the professors of the Sorbonne and the counselors of the King of France.

With the restoration of the Roman pontificate, all the old territorial claims, rights, and traditions of the Curia as an Italian state were brought forward. The ruined city of Rome and the surrounding country were divided among rival patrician families, each advancing its own feudal claim. In the town itself the middle classes and the populace clung to their old communal constitution, still represented by the Capitol, in opposition to the fortified papal city around St. Peter's and the Vatican. The same conditions existed in the old papal territories of central Italy reorganized by Cardinal Albornoz, but later disintegrated when petty tyrants reconquered one by one these old papal strongholds. For more than a hundred years the popes were compelled to pursue a more or less ruthless policy of conquest and consolidation in order to restore their political and spiritual prestige.

This development was ·a direct consequence of the isolation and weakness into which the Roman papacy had been drawn first by the Schism itself and then by the conciliary movement arising from a general solicitude to restore the unity and spiritual power of Christianity. The theological, ecclesiastical, and moral consequences of that movement were unimportant for Italy, which had not brought forth dogmatic questions, heretical scandals, or patriotic reactions such as Wycliffe had done in England, Huss in Bohemia, and Jeanne d'Arc in France. Nor was the country agitated by religious ferments or national political ambitions as were France, Spain, and, to a certain extent, England and Germany. The Italians saluted the restoration of the Roman pontificate with feelings of religious satisfaction and national pride. Yet as the papal power assumed the form of an Italian principality, the initial enthusiasm cooled, giving way to resentment, criticism, and open revolt. During the whole Schism the position of the popes in Rome was insecure, threatened both by the feudal nobles and the turbulent populace. They relied for protection on the armies of the King of Naples, still regarded as the shield of the popes. A bodyguard garrisoned the papal precinct of the town. In 1434 an insurrection of the Roman populace forced Pope Eugene IV to take refuge in Florence, where he remained for ten years. Braccio da Montone, a military adventurer emulating Cola di Rienzo, thwarted the return of Martin V to Rome in 1420. Nicholas V almost fell victim to a well-organized conspiracy led by Stefano Porcari, who was hanged with nine of his companions in 1453.

While the papacy was fighting for its political rights in its own territories, its spiritual authority was undermined abroad by the conciliary movement that had helped not only to restore the Roman pontificate, but also to keep alive the disturbing demand for an internal reform of the Church. The popes had resumed their sovereignty amid promises of reform and without the absolute power of the medieval pontificate, as represented by Gregory VII, Innocent III, Boniface VIII. The coexistence of two, at one time even three, popes, all advancing their argu-

ments of legality, practically nullified the pretensions to a papal
world monarchy put forward in the bull *Unam Sanctam* (18
November 1302). Furthermore, the spiritual and political forces
that imposed on the reluctant pontiffs the Councils of Pisa,
Constance, Pavia, Basel, Ferrara, and Florence between 1409
and 1439 shattered the foundations of papal absolutism and submitted the pope's personal authority to the control of general or
synodical assemblies.

With that, the famous 'Donation of Constantine,' which for
many centuries had supported papal pretensions to a temporal
world monarchy, became an empty relic of bygone times. When
in 1440 Lorenzo Valla in his famous pamphlet denounced the
Donation as a fraud, he was merely battling the dead, because
none of the post-Avignonese popes would have dared to invoke
the authority of that document for the restoration of old papal
rights and claims. The reconstruction of the papacy began on
an Italian rather than an ecumenical basis, and continued in
that direction despite the crowning of Emperor Sigismund in
St. Peter's by Pope Eugene IV, and the zeal displayed by that
pontiff for the reunion of the Greek and Latin churches and the
submission of Eastern Christian nations, such as the Armenians,
Copts, and Ethiopians, to the Roman Curia. Europe was becoming increasingly estranged from the papacy, which identified
itself more and more with Italian trends and interests.

The papal accomplishments of this period were political,
financial, artistic, and intellectual rather than religious. Of all
the countless documents that reflect the activity of the popes
from the end of the Great Schism until the Council of Trent
(1545), only two were devoted to fundamental dogmatic questions: namely, a bull on the sacraments of Eugene IV, published in 1439, and the constitution of Sixtus IV concerning the
Immaculate Conception (5 September 1483). The idea of the
Crusade against the Turks was the only vestige of the medieval
tradition of the militant Church. Amid general indifference, its
only active supporters were the Venetians, who in that case were
less interested in the cause of Christianity than in the protection
of their possessions and trade routes in the eastern Mediterranean, as had been made evident in 1204, when they diverted

the Fourth Crusade against the infidels to Zara and Constantinople.

After the loss of theological authority, the Roman Church took upon itself the spiritual leadership of Italian secular civilization. In 1406 Innocent VII restored the Roman university in line with the scholarly interests of the day. In 1420 Martin V initiated the gigantic work of reconstructing the town. Two centuries of uninterrupted architectural activity transformed into a magnificent metropolis what formerly had been an amorphous conglomeration of ruins, slums, and marshy wastes. The outstanding artists, scholars, poets, jurists, and orators of Italy gathered around the great pontiffs of that new era—Nicholas V, Pius II, Sixtus IV, Alexander VI, Julius II, and the Medici popes—who made their courts the most brilliant and diversified cultural centers of the world.

The most lasting and eloquent expression of papal ascendancy over the secular powers of the peninsula is to be found in the new Roman architecture, with its grandiose proportions so staunchly affirming the superior power of the Church and its efforts to surpass the majesty and prestige of ancient Rome. The Colosseum, the ruined Roman baths and temples became the standard for the new architectural development of the town. By erecting buildings of unsurpassed magnitude and splendor, the papacy demonstrated that it was Roman and no longer Avignonese, sovereign and not conciliary, universal and not merely Italian. This architectural revival deflected the Italian artists who flocked into Rome from their quaint and stubborn provincialism and molded their inspiration to the universal mission of the Church.

It was this idea, never renounced by the Italian popes, that lent color and meaning to the revival of classical Latinity initiated by Petrarca. What was elsewhere a literary hobby, an antiquarian passion, a remunerative employment, or a courtly ornament became in Rome an instrument of spiritual and political regeneration and a symbol of universal power. One has only to compare the limited, provincial horizons of Petrarca's first literary heir, Coluccio Salutati, who spent thirty years in the Florentine chancellery, with the scope of the younger hu-

manists, such as Leonardo Bruni, Poggio Bracciolini, Lorenzo
Valla, and Flavio Biondo, who were employed by the Roman
Curia as secretaries, orators, and writers. These men, and many
of their followers in the course of that eventful century, were
all involved in the great problems, controversies, and movements
in which the Church took a leading part as a political power
aiming to create an ecumenical Christian community and to
propagate the faith far beyond the limits of the medieval world.

This spirit lent such works as Biondo's *Italia Illustrata, Roma
Instaurata,* and *Roma Triumphans* a historical justification and
range that the other regional and local histories composed elsewhere in Italy could not approach. Valla's famous treatise on
the *Elegantiae* of the Latin language was far more than a philological manual for the use of professional scholars. In the Councils and in diplomatic dealings with the states of Europe, the
solemn, sonorous, elegant Latin of the papal representatives became a powerful weapon of persuasion and an awe-inspiring
symbol of papal dignity.

The increasing patronage accorded by the pontiffs to Greek
studies was no doubt bound up with the papal aspiration to
establish a unified church and to revive the Roman heritage in
its universal, religious, and profane totality. A characteristic expression of this trend can be found in the life and work of the
most representative and influential of those Latinized Greeks,
the learned Bessarion of Trebizon, who was made a cardinal
by Eugene IV in 1439 and held court like a prince of letters in
a palace on the Quirinal hill in the center of Rome. After the
capitulation in 1449 of Felix V, the last antipope, to the Roman
pontiff Nicholas V, and after the departure for Germany in 1452
of the last emperor ever to be crowned in Rome, the papacy
felt free to pursue the ecclesiastical task of rallying the Christian world around St. Peter's chair, the political aim of creating
an Italian papal monarchy and the cultural object of absorbing
antiquity into Christianity.

To this end the popes set themselves at the head of the patriotic and cultural renewal that had developed in Italy during
their absence. For the last time in its history the Roman Church
succeeded in channelizing and absorbing a powerful spiritual

current originating outside of its own orbit. It harnessed the growing pagan enthusiasm of the educated classes of Italian society with the same determination and flexibility that the great popes of the thirteenth century had displayed in assimilating Aristotelian doctrines to a Christian system.

Since the early period of that cultural renewal marked by a Petrarcan indifference to theological speculations, aesthetic enthusiasm for pagan art and literature seemed less dangerous to the soul than the heretical and corrosive maxims of Averroism. From a moral standpoint the Averroistic doctrine of double truth was certainly more corrupting and sterile than the frank humanistic statement of the identity of truth and beauty. In supporting this concept, totally ignored by the Scriptures and disregarded by scholastic philosophy, the Church added to its system a powerful element of faith and persuasion in harmony with the cultural trends of secular society.

Actually, the belief in the divine origin of beauty and the conviction that truth is embodied in the perfection of form have been the basic principles of Italian civilization ever since the throngs of the faithful were enraptured by a Madonna of Giotto or Simone Martini, not, as in earlier days, because of her miraculous power, but because of the supernatural charm emanating from those beautiful human images of a perfect divine creature. Dante, Petrarca, and their successors turned away from the dry, amorphous, and unimaginative language of the medieval theologians and philosophers in pursuit of the same revelation of transcendent truth through poetic vision and style. The general feeling that truth and beauty are equal attributes of the divinity led those generations to contemplate the external world with religious eyes and to express religious emotions in concrete, realistic forms.

This was the general state of mind that brought about the feverish, almost delirious, participation of the masses in the erection and decoration of new churches and sanctuaries all over Italy. It also led to the unprecedented flourishing of the figurative arts. The divine mysteries, the Biblical myths, the miracles of the saints, achieved a new palpable reality through the lifelike beauty of their artistic representations. It was from this corporeity of their spiritual nostalgia that the Italians drew their feeling of an intimate affinity with the ancients in the human realism of their artistic and literary heritage. In the Middle Ages the connection of antiquity with Christianity was felt, if at all, in the idea of a secret, apocalyptic, eschatological connection between the past, present, and future, *teste David cum Sibylla*. For the new generations that relation with the pagan world meant an actual, vital, symbiotic association of essentially congenial aspirations.

The cult of extrinsic form developed in all the artistic centers of Italy. The revival of pagan interests in art and culture was everywhere intended to add glory to the divinity and to intensify human efforts in the search for God. From the early years of the fifteenth century, when the Florentine Masaccio decorated the church of San Clemente in Rome (1417), until Raphael Sanzio finished the Vatican 'Stanze' (1520) and Michelangelo Buonarroti his formidable 'Last Judgment' in the Sistine Chapel (1541), the popes transformed the historical and apostolical, if no longer political, center of Christendom into an architectural and pictorial glorification of its mission.

The artistic reconquest of Rome and the world proceeded at a time when the Roman Church was losing ground abroad and establishing a temporal domain in Italy. The central Italian papal state was carved out and consolidated by the methods of violence and intrigue associated with the secular princes of that era. The adventures of such men as Cardinal Giovanni Vitelleschi are typical of the process. Dynastic plots, assassination by every known means, treachery, and bribery were common practices.

Yet it is an unjustified historical commonplace to attribute the policy of violence and corruption to the cultural revival of ancient paganism and skepticism as contaminating the pure source of medieval piety. In reality the papacy merely carried on the same methods of power politics that had characterized political life during the Middle Ages. In Italy the Church relinquished none of the rights acquired before the Schism; it was still beset by the same political powers, factional passions, and local groups and interests that had troubled the pontiffs for many centuries.

And the ecclesiastical and political means of fighting those adverse forces were very much the same. There is hardly an aspect of that temporal policy that does not have its counterpart in the earlier history of the papacy, when the world seemed entirely dominated by religious fervor. The methods of conquest and domination followed by Sixtus IV, for instance, were not far different from those of Boniface VIII. The assassination of Giuliano de' Medici in the cathedral of Florence, on 26 April 1478, organized by his rivals, the Pazzi, and sponsored by Pope Sixtus IV, was certainly no less a sacrilegious action than the killing of Thomas à Becket in Canterbury Cathedral three hundred years earlier.

In that age so often presumed to have been dominated by paganism and religious indifference, the popular protest against the worldliness of the Church was even more resolute than before the Schism. In Florence, where an uninterrupted series of eloquent preachers from Bernardino of Siena to Girolamo Savonarola challenged the cultural and political prestige of the papacy, Archbishop St. Antonino combined learning and piety to an extent scarcely achieved in the earlier history of the town. One of his successors, Archbishop Salviati, involved in the Pazzi conspiracy, was hanged by the outraged Florentine populace from a window of the Palazzo della Signoria. As late as 1498, when the political and religious drama of Savonarola reached its climax, the government permitted the local contest between the Franciscan and Dominican friars to be decided through an ordeal by fire, a custom fallen into disuse since St. Francis had offered it to the Sultan. On this occasion the ordeal was an appeal to divine authority in a question involving a papal verdict. Machiavelli was certainly on the Piazza among the agitated multitude, as was Giovanni Pico della Mirandola, the phoenix of Italian intellectuals and a devoted follower of the Friar. The heavy rain that prevented the ordeal surely did not mark the victory of Olympus over Golgotha.

In Rome, Valla's caustic attacks on the papal political pretensions and the failings of the Church brought no harm to that most independent and combative of the Italian humanists. Called to Rome as a professor by Nicholas V, and appointed a papal

secretary by Calixtus VII, he succumbed, like all Italian scholars, to the seduction of that courtly environment and, with all
his keen criticism and intellectual sagacity, remained an obedient and loyal servant of the Church. The same is true of the
enthusiastic, alert, and noisy literati of the Roman group around
Bartolomeo Platina and Pomponio Leto, the founders and leaders
of the Roman Academy. This institution was dissolved in 1468
by Paul II, allegedly as a den of heretics and libertines, in
reality because the eccentric and cantankerous pontiff feared
the resentment of quarrelsome scholars whom he had dismissed
from costly and purely decorative sinecures. Despite their pagan
attitudes and epicurean effusions, their secret gatherings in the
catacombs, their loose talk and antiquarian mummeries, none of
these scholarly luminaries gravitating around the papal throne
ever departed from a general orthodox adherence to the doctrines of the Church. In fact, Sixtus IV rehabilitated the whole
company and took them all back into the papal service.

Strictest devotion and obedience to canonical precepts were
traditional at Naples, the most corrupt and vicious of the Italian
courts, at first under the late Angevin rulers and afterwards
when in 1442 Alfonso of Aragon annexed the whole Italian Low
Country to his Hispano-Sicilian Kingdom. His political shrewd-
ness in countering the general hostility to that move, his cruelty
in suppressing the resisting barons of his kingdom, his ruinous
fiscal policy, his passion for the riches of this world and the
most spectacular aspects of ancient life—all his scandalous offenses against the moral order in state and family did not prevent that crafty and harsh ruler from being the most zealous
churchgoer and sedulous theologian. He was praised by his contemporary biographers as 'a mirror of penitence' and a model
of Christian virtue.[1] In all that, he surpassed King Robert II,
who, more than a century before him, inaugurated the Neapolitan courtly traditions of bigotry and frivolity. In that atmosphere
of unbridled license and penitential fastings, there was a balance between profane letters and religious practices. The same
King Alfonso who attended three masses daily, and could quote

[1] Vespasiano da Bisticci, Vite di uomini illustri del Secolo XV (Vita di
Alfonso, re di Napoli).

by heart the voluminous Bible commentary of Nicolaus de Lyra, called to his court from Milan the Palermian Antonio Beccadelli, the much admired author of a highly scandalous and salacious collection of Latin epigrams. Similarly, Poggio Bracciolini's impertinent and obscene *Facetiae*, first narrated in a group of papal functionaries, were never considered incompatible with the dignity of an apostolic secretary and the pious and austere attitudes inspired by his extended sojourn in England.

Finally Aeneas Sylvius Piccolomini, an opportunistic politician, author of an indecent comedy and a voluptuous love story, became Pope Pius II, an ardent protector of the faith and champion of papal authority. The frank worldliness and skepticism of Pontano's rationalistic moralism are rare among the literary men and courtly adventurers of that age. Sannazaro, for instance, who was his contemporary and belonged to the same Neapolitan circle around the disgraceful and cruel Ferdinand I of Aragon, divided his attentions between the amorous tortuosities of his pastoral novel *Arcadia* and *De Partu Virginis* (1490), a classical account of the birth of Christ.

This spiritual duality, rather than duplicity, is a common phenomenon in that era of expanding laical culture and secular civilization. As a characteristic aspect of Italian spiritual life it is not confined to a few leading courts or to a group of timorous, half-hearted literati, but rather constituted a general attitude toward reality and religion, life and faith, daily experience and eternal values. Those apparent contradictions, dissonances, incongruities in the general trends of a national civilization resulted from a complex of intellectual ferments, social conditions, habits of thought, and spiritual needs of which the historian has to take a synoptical view.

* * *

After Petrarca the impact of pagan culture was as powerful on the clergy as on the laity, but the foundations of Italian faith were not nearly as much shaken as they had been by the heretical movements of the Middle Ages. The great majority of the men who concerned themselves with the humanities were equally expert in the divinities. Most of them held ecclesiastical offices,

or belonged to the priesthood or the monastic or mendicant
orders. They rarely neglected the practice of religion and never
professed dogmatic non-conformity and spiritual independence.
In that early humanistic epoch there was hardly a man of letters as free from ecclesiastical allegiances as Dante had been in
an era held to be profoundly religious.

The increasing passion for pagan antiquity, accompanied by
the greatest development of religious art known to the history
of Christianity, was certainly not an expression of economic
prosperity and dwindling religious interest. The extraordinary
number of churches and shrines built during this period can
hardly be regarded as a formal and external manifestation of
mere traditional beliefs. Princes and despots, banking and trade
magnates, powerful governments and influential congregations
built churches, chapels, and monasteries throughout the country
as a matter of pride and prestige. But those monuments of faith
were certainly intended also as expressions of personal devotion
and appeals to divine intercession, as pantheons of earthly glory
and stepping-stones to eternal salvation. These were the feelings
and intentions that moved Gian Galeazzo Visconti, the most
daring and successful of Italian sovereigns, to found, after the
imprisonment and poisoning of his uncle Bernabò in 1386, the
cathedral of Milan as well as, ten years later, the famous Car-
thusian monastery near Pavia, which became the mausoleum
of the new Lombard dynasties and one of the most conspicuous
monuments of Italian religious art. In the midst of dynamic
secular activity, an increasing creative fervor stimulated the construction of the most impressive landmarks of Italian devotion.

The depth of the cultural problem may be revealed by the
example of the Florentine civilization of the early Medicean era,
when the town had become the focus of that literary paganism
and artistic naturalism generally designated as the Italian Renaissance. The enormous wealth accumulated by a few patrician
families through commercial monopolies led to the outburst of
architectural enthusiasm that transformed a medieval town into
a palatial modern city. Cosimo de' Medici, who added to the
fortune of his father Giovanni through his activities as a papal
banker, was an indefatigable builder and was emulated by the

still powerful families of the old commercial and patrician oligarchy, the Albizzi, Pazzi, Pitti, Acciaiuoli, Strozzi, Pucci, and many others whose names are still alive in the life and memories of the town. The inspiration of all those private palaces was no thought of comfort, intimacy, or joviality. Those Florentine bankers and businessmen invested their surplus funds in the shape of stone, marble, bronze, and iron. Surrounded by danger of violent death, they were passionately attached to life, and wished to survive through their families and buildings. Popes and princes, patricians and upstarts, all had the same concern.

All these men, inspired by a throng of learned humanists, mostly of low extraction, with an almost superstitious respect for classical architecture and for their ancient mythical ancestors, lavished unlimited sums on religious monuments. At the peak of the antiquarian passion, the churches of San Lorenzo and Santo Spirito, the monastery of San Marco, the chapels of the Brancacci and Pazzi, and other Florentine masterpieces by Brunelleschi, L. B. Alberti, Michelozzo, Rossellino, the Manettis, et cetera, represent not only new technical and artistic accomplishments but also the realization of a new approach to God and the faith.

Similar conditions prevailed in other Italian centers. Bartolomeo Colleoni, symbol of the conquering spirit in Verrocchio's equestrian statue, and in real life a ruthless warrior and astute opportunist, founded no less than three churches in addition to his famous memorial chapel at Bergamo. Sigismondo Malatesta was the most wicked of the princely *condottieri*, the man who called the Turks to Italy while his territorial enemy, the pope, was organizing a crusade. After 1445, he built in Rimini the Tempio Malatestiano, consecrated to St. Francis; here he and his mistress, the beautiful Isotta, contemplated their tombs and provided in time for perpetual masses for the peace of their souls. In that famous church, erected by Leon Battista Alberti, they rest among the scholars and poets who ennobled their court. The same architect sketched the imposing church of St. Andrea in Mantua, whose vast and noble proportions reveal the genius of the learned and versatile master who devoted the formal conceptions of Vitruvius to the glory of a Christian martyr. The same spirit emanates from the other churches of that age, whether small and tranquil like Piccolomini's Tuscan cathedral of Pienza, or spaciously vaulted like the Roman churches and the structures of Bramante. In either case the whole population participated in an architectural enthusiasm expressive of an unvaried cult.

To the modern mind affected by Protestant rigorism and philosophical rationalism, the coexistence then customary of crime and devotion, fear and faith, individualism and obedience, is hard to understand. It is historically unsound to suppose that this dualistic attitude was limited to the ruling classes. Even today, most users of profane language are fully submissive to the sacred objects of their blasphemy. The people who constituted the turbulent, unstable Italian society of that epoch were exposed to constant danger and therefore prone to take precautions for individual and collective salvation. The whole religious attitude of that society was consequently one of obedience rather than of rebellion and individualism. Organized heresies were almost nonexistent. Despite the moral and religious implications of Savonarola's movement, it did not stand for dogmatic or institutional reforms.

The paganism commonly held responsible for the corruption of the times was primarily of a cultural character and was always redeemed by works of piety. Lorenzo de' Medici's pagan carnivals, the lascivious imitations of Plautus and Terence by courtly literati and amateurs had their counterpart in the Lenten religious dramas—the *sacre rappresentazioni*—in which Lorenzo himself collaborated. Composed by the poets of his circle, they were performed with the greatest refinement, but also with the gravity and reverence of a religious rite. There was no skeptic or sinner so intractable as to refuse the sacraments of the Church. The pagan revival in art, poetry, scholarship, and philosophy never affected the Christian idea of salvation, which was totally unknown to the ancients. There was no substitute for it in any other religion or philosophy, and it still dominated the Italian mind even though enjoyment of this world's goods seemed to divert Italian society from piety and religious tradition.

Since the spiritual heritage of the Middle Ages did not include an ethical code to meet the exigencies of active life, and since the revived pagan philosophies did not concern themselves with redemption, divine mercy was the only refuge and hope of great and small sinners who wished to avoid eternal damnation and attain everlasting bliss. The whole of religion was concentrated on this hope of salvation through intercession and clemency. All religious life was dominated by the fear of an avenging Numen whose wrath and justice could be placated by oblations and the ritual practices of devotion. This was, of course, a pagan and superstitious approach to God, but so shrouded in Christian tenets and traditions that it never seemed to contradict the essence or even the canonical expression of the most orthodox faith. Religion remained an exclusively supernatural concern without any necessary implications for man's acts and values here on earth.

Thus religion and practical morals became mutually independent, the practice of life was detached from the control of conscience. Easy remittance of sins and the connivance of the priests legitimized this dissociation of morals and faith. Repentance for sins was deferred to Purgatory, where hope and punishment concurred in the work of ultimate salvation. The religious life of that epoch can be said to have been dominated by the idea of indulgence, just as that of the Middle Ages was dominated by the idea of damnation. Purgatory played a secondary role in medieval theology, ethics, and imagination; the alternative was rigid: damnation or salvation. As a temporary eschatological institution, it became the hope and concern of a society that had no transcendent ideals for which to fight and live. The new aristocracy of money and power assumed the legal and picturesque aspects of feudalism and chivalry, but ignored its ethical code. Power and religion became as amoral as the professions and personalities that embodied them.

The pilgrims who streamed by the millions to Rome and other Italian sanctuaries, particularly in the jubilee years, were empowered to release innumerable souls from Purgatory by paying a certain amount of money and reciting a canonical number of prayers. Every sinner who took care to die in a state of grace could count on an ultimate, if deferred, beatitude. The wealthy and influential availed themselves of this privilege by making pious bequests to charitable and religious institutions. A worldly minded clergy became increasingly liberal in administering sacraments and absolutions, which were readily accepted by poor and rich alike, from the hands of unworthy or simply secularized priests and prelates. Under these circumstances, Purgatory was the principal topic of the theological discussions during the Council of Florence, in 1439; it was the first Catholic stronghold assaulted by the Greeks and later by Luther in their respective movements of secession and reform.

Purgatory was so deeply anchored in the Italian consciousness and practice that its optimistic, utopian image withstood every theological or skeptical argument. It was the religious counterpart of that capricious and mysterious *Fortuna* popularly believed to govern the unsettled and undisciplined life of Italian society. Life seems to have developed in the shadow of Dante's *Purgatorio*, which had transformed a vague theological concept into a lifelike transcendent reality. The objectionable morality of those concepts and mental habits was compensated by the practical results both for human achievements and the greater glory of God.

✿   ✿   ✿

Into that moral vacuum the humanists stepped as a new cultural community interposed between the rigid dogmatism of the Church and the spiritual derangement of the laity. Humanism, which at first embodied the interests of only a few learned men, became a cultural force affecting all Italian life and civilization. As a towering cultural superstructure over the still unshaken traditions of medieval thought and customs, humanism promoted their intellectual and artistic renewal through the inspiration of the ancient world. With its countless variations and contradictory manifestations, humanism is a complex and sometimes confused phenomenon. It became a leading constructive force after the spiritual exhaustion of the Church had deprived the nation of its traditional intellectual and moral support.

Humanism was not merely a literary and aesthetic movement. Beginning with Petrarca, it was a determined secession from the Parisian intellectual hegemony, a break with the Arabo-

Hispanic traditions of High Medieval culture, a rejection of the Germanic traditions of suzerainty, and a return to the cultural heritage of the Roman and Mediterranean commonwealth. However divergent the definitions of humanism may be, it was indisputably a renascence of the classical values of the moral and aesthetic, seen as autonomous and profane expressions of the human mind. The interests of the new intellectual leaders extended to the whole of ancient civilization, only partly known until then and only conditionally appreciated. Humanism was not merely the hobby of a few scholars, but was supported by the greater part of active Italian society, which, indeed, played a decisive part in molding its moral and intellectual contents. It was only through the general participation of Italian society—secular as well as ecclesiastical—that the representatives of the new spirit were enabled to form a free association of cultural interests throughout the Italian peninsula and soon, also, beyond its frontiers.

Humanism was not a product of the schools, although the Italian universities were conquered one by one, at least in some of their faculties, by the new trends. Nor was it exclusively a courtly manifestation, although every Italian court soon became a center of the spiritual revival. The last two republican strongholds of Italy—Florence and Venice—remained the headquarters of its conquests and expansion. Universality was the characteristic feature of humanism that subjugated even those groups and individuals who vainly endeavored to stem the hegemony of pagan cultures. Consequently, humanism became the predominant expression of Italian civilization and the only cultural movement that submitted the whole Western World to its intellectual guidance.

Those were Petrarca's aims. They became a universal reality through his friends and correspondents in different parts of Italy, who formed the groups of scholars and enthusiasts from which, in the course of the fifteenth century, the first 'academies' arose. Those gatherings were originally simple, informal meetings, independent of the professional and ecclesiastical schools. In the early period of humanistic civilization, shortly after Petrarca's death, two different types of cultural meetings developed in Italy. The one—impressively described in *Il Paradiso degli Alberti,* a famous novel by Giovanni Gherardi—was of a courtly character after the pattern of Boccaccio's Neapolitan reminiscences. The other type represented by the meetings of scholars and laymen in the Augustinian monastery of Santo Spirito in Florence recalls Dante's more exclusive and masculine company of *filosofanti.*[2]

The humanist tradition of Petrarca was very much alive among the Venetian nobility. It found active adherents in Paduan university circles, and became a dominant feature of Milanese cultural life, first under the last Visconti and afterwards, in an increasing spirit of emulation, at the Lombard residences of the Sforzas. Florence, Rome, and Naples developed as its leading centers, but the smaller places, and a few courts that resisted the expansion of the five most powerful states, joined in the cultural renewal. Ferrara and Mantua, Rimini, Bologna, Pesaro, Urbino, and many provincial towns from the Alps to Sicily were driven along with the others by that scholarly infatuation and intellectual fervor. Every region, including Sicily, contributed to the throng of learned humanists. Consequently, the sociological aspects of the cultural revolution are of the greatest importance. Humanism began as an intellectual aristocracy more or less closely connected with its founder and master. It developed through a free spiritual organization of men active in very different branches of life. Talent and ability were its only conditions for success and renown. Its leaders, who rapidly rose to positions of influence and power in every section of public life, were mostly of humble origin.

In this way humanism became a national movement. It spread very much in the manner of religious or political organizations, with cells and groups forming around apostles, leaders, and teachers, with sponsors and propagandists in various sections of the population, and finally with gatherings, rituals, and a distinctive language symbolizing congenial aims and intellectual solidarity. With all the divergence of interests and activities in that vast ideological community, classical Latin was for all its

[2] Cf. above, ch. 7.

members the touchstone of that congeniality and the universal criterion that separated the humanists from all other intellectual groups. Thus, humanism and scholasticism became irrevocably divided in spite of their intimate coexistence and partial affinity. The humanists became a nation-wide intellectual caste, reaching into Church and State, courts and schools, workshops and guilds. As such it represented a cultural cross-section of the most diversified Italian social groups.

Humanism appears on the Italian scene as the first secular movement of the Christian era, comparable only to the penetration of Greek thought, customs, art, and poetry into Roman civilization toward the end of the republican era. But while that cultural revolution developed as a result of political conquests, Italian humanism arose as a spontaneous national concentration of spiritual interests and energies, totally independent of political circumstances. The Rome of the humanists was neither republican nor imperial, neither papal nor Italian, neither ancient nor modern, but a symbol, a sort of secular Jerusalem.

Yet, despite its Italian implications, humanism was universal from the start. With discernment Petrarca knew that the restoration of classical civilization required the revival of Greek thought and poetry and the inclusion of the Hellenic world in the orbit of Christian experience and Italian knowledge. While the last vestiges of medieval Byzantine influence were disappearing from Italian soil, the first humanists, fulfilling Petrarca's vague aspiration, were reconstructing ancient Greek civilization in their Italian environment. While the Ottoman Turks completely surrounded the poor territorial remnants of the Byzantine empire, the popular Florentine government appointed the imperial ambassador Manuel Chrysoloras to the chair of Greek language and letters. He was the first of an illustrious series of Greek scholars to unveil pagan and Christian Hellenism to the eager, if somewhat perplexed, Italian humanists. The Council of Florence and the fall of Constantinople, in 1453, attracted more apostles of a weary, eclectic, and ghostly Hellenism to Italy.

Italian scholars, however, brought more method and direction to the task of propagating Hellenism. Simultaneously with the restitution of the Latin classics, Leonardo Bruni, Poggio Brac-

ciolini, Guarino, Filelfo, Poliziano, Lorenzo Valla, and many
minor humanists translated the Greek authors and initiated collections of Greek manuscripts. Nevertheless, the process of Hellenization was slow and remained limited to a privileged scholarly class. Even though a sort of Graecomania raged for many
decades within the ranks of refined society and particularly
attracted the blue-stockings of the day, it could never compete
with the Latin classics in interest and influence. Even the large
and small editions of the Greek classics published by Aldus
Manutius at the end of the fifteenth century contributed little
to the cultural Hellenization of the country. Only those aspects
of Greek antiquity that could be absorbed by Christian thought
and Latin traditions became vital elements of the new national
civilization. While the Latin revival was a national destiny that
affected the whole of Italy, the Greek literary infiltration was
little more than a fashionable literary vogue.

Platonism, soon to become the laical religion of Italy, still followed the medieval patterns and traditions of Cicero, St. Augustine, and the Latin Platonists, although the efforts of a Greek
enthusiast, Georgios Gemistos Plethon, succeeded in interesting
the Medicean circle in the Alexandrian rather than the Christian
interpretation of the Platonic doctrines. An intimate knowledge
and historical understanding of ancient Greek civilization were
never attained on Italian soil in spite of all the scholars and their
teachings. The Greek epigrams, grammars, and published texts
of Poliziano and other scholars did not affect the general picture of early humanistic culture. What remained of all those
noble efforts was a shining mirage of human wisdom and the
alluring image of a laical religion rooted in philosophy and experience rather than in revelation.

From then on, anyone inclined to reconsider the great problems of man and the universe, of science and ethics and politics,
knew that he had to start with the Greeks. By the end of the
century all the Greek authors after Aristotle and Plato were
accessible in Italy, in the original text or in Latin, sometimes
also in vernacular translation. The moral equivalence of Greek
and Christian thought in the general acceptance was expressed
by Raphael of Urbino, who, in the Vatican's *Stanza della Seg-*

natura, painted his 'School of Athens' opposite a fresco in which he glorified the Christian faith. In that soul-stirring and thought-provoking fresco the sublime countenances of Plato and Aristotle dominate the crowd of philosophers, scientists, and empiricists who embody in the realm of thought and knowledge the immortal attainments of Greek and human civilization.

All the efforts toward its complete revival and understanding did not make Italy a country of philosophers, but they do show that humanism was more than a rhetorical and erudite fashion. The public opinion that supported humanism saw in it a secular religion that complemented Christianity in the moral and intellectual sphere. It was this feeling and not merely the widespread admiration of Latin eloquence that led republics and princes alike to place humanists in positions of distinction and responsibility.

Frequently, to be sure, words were taken for facts, and gestures for accomplishments. This is often the case when lofty ideals are transmuted into practice and reality. For those generations a man of letters represented the living embodiment of their cultural aspirations, even though as an individual he might prove intellectually mediocre or morally unworthy. So great was the reverence accorded men of letters that a scholar more learned than original, like Coluccio Salutati, could acquire a general popularity and a conspicuous influence in the political affairs of Florence by the simple power of his pen. His prestige resulted not only from his literary ability, but essentially from the abundance and aptness of his quotations from ancient authors.

The political influence and authority acquired by such scholars can be explained only by the lack of a common ideological basis in the diversified and fluctuating public life of Italy. Political power had ceased to imply the idea of a divine mission and had become, as in pagan times, a human profession, a mere game of fortune and expediency. Under such circumstances much could be learned from the political experience of the ancients.

This idea is clearly expressed by Cristoforo Landino in his *Disputationes Camaldulenses* (1468 I), one of the most comprehensive works of Italian humanistic literature, in which Lorenzo de'

K

Medici and leading members of his circle discuss some central problems of moral and practical philosophy. In the course of the discussion Leon Battista Alberti, the learned architect and moralist, eloquently affirms that 'if a man, led by a wrong ambition or moved by a great love for his native country, wants to take over the administration of the state, he must first know and thoroughly consider by what artifice and means he is to enter upon so important a task'; and Alberti compares this artifice with the technique of a painter or sculptor. In stating the purely secular and human origin of political power in personal ambition or patriotism, and by stressing the necessity of a theoretical and technical preparation for the exercise of that power, the scholarly architect anticipated Machiavelli.[3]

It had meanwhile become the general practice to entrust the education of young noblemen and scions of wealthy families to humanist scholars. Thus Guarino, one of the most learned and humane among the humanists, was called to the court of Ferrara, and Vittorino da Feltre, one of the few outstanding moral personalities in their ranks, became tutor to the children of Gianfrancesco Gonzaga in Mantua. All the scions of the new princely dynasties, such as Cosimo and Lorenzo de'Medici, the last Viscontis and the young Sforzas, the Montefeltros of Urbino, as well as many common citizens and upstarts in public life, were educated by more or less skilled, intelligent, and conscientious men of letters who conjured up before their pupils' eyes the glory of the ancient world, and consistently instilled into their minds the wisdom of the classics. This practice gave rise to an extensive humanistic literature devoted equally to the indoctrination of princes and the guidance of the common folk.

Like most humanistic writings these educational treatises had no firm philosophical foundation. The idea of antiquity embodied in them was fragmentary, eclectic, and factitious, despite the abundance of original texts available. Insistence on the use of classical Latin as a living language obstructed any direct appreciation of reality and fostered rhetorical, unsubstantial, and vainglorious attitudes. This linguistic alienation caused classical

[3] Cf. Machiavelli, *Discourses on Livy*, I, 25.

culture to appear as the secular appanage of a privileged class. The medieval duality of spiritual life, represented by ecclesiastical and scholastic Latinity on the one hand, and by a vernacular culture on the other, was now further complicated by the addition of an exclusive but thriving third sphere of taste and thought.

Although continuously clashing, those three spheres were clearly circumscribed, not only by their mode of expression, but also by their substance and aims. In that tripartite national civilization the social categories counted least of all. The fluctuation and equalization of the classes proceeded even more rapidly than in the Middle Ages. Plebeians rose to wealth, fame, and power while noblemen mingled with commoners and plebeians. Many of the outstanding *condottieri*, like Carmagnola, Gattamelata, and Niccolò Piccinino, all the great scholars and artists, some of the founders of the new dynasties, like Attendolo Sforza, were men of common and even rustic or low extraction, while most of the innumerable princely 'bastards' in the highest positions of the political, ecclesiastical, and social hierarchy, represented a popular contribution to aristocratic strains.

The aristocracy of classical culture was more aloof. Its polished, bookish Latin remained distinct from the cursory, hybrid, and desultory style of ecclesiastical professional routines. The intellectual aristocracy condescended to the use of the vernacular only for what they considered the lower forms of conversation and literature. The growing prestige and final preponderance of classical culture over the scholastic and vernacular was largely due to its courtly, laical, and national character. While religious thought was more and more limited to otherworldly objectives, humanism concerned itself increasingly with the formation of the worldly human personality. The common aim of the humanists in their diversified interests and activities was to create and to embody a new cultural nobility as advocated by Dante and initiated by Petrarca on the verge of the courts, in the home of the wealthy, and in the centers of power and influence. The humanistic trends and efforts were directed toward the perfection of earthly life through poetry, art, scholarship, and knowledge. Hence the extraordinary number of educational treatises, didactic works, and moralistic dissertations, all intended to establish models of individual or professional excellence.

In some essential points this literature was connected with the traditions of medieval doctrinalism. But in creating the standard for the perfect prince (Platina, Patrizi, Pontano, etc.), the perfect husband (F. Barbaro), the perfect citizen (Palmieri), the perfect courtier (Castiglione), or the ideal family (Alberti, etc.), all those moralists drew their inspiration, models, and maxims from ancient and pagan authors. The imaginary portraits of human perfection are moralistic rather than idealistic, and are abstractly composed in accordance with eclectic principles, maxims, and opinions drawn from the Aristotelian treatises, the Stoic writers of antiquity, and technical authors of every discipline. Medieval dialectical deductions are replaced by a discursive and constructive illustration of human accomplishments and ideals. Only a few vernacular masterpieces, such as Castiglione's *Cortegiano,* grant an insight—though wishfully idealized—into the realities of contemporary life.

The golden mean generally praised and taught in all those treatises is hardly in harmony with the intemperance, corruption, and cruelty of the era. Yet the moral teachings of the humanist writers are not entirely hollow, rhetorical, and insincere. Frequently enough, it is true, an oratorical gesture creates conviction, and a sonorous, well-balanced phrase evokes an opinion that vanishes with the last echo of the words. But the habit of idealization had a real basis in the Platonic trend of all this moralizing literature, eclectic as the bulk of its maxims and doctrines may appear to the modern reader. The creation of ideal types of human perfection by which to measure individual worth is a purely Platonic attitude, in strong contrast with the empirical Aristotelian approach to the problems of moral philosophy.

Throughout the humanistic period Platonism was a way of thinking rather than a doctrine, a temper of mind rather than a system. Plato's philosophy has never been correctly understood by its Italian translators and interpreters. But Platonism as an intellectual trend represents and typifies the humanities, in contrast with Aristotelian naturalism and the rational methods of scholasticism. The general spiritual inclination had moved away from the scientific, classifying empiricism of the Aristotelian and Averroistic tradition toward an intuitive, emotional, and comprehensive understanding of God and the world. The intellectual attitudes of that highly artistic and intensively creative era tended to substitute ideals for categories and to replace distinctions and definitions by images and symbols. The thinking of those generations revolved around ideal types substantiated by poetry and erudition, and not around experience explained by common sense or scientific abstractions. The Aristotelian tradition of thought remained unshaken in the schools. But where the individual was discussed as a member of human society or as an eternal soul, Platonism seemed the only alternative.

Lorenzo Valla had cleared the ground for a philosophical revival among scholars mainly devoted to literary work. In his famous treatise on free will (1439) and in *Dialectical Disputations,* he dissociated philosophy from theology and science from faith. There re-emerged the old dualistic approach to the fundamental spiritual problems, and the result was perplexity, moral indifference, eclecticism, and speculation for its own sake.

In that spirit the humanist writers and educators went on discussing, on a purely secular and erudite basis, such problems as the highest good (Bruni), tyranny and liberty (Salutati), nobility (Landino, etc.), avarice and fortune (Poggio), human dignity (Manetti, etc.), physical and intellectual pleasure (Valla), and other topics of moral philosophy that might have been subjects of serious reflection but actually became a pretext for oratorical performances and idle dissertations. The absence of a moral code in a society undergoing a violent process of transformation stimulated those interminable and generally inconclusive discussions of the ordinary problems of private and public life. The insurmountable perplexity in men's minds was due to their equivocal intellectual situation and to attitudes that were neither consistently Christian nor frankly pagan. Thinkers took refuge in dialectical tricks and oratorical evasions, while their moral intentions assumed a purely literary character. In spite of all these shortcomings, however, the humanists did accustom their contemporaries to an immanentistic approach to life and the world, supported by the belief that all that pertains to human destiny on earth is contained within man himself and embodied in the pagan but not godless ancient civilization.

*   *   *

A decisive step in this direction was made with Poggio's discovery, in 1411, of Lucretius' *On the Nature of Things*. The Epicurean philosophy and the materialistic doctrines of the Democritean school ceased then to be a moral bugbear for timorous minds and became a challenge to the revived Roman Stoicism as well as to Aristotelianism and Platonism. Democritean atomism and Epicurean hedonism were, it is true, irreconcilable with Christian tenets, yet Lucretius' poem contained ferments of a spiritual renewal. The aesthetic and intellectual enjoyment embodied in that noble inspired work was highly acceptable to the new pleasure-loving generations, and the Epicurean disregard for politics was most compatible with the indifference and aloofness imposed on the educated people of Italy by the current despotic trends. To a society obsessed by the fear of death, animated by a creative fervor, and engulfed in the uninhibited enjoyment of earthly goods, a philosophy that taught how to ignore the gods by respecting them, and how to perfect man by increasing his self-awareness, held a peculiar charm and a dangerous allure. All the poets and philosophers who strove to break out of the circle of approved or traditional systems of thought, and engage in free speculation, found their course charted by Lucretius. Later on the best of them, such as the Ferrarese Palingenio Stellato, the Roman Aonio Paleario, the Neapolitans Capece and Giordano Bruno, were burned at the stake or posthumously condemned for their attempts at a poetical and philosophical renewal of pagan opinions and maxims.

Nevertheless, the Lucretian tribute to intellectual and physical enjoyment became an important element in the formation of the Italian mind. Under the influence of Marsilio Ficino, vast sections of Italian society engaged in lively debates on sacred and profane love, on beauty in nature and perfection in art. One of their main concerns was the ticklish topic *de voluptate,* so frequently and thoroughly debated in those circles of worldly men of action and letters moved either by a bad conscience or by a more or less sincere desire for intellectual clarification.

Yet, even the art of Lucretius was unable to make the Epicurean doctrine palatable outside of a refined and restricted society yearning after luxury, pleasure, and ease. Similarly the Ciceronianism of the orators and teachers did not prevent the steady decline of the Stoic attitudes embodied in Dante's idealized portrait of Cato and considered by Petrarca as the highest heritage of Roman wisdom. All the efforts of the leading humanists in restoring and translating the original Aristotelian texts failed to discredit the Arabic and medieval interpretations of his doctrines. The Byzantine scholars who participated in the Councils and taught in Italian universities were not restrained by the Thomist tradition in their straightforward and sometimes passionate defense of Aristotle's philosophy. The dislike of logical formalism was so strong among the Italian humanists that they persistently neglected even the Greek Aristotle, whose authentic works they had published and translated. Moreover, the thinking and habits of the humanists were so deeply permeated with Christian spirit that none of them would have dared even to consider accepting a philosophy that, like Aristotelianism, ignored the ideas of individual immortality and divine creation, both of which were at least vaguely foreshadowed in the doctrines of Plato. Therefore, their preference was for Platonism, which developed from the eclectic philosophical experiences of their epoch into a sort of human religion and lay theology, whose priest and apostle, the Florentine Marsilio Ficino, sums up the spiritual attainments and aspirations of the whole humanistic era.

To the modern mind the philosophy of Marsilio Ficino appears in method and structure to be a mere outgrowth of late scholasticism, and as god-centered and spiritualistic as any other medieval system of thought. The extremely speculative character of that philosophy is marked by the almost complete absence, in Ficino's voluminous and numerous treatises, of the main topics of humanistic literature. To a society in search of an ethical code for its secular existence, to a nation deprived of any ideological basis for its public life, and engaged in a pas-

sionate effort at artistic and intellectual regeneration, Ficino
gave nothing but a mythical vision of the universe. In his writings and teachings there is no trace of Plato's political concerns.
Ficino also ignored the mathematical foundations of Plato's
metaphysics and cosmology and gave no thought to the cult of
the 'divine proportion' that inspired the aesthetic ideals of his
contemporaries.

Ficino's philosophy is a doctrine of faith with the Christian
goal of human salvation and the humanistic substance of a
'learned religion.' It is a human theology intended to provide a
metaphysical ground and a rational explanation for the exceptional position of man in the hierarchy of beings and in the
physical and spiritual structure of the universe. Ficino's great
popularity and profound influence were not due to his ontological speculations or his subtle and often purely dialectical
proofs of the immortality of the soul. Nor did he greatly impress
his contemporaries by his sincere, if not ascetic, contempt of
the world or by his mystical pantheism. His ultimate and orthodox object consisted in the deification of the human soul through
a contemplative ascent toward the divine source of goodness,
beauty, and illumination. Professional philosophers and mystical
writers, especially outside Italy, were stimulated by these doctrines in whose speculative tortuosities a learned reader could
easily find the reflections and sediments of all ancient and medieval currents of thought and, most definitely, the direct and
conscious influence of the Neoplatonic systems in their Alexandrine and Christian traditions and interpretations.

That high-flown doctrine that aspired to bring God to earth
beyond the altars and man to heaven before death became very
early the official philosophy of the Medicis and the spiritual
guide of the educated classes of Florence, at that time the uncontested intellectual capital of Italy. Ficino was revered as the
high priest of that ecstatic school long before he was ordained
a priest in 1473, and finally a canon of the cathedral of Florence.
What prompted the town's most successful money-maker and
shrewdest politician, Cosimo de' Medici, to give special protection to this one among the many excellent scholars gathered in
Florence? Was it possible for Lorenzo the Magnificent to be-

come the vernacular herald of those doctrines [4] and draw lyrical inspiration from concepts and trends apparently so far removed from the experience and ambitions of his countrymen? Those striking facts have complex psychological and spiritual causes that can only be touched upon in this context.

Ficino's doctrines and methods achieved a coherent and balanced fusion of the humanities and divinities, of pagan and Christian thought. Here philosophy is not the handmaiden but the partner of theology and, as in Dante and Petrarca, an inspired vision of the universe rather than a rational system of thought. It is an aristocratic doctrine that instills poetic substance and lofty motifs of contemplation into a religious practice usually contaminated by vulgar superstitions and the ignorance and corruption of the clergy. Moreover, it is a philosophy in which love is considered the essential principle of the universe, and, as such, spiritualizing beyond the consecrated process of procreation the physical communion of two human beings and of all beings existing in nature and the universe. It was this central motif of Ficino's speculation rather than the problematic consistency and fragile structure of his system that fascinated so many Italian poets, artists, and intellectuals.

Ficino's ecstatic philosophy of love spread over Italy like an intellectual poison. Its vague, sensual, and intellectual pan-eroticism rapidly became the spiritual substance of Italian civilization in one of the most extraordinary cultural movements in human history. It marked the triumph of Venus over Minerva, of the Platonic Eros over the Christian *caritas*, of the Italian mind over the French intellectual supremacy. That doctrine of love, with its cult of beauty in man and nature, replaced the medieval courtly love, which had never been truly understood and professed in Italy, by the Neoplatonic Eros, a more substantial and noble doctrine of cosmic scope and religious temper. It taught men to recognize in corporeal beauty a manifestation of divine perfection and to worship in physical and artistic forms a reflection of the divine mind.

The intellectual and erotic cult of beauty transformed the

[4] Especially in his *Altercazione* (1474) and the *Selve*.

K*

mercantile, learned, enterprising, and turbulent Italy of that creative era into an entranced and lovesick nation. This trend first developed as a courtly mood and fashion in the Medicean inner circle of men of letters, artists, and dandies who found in the lyricism of Lorenzo the Magnificent an echo of the early traditions of Florentine poetry. It was under the influence of Medicean Platonism that the learned and exclusive humanistic culture of Florentine scholars and noblemen turned into a vernacular, popular, and finally national civilization. The first impulse in that direction was provided by Cosimo de' Medici's Platonic hobbies. This first citizen of Florence invested a large part of his immense fortune in religious, public, and private buildings, and collected books and works of art on a royal scale. He can be readily compared with the nineteenth-century American magnates of iron, copper, railway, oil, and banking, who transformed their homes, libraries, and galleries into public institutions and endowed universities and museums for the advancement of culture and learning as well as for the benefit of their influence and reputation.

There is, however, a substantial difference between these modern patrons of arts and letters and their Italian forerunners. The latter did not lavish their means in the delusive expectation that buildings, objects, and institutions would create or inspire a civilization. Cosimo de' Medici, Palla Strozzi, Bernardo Rucellai, Luca Pitti, and many other conspicuous Florentine citizens; the Venetian Barbaros, Giustinian, Loredano, and other merchant patricians patronizing the arts and letters; and the innumerable provincial protectors of cultural undertakings, all participated personally in the intellectual currents and spiritual attitudes of their time. They did not immure their fortunes in anonymous and soulless institutions administered by functionaries and businessmen. Cosimo de' Medici laid the foundations of the Florentine Academy because he felt sincerely attracted to the Platonic doctrines revived by the scholars whom he protected and revered in a sincere impulse of intellectual ambition and in a sound estimate of spiritual values. Most of the great Italian patrons of the arts and letters won more lasting fame through the association of their persons and houses with a trend of thought, a school of art, a cultural movement, than through sepulchral monuments or stillborn literary eulogies.

Italian Platonism was not an academic solace or the exclusive cultural appanage of a privileged class. Developed first in Florence as a courtly doctrine, it marked and exalted the triumph of love over all sentiments and passions that can inspire, stir, deify, or ruin an individual, a class, a country. In the Italy of that era patriotism, heroism, piety, civic spirit, and other inspiring virtues did not count as constructive elements and emotional springs of action. There was a prophecy in Petrarca's vision of the best men of his country dragged in chains by Amor to an enchanted and enervating island of delight.[5] But while his Christian feeling made chastity overcome love, fame conquer death, and divinity triumph over time, the new generations idolized love as the divinity itself to which all other human values and virtues were subordinated. Only in such a mood could the most popular symbol of Christian and chivalric heroism be transformed into a lovesick swashbuckler, first in Boiardo's *Orlando Innamorato* (1474) and a generation later in Ariosto's *Orlando Furioso*.

The whole texture, development, and meaning of Ariosto's poem are drawn from the varied passion and experience of love, from tender devotion to abominable crimes, from enlightened wisdom to delirious lunacy. Love appears as the only moving and inspiring power in nature and mankind, as the only source of inspiration in life and poetry. The heroic paladin whose love-shattered brain is carried off to the wondrous landscape of the moon appears as a symbol of Italy creating an unreal world of beauty and delight in the midst of the most radical and destructive revolution of modern times. And, indeed, it would seem that this sensual, literary, artistic, and philosophical cult of love had become the dominant trend in Italian spiritual life.

Two great men reacted consistently against the amorous rapture that was corroding, so they thought, the vital energies of the Italian people. One was Savonarola, a vernacular and popular representative of the divinities; the other was Machiavelli, the

[5] *Triumph of Love.*

vernacular spokesman of the substantial, active, and not merely literary humanities. Savonarola organized the Florentine people, during the critical days of their history, into a political party opposed to that pagan philosophy and based on the common principles of Christian morality still alive, if not actually practiced, in vast sections of Italian society. He dared to defy the most worldly and authoritarian of all the popes of that age, and died at the stake, in 1498, a victim of intrigue, bigotry, and political subservience to the papal authority.

For the political and moral ruin of Italy, Machiavelli made responsible, first, the Italian princes 'adorning themselves with gems and gold, and sleeping and eating with more luxury than others'; [6] and then the corrupt Roman court that had made the Italians 'without religion and vile.' [7] He called for the resurgence of the Roman civic and military virtues in a people morally and physically disarmed by their spiritual and political leaders, just as Savonarola preached the restoration of the Christian virtues in public and private life. But the Dominican friar from Ferrara was unable to make the Italians more virtuous and religious, and the Florentine Secretary could not make them more patriotic and warlike. In the years of the country's worst catastrophes, between the French invasion in 1494 and the Sack of Rome by the mutinous imperial army in 1527, the cult of immortal love and mortal beauty was at its peak. Artists and poets were eager to materialize immortal love in a mortal beauty and mortal love in immortal beauty. During those years a more and more popular erotic philosophy systematized that amorous state of mind in vernacular treatises in which a speculative and ethical idealization of the natural instincts and human appetites was mingled with an elaborate casuistry of chivalric love and flirtation.

A Jewish physician from Spain, Jehuda Abarvanel, called Leone Ebreo by the Italians, who found refuge from religious persecution in Naples, built up in famous dialogues that amorous, seductive, but never impious philosophy.[8] About the same time

---

[6] *Arte della guerra*, end of book 7.
[7] *Discourses on Livy*, I, 12
[8] *Dialoghi d'amore*, published in 1535.

the Venetian Pietro Bembo, a follower of Ficino and a great lover and poet before he became a worldly cardinal and a revered scholar, composed the *Asolani,* a Neoplatonic revival of courtly love and gallant service. A few years earlier the learned Mario Equicola had taught the essence of love at the court of Mantua.[9] This is again a main topic of sober debates and lively repartee in Castiglione's ideal revival of the courtly conversations at Urbino. Other treatises and dialogues of the same nature were composed all over Italy. Innumerable courtiers, ladies, scholars, poets, and even courtesans joined in the observance of a cult which prompted the Italians to express their sentiments and passions in concrete, realistic forms and, at the same time, to spiritualize their sensual temptations and bodily enjoyments.

The tender motifs and melancholy introspection of Petrarca's lyrics inspired an epidemic of transcendental love poetry that became the delight of the courts, the pastime of noblemen, and the solace of lovesick women. The aging Michelangelo praised the noble Vittoria Colonna in this same Neoplatonic spirit that filled all minds with the vague and intriguing idea of the 'infinity of love.' In such a mood of secularized religion the Italians of that great century discussed the problems of love and art in a consistent effort to reconcile their attachment to the reality of life with their spiritual fervor, and their artistic enthusiasm with an instinctive piety.

Under the impact of a cultural revolution, Italy dissolved its Biblical faith in God into a vague Platonic theosophy in which God appears as a universal Numen and the human soul, eager to rejoin its divine source, as the most perfect and eternal emanation of that supreme being. The creative power of man is a divine appanage that ennobles earthly love and enables an artist to represent the eternal idea more adequately than nature, and a poet to attain through his feeling and imagination the highest stages of perfection. These doctrines and sentiments, consecrated by Dante and Petrarca and supported by ancient and humanistic authority, formed the spiritual climate of Italy in an era when Spain was organizing the fanatical and systematic

---

[9] *Libro di natura d'amore,* published in 1525.

vindication of Catholic orthodoxy, when Lutheran Germany was reinstating the Scriptures as the only guide to truth, and the French Huguenots were reforming Christianity in the spirit of Augustinian predestination.

Deprived of its dangerous pantheism and paganism, the Italian religion of love lost its philosophical support and Neoplatonic implications under the impact of the Counter-Reformation, which restored orthodoxy and ecclesiastical control over the spiritual life of the country. In that new trend of Italian civilization the Spaniards were instrumental. But they were not able to destroy a national tradition of thought and sentiment reflected in every great achievement of letters and art. The hegemony of love remained unshaken in the intellectual and artistic inspiration of Italians. Italy became a country of joy and delight under foreign rulers and domestic despots, while her few religious reformers, such as Diodati and Ochino, and independent philosophers, such as Bruno and Campanella, had to find refuge abroad in order to give free play and expression to their thoughts and purposes.

Italian amorous poetry, detached from its philosophical framework and drained of its ideological substance, shrank to mere gallantry and merriment, to intellectual play, and courtly flattery. Its intellectual quintessence dissolved in aphorisms and puns, its sentimental wisdom froze in stilted *concetti,* and its religious anxiety disappeared in the ornamental exuberance of lovelorn heroes and saints, rapturous courtiers, and idealized shepherds. This was the world of Tasso and Guarini, Marini and Bernini, of all the poets and artists who transformed the ascending and world-spanning 'erotic emotion' of the Neoplatonists into a sensuous, radiant, inebriate, amorous fantasy.

A few Italian thinkers tried to emancipate their minds from the yoke of that intellectual love of God and mystical love of man. In Florence Pico della Mirandola increased the potentialities of the human soul in Ficino's hierarchical order of the world, by making man 'the bond and knot of celestial and earthly things' [10] and by extending humanism beyond the classical heritage and Platonic traditions. He included the Scriptures, the Talmud, the

[10] Plotinus, *Enneads,* VI, Book 9, ch. 7 ff.

Cabbala, and the hermetic doctrines of antiquity in a syncretistic view of the universe and a comprehensive synthesis of God, Nature, and Man. Shortly after him Pietro Pomponazzi, in Padua, renewed the Averroistic and Parisian traditions of natural and moral philosophy in a spirit thoroughly adverse to humanistic trends of thought and to the inclinations of the public at large. This late revival of a school of philosophy was in greater conflict with basic Christian tenets than was the flexible and ecstatic pantheism of the humanists, the courts, and the 'academies.' Its principles were even more corrupting, misleading, and morally destructive because they revived the dangerous escape of the double truth that humanistic philosophy had eliminated by its inspiring belief in the essential identity of truth and beauty.

The whole evolution of Italian thought had been away from this 'double truth,' according to which what is true in philosophy need not be necessarily true in theology. On that ambiguous basis no philosophical faith could ever have developed beyond a play of dialectical subtleties. It was, however, a convenient attitude for certain professors in search of protection for their tenets and chairs against stiffening ecclesiastic control and mounting inquisitorial suspicion. A few independent thinkers freed themselves both from Neoplatonic speculations and the ambiguities of a restored scholasticism. The Calabrese Bernardino Telesio attempted to investigate the natural world 'after its own principles' in a system of knowledge based on a consideration of the active forces in nature and life; the result was a hybrid philosophy and a threadbare science.

Humanistic philosophy died in the Campo dei Fiori of Rome on 16 February 1600, on the pyre that destroyed the physical existence of Giordano Bruno. He was the only thinker who broke completely with Christianity in a passionate attempt to establish the unity and infinity of the universe on the principles of ancient philosophy. Bruno's personality was greater than his philosophy, which soon became little more than an object of intellectual curiosity. But in dissociating the divinities from the humanities in his 'heroic fury,' he prepared involuntarily but fatally the rise and triumph of modern science.

XIII. *The Arts and Crafts in Italian Life*

THE Italian masters who inaugurated a new style and perfected a new technique in every field of the fine arts in the first decades of the fifteenth century were aware from the first of the novelty and nobility of their intentions and accomplishments. The prominence acquired by the arts in that period, particularly in Florence, is emphasized by the constant theoretical and speculative interest of those masters in the scientific principles and technical artifices of their work. The reflections and precepts formulated in more or less systematic treatises on these subjects reveal a new, clear consciousness of the function of the arts and the position of the artist in society and intellectual life. Thus, for instance, Cennino Cennini, a Florentine who worked in Padua at the end of the fourteenth century and still clung to the more workmanly than artistic practice of the school of Giotto, insisted on designating that style as Latin and modern, although for an observer of our day the profusion of gold, the color symbolism, and the Gothic features in figures, draperies, and structure still link the frescoes and paintings of that era with Byzantine models, and the traditions of medieval iconography. What Cennini and his circle designated as Latin and modern was certainly the drastic expression, the dynamic effect, and the attempted pictorial relief of Giotto's narrative, illustrative, and allegorical paintings. Although still enmeshed in the traditions of the medieval workshops, Cennini was so convinced of the creative power of artistic inspiration that he broke with the old classification of painting as a mechanical profession, and designated the arts as an activity of the human imagination, as free as poetry, and second only to science in the grasp and intuition of reality.[1]

Thereby the generation of 1400 confirmed in theory what the people of Florence had in practice decreed more than a century earlier, when the charter of 1293 assigned to artists the same constitutional rights as those granted to physicians, pharmacists, and men of letters as representatives of a higher culture. The arts were acquiring a position of prime importance in public and private life, while the masters and workshops were becoming a powerful force in the spiritual and practical education of the people as a whole. Thirty years later that evolution was completed: the treatises of Leon Battista Alberti placed painting and sculpture on the level of scientific studies, and the attitudes of the artists themselves had undergone a radical change. The new concept of the essence and function of the fine arts permeated every aspect of artistic activity as well as the general appreciation of painting and sculpture. It was this general consciousness of the universal nature of the arts that led the new generation to think disparagingly of the barbarous past, to despise the old workshop traditions, and to exalt the new style and concept of art as a revival of the noble and perfect achievements of Greece and Rome.

The zeal that incited the first humanists to recover forgotten manuscripts from medieval libraries and to hunt for Greek and Latin texts in all their travels prompted the artists of that day to disinter statues and other relics of ancient art. The princes, despots, and money-magnates who built up large libraries for private and public use feverishly collected the rediscovered remains of classical sculpture, craftsmanship, and decoration which everyone—as Machiavelli reports—was 'eager to possess to ornament our house with, or to give to artists who strive to imitate them in their own works.'[2]

This antiquarian enthusiasm was transferred to the field of the arts by the Florentine masters Ghiberti, Brunelleschi, Donatello, Masaccio, Alberti, and some minor artists of the same group.

[1] *Libro dell' arte*, ch. 1 and 28.
[2] *Discourses on Livy*, Introduction.

Their intense study of ancient monuments among the ruins of Rome, and of the statues and fragments recently unearthed all over Italy, confirmed them in their determination to revive the style, dignity, and perfection of the ancients.

The idea of the perfection of Greek art was already a commonplace in medieval literature and had been kept alive by Pliny and some popular compendia from which the illiterate drew a rudimentary knowledge in various fields of science, history, and the liberal arts. Polycletus is for Dante the apex and paragon of the art of portraiture.[3] Romanesque churches preserved many classical decorative motifs that became a source of artistic inspiration to the Gothic masters of the late Middle Ages. The classical reminiscences in some of the masterpieces of Niccolò Pisano did not escape the attention of his Florentine successors and emulators. Consequently general praise of what was called in contemporary documents, epitaphs, and treatises 'the ancient way of building,' [4] is as perplexing to a modern connoisseur as the emphatic and insistent statements of those masters that they were imitating the ancients in every field of the figurative arts.

The modern critic is more inclined to connect the architectural, sculptural, and pictorial works of the Florentine masters with the style and technique of the medieval era than with the rediscovered monuments of classical antiquity. The Madeleine in Paris is more like a Greek temple and the Union Station in Washington, D. C., more like a Roman building than any religious or profane edifice erected in Italy in the long period of the classical revival. There are closer connections with Graeco-Roman models in the figures of Niccolò Pisano's sculptural reliefs than in any of the numerous works of that kind created in marble and bronze by the Florentine masters of the *Quattrocento*. Despite some classical reminiscences and intentional imitations, the panels of the east bronze door of the Florentine Baptistery, wrought by Ghiberti between 1425 and 1452, which Michelangelo considered worthy to be the gates of Paradise, reveal the influence of Giotto and of Masaccio and his group, rather than of any Greek or Roman models.

[3] *Purgatorio*, x, 32.
[4] 'Il modo dello edificare antico,' Manetti, *Vita di Brunellesco*.

It was not until 1434 that Donatello dared to execute the first free-standing nude statue modeled since classical times. He called it 'David,' but that slender, shy, delicate boy might just as well have been designated as Narcissus or Apollo and still he would be neither a Biblical hero nor a pagan mythological figure. David has the expressive delicacy and thoughtful chastity of a Gothic statue, combined with the natural candor and the noble poise of an ancient god. Yet though that charming nude reflects classical influences or vanishing Gothic traditions, it is not an imitation of any prototype, but rather an original conception of a creative artist who looked at nature and art with his own eyes.

At the same time, the youthful genius nicknamed Masaccio, who in his stirring frescoes inaugurated the modern pictorial concepts of space and proportion, also created, through a scientific conception of aerial perspective and anatomic corporeity, the illusionistic style of painting that remained dominant until the decline of the nineteenth century. His architectural organization of space and deepset construction of pictorial scenery and backgrounds may represent the turning point in the evolution of the arts toward natural similitude, but it also marks the complete independence of the new artistic vision, principles, and aims from classical patterns and medieval traditions.

All the Florentine artists of this period moved in perfect synchronization toward the discovery of geometrical space, that is, the objective world, as it appears to the human mind and eye in its invariable spatial dimensions. It was into that measurable, finite, physical world that the Florentine masters projected their scenic inventions, each one in a personal style but all in a concordant effort toward a correct, stereoscopic, and tangible rendering of a transcendent reality or a consecrated story. All the subjects represented in that first outburst of local artistic enthusiasm were Biblical and religious. But the interpretation was laical, the episodes were transferred into the sphere of human experience and understanding.

In the medieval arts, including Giotto's frescoes, the relations between the principal figures in a scene are intrinsic, and determined by religious symbolism. This phenomenon can be easily observed in such subjects as the Crucifixion, the Adoration of the Magi, the Last Supper, in some figurations of the 'Majesty,' and in the representation of Biblical and hagiographical episodes. After 1400, in Florence, the same subjects and others of that kind appear as dramatic actions in groupings and compositions gravitating toward fixed points conceived as ideal centers of the scene. The artistic conception of an episode depended from then on upon a new science of linear perspective whose rules established this reference point and underlay the three-dimensional balance of every composition.

The realistic transfiguration of spiritual values and religious subjects certainly implies a secularization of the faith and an extroversion of sentiments and inspiration, but not necessarily in the ancient pagan sense. The new approach to art, faith, and nature was not primarily determined by bookish influences or economic factors. Such a vital and lasting phenomenon in the cultural development of a nation is necessarily of deeper origin in that it involves the whole life and civilization of which it becomes the most characteristic and universal expression. The great artistic revolution generally designated as the Italian Renaissance manifests in the field of the arts the same ascendancy of the Italian laical spirit that had previously revealed its creative power in Dante's poetry, in Petrarca's scholarship, and in the theory and practice of politics. The Italian artistic renewal was still exclusively religious and all the works of art that inaugurated the new style of architecture, sculpture, and painting were a *laicorum literatura* as in the Romanesque and early Gothic period, but with the difference that in the new times the selection of subjects and artists, the interpretation and illustration of episodes, topics, and symbols, the individual inspiration and stylistic realization were no longer determined by ecclesiastical authority and tutelage but by laical initiative, through governmental bodies and popular vote.

This democratization of the arts began in Florence when the main churches of the mendicant orders were almost completed. By the end of the fourteenth century the walls of the chapels of Santa Croce and Santa Maria Novella were covered from top to bottom with shining frescoes. From then on the artistic activity of the industrious and wealthy town was concentrated around the three buildings in which the political and religious life of the lay population had been concentrated for centuries: the Cathedral, whose erection was decreed by popular vote in 1294, and which remained from that time on the focus of Florentine civic pride; the Baptistery, devoted to the patron saint of the town and a landmark since its earliest times; the Campanile, begun by Giotto in 1334, and completed in 1387.

The history of modern art begins with the competition for the north doors of the Baptistery, decreed in 1402, and won by Ghiberti over the most renowned young masters of that time; and with the competition for the vaulting of the dome, won by Brunelleschi, in 1418, amid the feverish participation of the entire population. Meanwhile, Donatello, the third in that triad of leading masters, had revealed in five statues for the Campanile and others for the Cathedral the new spirit that brought life and motion into dead marble and rugged stone. For more than a century the artistic interest of the whole population was kept alive by its incessant association with those mighty monuments of municipal prestige that swallowed enormous amounts of money from public funds and occupied an army of masons, stonecutters, carpenters, foundrymen, and other craftsmen. Since the whole façade and the cornice of the cathedral had to be covered with statues in the Gothic tradition, that building became the seed-bed of all the local talents who found there a field of activity, a source of income, an opportunity for success and glory. There was a common trend in that colossal enterprise. It aimed at substituting for the *cose tedesche*—the German stuff— what was intended to be a Latin style of ornamentation.

All these artists and craftsmen and the powerful committee of the *opera del duomo* were responsible to the whole community and to the political and administrative authorities of the republic, who, however, left them ample freedom to show their mettle. It was a sign of the new spirit that the Biblical subjects of the ten panels of Ghiberti's most celebrated bronze doors were not selected by a bishop but by the humanist Leonardo Bruni, then a chancellor of the republic and the official historian of the town. For the people of Florence, every bit of progress in those buildings, every new problem and competition connected with the artistic life of the town, or the appearance of a new talent in that arsenal of municipal devotion, was an event of the first magnitude. The enthusiasm for art and architecture helped to divert the general attention from political affairs and intellectual controversies, clearing the way for the hegemony of professional politicians.

The wealthy and influential families began to employ these artists to build and decorate places of worship all over the town. Long before the Medicis assumed the *de facto* leadership of the state, their ancestor Giovanni had charged Brunelleschi with the rebuilding, and Donatello with the decoration, of the old church of San Lorenzo, which became the family mausoleum and, with its chapels, cloisters, and the Medicean library, still represents one of the most venerable centers of Italian art and culture. The bitterest rivals of the Medicis employed the same artists on the famous Pazzi chapel near Santa Croce, one of the first examples of the new architectural style. In those years young Masaccio decorated the Brancacci chapel with his celebrated frescoes. Borough fraternities, conventual communities, private citizens, the guilds that decorated the corn exchange and granary of the town [5] with statues of their patron saints, some suburban parishes and, more than anyone else, the crafty and devout Cosimo de' Medici, contributed in transforming the turbulent trading city of Florence into a religious shrine and a sanctuary of devotion in the very midst of the classical and pagan revival. The same Cosimo who had to appease the always influential, if largely despised, mendicant orders made the newly rebuilt convent of San Marco the home and refuge of the dwindling Dominican traditions in art and gave Fra Angelico the unique opportunity to immortalize his radiant visions of piety on the walls of cloisters and cells.

The great variety of artistic activity in so small an area enabled the private patrons to choose their artists after their taste and interests, and gave the artist a certain liberty in choosing his commissions. It raised the social and economic status of the artist and stimulated competition. It made possible the coexistence of

[5] Or San Michele.

many diversified styles and trends. There was room for Fra Angelico's visionary, ecstatic, and claustral approach to art and reality side by side with the worldly, objective, and experimental concepts of the sculptural and illusionistic painters, such as Paolo Uccello or Piero della Francesca.

While the painters of all these trends and traditions were striving to obtain plastic relief by a new distribution of colors and shadows or by tricks of perspective, Luca della Robbia was bringing new chromatic effects to sculpture. Despite the decided classicistic inclinations of the leading masters, many artists were sensitive to the revival of painting in Flanders and Burgundy, which had become known through Florentine agents and travelers. They were impressed by the suave, florid, and vigorous religious realism of the Brothers van Eyck, and by the shining and colorful Franco-Flemish miniatures of precious prayer books. As late as 1476, the Florentine population flocked together in amazement to comment upon Hugo van der Goes' huge tryptic of the Adoration of the Shepherds, donated by Tommaso Portinari to the small church of Sant' Egidio.

The history of art has detected in painstaking scrutiny the individual note, the stylistic interferences, the technical peculiarities, the traditional connections of every one of the many artistic personalities at work in that general renewal of taste, tasks, and purposes. It is always possible to determine whether a Florentine master received his artistic training in the workshop of a goldsmith, like the Brothers Pollaiuolo and Domenico del Ghirlandaio, or like Lorenzo Monaco and Fra Angelico in that of a miniaturist; whether he grew up in a clerical environment, like Filippo Lippi, who discarded the frock and married the nun whom he portrayed and seduced, or like Andrea del Castagno and Verrocchio in the lay, technological, and scientific world of the sculptors and bronze-workers. A trained eye easily discovers the relations between the schools and the masters, the ramifications of their concepts and style in other centers of Italian art, such as Padua, Venice, Bologna, Ferrara, and later Milan, Parma, Umbria, Rome, and central Italy. The art historian knows the debt of Florentine and Venetian painters to the gracious, serene, meticulous, and provincial Gentile de Fabriano; the tempering influence of the

conservative Sienese tradition upon the turbulent artistic milieu
of Florence; Mantegna's daring innovations in pictorial fore-
shortening and draftsmanship.

The continued leadership of Florence in the nation-wide renewal and flowering of the arts despite the extraordinary activity
of artists and craftsmen in every center of Italy has always appeared to be a historical enigma. Influenced by the Aristotelian
climatology, which was very popular in his day, Giorgio Vasari,
the first historian of the Italian arts, attributed the striking
artistic fertility of Florence to its pure and invigorating air. More
recently a latent or conscious racialism invented the absurd explanation of an Etruscan revival in Tuscany, as if there had not
been strong Greek influence in Etruria and Etruscan domination
in the rest of the peninsula. The economic theory that treats the
arts as commodities and artists as workmen ignores the fact that
Genoa and Venice were commercial centers no less flourishing
than Florence. Both mercantile republics remained subject to
Florentine influence and stimulation. No Genoese ever attained
a mastery in these fields of the arts even when, in the seventeenth
century, Spanish gold flowed into the coffers of the Genoese
bankers and traders who built the magnificent palaces and
villas on the bright and busy gulf.

A superior craftsmanship, especially in marble and metals,
was traditional in Florence and contributed decisively to the
rapid flowering of sculpture. Ghiberti's training as a goldsmith,
Donatello's mastery in stone and bronze, the technological ability
of Brunelleschi, the patient and minute technique of all Florentine painters reflect a long routine in refined handicraft and an
age-old tender familiarity with all kinds of materials that is still
characteristic of the Florentine artisan. There is an intimacy
between his hands and the stuff he works in.

But that refinement of craftsmanship was not limited to
Florence. The stonemasons of Venice learned much earlier how
to knock the weight off marble blocks and to give the façades
and loggias of public and private palaces the grace, transparence,
and lightness of lacework. Venetian artisans had specialized since
the eleventh century in mosaics and inlays after the Byzantine
manner, but with Romanesque and Gothic modifications of pat-

tern and with motifs of Western or local origin. They also developed to the highest perfection the manufacture of glass, once a priceless material, and still the most celebrated local product. The decorative sense and skill of the Venetians emerged at an early date and were already well developed when, after 1204, the maritime city began to adorn its squares and buildings with the most valuable monuments of Byzantium and the first antiques imported into Italy for merely decorative purposes, such as the bronze quadriga in front of St. Mark's Cathedral. With their colorful interlacing of brick and stone, of agile columns and polychromatic ornaments, of iridescent stone-slabs and airy pinnacles, with their golden crosses and vanes, the Gothic churches and secular edifices of Venice reveal the almost instinctive tendency of the local craftsmen and architects to catch up, to polarize and reflect the reverberations of the sun-flooded waters, the gleaming blue air, and the play of light and shadow in the clouds, walls, courts, and canals.

Other Italian cities were likewise advanced in different kinds of decorative and industrial handicraft. Milan excelled in the manufacture of metal tools and weapons out of iron extracted from Lombard ores. Brescia became famous for the skill of her woodcarvers, while the late medieval Lombard sculptors, called the *Campionesi* after a village on the Lake of Lugano or the *maestri comacini* after the city of Como, specialized in marble decoration and stone-masonry. Decorative bronze casting, the production of artistic objects for practical use, and of medals like those of the Veronese Pisanello, were North Italian specialties in which the Florentine connoisseurs were less interested than the petty sovereigns and wealthy amateurs elsewhere in the country.

In Rome and southern Italy the Cosmati developed an independent decorative technique in which small slabs of colored marble were alternated with pieces of stained glass and glittering gilt cubes. Mosaic painting was at its height in Sicily in the Norman era and from there spread to such wealthy centers of the Low Country as Amalfi and Ravello. But it was in Rome that the mosaicists displayed their greatest mastery. In their magnificent mosaics for the apse of Santa Maria Maggiore and the chancel of Santa Maria in Trastevere, the thirteenth-century

artists Jacopo Torriti and Pietro Cavallini overcame the anonymity of the medieval craftsman.

But the priority of Florence in emancipating the arts from
workshop traditions and in giving the artist the scope and dignity
of a creative autonomy is an indisputable historical fact. It is
equally incontestable that the great artistic revolution took place,
after 1402, in an exclusively religious framework. Consequently,
it is in the light of that religious meaning and not of natural
conditions or such external circumstances as economic prosperity
and craftsmanship that the Florentine renewal of the arts can
best be understood.

The religious realism that characterizes the Florentine artistic
revival was not suggested by theological doctrines or mystical
influences. Brunelleschi, Ghiberti, Donatello, Luca della Robbia,
Mino da Fiesole, Masaccio, Masolino, Paolo Uccello, and all the
masters and artificers of that first generation of inspired realists
were simple unscholarly men of common extraction, without
speculative preoccupations. Despite all the scientific ambitions
that grew out of their approach to art and nature, they were
artisans by birth and breeding, commoners by rank and education. Free to express their visions unhampered by any hierarchy
or authority, those artificers recognized no other judge or patron
than the general public whose sentiments and needs they were
able to express.

Supported by the enthusiasm and confidence of the people,
the artists felt free to expand their talents and mastery in an
epoch when triumphant humanism was becoming more and more
hostile to the people. The Florentines did not, like the artisans
of Naples and Milan, have to submit to courtly exigencies and
traditions, or to the conservative preferences of the Venetian
nobility. Their activity did not depend upon the taste and whims
of princelets and provincial despots. In Florence they depended
only upon public favor. In that democratic environment and
spirit they were able to give free expression to their workmanlike
intentions and to the religious and artistic feelings of their contemporaries. Only in that free atmosphere could personal talents
develop an individual style and impose it on the people they
served.

In this spirit and practice art lost its mystery, its traditional symbolism and magic power. In their eagerness to make the Biblical figures and episodes more evident, the artists made divinity more human, religion more worldly, and sacred history more familiar. Christ, the Virgin, Moses, David, the prophets, and the saints lost their aloofness and glory and mingled with the crowds. The divine was adjusted to the mortal eye, sanctity was attuned to the human imagination, portents and miracles were brought down to the level of man's vision, and the beatific attitudes were seen in terms of corporeal beauty.

Thus the evolution, beginning with Dante, that had led God back to the world completed its cycle in the field of the arts. Soon the donors, realistically portrayed, were to appear in religious scenes as participants in the holiness of the events represented. One step farther, with Filippo Lippi, and pretty Florentine girls appeared as portraits of the Virgin, while friends and fellow-citizens of the artists became the witnesses to sacred scenes. Beginning with Masaccio's 'Expulsion from Eden' and Ghiberti's dramatic relief, the Biblical episodes developed a purely artistic symbolism of human passions and experiences embracing the whole gamut of sentiments and emotions from jubilation to despair, from tranquil, pathetic solemnity to turmoil and frenzy. This art reveals not divine mysteries, but human realities. The episodes of the great drama from the fall of man to his redemption now tell the story of human misery and glory presented in the familiar environment of an architectural structure or a scenic panorama. The artificial or natural framework is always imaginary, but composed with the elements of reality familiar to the artists and their milieu.

Donatello's prophets looking down from the cathedral tower of Florence, his patriarchs, his St. John and David are all living types modeled either directly from nature or in an imagined synthesis of real human features and attitudes. For the Florentine people, Donatello's marble David was simply 'the pumpkin-head,' *lo Zuccone*, a designation certainly more appropriate to that famous statue than the Biblical name carved on its base. The celebrated St. George looked down from his niche in the civic granary of Orsanmichele, on the most commercial street of

Florence, as an embodiment of chivalrous self-confidence and youthful spirit of enterprise, as a perfectly balanced symbol of charm and valor with no other implications than the artistic intentions of the master and the human meaning carved into its traits.

In the place of ethereal, gilded, and highly draped angels, garlands of healthy, exuberant, naked children display a joyous vitality in singing, dancing, and playing around altars, tabernacles, and pulpits. Such are the roly-poly infants intended to whirl around an open-air preacher thundering down his Lenten sermon in front of Prato's cathedral. The public squares of the Italian towns began to be filled with sculptures, sacred and profane, such as Donatello's 'Judith' before the town hall of Florence and his Paduan 'Gattamelata,' the first equestrian statue to be cast in bronze since antiquity.

The democratic disenchantment of religious art was compensated by the glorification, idealization, and spiritualization of the human figure and mind. The nude that in medieval art represented the fall of man (Adam and Eve), his redemption on the Cross and his ultimate destiny (the Last Judgment) now became the object of intense study and speculation as an emblem of the perfect creature and as the fulcrum and measure of all corporeal form. Figures from sacred and profane history were reproduced as naked as possible, even when an abundantly draped garment seemed to conceal their bodily features. In that emotional, dramatic, and dynamic interpretation of Biblical episodes every trait, muscle, limb, and sinew of the human body concur in the composite effect of the scenes and participate in the single expression of religious sentiments, passions, and experiences. An intimate knowledge of physical proportions and shapes, a systematic insight into their structure and function, and a minute observation of human anatomy and movement were necessary conditions for a style intended to convince through corporeal reality and not to teach by example and allegory. Before anatomy became an empirical science in Pollaiuolo's workshop and in Leonardo da Vinci's treatises and drawings, it developed as a technique of muscular expression with the precise objective of fully exploiting the expressiveness of the human form.

This was what the masters and theorists of the new trend in the arts sought in the statues and fragments of classical antiquity. They were much more interested in the treatment of the human form by ancient sculptors than in the significance of the preserved or unearthed monuments. The famous torso of the Vatican 'Belvedere' served generations of artists as a model for muscular expression. It taught sculptors how to evoke life, energy, and action from a block of marble. Before the founding of scientific archaeology by Winckelmann, no one cared very much about the correct interpretation of an antique fragment or monument, which was mainly contemplated for its intrinsic expressiveness and technical mastery. The statues and ruins that inspired the popular imagination during the Middle Ages and that, like the famous horses on the Quirinal, had become the source of legends, fairy tales, and nonsensical talk, now fascinated onlookers mainly for the formal qualities and aesthetic effect of structural elements, gestures, contours, and ornamental detail. The theoretical insistence on the imitation of the ancients concerned mainly these technical aspects of the arts and not the invention and arrangement of subjects and figures.

The artists were concerned exclusively with giving life, form, fitness, and vigor to their plastic or pictorial revival of saints, patriarchs, heroes, and prophets. Their paganism is purely artistic and their Christian feeling purely human. The mythological motifs that profusely surround the sacred episodes on the panels of St. Peter's bronze doors, executed around 1440 by Antonio Averlino, called Filarete, have a merely decorative purpose, as have Donatello's eight classic reliefs from antique gems, preserved in Cosimo's Florentine residence. Even in the later development of classical subjects and myths, including those painted with almost furious energy by Antonio Pollaiuolo, the admiration of corporeal forms and expressive action far exceeded the interest in pagan life and symbolism.

The stagelike recession of the scenes and the proportionate groupings of figures are in keeping with this plastic corporeity. In the new artistic trends inaugurated by Brunellesco and accepted by all the masters and schools of his generation, an optical realism was systematically elaborated as a structural complement of the plastic realism in painting and sculpture. This optical realism was attained by geometrical perspective and a mathematical distribution of space through exact measurement of proportions.

Attempts to give plastic evidence to a main subject through contrast with a natural or imaginary background were made at different times and by different means. Ambrogio Lorenzetti, for whom Brunelleschi felt a profound affinity, attained surprisingly deep effects in his monumental allegories painted in Siena between 1337 and 1339. Later on, the miniaturists of the Franco-Flemish domain developed a successful technique in detaching figures from their background by an ideal succession of progressing surfaces and an effective distribution of colors. The shortening of paving-tiles in an interior was another trick for the apparent isolation of figures and objects. But the Florentine device was not a simple technical artifice. The new optical realism was achieved through a unity of composition attained by the measurable interrelations of figures and objects on the one hand, and the ambient on the other. Ideas are expressed by symmetrical juxtapositions, parallelisms, polarity, gradation, and the proportionate situation of a determined figure within the pictorial space. Accordingly, even the most dramatic episodes, such as Donatello's figuration of Herod's feast, Masaccio's 'Crucifixion,' Piero della Francesca's Biblical and historical frescoes in Arezzo, and innumerable others down to Raphael's 'Stanze' and Leonardo's 'Last Supper,' are all structurally oriented toward a vanishing point, which assembles and diverts the forces displayed in the scene and resolves the whole composition in a restful and disciplined order.

It was in that equilibrium of dramatic tension and structural harmony and in that geometrical proportion of the parts to each other that the new generations found beauty, sought inspiration, and discovered the true significance and function of the arts. The common goal of all the masters was to create an artistic reality, religious or profane, which summarized and materialized the spiritual needs and aspirations of their contemporaries. Most of their works were intended for places of public worship, even when the subjects were mundane. Hence, those sculptures, reliefs, frescoes, and paintings do not reveal the whims of individual amateurs, but rather disclose the mood and preferences of the multitudes for whom those works were intended. That ideal reality displayed before the eyes of the people was not, as has sometimes been supposed, an escape. On the contrary, it was a striking synthesis of divine and human reality, a constructive and noble attempt to create an artistic hypostasis of human experiences in the light of faith and knowledge.

The scientific interest that accompanied this artistic activity is inspired by the belief that the evidence of the outward shape is also the warrant of its internal truth. The intense, systematic study of anatomy and geometry culminating in the investigations of Leonardo da Vinci shows clearly that the artistic naturalism of those generations did not derive from the interests and mental habits of merchants and bookkeepers, as is sometimes represented, but was rather the expression of a general spiritual desire for order, balance, clarity, and truth. This tendency was not a manifestation of bourgeois pretensions and prerogatives; it was the expression of a living lay society that created its own form of worship in art and its own cultural substance in poetry. The same desire for order, regularity, and systematic arrangement existed in many other fields of human activity, as, for instance, in the orderly public administration of Florence, Venice, and other towns, in commercial organization and the operation of the legal system.

＊　＊　＊

One of the first and most striking indications of the growing spirit of systematization can be found in the development of Italian architecture and in the gradual appearance of geometric ideas in town planning. The transformation of medieval towns from an intricate maze of angular lanes and narrow winding streets into a regular network of parallel avenues and spacious squares began in Florence in the late fourteenth century, when the houses and slums around the imposing town hall were demolished to make room for the great *piazza*. Some of the thoroughfares and squares in Florence and other Italian centers show the same desire for space, light, vista, and movement breaking through the irregular, dark, and crowded sections of old. Economic considerations and circumstances of tenure prevented the complete reconstruction of the towns after a geometrical scheme, as projected for several urban centers and especially for Rome at the time of Pope Sixtus IV (1471-84). A similar plan executed at the same period in Ferrara and, after 1539, in the small Lombard residence of Sabbioneta near Mantua was characterized by straight streets, airy vistas, and rectangular sections.

Only the towns situated in the plains were susceptible to such far-reaching structural changes. Sometimes, however, old-fashioned medieval hilltop towns like Bergamo built their new quarters in the plain and showed a decided trend toward an architectural renascence. It would be wrong to attribute this new style of city planning to an increase in traffic and an improvement in the means of communication. In the mountainous regions of Italy commercial intercourse and ordinary travel were accomplished almost exclusively on horseback, and this was the case up to the eighteenth and nineteenth centuries. The extraordinary development of industrial and economic life in the late Middle Ages had little effect on the urban structure of the great commercial centers. As a matter of fact, most of the thoroughfares and business sections of the towns preserved their traditional character for a long time, even up to our day; while the most sweeping changes in the shape of such teeming centers as Florence, Rome, Milan, and later of Bologna and Turin, were largely brought about by considerations of beauty and grandeur. The main purpose was to open broad residential avenues through the noisy, squalid, overcrowded maze of gloomy medieval mansions and towers.

The slow and necessarily incomplete architectural revolution was preceded and accompanied by theoretical discussions and archaeological investigations intended as a systematic revival of the classical concepts of balance, harmony, and grandeur which seemed to express the needs and predilections of the new times. The column replaced the pilaster, the Roman arch replaced the ogive, the dome replaced the pointed roof, and symmetry supplanted the irregular and amorphous character of medieval buildings and towns. Roman monuments, like the Colosseum,

the Pantheon, the Theatre of Marcellus, and some of the minor
buildings still standing in those days, not only aroused a spiritual
nostalgia for a better world, as expressed in Petrarca's soft-
hearted letters and Alberti's learned books on architecture, but
also became the school of an architectural and aesthetic renewal.
One after another, all the Florentine masters went to Rome on
an artistic pilgrimage. The works of Vitruvius, so little known
in the previous era, were studied by painters, who now set well-
proportioned architectural structures in the background of their
sacred scenes.

This architectural painting offered an easy, inexpensive means
of expressing the new structural ideals. The Italian painters developed numerous types of 'ideal city' in an evident effort to
create an artistic reality that could not be achieved in practice.
The passion for building was by no means limited to despots or
merchant-princes like the Montefeltros in Urbino, the Malatestas
in Rimini, the Sforzas in Milan, Pius II in Pienza, and the popes
in Rome. The enthusiasm for architecture was general, as is
shown by the dramatic story of the ecclesiastical and public
buildings in Florence, Siena, Orvieto, Bologna, and Milan and
by the eager participation of the whole population in the rebuilding of towns.

The treatises on architecture composed at that time are documents of cultural trends rather than practical manuals for builders and technicians. Alberti's ten famous books on architecture
composed around 1450, but published only in 1485 by Poliziano,
are a compilation of humanistic essays on different subjects,
although the main emphasis is on architecture and archaeology.
In his many digressions on historical and aesthetic generalities,
and in learned commentaries on the various aspects of public
and private life, Alberti expresses the moral and cultural importance of the arts for family life, the community, and the
whole of mankind. The noble and versatile Florentine raises
architecture to the rank of the liberal arts by the moral value he
ascribes to it. Architects who, like Alberti himself, had not many
opportunities of realizing the monumental ambitions and the
new aesthetic feelings of their contemporaries in original buildings and urban reconstruction gave vent to their passion by

L

projecting all sorts of architectural inventions in drawings and descriptions. The most curious and eloquent manifestation of that romantic and literary frenzy is Averlino's architectural utopia, written after 1451, sketching the plan of an entire imaginary town called 'Sforzinda,' after Francesco Sforza, his Milanese protector, for which he calculated all the measurements and recorded all the structural and ornamental details. Such treatises reveal the civic spirit that animated the most representative personalities of that Florentine artistic democracy, even when they worked and planned at the court of an Italian despot. Alberti's insistence on the moral value of architecture and Averlino's painstaking accuracy in fancying an ideal town reveal the deep interest of those artists in the welfare of their countrymen and the improvement of human conditions.

The monumental will that stimulated that general renewal of taste and interests found a more consistent and durable expression in the architectural undertakings that created the new landmarks of Italian towns and the new centers of cultural and civil life. A new type of palace was created by Brunelleschi and his contemporaries and pupils when the Florentine merchant-princes and money-magnates began to vie with one another in building impressive palaces in the same spirit of emulation that prompted the medieval patricians to erect their urban fortresses overtowering one another in a wilderness of defiant skyscrapers. An architectural competition of that kind was possible only in a republican environment, such as still existed in Florence and Venice, because no despot would ever allow a private citizen to build a residence surpassing his own.

All the first civic buildings of that architectural renascence still preserve the sturdy, grim, fortress-like character of medieval castles, as for instance the massive Palazzo Pitti in Florence, the battlemented Palazzo Venezia in Rome, or the turreted residence of Federico da Montefeltro in Urbino. They have none of the airy elegance and color of the contemporary Venetian Ca' d'Oro; but they do represent an independent spirit and a serene grandeur when compared with the gloomy castle of the Este dynasty in Ferrara or the fortified residence of Francesco Sforza in Milan. The new style of the patrician mansion was inaugurated, between 1442 and 1452, when Michelozzo built the first Medicean palace for Cosimo, and Leon Battista Alberti and Rossellino erected the home of Bernardo Rucellai. One by one the wealthy Florentines reconstructed their residences in the rectilinear alignment of palatial avenues, reflected in the interior by the long rows of spacious rooms running parallel to the streets or leading off in symmetrical order from a monumental, vaulted courtyard.

Life was not comfortable in those large halls, with their scanty furniture and austere, almost claustral ornamentation. Only the wealthiest of the wealthy could afford glass panes in their vast windows. Wooden boards protected residents from the cold, the damp, and the noise of the narrow, resounding streets. An iron generation grew up in this severe environment of stone and marble; still, they were animated by a desire to live in beauty and dignity as cultivated men.

It was only toward the end of the century, in the best days of Lorenzo de' Medici, that paintings instead of frescoes began to adorn the walls of the stately rooms, but they appear first in the suburban country-houses for which Botticelli created his graceful 'Primavera' and the mythological allegories inspired by a lyrical rather than a decorative impulse. Just as in Borso d'Este's Palazzo Schifanoia on the periphery of Ferrara, profane subjects like these seemed fitting for an informal country-seat devoted to intellectual enjoyment and a courtly mode of life. They would have appeared misplaced and even disturbing in an urban residence, where political affairs and commercial transactions left little opportunity for leisure. A display of luxury and lavish decoration was reserved for banquet halls and bedrooms. Benozzo Gózzoli's famous 'Procession of the Magi' (painted around 1460) in the private chapel of Cosimo's sumptuous urban residence transforms a Biblical subject into a purely decorative display of sumptuous pageantry. Yet the chapel is still a chapel.

❊ ❊ ❊

On the whole, it can be said that in the Italy of the *Quattrocento* the monumental and structural sense of art greatly prevailed over decorative and ornamental concerns. A sense of rhythm in movement and of balance in action is the aesthetic expression of the same spirit that in politics suggested Lorenzo de' Medici's idea of the balance of power and in practical life inspired the general endeavor toward a social equilibrium. The growing authority of Platonism represents the intellectual manifestation of that general solicitude for order and symmetry. The geometrical concerns of the leading masters from Brunelleschi to Leonardo da Vinci embody an evident Platonic trend. It consists in the general conviction that surfaces and figures, which are determined by rule and square, are not relatively, but absolutely, beautiful and reflect in their structural proportions the beauty and perfection of the universe.

The artists who projected their pictorial and architectural concepts into a Euclidean space and consistently strove toward an internal and extrinsic symmetry of composition and detail openly professed and instinctively felt that the cosmic principles of the divine order were reflected in the objective structure and harmonious proportions of their works. Thus painting became in Leonardo da Vinci's mind a speculative science, not only because, in his own words, 'it considers with subtle philosophical speculation the qualities of forms, aspects, sites, plants, animals, herbs, and flowers surrounded by light and shade,' but mainly because all those things appeared in a geometrically correct pictorial space. In a perfect work of art the intrinsic beauty of spatial proportions is coupled with the objective evidence of the figures and forms. Thus, the interdependence of truth and beauty was established in the field of the arts both in empirical practice and in its theoretical foundations.

Leonardo da Vinci is the greatest and universal representative of this scientific realism, not only because of his artistic mastery and intellectual versatility, but mainly because he extended the aesthetic synthesis of truth and beauty to everything in nature and life. His penetrating mind and speculative approach to art did not confine his scientific interests and artistic inspiration to idealized expressions of divine perfection and human reality, but they made every apparently insignificant thing, such as a stone, a grass-flower, a reed, an empty shell, problematic and meaningful. Even what was generally regarded as ugly stimulated his curiosity and imagination. His interests and activities embraced all reality.

The eagerness for knowledge, insight, and experience, the aspiration to universality in artistic practice and in science were a direct heritage of the cultural environment of the Florentine masters whose workshops had become centers of the town's productive and creative life. Conscious of the leading importance of the figurative arts in the civilization of the day, Ghiberti in his *Commentaries* insisted that a skilled artist be versed in all the vast store of knowledge proclaimed by Vitruvius as indispensable for an architect; he even added to the many disciplines enumerated by the Roman theorists the study of anatomy, optics, and other branches of mathematical theory and practice. Very few painters and sculptors, however, took that maximum program of artistic training seriously but contented themselves with skill in draftsmanship and proficiency in the new technique of linear perspective.

Yet interest in all the auxiliary branches of artistic practice was widespread. The workshop of Andrea del Verrocchio in the heart of Florence was the center of the local artistic traditions and also of the scientific activities of the town. Verrocchio was an artist and craftsman of extraordinary inventiveness, creating masterpieces in many fields, and perpetuating the medieval tradition of the versatile master artist. Most of the painters, it is true, limited themselves to painting, as did Ghirlandaio, Filippino Lippi, Perugino, and Lorenzo di Credi. However, from Brunelleschi to Leonardo and Michelangelo, the leading masters worked as painters, sculptors, architects, engineers, military advisers, metal-founders, and hydraulic experts, making their workshops the center of the most diversified cultural and technical activities.

Thus the workshop of Verrocchio was not only a center of art but also a school of science, probably the only such school in the country. In fact, such a communion of artistic and scientific activities did not exist in any other part of the world. The 'mechanical arts' were not at this time taught at any institution of higher learning. Artists availed themselves of the knowledge and skill of the best mathematician in town, Paolo Toscanelli, whose map is said to have helped Columbus to chart his first transatlantic voyage. Outstanding medical authorities helped the Florentine artists in their study of anatomy. Painters like Pollaiuolo and Leonardo became skilled dissectors of the human body.

In a comparatively small town, where people called each other by their first names, there was an intimacy of intercourse that brought all kinds of interests closely together and transformed a busy workshop, open to the street, into a cross-section of all the town's vital activities. It was in these workshops that the works of science rediscovered by the humanists found the most interested public. Yet the artists were all self-educated and none of them ever attended a university or carried on a methodical study of science and letters. Lacking the systematic routine of those institutions, the artists applied themselves to their tasks with natural genius and assiduity. The pragmatic approach to science and learning made the artists antagonistic to the scholastic concepts and methods of science. They shared the humanist's aversion to the logical formalism of official learning, but did not share his contempt for scientific knowledge and mechanical practice.

Thus, the intellectual life of Italy became polarized around three independent centers of cultural and artistic activity. Vocational and traditional education was organized after medieval principles and under ecclesiastical control in the universities, which contributed very little to the vital ferments of spiritual renewal. The literary interests expressed in the dignified and exclusive Latin manner of the humanists or in the unassuming but ornate style of the vernacular poets gravitated, as in the Middle Ages, toward the courts, by which most of the poets and writers were supported. Empirical and scientific knowledge centered around the workshops of the great masters, whose creative imagination transformed technological achievements into works of art and an artistic creation into a scientific problem.

Leonardo da Vinci, the illegitimate son of a highly esteemed notary and a peasant girl from a Tuscan village, entered the workshop of Verrocchio at the age of thirteen. During his long apprenticeship and collaboration with that versatile master, Leonardo had ample opportunity to develop his extraordinary talents. The center of his extensive activities was draftsmanship, in which he achieved a skill and daring that served him all his life in capturing the most diversified aspects of the physical world, the most delicate nuances in human features and expressions, the strangest vagaries of a combinative and inventive imagination. Some of these sketches were so exhaustive and perfect as to satisfy his highest artistic ambitions, and caused him to leave elaborate compositions in a preparatory, yet definitive, stage.[6] The earliest of his drawings reveal, with a personal intensity of his own, the geometrical sense of proportion and the scientific realism characteristic of the Florentine tradition.

There is hardly a phenomenon on earth or sea, even in the air, that escaped him. The notebooks he carried with him on his wanderings to Milan, Rome, and France are filled with innumerable sketches of anatomy and mechanics, plants and animals, hydraulics and technology, landscapes and monuments, architecture, guns and war machines, all enlivened by an inspired élan, but often technical beyond any possibility of artistic development. And indeed, after his removal to Milan, in 1482, his scientific and technical interests extended and deepened in the more pragmatic than aesthetic environment of his patron Lodovico Sforza. Here there flourished a group of prominent scholars and professional men including some professors of Pavia, the mathematician Luca Pacioli; the greatest living architect, Donato Bramante; the Duke's military adviser, Galeazzo da Sanseverino; and his chief astrologer, Ambrogio da Rosate. All these officials and dignitaries frequented the master's workshop, which he transformed into a bustling center of arts and sciences and called, after the Florentine manner, the 'Academia Leonardi Vinci.'

From then on the master went on filling his notebooks with innumerable remarks and records reflecting the whole extent of his observations, meditations, studies, and experiments. But while his increasing preoccupation with intellectual, scientific, and technical interests becomes evident from the quantity and the content of those literary fragments, Leonardo emancipated himself as a painter more and more from the exact and some-

6 For instance his St. Jerome, Vatican Picture Gallery.

times crude naturalism of the Florentine tradition and concentrated his artistic inspiration on the study and revelation of the Human, as manifested in religious or mundane experiences, and even in simple reactions of a psychological or physical nature.

It was this inexpressible but eloquent concentration of visible and problematic humanity, of revealing and mysterious introspection, of troubling and lucid confession that gave such power to his few authentic masterpieces: his 'Virgin of the Rocks,' 'The Last Supper,' 'Mona Lisa,' and the group of 'St. Anne.' If the background of all his human imagery is considered, it becomes evident that the scientific realism of Leonardo's early years and of the Florentine tradition has been replaced by a visionary, romanticized, and anti-classical inspiration announcing a new spiritual orientation, and not merely a new, personal trend in the arts. At the same time Leonardo's countryman, Botticelli, whom he greatly admired, reacted in his own exquisite, fanciful way to the naturalistic crudity, classicistic rigidity, and growing conventionalism of the prevailing style. Yet, it is arresting and symptomatic that the unreal, almost elfin, background of Leonardo's portraits and sacred scenes was conceived by an artist who as a naturalist and geologist had studied the tectonic structure of the Alps and Apennines and had described in numerous sketches and notes the formation of slopes, rocks, and riverbanks, the shapes of the lakes, swamps, and hills of Tuscany and Lombardy.

It is evident to every connoisseur that these landscapes of Leonardo's, from the early 'Annunciation' in the Uffizi to his 'St. Anne' in the Louvre (1510), are more closely related to the imaginary landscapes of early Flemish painters than to any mountainous region ever visited or sketched by the master. Around those human figures he composed a fictitious scenery fashioned more from his soul than from any geographical reality. He liked to portray human beings with an ambiguous, problematic smile, with indefinite gestures and expressions, and shroud them in a vaporous atmosphere. It was in harmony with these softly drawn features, vanishing perspectives, and veiled tonalities that he invented his famous technique of *sfumato*. With its subtle transitions from light to shadow and its almost imperceptible gradation of colors, that technique added a touch of pictorial indetermination and a veil of mysterious haze to his drooping, somewhat ambiguous, or definitely hermaphroditical women and saints.

The 'Last Supper' does not contradict that impression. The sacred event is represented as a dramatic conflict between exploding human emotions and the impassive resignation of a transcendent wisdom. That is what makes the famous fresco appear as the most characteristic Italian expression of religious sentiment and artistic inspiration. It became universal because the features and gesture of the Saviour in that striking scene embody His double nature in the most convincing fusion of divine sublimity and human consecration. Despite the perfect geometrical symmetry of the composition, the vanishing point of its perspective is slightly removed from its mathematical axis, and this has the magical effect of giving an imperceptible motion to the calm, dominating solemnity of the central figure of Christ. These artifices brought entirely new accents and possibilities to the figurative arts. Through interferences of colors and rhythms the monumental and plastic character of the earlier Florentine painting was mitigated for the sake of a more picturesque revelation of an ideal reality. The sharp contrast between light and shadow, characteristic of the natural, human, and artistic Italian atmosphere, began to dissolve in a more flexible and smooth modulation of forms and tones, probably similar in structure and temper to Leonardo's musical compositions so much appreciated in the courtly environment of Florence and Milan.

This style appealed so much to his contemporaries that, despite the small number of his works, Leonardo's popularity as a prince of painting rapidly became universal and even proverbial. The extremely aristocratic refinement of his inspiration and artistic method was no hindrance to that uncontested admiration. Evidently his characteristic softness of contours and tenderness of tones were well-suited to the taste and mood of an artistic-minded society that had experienced, at the turn of the century, the collapse of its political and cultural foundations with the end of the Medicean hegemony in Florence and the annexation of Lombardy to the kingdom of France. Leonardo's

L*

popularity reached its peak when the Signory of Florence entrusted him with the decoration of the main hall of the governmental palace in competition with Michelangelo Buonarroti. Significantly, the political authorities had selected two episodes from the military history of Florence whose pictorial glorification was to compensate for the loss of prestige suffered, in 1494 and afterwards, when foreign armies conquered Italy by simply chalking their billets on the houses along their advance, as a contemporary French observer maliciously reported.

However, when the cartoons of the two masters were publicly exhibited, the patriotic intentions of the government counted little in the general enthusiasm aroused by those masterpieces. With an instinctively sound interpretation of the artists' very intentions, far beyond any political provincialism and warlike enthusiasm, the public interest concentrated in boundless admiration on a group of horses in Leonardo's project and on Michelangelo's gang of bathing soldiers. The independence and intensity of artistic feeling had become so strong that, for the Milanese, Leonardo's heroic plaster monument of Francesco Sforza was nothing more than 'The Horse,' and Michelangelo's David in front of the Florentine town hall, simply 'The Giant.' The excitement produced among the Florentine population by the public discussions on the situation of that admirable statue was increased by the competition for the two patriotic frescoes in the first years of the sixteenth century when foreign interests, the conquests of Cesare Borgia, and the appearance of Medicean pretenders presaged the fall and end of the weak republic. It even seems that the artistic enthusiasm of the Italians grew in proportion to the decay and disintegration of the country, when more destructive and humiliating foreign invasions, new papal conquests, and a general political derangement drove Italy into a state of irreparable national disruption.

A few years earlier that general collapse had been prophesied by Girolamo Savonarola as a divine punishment for all those vanities of the arts and profanities of the mind. But no trace remained of the sudden revolutionary upheaval that brought Florence under the rule of his partisans and prompted many artists to destroy their works and to disavow their predilections. A new artistic fervor swept the country, from the Alps to Naples, and produced even higher waves of enthusiasm and activity, despite Machiavelli's warning of the impending ruin of a society entirely devoted to intellectual enjoyment and generally indifferent to the urgent moral needs and imminent social dangers. Of that spiritual aloofness and high-flown aestheticism Leonardo da Vinci is the most impressive and almost sublime representative. In his voluminous notebooks there is no trace of the shame and despair over the political ruin of his country that inspired Michelangelo's immortal quatrain on his statue of the Night.[7] In a simple, crude, almost cynical statement Leonardo declared: 'Io servo chi mi paga.'[8] In fact, he accepted work as a military engineer for Cesare Borgia in 1502 when the ambitious papal prince was preparing to conquer Tuscany and subjugate the Florentines, who—as Machiavelli declared—'would stand helpless against him.'[9] With the same sovereign unconcern he joined in Milan, a few years later, the governor of the French king who, in 1499, had defeated and imprisoned for life his munificent patron, Ludovico Sforza, il Moro. When in 1516 the son of the Duke, Massimiliano Sforza, surrendered his whole domain to Francis I, Leonardo followed the conqueror to France as his chief engineer. There he died on 2 May 1519, a stranger, a fugitive, and already a legendary figure in the realm of art and science. ˙

For Leonardo, *saper vedere*—to know how to see—was the common basis and goal of both the arts and the sciences. As a speculative painter, he believed that knowledge and likeness were only two different terms of the same approach to the empirical reality that he studied and portrayed. This professional and sensualistic concept of the essence and method of knowledge also marked the limits of his scientific understanding and achievements. With his deep and consistent distrust of what he called 'le bugiarde scienze mentali,' i.e. the lying sciences of the mind,

[7] Sweet is this sleep, still more of stone to be,
 While loss and shame here all around remain;
 To see not, hear not, is my greatest gain
 So pray speak low, and do not waken me.
[8] 'I serve the one who pays me.'
[9] Machiavelli, *The Prince*, ch. 7.

and with his visual attachment to the outward world, he expressed the general critical attitude of his contemporaries toward bookish knowledge and purely mental procedures. But without an abstract common principle by which to co-ordinate the prodigious variety of phenomena he observed, described, or reproduced in countless rudimentary experiments, Leonardo was unable to find what he called a 'regola generale,' i.e. the intrinsic laws governing the mechanical process of his machines, the physiological function of organisms dissected, the secrets of that nature he depicted with as much passion as skill and imagination. He felt almost religiously the cosmic connection of all things in heaven and earth, but he never attempted to transform the immense number of heterogenous facts collected in his notes into a coherent body of scientific or empirical knowledge. He had a clear intuition of the universal value of mathematics as a leading science, but his geometrical horizon was limited by the cult of the *divina proporzione* and his arithmetical practice hardly extended beyond elementary operations, measurements, and verifications. His mathematical knowledge never stimulated new investigations or promoted the discovery of a general principle or of new methods of physical procedure.

Leonardo's achievements as a military engineer, in hydraulics and other fields of practical mechanics, were certainly remarkable. But his technology still belongs to the traditional type of antiquity and the Middle Ages; it was a highly developed craftsmanship, with no attempt to apply scientific principles. For the most part his elaborate sketches of war machines represent models described by Vitruvius and Valturius, blown up to unusual proportions; they could scarcely have been constructed or, if constructed, put to any use. Here, as in his systematic studies of flying, he did not take into practical consideration the essential problems of motion and resistance, or the physical properties of materials. He never overcame the static concepts and traditions of the Aristotelian and scholastic mechanics. The concept of inertia, the principles of friction, the notions of momentum and acceleration on which mechanics and practical engineering are based, were unknown to him. Consequently his scientific and technological work is little more than a mass of eloquent literary fragments and realistic drawings, of ingenious projects that would hardly have withstood a practical test. What Leonardo did accomplish in behalf of science as well as art was the final mathematization of space. That notion, made familiar by his forerunners—Brunelleschi, L. B. Alberti, Francesco di Giorgio, and Piero della Francesca—initiated a profound change in human thinking and revolutionized the concept of motion.

In praising experience and common sense as the basis and condition of human knowledge, Leonardo was not far from the common Aristotelian approach to natural philosophy and scientific problems prevailing in his period. Even his accumulation of facts by perception and description was in line with traditional Aristotelian classification. But in his adoption of the abstract space of Euclidean geometry for the observation and reproduction of natural phenomena and in his insistence on mathematics as a universal criterion of scientific reality and knowledge, Leonardo abandoned the mental habits of scholars and schoolmen in a decisive step toward a Platonic vision of science. As an artist he was not greatly interested in ancient monuments and models. But the impact of humanism is evident in his many attempts to revive and practice the mechanical principles of Archimedes and to materialize the suggestions and projects of Vitruvius in the light of pragmatic experience.

None of the architects and engineers of his century went so far toward overcoming the age-old separation of the 'mechanical' from the 'liberal' arts. In Leonardo's circle and school the problems of statics and dynamics, of motion and projection, of trajectories and falling bodies, of lines and figures, emerged from the books, treatises, commentaries, and academic discussions and for the first time since antiquity entered the domain of direct observation. This workshop tradition lay at the base of the activity and discoveries of Niccolò Tartaglia, the Lombard mathematician of the sixteenth century who gave more coherent scientific shape to the practical problems of artillery, hydraulics, and empirical mechanics. None of the Averroists and Ockhamists of Paris and Padua, or any other professor of natural philosophy in a European university, had ever been interested in firing a gun or releasing an arrow in order to consider, as Tartaglia did, the curve traced by a projectile, or to calculate its range. Only the practical engineer knew how to move a body down an inclined plane, how to hoist a crane or pulley, how to establish the specific weight of a body immersed in water, how to raise a wreck, to launch a boat, and to make a pump work. Leonardo da Vinci is the most famous and ingenious representative of those scientific empiricists, who renewed the methods of Archimedes and came to realize that implements and machines cannot be devised without a rational system of rules and laws. It is certainly not by pure chance that Plato's concept of 'natural laws' reappears for the first time in Leonardo's notes.[10]

In Leonardo's day the Germans were highly praised for technological achievements and engineering skill. The invention of gunpowder and printing confirmed the popularity of German technicians who worked as architects and craftsmen in Milan, Venice, Florence, and other centers as far south as Orvieto. After 1465, Germans established their printing workshops in every Italian town, and provided private and public libraries, convents, and schools with the incunabula of theological, classical, and vernacular texts. Until 1490 when the Roman Aldus Manutius established his *officine* in Venice for the complete Italianization of the art of printing, the German competition was consistent and successful. It operated dramatically in the architectural field, as is evident in the history of the Milanese cathedral. Artillery was a particular field of German technology, in which only Leonardo da Vinci and the Florentine gun-founders were able to compete. But the theoretical penetration of practical mechanics and the transformation of craftsmanship into science was an Italian achievement of those days. The problems and findings of Leonardo were handed down to the school of Galileo Galilei.

*   *   *

The intellectual approach to the arts is a typical feature of the Florentine spiritual climate. The Platonic cult of the 'divine proportion' in man and nature, the insistence on measure and evidence, and finally the speculative intentions of some of the

[10] MS. c, fol. 28; Plato, *Timaeus*, 83E.

leading masters are characteristic expressions of an artistic style substantially related to the *docta poësis* of Dante, Petrarca, and the humanists. The whole of Italy was rapidly drawn into that intellectual and artistic orbit and the Florentine masters were able to impose their taste and technique on the whole country. By 1500, after more than 150 years of uncontested Florentine hegemony, an Italian style of art had developed, very much as the Tuscan literary idiom had become, at approximately the same date, the national language.

During that evolution every important center matured its peculiar style of art and decoration, branching out into the surrounding areas. The small Lombard village of Castiglione Olona reveals frescoes and buildings in the Florentine manner as early as 1435. And while the Certosa of Pavia developed into a showpiece of ornamental grandeur, Pienza—the native village of Pope Pius II, near Siena—realized, shortly after 1450, in small but perfect proportions the aesthetic ideals of its learned patron and his generation. Florentine scientific realism rapidly assimilated the devotional spirit of neighboring Umbria, culminating in Perugino's religious masterpieces of charm and dignity, of lyricism and measure. That vivifying spirit transformed the Venetian traditions of artistic craftsmanship and decoration into a pictorial conquest of air, space, landscape, and life, initiated by the Bellinis.

Many elements distinguish the Venetian artistic taste. Antonello da Messina, a Sicilian vagabond of natural genius and free education, introduced into the Venetian circle the technique of oil painting that he had learned from Flemish painters and developed in masterful compositions and portraits of his own, characterized by mellow tones and a harmonious spaciousness. Andrea Mantegna of Vicenza, educated in Padua, stirred and frightened the pleasure-loving Venetians with an impetuous classicism and a drastic, almost inexorable realism of posture and gesture within a framework of monumental Roman architecture. His plastic energy and archaeological passion exceeded those of the Florentines and found a more appreciative understanding at the court of Mantua and on the Venetian mainland than in Venice itself, where the dramatic excitement and bold perspective of his painting appeared disquieting and inconsistent with the local style and mood.

With its Roman monuments and memories, Verona became the classicist center of the Venetian mainland and northern Italy as a whole. It was there that the bizarre and learned *Polifilo* was written by an anonymous humanist and illustrated by an anonymous artist, both equally addicted to architectural extravaganzas and allegorical allusions.[11] Printed by Aldus Manutius, the book was a masterpiece of Italian typography and illustration, one of the most attractive documents of the Italian culture and aesthetic ideals of the day. The busy *officine* of Aldus had already become the humanistic center of the country, after the fall of the Medici and Sforza, the military expansion of the papacy at the expense of minor dynasties, when foreign influences and domination had committed to Venice the protection of the humanists, the development of the arts, and the advancement of learning.

In that evolution from insularity to cultural domination, from traditional craftsmanship to creative artistic independence, Venice attracted to its orbit the talents burgeoning in the newly annexed Venetian mainland, as Florence had done in its own domain since the days of Giotto. Yet with all the splendor of Titian's genius, the subtlety of Giorgione's inventions, with all the versatility and daring of Carpaccio, Sebastiano del Piombo, Paolo Veronese, and Tintoretto, none of the Venetian artists ever attained the universal volumen, the intellectual power, the speculative inquisitiveness characteristic of the leading Florentine masters.

Religious subjects were no less favored than elsewhere. Among the Venetians, and in North Italian painting in general, there was a common tendency to remove cult and devotion from the worldliness and familiarity that prompted the Florentines to reduce divine persons to the level of human experience. The Venetians avoided that intimacy of intercourse with the other world that the Florentines had learned from Dante. Gentile Bellini and Vittore Carpaccio treated certain sacred subjects as a colorful display of local motifs and events. But those were

[11] F. Colonna (or F. Feliciano), *Hypnerotomachia Polyphili*, Venice, 1499.

minor works, hardly intended for religious edification. Carlo Crivelli who, in the same period, carried Venetian craftsmanship down to Ascoli Piceno in the southernmost section of the Adriatic Marches, produced a remarkable number of elaborate and highly ornamented icons. It was Giorgione's stupendous Madonna of Castelfranco that removed the holy image from direct and indiscreet human glances and enthroned her between heaven and earth in the infinite and delicately spiritualized clarity of a diaphanous, vanishing landscape. Titian's 'Assumption' dramatizes the contrast between the luminous calm of a superior world and the frenzied devotion of beings left in the darkness here below. Ten years later the same subject was treated by Correggio in the dome of the cathedral of Parma as a rapturous flight into vaporous clouds. In the second half of the century the first impact of the Counter-Reformation brought all those holy creatures back to earth and surrounded them, in the spectacular compositions of Veronese and Tintoretto, with all the riches of the world and all the fancies of the arts.

Until then the greater autonomy of the profane world turned artistic talents north of the Apennines toward the most varied aspects of human and animal life; striking examples of this are Bellini's famous sketchbooks and Pisanello's drawings of everyday life. That particular attitude favored the development of certain artistic genres neglected, if not entirely ignored, by contemporary Florentine artists. Individual portraiture, for example, was of little importance among the Tuscans at a time when Gentile Bellini had already attained such mastery and fame as a portraitist that Emperor Frederick III conferred on him the title of Count Palatine, and Sultan Mahomet II called him to Constantinople, in 1479, to paint his likeness and many other pictures. It is a strange fact, indeed, that the features of doges and princes, of statesmen and writers, of ladies and notables, of merchants, artists, and distinguished personages in all fields of life were immortalized in an extraordinary number of masterpieces by North Italian artists, while very few of the innumerable outstanding men of Florence had their portraits painted by local masters.

There are, of course, numerous portraits of military leaders, such as Pippo Spano painted by Andrea del Castagno in the oratory of St. Apollonia, or of Sir John Hawkwood and the *condottiere* Niccolò da Tolentino in the cathedral of Florence. The features of political leaders or famous humanists are shown in many sepulchral monuments, as in the Florentine memorial church of Santa Croce, now Italy's most solemn mausoleum of national glories. But all those portraits, as well as the monuments and statues in Venice and other Italian historical towns, show the local heroes and leaders transfigured in the peace of death or in rigid, heroic, idealized, and artistically altered forms. This kind of memorial and monumental portraiture, so characteristic of Italian art and of the national cult of great men, was not substantially different from the general medieval practice of extolling the memory of sovereigns, prelates, and knights by posthumous equestrian statues and ornamented marble slabs showing their features and insignia of rank. The last and most famous of these ideal portraits presenting an abstract type rather than a personal likeness were Michelangelo's statues of Giuliano and Lorenzo de' Medici in the New Sacristy of San Lorenzo in Florence, both conceived as symbols of a sovereign and human power never truly embodied by those mediocre scions of the young Medicean dynasty.

None of their ancestors and none of the older Florentine patricians and merchant-princes, who spent their fortunes building palaces and decorating churches, ever commissioned an artist to paint an individual portrait or was ever represented by a contemporary master in a lifelike figure of marble or bronze, such as those executed by Donatello, Verrocchio, and other Florentine masters for their foreign patrons. The outstanding men of Florence were satisfied to appear as actors in holy scenes painted by their favorite artists for local churches and chapels. It was not until the end of the century, and then only occasionally, that Botticelli, Ghirlandaio, and other Florentine masters, in line with the courtly spirit that had recently overtaken certain leading circles, provided idealized portraits of beautiful women and local noblemen.

The disproportionate prevalence of beautiful women in that Florentine portrait gallery, climaxed by Leonardo's 'Mona Lisa,' shows the latent vitality of the courtly medieval cult of feminine beauty as reflected by the love poetry of the Medicean circle. But, at a period during which the Duke of Urbino and his wife were portrayed by Piero della Francesca in a famous diptych (1465), and innumerable medals, coins, and paintings preserved for future generations the likenesses of all the Viscontis, Estes, Sforzas, Gonzagas, and members of minor North Italian dynasties, neither Cosimo nor Lorenzo de' Medici, nor any of their rivals in the Florentine patriciate, ever dared to challenge the democratic feeling of their countrymen by such acts of self-glorification.

The human portrait was considered an aristocratic privilege, as is attested in unmistakable statements by contemporary Italian writers on art, particularly by a well-known letter of Pietro Aretino, the famous playwright, pornographer, and scandalmonger who, in 1545, bitterly complained that in his day even tailors and butchers dared to have themselves portrayed by painters and sculptors. The development of portraiture in North Italy is certainly connected with the feudal character of that region, where a great number of young and old dynasties clung to an aristocratic way of life and a conservative courtly spirit.

It was the lively artistic interest of the Venetian nobility that created the conditions favorable to the extraordinary development of portraiture in the Venetian territories. In that aristocratic environment the lower classes tried to imitate and emulate the behavior, tastes, and interests of the ruling nobility. Refined craftsmen like Vivarini, experienced painters like Antonello da Messina and Gentile Bellini, and finally the leading masters of Venetian art, such as Giorgione, Titian, Lorenzo Lotto, and Sebastiano del Piombo, became professional portraitists of sovereigns, noblemen, courtly ladies, and famous men. The sixteenth century became the grand epoch of the portrait. Interest in man was greater than in ideas, and individual self-complacency was at its height. Painters and sculptors specialized more and more in that branch of the arts in order to satisfy the growing public interest in human likeness and the widespread solicitude for this form of eternity. The noblest painters of that century became the most celebrated portraitists, as is eloquently shown by the immortal works of Raphael. Of the two greatest Italian artists of that epoch, perhaps of all time, Titian the Venetian became the most prolific portraitist, while Michelangelo the Florentine never painted the likeness of anyone.

The unwarlike, commercial Venetian nobility were especially addicted to the refined pleasures of the world. In this they were joined by the population, which participated in the prosperity of the ruling class and accepted without resistance the political and social sway of the local aristocracy. There was never a Savonarola or a Simon Boccanegra in Venice. Consequently, its patricians needed only a well-organized police force to hold the masses in subjection, while the Italian despots required armed bodyguards of foreign lansquenets. For external security and the preservation of their possessions overseas, the Venetian noblemen thought they could rely upon the ability of their diplomats, the power of their mercenary armies, and the experience of the fleet.

The ominous events at the turn of the century did not change the temper and structure of this self-indulgent, pleasure-loving, if not yet dissolute society. Its most glorious cultural development coincided with the fatal blow given its commercial expansion by the discovery of America and the Portuguese conquests in the East Indies. It reached its peak after the League of Cambrai had rallied, in 1508, all the European powers and some of the Italian potentates against the republic, and after the relentless advance of the Turks into the Western World deprived Venice of its Mediterranean territories. In that critical phase of its eventful history the Venetian nobility and its entourage of commoners and protégés strove to maintain in external forms what it was losing in real power. The religious concerns, the intellectual ambitions, the political strife that always made life in Florence tense, austere, and dangerous never aroused the feelings of the Venetians.

In this atmosphere the decorative type of art soon prevailed over the substantial, and profane interests and inspiration over the religious. Mythological subjects of an erotic and idyllic nature delighted such painters as Giorgione, Titian, and Palma Vecchio, who adorned the villas of the Venetian patricians with nude goddesses or nymphs in pastoral settings. The heroic mythology and its symbolism that inspired Andrea del Castagno, Piero di Cosimo, and young Michelangelo in Florence were little appreciated in Venice and northern Italy, where the ancient fables and figures came to be regarded largely from a decorative point of view. In the Florentine sphere of art and poetry, mythological allegories retained much of their medieval character. They were often acted out in a more carnivalesque than humanistic spirit in the public festivals, triumphs, and masquerades organized by the ruling families with the collaboration of leading artists. All the masters, Leonardo no less than Raphael, were called upon to embellish those mythological pageants with their inventive talents and artistic skill, only to see their ephemeral works destroyed or forgotten in the Lenten mood after the feast. It was probably only in that festive and transient form that the Florentine population tolerated, at least during the *Quattrocento*, this artistic revival of the ancient gods and the pleasant fables that later inspired the Venetian artists and delighted Italian courts.

The Venetian nobility extended to a whole class that particular aspect of a courtly civilization. The society that liked to contemplate the figures and episodes of that amorous and idyllic mythology held court in palaces and country houses and made a habit of composing love poems characterized by the same elegiac lyricism and sweet languor as so many canvasses of contemporary Venetian painters. The public that was fascinated by the soft brilliancy of Giorgione's 'Pastoral Symphony,' by Titian's 'Sacred and Profane Love,' and by the many mythological allegories of these and other masters, had, since 1502, passionately read Bembo's *Asolani* and Sannazaro's *Arcadia* and discussed for hours in drawing-rooms and at garden parties the new canon of feminine beauty. The Florentines accepted late and reluctantly the corporeal idealization of feminine beauty, as copiously and intricately debated by Agnolo Firenzuola and some minor theorists of the late sixteenth century.[12] For the older generations of Florentine artists and connoisseurs the perfection of bodily proportions was an exclusively male attribute, not granted to women who, imperfect by nature, were held to occupy the rank of ani-

[12] A. Firenzuola, *Delle Bellezze delle Donne*, written around 1530.

mals.[13] Florentine civilization considered itself strictly masculine. Botticelli's 'Venus' is a chaste, timid young girl compared to the voluptuous Venetian versions that show the goddess in languorous relaxation, in the sensuous luxury of a nuptial bed, or in the softening warmth of a luxuriant summer landscape.

The Madonnas of the Venetians have the same luminous complexions, the same sumptuous flesh, as their goddesses. A Venus or a Madonna, a mythological episode or a holy scene, was felt to be but a different expression of the same divine power, a congruent emanation of the universal love that rules the world. No dramatic explosions and no soul-stirring conflicts could come of the conciliatory attitude that allowed Pietro Bembo, fortunate lover and refined love poet, to become a Cardinal of the Roman Church in the most critical days of its religious and political history.

❖   ❖   ❖

At the turn of the century a new palatial style of architecture developed in the main Italian centers. The new sense of proportion, dignity, and art that inspired architectural concepts and projects and changed the external features of patrician residences was accompanied by a desire for more comfort, luxury, and ease to replace the austere and simple life of the past. This architectural renewal gave painters and sculptors an almost unlimited field for artistic and decorative invention. In Venice, private palaces were built in the new style that harmonized heavy but well-balanced masses of stone and marble with colorful decorative motifs and ornamental details. The love of color and magnificence was pushed to the point of frenzy when, in 1506, Giorgione and Titian covered the façade of the German warehouse near Rialto with sumptuous frescoes.

Rows of patrician palaces forced the new style through the medieval labyrinths of Bologna. Entire sections were rebuilt in Florence in a spirit less aggressive and pretentious than that which had created the monumental, massive, and somber residence of the Strozzi as a challenge to the Medicean palaces in the town. A considerable number of excellent architects trained

---

[13] Cennino Cennini, *Trattato*, ch. 70; Ghiberti, *Commentarii*, etc.

in the workshop of the old masters, Michelozzo, Rossellino, the Sangallos, Baccio d'Agnolo, showed how smaller, more modest buildings could be enhanced with a gravity and nobility that would stand comparison with the colossi of former generations. This transition from mass to elegance, from linear severity to decorative grace, from aloofness to amenity, marked a new epoch of taste and civilization.

There were no radical social changes in the background of that development. The transformation of the outward aspects and spiritual currents of Italian life took place in a time of crushing political collapse, in the course of which the structure of Italian society was definitely consolidated. Wherever the Italians were free to organize in comparative autonomy, as in Venetia, Tuscany, the Duchy of Ferrara, and a few small independent domains of the Upper Country, all artistic inspiration assumed a courtly and patrician character. Every wealthy man who made money by trading or through the favor of the potentates expressed his success in architectural undertakings, a palace in town and a villa in the country. He made each of his houses into a sort of miniature court for the renown of his name and family and for the advancement of culture, learning, and the arts. Thus for the first time in her social history, Italy developed a common ideal of life and dignity. It is still alive in the general respect and esteem for the *signore,* the urban gentleman who can devote himself to the enjoyment of all the pleasures of life in an environment suitable to his rank and requirements. The *signore* has only what public or military obligations he desires. He is free to become a soldier or a prelate, a merchant or a statesman. At one time he was required to be an educated man with courtly manners and cultural ambitions.

In those days the whole country participated in the flourishing of the arts and letters. Italy was conquered by the arts and invaded by an army of skilled, daring, sensitive, and prolific artists who served their patrons and the Muses in the face of the German, French, Spanish, and Swiss armies that assured the foreign domination of the country for centuries to come. While the Venetian arts developed more and more along lines of pomp and festivity, Florence manifested the first symptoms of an academic and decorative classicism, to which its greatest masters, Benvenuto Cellini and Bartolomeo Ammanati, brought a certain ornamental grandeur. For a century all the creative talents of Central Italy were concentrated in the dramatic effort to rebuild Rome as the center of Christianity and the focus of a religious and mundane civilization.

The outlines of that task were laid down by indestructible historical memories, the monumental remains of antiquity, and the energetic affirmation of a renewed papal authority. Just as in antiquity, the spiritual and artistic builders of Rome came from the neighboring provinces and especially from that old Umbro-Etruscan region whose men and customs had impressed the first indelible mark upon the early city, its spirit, and institutions. Florence, noblest daughter of Rome, as its historians used to repeat, became her artistic mother and cultural guide. Yet the first architects and sculptors of the era of Brunelleschi and Ghiberti, who had come to the city in order to study its monuments and unearth statues, reliefs, and ornaments, contributed nothing directly to the transformation of the disorganized, impoverished, and depopulated town into a leading center of the Italian arts. The initiative came from the pontiffs whose long sojourn in Florence had taught them to appreciate the vision and skill of Florentine artists and craftsmen.

The task of making Rome the uncontested religious and cultural center of the world was conceived by Nicholas V. He had spent his youth in Florence as a scholar and teacher, and he employed the Florentine artists he had seen at work to fulfill his gigantic project of rebuilding the Vatican and St. Peter's in accordance with his conception of the pontificate as a national and universal power. Until Bramante came from Milan to Rome, in 1499, that truly Roman task was entrusted exclusively to Florentine masters and craftsmen, sculptors and painters. Sixtus IV continued the work, extending his architectural ambitions to the whole city. Between 1473 and 1481, he erected the Sistine Chapel, where for more than sixty years, until Michelangelo completed his 'Last Judgment' on its altar wall, Italian painters expressed their highest genius. During all those decades of intense architectural renewal it became a matter of course for every resident cardinal to build a magnificent palace and appoint himself a patron of the arts.

That incomparable architectural development reached its culmination in the seventeenth century, when the splendid suburban villas and new palatial residences surpassed in number, size, and refinement anything erected before in the Roman area. But the first impulse toward a monumental reconstruction of the town was directed by the humanistic idea of the *Roma instaurata* with all its political, religious, antiquarian, and rhetorical implications. The Tuscan architects who carried out the task adapted that leading idea to the new Florentine concepts of style, mass, space, and proportion. The problem of adjusting Florentine simplicity of form to Roman ideas of grandeur was solved by individual artists in a variety of ways.

The great era of Roman architecture was inaugurated when Bramante, Raphael, and Michelangelo found in Pope Julius II a congenial patron, the resolute heir to the highest architectural ambitions of his predecessors. His affected dislike of letters shows a new type of pontiff. He was the only warlike potentate in the country and so utterly possessed by the idea of absolute sovereignty that, like Caligula, he 'never worried about being hated, so long as he was feared and respected.' [14] Only a man of that unbending energy could have accepted, and realized despite the general, almost superstitious opposition, the quixotic proposal of a megalomaniac craftsman to destroy the dilapidated Constantinian basilica of St. Peter and replace it by the most spectacular edifice of all time. This was the origin of the greatest temple of Christianity, a building that still represents the earthly expansion and pontifical attributes of the papal power, just as the Sistine Chapel in the innermost recesses of the Vatican expressed in its merely religious function and symbolism the sacerdotal sway and dignity of the popes.

The efforts of that unique triumvirate of creative masters succeeded in overcoming the tenacious provincialism of Italian artistic traditions, technique, and inspiration. For the literary dreams of the humanists and the clerical concepts of the Middle

[14] N. Machiavelli, *Letter to Francesco Vettori*, 20 December 1514.

Ages those great men and artists substituted an architectural vision of Roman grandeur. The co-ordination of efforts and intentions in their overwhelming materialization of that leading idea is especially striking when their Roman accomplishments are compared with the scattered attempts of their predecessors. The eclectic yet provincial decoration of the Sistine Chapel, in which all the Florentine and Umbrian painters before Michelangelo tried to outdo each other in skill and invention, had now been supplanted by a national and universal style.

In 1500 Bramante began his systematic studies of the ruins of ancient buildings after a long apprenticeship and architectural practice, first at the ducal palace of his native town Urbino, and finally in numerous churches in Lombardy. His most memorable achievement was his concept of the monumental dome-crowned central structure, exemplified in innumerable churches and sanctuaries in Italy and the whole Western World. Michelangelo perfected Bramante's majestic vision of the dome of St. Peter by the design of its curvature, a stroke of genius that gave to an architectonic mass of gigantic proportions the abstraction of a mathematical curve and a symmetrical solidity, the monumental weight of rock and the airy lightness of a cloud.

The combination of these different elements and qualtities characterizes the masterpieces of Italian architecture. In the Roman domain of that artistic triumvirate no trace was left of Gothic angularity and verticality. Yet in their work the massive splendor of ancient Roman monuments appears spiritualized and animated by an immanent structural idea that is neither entirely Christian nor definitely pagan. It is purely artistic and ultimately determined by a faith in man no less sincere and vigorous than the faith in God.

It was in Rome, whither he was called in 1508, at the age of twenty-five, that Raphael Santi of Urbino displayed the unsurpassed versatility of his artistic genius. At that time he was already in full possession of his extraordinary talents and all the secrets of the arts. In the service of two luxurious and extravagant popes, Julius II and Leo X, he decorated the Vatican rooms of state with gigantic frescoes, designed unusually large tapestries for the walls of the Sistine Chapel, replaced his late fellow-towns-man Bramante in the reconstruction of St. Peter's, furnished devotional paintings and sepulchral monuments for Roman churches and chapels, decorated the palatial residence of Alessandro Chigi, the papal banker, painted portraits of popes, cardinals, and courtly ladies, and, finally, advised an army of artists, craftsmen, and engineers engaged under his direction in the most diversified artistic undertakings.

Thus, the whole of Italy's memories, glories, accomplishments, and creative energies seem to have been concentrated in the brisk, slender person of that young master, whose sagacity penetrated with the same essential understanding the mysteries of theology and the wisdom of ancient philosophers, the world of Dante and the poetic atmosphere of his own day. He drew the innermost psychological secrets out of a human personality as easily as he adapted his youthful forces to the physical and spiritual proportions of his Roman undertakings. The inconceivable fertility of his natural talents is comparable only to that of certain eighteenth-century composers, and what adds to our amazement is the maturity of his work in the different gradations of his short but glorious career. It is as evident in a simple sketch as in oversized cartoons; in the bold project for transforming Bramante's plan of St. Peter's or in his innumerable canvasses, murals, portraits, and decorative designs; in his architectural planning in Rome and Florence, or wherever he set his magic hand until his untimely death at the age of thirty-seven.

In the variety and maturity of his accomplishments Raphael embodied the traditional aspiration of Italian artists to a universal mastery of art and life. He was able to achieve it in expressions so complete and perfect that both life and art seem to be concentrated in his work to the fullest possible extent. In his pictorial visions the calm, unproblematic, satisfying devotion of his Umbrian masters is coupled with the scientific precision and architectural balance he acquired through his association with the Florentines. From Leonardo da Vinci he learned the grand manner of dramatic composition and intense insight into the human soul. He vied with the Venetians in surrounding his sacred scenes and maternal Madonnas with an airy scenery of purest transparence and atmospheric infinity. He kept

pace with Titian in the objective likeness and subjective interpretation of his portraiture. In the grandiose style of his allegories
and sacred scenes, in his mastery of mural paintings, in the
emphatic dignity of certain oversized figures, he equaled Michelangelo and surpassed every other painter of his period. And there
is in some of his famous works just a touch of exquisite unctuosity
and sublime vulgarity in conformance with popular taste. These
traits of his genius contributed not least in establishing Raphael's
world-wide reputation as the greatest artist of all time.

Michelangelo's universal genius arose from attitudes totally
different and essentially antagonistic to those of Raphael. He
never painted a landscape and never portrayed a living being.
He showed indifference to natural forms and phenomena, be-
littled the scientific preoccupations of contemporary artists, despised the paint brush he was compelled to use in obedience to
his papal patrons, and felt an affinity only to the environment
of stone and marble, whether in Lorenzo de' Medici's collection
of antiques, in the workshop of the Florentine cathedral, in the
quarries of Carrara, or the stony world around St. Peter's. His
favorite tools were the chisel that materialized his corporeal
visions and the pen that traced his thoughts and emotions in
elaborate, if rude, verses. He gave his paintings the massive
density of his sculptural compositions and the passionate thought-
fulness of his wistful sonnets.

Every trace of craftsmanship was absent from his concept and
practice of the arts. His universality is not that of his great
forerunners and competitors, of Donatello, Alberti, Leonardo,
Raphael, and Titian. Michelangelo's universality consists in his
belief in the superhuman as the only worthy subject and motive
of artistic creation. His sculptures and paintings are not attractive but awe-inspiring, never didactic but always symbolic, never
edifying but always transcendent. He impressed that mark of
the superhuman, that spiritual vitality, and gigantic energy on
all his work. He gave a Promethean spirit to mythological figures
and Biblical heroes, to the prophets and Sibyls of the Sistine
vault, and to the unworthy members of the Medicean dynasty, to
devotional sculptures and reliefs, and to his allegorical colossi
shrouded in a sacred arcanum of transcendent innuendos.

A religious aura surrounds all his works, even his profane architectural accomplishments. And the tragic sense of life that never inspired a contemporary Italian poet pervades his pictorial, sculptural, and lyrical compositions. In his frescoes and statues every corporeal feature concurs with the expressiveness of the least anatomical details in the glorification of the human body as the divine receptacle of all the mysteries and destinies of the universe. Michelangelo was possessed by the great drama of creation, redemption, and salvation, which he embodied with a life-long ascetic labor in statuary figures, eschatological scenes, and a tense poetic contemplation of death. In all that he was the heir and culmination of Florentine cultural traditions and spiritual ambitions. He followed Dante in his intense effort to spiritualize his experience of human reality and to attain as a mortal an intuitive cognition of eternal and transcendent truth.

The generations seduced by Raphael's polished realism and fascinated by Titian's sensuous brilliancy were struck by Michelangelo's impetuous unrest and tormented sublimity. They called his style 'terrifying,' *il terribile*. A feeling developed among artists and the general public that his works marked the highest possible accomplishments granted to human skill and imagination. The expressive power of every detail, the stirring vehemence of every gesture, the profound significance of his human symbolism, filled the minds of his contemporaries with the conviction that the essence of life, art, and beauty could be discovered through Michelangelo's insight and teaching. But no one ever attained his spiritual standards and earnestness, not even the great Venetian virtuosi of painting and drawing, such as Paolo Veronese and Jacopo Tintoretto, the daring and imaginative masters who translated Michelangelo's tense inward drama into colorful decoration, worldly splendor, and theatrical animation.

A feeling that the limits of human power in art had been attained determined Giorgio Vasari to retrace the whole development of the Italian arts in his famous biographies.[15] At the same time Cosimo I, Duke of Florence, began collecting the paintings and sculptures of great masters, which were becoming

[15] G. Vasari, *Le vite de' più eccellenti pittori, scultori e architetti.* First edition, Florence, 1550; second edition, 1568.

increasingly valued as showpieces and objects of trade. He was
soon imitated by the Italian nobility and by foreign sovereigns.
The collections of antiques organized by Italian potentates and
connoisseurs in the preceding century developed into galleries
giving more and more place to modern masters now elevated to
the rank of classics.

In co-operation with the foremost contemporary masters,
Vasari established in Florence the first academy of arts intended
to perpetuate the traditions of a glorious past as well as more
recent doctrines and techniques. With the solemn inauguration
of that institution, in February 1563, artistic production in
Tuscany came under the protection and supervision of the Duke,
who was now the absolute arbiter of public life and interests
in his domain. The old guild of free artists was transformed into
an official institution and a school of artistic practice supported
by an increasing literature of manuals and precepts. A conservative uniformity succeeded individual expression.

When Cosimo I founded that first academy of the fine arts,
and when a few years later the inquisitorial tribunal of Venice
summoned Paolo Veronese to defend his paintings, the State
and the Inquisition became the supreme regulating instances of
all the spiritual trends and cultural interests of Italy. This was
only one of the many symptoms of the profound changes that
had transformed the public and its intellectual life. Talent did
not disappear. Great monuments of the arts continued to beautify
Italian towns, churches, palaces, and private homes. The creative energies were not exhausted and the enthusiasm for beauty
and grandeur neither languished nor went astray. Rome, Genoa,
Turin, and many small towns as far as Lecce in southern Apulia
perpetuated the monumental sense and decorative passion of the
Italian artists and people. Nevertheless, the power and prestige
of the arts as the dominant manifestation of the national civilization were shifted to other fields of intellectual activity, equally
dependent upon princely favor and the agreement of the public
at large.

XIV. *Political Servitude and*
Intellectual Alignment

THE tragic inconsistency that marks the history of the Italian people manifests itself in the events around 1500, when the country acquired cultural and artistic unity while losing its political independence. From that time on, the Italian people were eliminated as an effective factor in shaping the political destinies of Italy, the European continent, and the colonized territories overseas. In the preceding era, it is true, Italy had counted for little in the continental political scene. But at that time her isolation in European affairs was compensated for by her commercial and financial power, the trend toward a balance of the five leading states, and, above all, by the weakness and disorganization of all the continental countries. The convulsive events in fifteenth-century Spain, the conflicts of France with England and Burgundy, and the instability of the general situation in Germany had deflected the interests of the leading European powers toward other goals and conquests. The Italians who profited by this state of affairs to achieve the cultural and economic reconstruction of their country were deluded into a feeling of security and into the belief that favorable circumstances would continue indefinitely.

In the short era of the foreign invasions, 1494-1527, Italy was besieged and conquered by armies of European potentates, whose internal policy was to combine the creation of national entities with the consolidation of their dynastic power as absolute sovereigns. In the course of one generation a politically unprepared Italy without effective armies was invaded by a whole series of ruthless and successful foreign sovereigns. After having settled the internal affairs of Spain with an implacable cruelty that provoked the indignation even of Machiavelli, Ferdinand the Catholic snatched the Kingdom of Naples from the French and incorporated it, as an Aragonese fief, into his expanding intercontinental domain. After 1503 the Low Country, Sicily, and Sardinia became Spanish provinces administered by viceroys and foreign functionaries, and the native population was deprived of all direct participation in the political organization of the country. The situation did not change when, two hundred years later, the Austrian viceroys replaced the Spaniards after the War of the Spanish Succession. The Bourbons, who ruled with short interruptions from 1748 to 1860, acquired through their laxity, sense of expediency, and good humor a certain popularity interrupted only occasionally by insurrections and outbursts of general dissatisfaction.

The worst forms of fiscal and tributary feudalism developed in the whole domain, without the compensation that a well-organized feudal hierarchy could have offered in terms of responsible administration and a courtly civilization. The whole Neapolitan kingdom was vitiated and perverted by terrorism, misgovernment, ignorance, corruption, and the mental and physical brutalization of the rural masses. Brigandage in the open country and a widely ramified urban underworld were the direct and lasting consequences of that state of affairs. Deprived of all political rights, the population learned to fear and to endure, but never to respect, the royal authority and its adjunct, the higher clergy. The conspiracies of the lower nobility against the kings, the popular insurrection led by Masaniello, in 1647, and the revolutionary unrest of the Napoleonic era were sporadic acts of despair, temporary political adventures without ideological impulse or intellectual preparation. They did not noticeably alter the passivity and resignation of the people. Thus, the Low Country disappeared from the political scene as a constructive element in national organization, while in North Italy a similar course of events deprived a highly developed and prosperous society of its political rights and the benefits of responsible self-rule.

While the kingdom in the South lost its independence to the Spaniards, the Milan of the Sforzas and their Lombard domain fell a prey of three exceptionally energetic French kings. Between 1494 and 1525 three well-organized Italian campaigns were undertaken, first by Charles VIII, then by his successor, Louis XII, and finally by Francis I, whose defeat at the battle of Pavia, on 24 February 1525, ended thirty years of French expansion into Italy. These incursions, first provoked by Lodovico Sforza's call for the invasion of the Kingdom of Naples, were purportedly legalized by the dynastic claim to Lombardy through Valentina Visconti, wife of Louis, Duke of Orleans. In this, as in other cases, the Italian despots paid with the loss of their territories for their belief that they would be able to protect their newly acquired power and create a dynasty of their own through matrimonial alliances and foreign help. Consequently, most of the Italian ruling houses became involved in foreign affairs wholly remote from the direct interests of their own domain. The perpetuation of feudal rights of succession in a society transformed by social changes and a national cultural renewal, subjected most of the Italian people to foreign domination and undermined the relation between the ruling houses and their generally loyal or merely passive subjects.

The French invasions revealed the instability of the whole political structure of Italy and let loose all the dynastic, regional, local, and factious energies that had been temporarily held in check by a general but delusive feeling of security. The fear of French hegemony seemed to justify Cesare Borgia's determination to protect the papal power and to extend his personal conquests by the savage methods of political repression and extermination that had been customary in his native Spain since the time of Peter the Cruel, but which surpassed in brutality and callousness anything the Italians had experienced in their long and bloody dynastic struggles.   •

At the same time, the actions of the French alarmed Emperor Maximilian I, a shrewd and resolute sovereign who succeeded a series of mediocrities on the German throne. Asked by the Florentines to help them against Milan, he responded with an invasion of northern Italy and was able to reconquer the old

M

imperial territories on the Venetian mainland through a short-
lived coalition of the major European powers with the Pope and
some minor Italian potentates. Although only temporarily successful, this reconquest of the former imperial territories around
the towns of Verona, Vicenza, and Padua served to revive super-
annuated claims and long-forgotten rights. These medieval phantoms reappeared on the political scene when an Italian national
consciousness was dawning and Italian cultural development
was at its height. The fatal drama that ended with Italy's political death was enacted on her soil by two foreign sovereigns
personifying different concepts of the resuscitated imperial idea:
Francis I of France and, after Maximilian's death in 1519, Charles
V of Spain, Emperor-elect of Germany.

Much to the world's surprise, Francis I, a dissolute, light-
hearted, but shrewd and highly educated sovereign, forgot all
petty dynastic claims to individual territories and boldly asserted
his imperial rights over Italy, as a descendant of Charlemagne.
With this venerable pretext, the enterprising young king inaugurated an imperialistic policy of conquest opposed to the
imperial rights and legal power embodied by Charles V. The
two sovereigns fought four wars for the possession of Milan and
Lombardy as an imperial fief, until Charles V invested his son
Philip II, King of Spain, with those prosperous territories. With
many destructive vicissitudes they became, in turn, a Spanish
province after 1545, an Austrian appanage after 1714, a Napoleonic department in 1796, and, finally, from 1814 to 1859, an
administrative section of the Hapsburg kingdom of Lombardy-
Venetia.

The few Italian principalities that survived the papal expansion as far as Bologna and Parma, the Venetian reconquest of the
mainland, and the foreign invasions, accepted the imperial
suzerainty with the same opportunistic obsequiousness that their
predecessors and many other princelets had shown toward the
victorious kings of France. The regional or local dynasty and the
courtly nobility around it pledged allegiance to a successful conqueror with the same ready adaptability that allowed a hired
military leader or an appointed official to serve an Italian tyrant
or a foreign sovereign. A Roman nobleman, Prospero Colonna,

commanded the imperial army in Lombardy, and an exiled Florentine patrician, Piero Strozzi, became a Marshal of France. The man who represented Italian courtly civilization at its best, Baldassar Castiglione, dedicated his famous *Book of the Courtier* to Francis I, and after having served the Dukes of Urbino and Mantua as a political agent and Pope Clement VII as an apostolic prothonotary, died in Toledo, in 1529, as an honorary Spanish subject of Charles V.

The next year Charles V came to Bologna for his coronation by the same pope. There he received from the crowds, swelled by visitors who flocked from all Italy, a welcome that exceeded in magnificence and enthusiasm any demonstration ever staged by the Italians in honor of a sovereign come from beyond the Alps to enslave them. The Emperor, irritated and amused by the noisy importunity of the crowds asking for titles of nobility, made peers of them all. 'Todos, todos,' he shouted to the throngs, and left behind him a people satisfied with having acquired an empty title of nobility at the price of a worthless political liberty.

Of all the Italian regions, only Tuscany opposed a scattered, but stout and sometimes heroic, resistance to internal and foreign servitude. Florence was a disarmed city-state when the powerful and colorful army of Charles VIII arrived on its frontiers in October 1494. The population made Piero de' Medici, son of Lorenzo the Magnificent, responsible for a premature capitulation that had been an act of expediency performed in accordance with the customary Italian tradition of purchasing a political franchise. For once the old expedient did not work. Every Italian schoolboy knows the quick, defiant retort of the Florentine delegate, Pier Capponi, as he tore up the humiliating treaty in the face of the victorious king.[1] His words were as effective as a victory in battle. The Medici family was treated as a scapegoat and driven out of the city, and the crucial period of the city's tumultuous history was initiated. A wave of enthusiasm swept through Florence when Girolamo Savonarola, who had predicted the catastrophe in his sermons, organized a sort of theocratic government incorporating the old republican tradi-

---

[1] '*Voi sonate le vostre trombe; noi soneremo le nostre campane*' ('You may blow your trumpets; we will ring our church bells').

tions of the town and taking account of the religious fervor of its population. Through certain unlawful acts of repression, however, the friar disappointed many of his adherents, and he lost ground by provoking resistance against papal intervention. His execution in 1498 marked the beginning of a long series of expedients adopted in order to safeguard civic liberties against foreign domination, Medicean claims, and internal troubles.

It was under these circumstances that Machiavelli convinced his fellow-townsmen that even the customary diplomacy of watchful opportunism and middle-course compromise had to be sustained by the organization of patriotic citizens into an efficient army. But this, also, was almost a counsel of despair so long as the small republic was beset by French, imperial, and papal armies, Medicean intrigues, and Venetian ambitions. The old spirit of municipal independence that seemed exhausted and forgotten flared up in Pisa's stubborn yet hopeless revolt against the century-old Florentine yoke. Siena, torn by internal conflicts, fought desperately for the traditional right to settle its own affairs without foreign domination or intervention. But this last bulwark of medieval civic home rule also had to capitulate to the coalition of imperial forces, papal authority, and Medicean pressure. The heroic episodes that marked the end of Sienese independence are still remembered in the quaint and gloomy lanes of the Gothic town so little cheered by the glaring sun of Tuscany. The cause of Florentine independence was lost when two Medicean popes, Leo X and Clement VII, succeeded in their determination to win for their dynasty this most precious possession in Italy which the pontiffs had always regarded as the legitimate fief of the Church.

The task of taking Florence by force was entrusted to the same imperial army that had sacked and profaned Rome in 1527. Michelangelo's walls and the city's small regular soldiery commanded by Malatesta Baglioni of Perugia, a half-hearted and later treacherous mercenary, could oppose little resistance to the seasoned troops of the world's most powerful sovereign. The final defeat was followed by surrender, on 12 August 1530, and by the abolition of republican institutions and the proclamation of Alessandro de' Medici as a hereditary duke. These dark events are illuminated by the memory of Francesco Ferrucci, a Florentine merchant, who in the hour of danger organized an army of citizens and fought a losing battle of resistance until he was killed by an Italian captain of the imperial troops. The end of the last independent, republican state in continental Italy gave the country at least one national hero in whom to take pride. And he is still unforgotten.

Duke Alessandro was assassinated by a relative, in 1537, after the tradition of Italian tyrants. He was succeeded by Cosimo, who became by papal grace, in 1569, the first Grand Duke of Tuscany. The price he had to pay Pope Pius V for the title, refused him by the Emperor as well as by the King of France, was the institution of the first Florentine 'ghetto,' a Jewish quarter whose last architectural vestiges disappeared only at the end of the nineteenth century. For two hundred years the Medicean dynasty ruled without interruption in the extended territory of Florentine domination, and was followed, after its extinction, by the Lorrainese branch of the house of Austria.

When, in 1530, Charles V became the legitimate and consecrated sovereign of the Neapolitan kingdom and of Lombardy, Naples and Milan came under a single domination for the first time in modern history. After opposing that territorial encirclement for centuries by every political and ecclesiastical means at its disposal, the papacy made the best of the situation, extending and consolidating its possessions through annexation of Ravenna, Perugia, Ancona, Rimini, and the whole region of the old Marches, followed in 1597 by Ferrara and finally by Urbino. Rome, spiritually shaken by the gains of the Lutheran and Calvinist Reformation, dominated effectively, as an Italian principality, the homogeneous and rich territory extending from the mouth of the Po down to a line connecting Ascoli Piceno with Gaeta. The remaining petty states of Modena, Parma, and Mantua, the small republics of Genoa, Lucca, and San Marino, although suffering many vicissitudes and always in a precarious situation, survived the foreign invasions of the sixteenth century. They maintained an apparent, and sometimes only nominal, administrative independence by subordinating themselves to the policy and orders of the Pontifical State. The Duke of Savoy, always an outsider in Italian affairs, was compelled also to take sides with one or the other of the leading European potentates. A new administrative, provincial, and bureaucratic feudalism was thus extended to the whole country as a social and official guarantee of political conservatism and popular obedience. By restricting the number of noble families entitled to political activity after 1506, the Venetian republic also adjusted itself to the general anti-democratic trend.

In some parts of the country the new state of affairs contributed to a regional or local prosperity. But despite the introduction of Indian corn from America and citrus plants from the East, foreign rule and agrarian feudalism did not contribute to the welfare of the poverty-stricken rural population or to general economic improvement. More than ever, prosperity was an urban blessing, limited to a section of the upper classes. The first Spanish governors of Naples and Milan undertook important public works in their residential districts. Rome slowly recovered from the ravages wrought by Charles V and was recast in its present contours, according to the patterns and spirit of Michelangelo, when Sixtus V entrusted the replanning of the town to the most imaginative architects and resourceful engineers. The development of Leghorn as a leading maritime emporium contributed to the stabilization of the Tuscan economy. Genoa's oligarchic constitution, shaped by Andrea Doria, withstood the famous conspiracy of the Fieschi in 1547, and provided the favorable circumstances that made the town the first banking center and financial capital of Western Europe. With Spanish gold flowing from America into the strong-boxes of the local money-magnates, superb palaces were erected as involuntary but eloquent monuments to Genoa's greatest son who conquered the New World for Spain. Foreign domination and growing dependence on foreign interests failed to hamper the expression of Italian genius. The *Cinquecento* was the most brilliant epoch of Italian civilization. But the country was politically dead.

✻   ✻   ✻

It fits into the picture of Italian destinies that the life and work of leading political thinkers of Italy coincided with her long and dreadful political agony. Niccolò Machiavelli died in the year of the Sack of Rome; Francesco Guicciardini, in 1540, after the final subjection of Italy to foreign rule. Both of these great political theorists were Florentines and took part for many years in the events that led to the establishment of the Medicean dynasty in Florence and of Spanish supremacy in the rest of the country. Machiavelli was a functionary of the Florentine republic from the year of Savonarola's execution to the temporary but ominous return of the Medici in 1512. Guicciardini, who started his career as a lawyer, became a papal agent and diplomat, and finally a loyal supporter of the first Medicean dukes.

Both men obtained a deep insight into political matters by active participation in public affairs in the crucial epoch of the Florentine republic and the Roman pontificate. And both became the leading historians of their time: Machiavelli by writing the history of his native town from its legendary origin to the death of Lorenzo de' Medici; [2] Guicciardini by narrating contemporary events in the first comprehensive representation of Italy's common political experiences.[3] The overwhelming spectacle of national tragedy which they observed inspired their meditations upon political affairs and human destiny and constituted the substance of their theoretical works. Machiavelli formulated his political thought in elaborate systematic treatises; Guicciardini, mainly in scattered notes of a personal and aphoristic character. Machiavelli complained bitterly that the state of Italian affairs prevented him from putting his political wisdom and experience at the service of his country. There is in Guicciardini's writings a touch of melancholy and an air of resigned pessimism, the sadness of a man who knows that his cause is lost and that he must bow to fate.

Neither of the two men ever sought consolation or enlightenment in the acceptance of God's will. For both of them faith, whether Christian or pagan, was not submission to divine decree, but a moral force of human order and power,[4] and the

---

[2] *Storie Fiorentine*, finished in 1525, published in 1532.
[3] *Istoria d'Italia* (1492-1534), published in 1561.
[4] F. Guicciardini, *Ricordi*, I, 1.

source of good laws and customs.[5] Neither of them believed in divine intervention in human affairs. For Guicciardini miracles existed as 'secrets of Nature to the depth of which the mind of man cannot attain'; [6] while for Machiavelli they were important also 'in false religions,' because a wise ruler could exalt them, 'no matter whence they originate,' and lend them credence through his own authority.[7] The whole philosophy of history and political science of these Florentine laymen is pervaded with this frank secular spirit. Both were imbued with humanistic culture and familiar with the classics of Greece and Rome. But their radical humanism was free from the scholasticism and literary formalism of their medieval and humanistic forerunners.

These two tendencies of earlier political writings are particularly evident in the numerous clerical and courtly treatises on political theory that were mainly devoted to delineating the didactic and moralistic image of a perfect prince bearing little resemblance to actual rulers of the time. These treatises were chiefly concerned with the final salvation or the earthly glory of a prince, without regard for his manner of acquiring power or his conduct of public affairs. The professional and technical aspects of state administration, political and military problems, and the pursuit of public welfare are totally absent from those erudite and polished compositions. Moreover, they ignore the extensive historical literature in the vernacular, such as the Venetian chronicles of Marin Sanudo and the Milanese history of Bernardino Corio.

The originality of the two Florentine historians appears more striking if considered against this background and the great variety of historical works composed in the preceding era. The father and master of humanistic historiography, Leonardo Bruni, was a classical annalist equipped with bourgeois common sense and a balanced discernment of the importance of events, but in his writings literary makeshifts take the place of an insight into the forces of history and the passions of men. Lorenzo Valla and Bartolomeo Plàtina had a keener sense of these human realities and made more discriminating use of sources and documents.

[5] N. Machiavelli, *Discorsi*, I, 11, etc.　　[7] *Discorsi*, I, 12.
[6] *Ricordi*, II, 123.

But in narrating, respectively, the deeds of a king and the lives of the pontiffs, they contented themselves with bare and rather crude accounts of words and deeds. Their follower, Paolo Giovio, was little more than a professional reporter, and the Venetian Pietro Bembo was a pompous herald of the glories of his native town.

There is in the work of all these and other minor contemporaries much dignity and a high degree of literary polish, but no clear insight into the nature of power and the historical process. Inspired and moved by catastrophes and failures, as well as by the grand and impressive events he witnessed, Guicciardini conceived of history as experience of the past and present, and of his narrative as an explanation of happenings in public life through an orderly clarification and co-ordination of facts. Machiavelli was never particularly interested in establishing facts and in checking the authenticity of reports. The legendary history of Rome, Xenophon's fictional biography of Cyrus, and his own interpretation of the personality of Castruccio Castracani afforded him fully as revealing an insight into the intricacies of history and politics as the most reliable documentary sources might have done. He was no more concerned with historical research than with the polished literary style of contemporary historiography. In both his sources and his own experiments he sought relations that would serve as a basis for the understanding of historical events and political developments.

His historical concept and method was, therefore, speculative and scientific in contrast with the pragmatic and empirical character of Guicciardini's works. This philosophical approach to the realities of history and life made Machiavelli the first political theorist of modern times, rather than the founder of a new method of historical investigation. Like his direct experience of contemporary events, history was for him a proving ground for theories and doctrines, providing an essential knowledge of the facts and a sound basis for the practice of politics. He aspired to the knowledge of a general rule for the explanation and exploitation of political acts and historical events. He did not find it in a pious belief in Divine Providence and grace, but rather

M*

in the naturalistic conviction that men are always the same and are always animated by the same passions that lead them fatally to the same decisions, acts, and results.[8] The attitude of a historian toward the political process would then be similar to that of an astronomer who plots the course of the stars and predicts the cycles of their course. While Savonarola believed he could predict the political ruin of Italy because he held converse with God, Machiavelli thought he could foresee the course of political developments by meditating upon the cycles and phases of historical events.

The result of this purely secular and scientific attitude is contained in his *Discourses on Livy,* begun in 1513 and published in 1531, in which the author discusses the conditions and circumstances, successes and failures, crises and accomplishments, that determined the power, expansion, and decay of the Roman people, the evolution, stability, and efficiency of their institutions, the wisdom, virtues, and achievements of their military leaders and political organizers. All these aspects and events of Roman history are integrated with the corresponding Greek traditions and experience, and are also considered in the light of contemporary developments in Florence, Italy, and the leading nations of Europe. And while he avails himself of the maxims and doctrines of Greek political writers, such as Thucydides and Xenophon, Plutarch and Polybius, he modernizes ancient history to such a degree that the Gauls of Brennus and Caesar seem to be Frenchmen, while the Etruscans closely resemble the Tuscans of his day.

On that universal basis Machiavelli attempted a political science substantiated, as he said, by 'a long experience of modern events and a constant study of the past,' and developed on the assumption that the historical process is determined by invariable human nature and an unpredictable fatality of fortuitous events. The practical value of this philosophy consists in the examples and maxims that teach how to tame the human passions by force, laws, and expedients, and how to master the whims of fortune by timely precautions against unpredictable but inevi-

[8] *Discourses,* III, 43.

table events. The moral implications of the doctrines and measures concern, in general, the welfare of a political community, and in particular, the independence and liberty of his native country, which Machiavelli professed to love more than his soul.[9]

Like Dante's poem, Petrarca's humanism, the Roman Church, and the new style in art, this system of political thought is at once Italian and universal. For, though Machiavelli's works were stimulated by the particular conditions prevailing in his country and intended to enlighten and strengthen his countrymen, his doctrines take into account political developments in every country and epoch, from Biblical times down to his own day, and are concerned with the future of nations. A synoptic and secular interpretation of the destiny of man is substituted for the transcendent and mythical vision of human history. To the universal city of God Machiavelli opposed the political city of man. His universalism results from the analogies he discovered in the historical developments of all countries and times. It has its philosophical foundation in the belief that men have always and everywhere been the same, all bad 'and ever ready to display their vicious nature.'[10] Consequently the general rules he formulates on that basis for the organization of a political community are not utopian and prophetic, but philosophical and pragmatic. Their objective was not human salvation but the 'common good.'

Wherein consists the common good of naturally bad men Machiavelli never explained in detail, because its definition is a matter of common sense and not of a particular philosophy. But he believed it could be attained in a free political organization based on three indispensable conditions: religion, law, and an army of citizens ready to fight for their town and country.[11] History and personal experience convinced him that 'the common good is regarded nowhere but in republics' because even a clever, courageous, and enterprising despot will always preserve his power by keeping the state disunited and will take

[9] Letter to Francesco Vettori, 16 April 1527.
[10] *The Prince*, ch. 17, 23, etc.
[11] *Discourses*, Introduction, etc.

advantage of the weakness of his subjects.[12] With these opinions and sentiments of a liberty-loving republican, Machiavelli expressed his contempt for the Italian princelets 'elaborating in their offices an argute answer, composing a fine letter, showing wit and readiness in their words, contriving a fraud,' clad in silk and gold, living in luxury and ease, and running away in time of distress.

To the corrupting influence of these princelets and to 'the wicked habits of the papal court' he attributed the sad circumstance that the once valiant Italian people had been disarmed and enslaved to the point of becoming 'poor, ambitious, and cowardly.' When in March 1513, shortly after the overthrow of the republican regime in Florence, Giovanni de' Medici became Pope, Machiavelli, who had lost his government office, realized that his native town and country had come under the double yoke of a resentful despot and a crafty, worldly, and powerful pontiff. He saw that democracy had disappeared from the political scene and from the public consciousness of the majority of his contemporaries. He was convinced that in his time there was only one country where free communities could exist, namely, Switzerland, which he so much admired for her republican institutions and equally feared as a potential conqueror of Italian territories.

Thus, when Lorenzo de' Medici, the Pope's nephew and a grandson of the Magnificent, became ruler of Florence under papal protection and with Spanish military support, Machiavelli made a virtue of necessity and composed his famous treatise on *The Prince*. This little book was intended to teach the new sovereign not to become a selfish despot and run the state as a private business at the expense of the people, but to become instead a ruler who would fulfill with dignity his political mission by establishing an orderly administration, by organizing a loyal and powerful army, and, finally, by redeeming his country from the foreign yoke. In debating 'what a principate is, what the species are, how they are gained, how they are kept, and how they are lost,' he teaches his prince a grammar

[12] *Discourses*, II, ch. 2.

of power by general rules and historical examples culminating in practical maxims for the attainment of a lasting success and the prevention of deadly failures. He urges that one condition is indispensable to an efficient and farsighted ruler: that he be an able, courageous, and experienced military leader who subordinates every other aim and thought to the military efficiency of the state.[13] With that, statecraft became a sort of human strategy directed to keeping the subjects united and faithful to their rulers,[14] even at the cost of acting against faith, charity, humanity, and religion.[15] Political power and the whole life of a ruler are conceived here as a perpetual struggle against the adverse forces of men and fortune. Thus the moral obligations of a prince are not those of the common man, but those of a soldier who has to achieve victory at any price and who justifies as strategic necessities the inexorable fulfillment of his professional duties. 'A war is just to whom it is necessary'—Machiavelli concludes, quoting Livy—'and arms are holy when arms are the last hope.'[16]

This is authentic Machiavellianism, free from bigoted distortions and patriotic glorification, a clear, honest, uncompromising formulation of the age-old concepts and universal practice of power and politics. The Italian theorists who elaborated this doctrine in the light of political practice and moral thought called it *ragione di stato*, but they saw it applied to the detriment of their country by the foreign and internal powers that kept it in political and moral subjection. This doctrine raises and solves within a strict political field the grave moral problem of necessity and power. Matured as an embodiment of humanistic culture, Machiavellianism is a system of thought conceived in the rational, scientific, and inquisitive spirit that characterizes the art, life, and cultural achievements of Florentine laical society. It is an outgrowth of a secular civilization no less portentous, revolutionary, and controversial than the Protestant reformation in the field of theology and religion. Both philosophies and attitudes represent the vernacular activation of humanism and the transmutation of scholarly and antiquarian ambitions into doc-

[13] Ch. 14.　　　　　　　[15] Ch. 18.
[14] Ch. 17.　　　　　　　[16] Ch. 26.

trines of life and action. In Italy this activation of humanism took place in the secular sphere. Machiavelli expresses the laical spirit of the Italian people always alive and active behind the sumptuous façade of its ecclesiastical monuments and institutions. While the religious conscience of Europe was jolted by the persuasive insinuation of Erasmus and the thundering rebellion of Luther, the moral consciousness of Italy was shaken and awakened by the spectacle of political misery and depravity unveiled in Machiavelli's pitiless picture of human stupidity, general corruption, and national degradation.

Yet in contrast with Machiavelli's widespread influence upon French and English philosophers and political writers, there is little evidence of its impact on the Italian spirit. In most of Italy, political passions, religious controversies, civic interests, and moral concerns had vanished from the public scene, if not from individual life, making way for two lasting and characteristic attitudes of the Italian masses: a patient fatalism derived from practical wisdom and moral indolence, and—on the other side— an almost anarchical individualism developed from the same sources of human experience, but expressed in creative and adventurous outbursts of natural vitality. No document of that epoch and attitude is more eloquent than Benvenuto Cellini's unreserved, graphic, and self-indulgent autobiography. Like it, Machiavelli's clever and facetious *Mandragola,* Ariosto's stories, Aretino's letters, and innumerable tales show how the arts, sciences, music, poetry, scholarship, even trade and industry could flourish in that turmoil of unbridled individualism that Machiavelli wanted to replace by a higher concept of freedom and society. But public concerns as well as religious aspirations could express themselves only in the soliloquies of solitary souls like Michelangelo and Machiavelli. The real world and the fruits of success belonged to professional literary adventurers and blackmailers like the defiant opportunist Pietro Aretino; to inspired jugglers like Lodovico Ariosto, who reflects human madness in artistic perfection; to ludicrous authors of macaronic verse, like Teofilo Folengo; to nasty rather than discerning playwrights; to sensuous painters and amusing authors. In such an environment a man like Machiavelli could only live in poverty and seclusion, dispelling the evil reality of his days with the noble visions of the past and the comforting phantoms of poetry.[17]

*   *   *

Machiavelli accused the Roman Church of responsibility for Italy's moral collapse and political disintegration. His bitter criticism is in line with Dante's violent charges and Petrarca's recriminations. But no one had yet dared to discuss the very essence of Christian religion in relation to political needs, experience, and practice. Machiavelli indeed believed that its 'principles have made men feeble and caused them to become an easy prey of evil-minded men.' A religion that places supreme happiness in humility and contempt of the world, he said, is unfit to become a pillar of a free human community, because 'the generality of men, for the sake of gaining Paradise, are more disposed to endure injuries than to avenge them.' He showed that the Church had made Christian doctrines an instrument of political power with which to establish its authority by money and force and to keep Italy divided and open to foreign conquests and political domination. Four years before Luther nailed his ninety-five theses on the door of the court church in Wittenberg, Machiavelli asserted that 'if the rulers of Christendom had kept their religion in the form in which its founder established it, Christian states and republics would be much more united and more prosperous than they are.'[18]

That criticism involved both the political failure and the spiritual exhaustion of the Church, without entering into dogmatic questions or discussing the institution of the papacy. Guicciardini, who dissented from his friend and countryman in some essential points of political philosophy, joined him in these sentiments as a Christian and a patriot. 'Three things I would willingly see before I die,' he wrote around 1530; namely, 'a well ordered republic established in Florence; Italy free from all her barbarian invaders; and the world delivered from the tyranny of these rascally priests.'[19] So disgusted was he by the 'ambition,

[17] Letter to Francesco Vettori, 10 December 1513.
[18] *Discourses*, I, 10, 12; II, 2.
[19] F. Guicciardini, *Ricordi politici e civili*, No. 236.

avarice, and profligacy' of the priesthood that, had he not felt obliged, as a functionary in their dependence, to desire the greatness of the popes he served, he would have loved Martin Luther as himself.[20] 'Not that I would be loosed from the laws prescribed by the Christian religion as commonly interpreted and understood,' he added, 'but because I long to see this pack of scoundrels brought within due bonds, that is to say, purged of their vices or stripped of their authority.'

Guicciardini's words can be complemented with the roguish anti-clerical remarks of Lorenzo the Magnificent and Marsilio Ficino, or by Ariosto's first satire on the scandals of Rome (1516) and many other allusions in contemporary literature. All these indignant effusions can be summed up in Machiavelli's assertion that 'we Italians owe it to the Church and the priests that we have become faithless and wicked.'[21] Indeed, vast sections, and probably the majority, of the Italian population contented themselves with the same passive, habitual, external, superstitious, and thoughtless practice of religion that more than once has deprived their faith of spiritual power and their social and individual life of moral consciousness and responsibility. The direct, lasting, and positive consequences of this metaphysical indifference were the extraordinary development of an autonomous laical civilization and the complete absence of the religious and dogmatic bigotry that brought moral debasement and physical destruction to most other European nations. Italy never was the scene of that organized fury and perverted fanaticism that led Spain to her *auto-da-fés*; England to the sanguinary outbursts of Henry VIII; France to the Eve of Saint Bartholomew; Germany to the Thirty Years' War. The average Italian looked with horror and fear on that universal spectacle of human perversity, and were strengthened in their national pride and customary inclinations when they compared their urban sense of decency and measure to the 'barbarous furor' of other nations.

At first the Lutheran rebellion and the Catholic reaction did not seriously affect the Italian public at large, although the events in Germany stirred up lively interest in many sections of

[20] Ibid. No. 28.
[21] *Discourses*, I, 12.

Italian society. The theological foundations of the Reformation, condemned by Leo X in 1520, became an object of widespread curiosity, it is true, and there is evidence enough to prove that there was much talk even among apothecaries, craftsmen, and marketwomen about free will, predestination, and justification by faith—much talk, but little consequence. The success and influence of Savonarola, the frequent emergence of petty prophets, zealots, and possessed seers in Italian towns and villages, the great flocking together of people to hear famous preachers, the impressive number of religious books and pamphlets published in Italy at that time, clearly show the general interest in ecclesiastical matters beyond the customary practices of devotion. Yet the basic principles of the new doctrines raised too many theological questions to be understood, let alone taken into consideration, by people who had brought the highest perfection and most convincing expression to the external, visible, and concrete manifestations of orthodox doctrines. To deprive the Italians of purgatory would have eliminated the only hope of salvation left them by a triumphant secular civilization built up with the active participation of the papacy, the congregations, and other ecclesiastical institutions. Ficino's Platonic theology and the worship of God in beauty or charity seemed to satisfy the rational, aesthetic, and practical interests of the population in their relation to the divinity and the after-life.

To a people trained in the virtues of obedience and respect for authority, the intercession of the Saints was as indispensable as the worship of their painted and sculptured images. And if the very realism of the arts excluded the miraculous power of such images, the innumerable relics preserved everywhere in elaborate shrines replaced the old images of Christ, the Virgin, and the Saints in working miracles and in protecting communities and individuals. As for the pope, the Italian people preferred a bad one to none at all. There was extended grumbling against the habits of the papal court, and satires, pasquinades, and loud protests against the vices of the clergy and the orders increased in number and virulence. Yet the new doctrines had no noticeable effect on contemporary literature. Several translations of the Bible were widely circulated in manuscript and printed editions, and it is probable that the great masters who painted or sculptured Biblical figures and episodes were directly inspired by the Scriptures and not by an ecclesiastical and iconographic tradition. There was no trace in Italy of that sudden flourishing of religious lyrics that accompanied the spread of the new doctrines in Germany and France. Even the poems of Vittoria Colonna, who was under serious suspicion of heresy, are unobjectionable from the standpoint of the strictest orthodoxy and show less direct Biblical inspiration than, for example, Michelangelo's frescoes in Rome. In Italy, however, the figurative arts reflect no influence of doctrines not entirely approved and traditional.

The reform movement in Italy showed no signs of giving rise to a political organization, as it did in Germany, or to a social revolution, as in France. In those very years the social structure of Italy acquired a degree of stability that the wealthy classes strove to maintain and that the overwhelming multitudes of the poor accepted without any attempt at organized resistance. The Spanish armies and the unshaken ecclesiastical hierarchy were the safeguards of the established social order, which continued to offer the only available awards to intelligence, ambition, and skill. Consequently any faint strivings toward reform remained confined to individuals or small groups inspired by mystical and philosophical aspirations rather than by revolutionary and radical ideas. However popular and successful the Lutheran influence may have been in the first half of the century, it never contributed to the creative expansion of Italian genius or to the development of Italian society. The fatal break in the European religious community did not affect Italy in the religious sphere but did indirectly influence every other field of life and activity.

The fight against heretical ideas was limited to small ecclesiastical communities, and doctrinal discussions were avoided. The new order of the Theatins, founded in southern Italy in 1524, was merely a clerical organization composed of churchmen of different ranks, while the Lombard Barnabites, created in 1530, maintained an aristocratic character and orthodox educational trend. The Capuchins and other new branches of a rigorous Franciscan monasticism were relatively few in number but supplied the reform movement with influential sympathizers, especially in the Venetian domain, and even with a great pioneer, Calvin's friend and follower, Bernardino Ochino of Siena. The papacy carried on the struggle in the political rather than doctrinal field, while involved in the struggle between France and Spain and in the conquest of Italian territories. Clement VII gave more thought to consolidation of the Medicean dynasty than to the increasing pressure for thoroughgoing ecclesiastical reform. While preparing for the first sessions of the Council of Trent, begun in 1545, and instituting, in 1542, the Holy Office for the repression of heretical and secessional movements, Paul III pursued the policy of his predecessors in patronizing the arts, beautifying Rome, and securing for his illegitimate children the dynastic power and dignity of the house of Farnese. No one was aware of the powerful social undercurrents and economic implications of the reform movement, although Machiavelli and a few theorists of public life had begun to consider this aspect of politics and history, which had been utterly neglected by writers of the preceding era. While Charles V solved his chronic financial problems by minting base coins, the papacy continued its policy of fiscal oppression and sale of benefices and feudal titles.

The widespread spiritual unrest finally became centered around two foreigners and two leading groups of courtly character and refined culture. One of the groups gathered in Naples, between 1535 and 1540, around Giulia Gonzaga, Countess of Fondi, a woman celebrated beyond Italy's frontiers for her beauty, intelligence, and moral integrity. Its spiritual leader was a Spanish theologian, Juan Valdès, a nobleman in the retinue of Charles V, inspired by the philosophy of Erasmus and by the Lutheran theology. The second group was directed by Renée de France, the wife of Duke Alfonso of Ferrara, a passionate adherent of Calvin, who had been for a short time, in 1536, a guest at her court. In both circles the Italian aristocracy was represented by the most illustrious and distinguished ladies of ruling families and ancient houses, who in many cases felt impelled to make amends by fervent devotion for the adulteries, murders, rapes, and armed robberies that had come to be tolerated as a privilege of their caste. The absence of men of equal rank in those lay religious conventicles suggests that the spiritual fervor displayed by the ladies of the courts was considered little more than a harmless feminine pastime and fancy.

These groups were actually a revival of the medieval courts of love, with the difference that divine love and an elaborate theological casuistry had replaced the old courtly custom of chivalrous and literary entertainment. In structure and form they recalled the numerous courtly sodalities in which, since the day of Lorenzo the Magnificent, Platonic doctrines and ecstatic musings cast a mystical twilight over the hardships and luster of that tense and eventful period. In the Neapolitan and Ferrarese groups the speculative ambiguities of a more or less intellectual eroticism had given way to a sincere and tormenting search for God. It was stimulated by two brilliant preachers. Ochino and Peter Martyr Vermigli, supported by adroit courtiers like the Florentine Carnesecchi and the Neapolitan Caracciolo, substantiated by versatile scholars like Marco Antonio Flaminio and Aonio Paleario, and finally consecrated by high prelates such as Pier Paolo Vergerio and those cardinals openly in favor of an internal but drastic reform of the Church.

The doctrines prevailing in both circles were definitely Protestant, but only the clever and experienced men of the company were really conscious of their heretical and revolutionary character. For many years all of them indulged in the fallacious hope that it would be possible to deny free will, purgatory, the efficacy of good works, or to abolish confession, mass, and religious orders and yet preserve the authority and mission of the Church. In their efforts to save the forms for the sake of the substance, Ochino, Vermigli, Vergerio and their protectors and pupils followed an ambiguous course and used an equivocal, but eloquent and soul-stirring, language. All of them profited from the same evasions, hesitations, illusions, and accommodating laxity that had brought Italy to moral and political ruin. Moreover, the new doctrines seemed to embody the same themes that for almost two centuries had determined the most vital aspects of Italian civilization. An aversion to scholastic and doctrinal orthodoxy and a striving toward a spiritual renewal of the whole system of thought and morals had existed unabated since Petrarca's day. The concern over salvation, which was at the root of the new doctrines, was not confined to devout souls, but was a pervasive element of religious and artistic life. The problem of free will had been discussed in connection with astrology, salvation, love, and morals by the humanist philosophers who followed the rational way of Valla [22] or the metaphysical trend of Ficino.[23] The new generations strove to free themselves from the ambiguous conclusions of both schools, but never found the moral courage necessary for an unequivocal statement.

Those self-deceived persons who believed they could serve Christ and the Pope at the same time, as they said, had to take sides when, around 1540, a harsh papal policy of repression replaced the half-measures and tactics of procrastination and evasion. This sudden change in papal policy owed its origin and character to foreign influences. Its adoption followed the sending of a memorandum, in 1537, to Pope Paul III by nine cardinals and bishops who were convinced of the necessity of an immediate and thorough reform of the Church. Some of the authors were well known for their personal and friendly connections with religious circles in Naples, Ferrara, and Venice. Reginald Pole was the only foreigner in that group in which the Neapolitan Cardinal Carafa represented the Spanish and radical wing of the Catholic orthodoxy.

Although the memorandum condemned the professors of philosophy in Italian universities who propagated impious doctrines, and protested against irreverent public discussions in churches, it was essentially a long and elaborate indictment of the abuses, scandals, corruption, and demoralization of the papal court, the clergy, the religious orders, and the entire ecclesiastical administration. There is no more circumstantial account of the Italian civilization of that time than this lucid, matter-of-fact recital of disorder and confusion. The document is at the same time an appeal to the Christian conscience and a call to human decency, cast in a form entirely free from the violent language of the Lutherans, the rigid dialectic of the Calvinists, and the harsh fanaticism of Spanish orthodoxy. As such, the document, which avoids doctrinal questions and contains the agenda of the im-

[22] *De libero arbitrio.*
[23] *De amore.*

pending Council of Trent, constitutes an outstanding expression
of the spirit of compromise, moderation, and practical wisdom
that distinguished the Italian reform movement. The attempt to
entrust the supervision of schools and books to the bishops rather
than to a central authority was the last manifestation of the comparative cultural freedom that so much favored intellectual life
in pre-Tridentine Italy.

Upon that conciliatory Italian trend Spanish radicalism was
finally superimposed in a sudden move to complete in the religious field the political and spiritual subjugation of the Italian
people. Spanish absolutism was firmly established in Italy, mainly
through the Company of Jesus and the Roman Inquisition, two
ecclesiastical organizations that controlled the entire life and cultural activities of the nation, directed the individual conscience,
and strengthened the papal power to an extent never realized in
the Middle Ages. Almost twenty years were needed before the
two organizations attained the full degree of efficiency and expansion that brought the whole of Italy, religious and secular,
under their sway. It was during that time that the Council of
Trent elaborated the doctrinal, juridical, and administrative foundations on which the authority of the Church could be legally
exercised in all fields of public and cultural life. But when, in
1542, a supreme inquisitorial tribunal was established in Rome
as the headquarters in the struggle against heretical doctrines, it
became apparent that from then on religious conformity and
uncompromising submission were matters of life or death. All
the Italian sovereigns were at that time papal vassals and had to
lend the 'secular arm' to the supreme tribunal presided over by
the Pope. The methods of moral and physical torture, the constant denunciations, the subtle techniques of intellectual spying
and secret prosecution perfected by the Spanish Inquisition in
the many decades of its activity, left no alternative but submission or exile. The groups at Naples and Ferrara were rapidly
dissolved, their spiritual leaders left for Switzerland, England,
Germany, and France, while a few communities of determined
Protestants, especially from Lucca and Modena, followed them
with bag and baggage; those who remained and defied the Holy

Office were subjected to its ordeals and burned at the stake on the banks of the Tiber.

There is no need to recall here the means that brought the Italian religious renewal to a bitter and bloody end. The methods of moral coercion, intimidation, and torture were much the same as those practiced by the secret police and political tribunals in modern 'totalitarian' countries. We are able now to appreciate the human tragedies of persons living under suspicion, of those who go through the anguish of interrogations, the torments of torture-chambers, the horrors of execution. We can apprehend the feelings of the émigrés, received with suspicion or hostility by foreign communities, struggling for a living, and finding abroad the same bigotry, intolerance, and dangers from which they had fled. Only impenitents had the heart to face those hardships. Most of those who had become devotees at the promptings of eloquent preachers, foreign influence, and a vast reform literature gave up the fight and preferred a quiet life on this earth and in their own country to the insecurity of grace and predestination or what was called the liberty of a Christian soul. The policy of two popes, Paul IV and Pius V, who had been Grand Inquisitors before ascending St. Peter's throne, cleared Italy of the last remnants of reform ideas.

The Italian character, abhorring conflict and inclined to compromise, did as much toward achieving that end as the rigors of the Holy Office and the zeal of ecclesiastical and secular henchmen. In fact, the attempts to introduce the Spanish Inquisition into Italy provoked popular revolts in Naples, Milan, and even Rome, where the palace and prisons of the Holy Office were attacked and ransacked more than once. Seeking to preserve its independence, public order, and commercial relations with foreign countries, the Venetian republic prevented any strict and consistent application of inquisitorial procedures, while St. Charles Borromeo, the greatest figure of the Italian Counter-Reformation, was restrained from violent, wholesale repression of heretical movements by widespread popular resentment against the methods of the Spanish Inquisition. From the Alps to Sicily, it is true, many hundreds of heretics were imprisoned, tortured, hanged, immured, and burned alive, but Italy never witnessed mass executions like those organized in Madrid's *Plaza Mayor*, going on from morning to midnight and attended by banqueting sovereigns, the court, prelates, and a brutishly excited throng of *aficionados*.

Even without such excesses the Protestant movement was entirely extinguished by the end of the century. But general uneasiness, moral pressure, and fear also destroyed the intellectual ferments and spiritual *élan* of the nation. Recent experiences with similar methods of constraint and intimidation practiced in regimes of organized tyranny show how the limitation of freedom in one essential field of human civilization finally affects all intellectual creation and national life. The great rise of interest in science and music and the production of architectural masterpieces in that epoch of apparent decline of Italian civilization prove that the creative vitality of the Italian people had not been exhausted through a process of natural decline but had only shifted to fields of activity considered harmless to Church, state, and moral life. The further development of Italian civilization shows however that the apparently innocuous practices of mathematics and music could act as ferments of intellectual, religious, and moral disintegration when detached from the cultural commonwealth of art and thought.

*   *   *

In the preceding era of Italian cultural renewal, the neutrality of the ecclesiastical and political authorities and their active cooperation with secular society had lent wings to the imagination, and boldness to creative endeavors. The Italian despots of the past era never supported any attempts to restrict cultural interests and activities. The medieval inquisition had become impotent, disorganized, and obsolete. In the following Spanish regime of terror and submission, the Roman Church stiffened into a centralized priestly and political organization, whose absolute power was felt in the remotest intellectual and spiritual spheres. Just so, in 'totalitarian' communities of our day the alternative of total obedience or extreme punishment rendered any individualization of spiritual attitudes a capital crime and a useless challenge. The sudden interruption of doctrinal discussions by Inquisitors armed with the conclusive dogmatic definitions of the Council of Trent paralyzed the spiritual life of Italy to the point that Italians never again participated in religious controversies such as those which, since the early Middle Ages, had produced a renewing and enlivening effect on the country's civilization.

The great majority of the Italian people still clung to the faith, its doctrines, and institutions, which withstood all human errors and contingencies. Bequests and donations continued to enlarge the ecclesiastical and monastic states until much of the Italian soil became the property of churches and convents. Yet the enforced conformity of the Counter-Reformation made the Italian people religiously apathetic and satisfied with a conventional and sterile formalism. It did not prevent individual piety and exemplary acts of devotion and sacrifice, but it deprived the Italians of the spiritual advancement and religious refinement of French Catholicism and Spanish mysticism, of the moral and philosophical influence of Jansenism, of the substantial and vigorous eloquence of great preachers and educators trained in the dialectical competitions of stirring religious controversies. The tragic destiny of Italy is manifested in the pathetic circumstance that her religious inertia coincided with the attainment of her highest ecclesiastical power, just as her political effacement concurred with the maturity of her political thought and experience.

The extent of that human and national tragedy cannot be measured by the brilliant monuments of devotion enlivened by multitudes of gesticulating saints or by the pompous courtly and florid civilization displayed in palatial residences and gardens. It does not even find its full expression in the timorous scruples and maniacal self-persecution of Torquato Tasso, a ponderous but not vigorous, languishing but not convincing, poet of love and heroism, of sensuous faith and devout jousting, of refined candor and solemn submission. Poetic license and an unusual metaphorical ingenuity granted his learned imagination an escape from the conflicts of conscience and the risks of individualism to which he was exposed both by the originality of his literary innovations and an indiscreet philosophical dilettantism. The Inquisition twice certified his orthodoxy, but a poet who has to work on probation never feels like a free man, sovereign in the realm of his fantasies. And so he transformed a noble poem of chivalrous inspiration, his *Gerusalemme liberata,* into a devout narrative of historical events, his *Gerusalemme conquistata.* Poetry in his day was reduced to a skilled form of literary craftsmanship for the delight of intellectual idlers and refined dilettantes. It was a game and an evasion, a profession and an entertainment, mostly deprived of human elements, natural features, and lyrical feelings which gave evidence and persuasive eloquence even to Ariosto's fictional extravaganza.

Although poetry had ceased to work as a constructive element and revelation of the human soul, it still had its justification in the aesthetic sense of the Italians, in the ability and sagacity of many courtly rhymers, and in the appreciation of refined connoisseurs. Poetry had become an indispensable ornament of life, an essential element of civilization, ennobling and beautifying even the hardest and most shocking aspects of the world. Thus Girolamo Fracastoro, a great Veronese physician celebrated as the first of the modern epidemiologists, devoted Latin hexameters of noble sound and structure to the appalling story of the disease that, in his day of public calamities and spiritual revolutions, had cast a pall of misery and anxiety on the relations between the sexes.[24] Husbandry and nautical science, beekeeping and hunting, chess playing, silk production, and other prosaic topics of human activity and literary composition were the pretext for a much admired display of poetical virtuosity. Literary history gives a discriminating appreciation of these didactic poems and discusses the purposes and accomplishments of that frigid Muse. As a cultural phenomenon the expansion of poetical polish over so many professional interests reveals both the generalization of the artistic sense and passion of the Italians, and the supremacy of literary technique over a human and spiritual substance of inspiration.

A humanist enthusiasm inspired the Latin and vernacular poems of the contemporary philosophers who were prompted by a moral anxiety and a lyrical love of knowledge and truth to give

---

[24] *Syphilis, sive de Morbo Gallico,* published in 1530.

their doctrines the support and glamor of poetic language. The greatest of those philosophers, such as Bruno and Campanella, are universally known for their works and fate. They were preceded by a few bold apostles of pantheism and naturalism, whose religious contemplation of nature and enthusiastic confidence in the human mind transformed a loose system of thought into a poetically harmonious vision of the world. In this mood and form the Ferrarese Palingenio Stellato attempted to teach a philosophical communion between man and God, only to be condemned as a heretic and posthumously burned at the stake; he was one of the first philosophical victims of the Inquisition. A profound religious solicitude and a vast eclectic culture substantiate the didactic efforts of Aonio Paleario, another poet who ended his life on the Roman scaffold because of his poem on the immortality of the soul and some eloquent treatises and letters that revealed the intimate co-ordination of humanistic culture with frankly Protestant trends. The same mental agitation and moral concerns are evident in the fluid hexameters of Scipione Capece's poems on the elements, in which the basic concepts of a naturalistic philosophy appear as poetic motifs, constituting an overture to a physical explanation of the cosmic order. He was condemned, with his books and doctrines, after the suppression of his Neapolitan scholarly group, the *Accademia Pontaniana.*

Until his flight to Paris, Campanella, crippled by torture but unbroken in faith and hope, paid with twenty-seven years of solitary confinement in political and inquisitorial prisons for his visionary projects for the moral redemption of mankind in a communistic 'City of the Sun,' or in a Spanish monarchy conceived as a universal human brotherhood. Giordano Bruno's attitude of defiance up to his last breath showed a world grown used to casuistry, ambiguity, and passive obedience how a man could die for his opinions and for the human right to express them in a form free and honest, even if substantially objectionable. Together with all those philosophers and poets who did not bow to contemporary conformity, he represents the spiritual heroism and fighting spirit of men who had a cause to defend. The naval battle of Lepanto against the Turks, on 7 October 1573, had shown that the Italians could also rekindle their fighting spirit in warlike undertakings, when the cause for which they fought seemed deserving of the sacrifice.

The usual designation of this epoch as an era of intellectual and moral decadence seems to be inappropriate and unfair, especially if we consider the multitude of widely diversified talents and the narrow framework within which they were constrained to work and teach. The institution of the Index of prohibited books and the individual condemnation of old and new authors by the ecclesiastical and political authorities deprived the Italian public of such poets, storytellers, humanists, and philosophers as Dante, Boccaccio, Lorenzo Valla, and Machiavelli, who represented the very substance of Italian civilization. None of the contemporary thinkers and teachers whose doctrines and interpretations differed in content or methods from the approved system of theological or scientific knowledge escaped molestation or condemnation by the Church, and in many cases also by the secular authorities. A revival of independent scholasticism had started with Pomponazzi in Padua and Bologna, and developed as an academic trend of thought in the very years when Protestant doctrines and humanistic philosophical poetry dominated Italian intellectual interests and life. This new scholasticism reacted against the hegemony of Ficino's Platonism and revived the speculative naturalism of the medieval Averroistic school of thought, especially in the medical faculties. It opposed to the Christianized system of Aristotelian doctrines some definitely pagan and heretical views: for instance, the basic assumption of the mortality of the individual soul and the questioning of eternity and creation. Those principles involved all the problems of fate, free will, and salvation then intensively discussed by those favoring the doctrinal reformation of the Church.

To break this philosophical conspiracy against its dogmatic structure the Church proceeded with vigor against all these currents of thought. All the outstanding representatives of the renewed Averroism, such as Agostino Nifo and Cremonini, perpetuated in their chairs at Padua the old subterfuge of 'double truth' that worked as a source of intellectual ambiguities, of disintegrating skepticism, and moral opportunism. That professorial attitude of self-protection was the counterpart of the spirit of sacrifice that exposed the independent thinkers of that era to the rigors of the Inquisition. That the protection of the only independent Italian republic was not sufficient to save a free spirit from persecution is shown by the case of Paolo Sarpi, the critical historian of the Council of Trent and follower of the condemned doctrines of Ockham, who in 1607 was crippled by five assassins hired by the vengeful adversaries.

It was under that regime of spiritual constraint and suspicion that Andrea Cesalpino and Ulisse Aldrovandi preferred to specialize in the descriptive natural sciences—botany and zoology—rather than devote themselves to philosophical speculations that would bring them into conflict with the authorities. Gerolamo Cardano, the talented mathematician and prolific author, slipped through the nets of the intellectual police by emphasizing the practical aspects of his scientific versatility, as did the masters of the *magia naturalis*, Francesco Patrizi and G. B. Porta, although they made no secret of their hatred of the verbalism and abstruse formalism of the official philosophy taught in schools and universities. It is an eloquent expression of the general uneasiness provoked by the policy of intellectual control and scientific conformity that Andreas Vesalius, the Flemish founder of modern anatomy, preferred to have his famous treatise printed in Basel, in 1543, rather than in Italy, where he had taught for many years with remarkable success. In that atmosphere of general insecurity, impersonal erudition and encyclopaedic compilation replaced the humanistic spirit of discovery and moral renewal that had inspired vast sections of Italian society in the preceding era.

It would be erroneous to consider all those trends and undertakings as mere scholarly concerns. The participation of all kinds of people in the intellectual interests is attested by the increasing number of active publishers and of typographical workshops directed by learned men and skilled craftsmen. The production of the Aldi in Venice, the Giunti in Florence, the Baldo in Rome, and of numerous provincial printers was immense, and extended to all kinds of knowledge and interests. The new regulations governing authors and books came as a blow to all parties involved and promoted the clandestine printing and selling of works of literature and philosophy, adding a new element of

moral corruption and public insincerity to the many that already
troubled the Italian conscience and mind. Strange practices of
witchcraft and a swarm of pseudoscientific superstitions spread
over the country in that epoch of intellectual turmoil. These
underground activities of religion and science represent a popular
and natural process of cultural disintegration in the sudden
evolution of Italian society from anarchy to bigotry.

In that evolution the Jesuits were the motive power. It is one
of the most singular events in Italian history that an organization
created and dominated by foreigners should have become a
decisive factor in national culture and the most powerful instrument of Italian cultural expansion in the rest of the world. In
its early stage the Company of Jesus was a typical Spanish institution characterized by its military organization and by the
fighting spirit and fanatical devotion of its founders. Spain was at
that time a nation of soldiers and conquerors, whose national
discipline, unconditional obedience, and fighting experience were
the antithesis of the anarchic individualism, regional particularism, and military weakness of the contemporary Italians. Ignatius
of Loyola, a former warrior, conceived of his organization as a
papal militia, with military virtues and religious forbearance co-
operating in a systematic conquest of souls for Christ. His institutions are centered in his *exercitia,* a devotional training and
spiritual drill opposed to the free expansion of religious feelings
fostered by humanist influence and Protestant trends. Therefore,
the principal task of the new order, approved by Paul III in 1540,
was the establishment of religious and laical education based on
a firm mental discipline and a clear consciousness of its final
objective: the organization of mankind as a city of Jesus governed
by His vicar, the pope.

The nucleus of the company consisted of Spaniards with an
inconspicuous minority of Frenchmen who had followed Loyola
from Paris. No Italians were represented in the group. The first
generals of the order were Spaniards, as were its spiritual leaders
after Loyola's death—Mariana, Suarez, Medina, and Escobar.
Several circumstances concurred in the establishment of headquarters in Rome instead of Spain, although the protection of the
powerful and far-flung Spanish monarchy would have helped the

missionary activities of the order. The reason for that strategic
move lay apparently in the desire to reconquer Italy for the faith,
in the growing French resistance to Jesuit influence, in the opposition of the powerful mendicant orders in Spain to a potential
competitor, and finally in the prestige of a Roman institution
under direct papal protection. Although the Spaniards could
offer their zealous devotion, the *esprit de corps* of a military
order, the age-old fanaticism of the Spanish *reconquista*, and
the recent experiences of conquest and domination, they were at
a loss in the educational field. At that time Spain had little
scholarship, no humanist tradition, no scientific interests or artistic
production, no secular civilization comparable in variety and
influence to that of Italy. Consequently, the cultural substance
of Jesuit education was definitely Italian and directly dependent
upon Italian trends, interests, and accomplishments.

The rapid expansion of the order in a country already satu-
rated with monastic organizations was a direct result of the position accorded scholarship and culture in Jesuit activities. In their
systematic ardor to place all human achievements in the service
of God, the Jesuits from the very beginning absorbed the humanist traditions, the philosophical and scientific interests, the artistic
enthusiasm, and all the other secular aspirations and concerns
that had led Italian civilization away from Catholic orthodoxy,
Christian morality, and religious devotion. The Italians felt attracted by the peculiar character of this organization which was
able to reconcile strict obedience with a certain amount of personal independence, active piety with secular activities, military
discipline with intellectual pursuits, sedentary occupations with
travel and exploration. Furthermore, the Jesuits represented a
sort of ecclesiastical and cultural nobility enjoying all the privileges of the monastic and mendicant orders but at the same time
stressing their militant and military character. Thus they preserved themselves from the animosity to the traditional orders
and their *frati* felt by most cultivated Italians and large sections
of the Italian society.

Although highly instrumental in the repression of heretical
movements, the Jesuits kept aloof from the inquisitorial tribunals,
ordinarily composed of members of the mendicant orders, par-

ticularly Dominicans. In this way the company evaded responsibility for the widely detested and generally feared activities of
the Holy Office. What the Inquisition achieved by terror and
legalism, the Jesuits attempted by persuasion and education.
Within a short time they became the religious élite of Italy and
the wealthiest and most powerful organization in the country.
Ten years after Loyola's death they began construction of their
most imposing bulwarks, churches, and colleges, expressing in a
new architectural language the profound influence of the order
on the national civilization and the powerful support given to
the revival of religious orthodoxy by the leading classes of Italian
society.

That new style was inaugurated by Giacomo Barozzi of Vignola, who, with Giacomo della Porta, planned and built, between 1568 and 1575, the first monumental Jesuit church, the
famous Gesù of Rome. Like all other monuments of that type, this
structure preserves the traditional dignity and regularity of Italian
architecture, but relinquishes its austerity and linear straightness
for the sake of a colorful, agitated richness. The visitor stepping
into that sanctuary is caught in an enchanted world of marvels
and mystery created by a magic co-ordination of the most diversified artistic effects: resplendent decoration, a surprising variety
of architectural and ornamental features, intense flashes of
gleaming gold, vari-colored marbles, pantomimes of gesticulating statues in startling and convulsive attitudes, and shining
frescoes teeming with figures, all embraced in a whirlwind of
thundering music from powerful organs and concealed choirs.
In other churches of the same type erected in great number in
Rome and imitated all over Italy and the Catholic world, highly
ornamented loggias and niches, chapels and recesses, spiral
columns, gilded stuccos, canopies, and festoons complete the
spectacular display of wealth, pomp, and charm characteristic
of the 'baroque.'

The 'magic' illusion of that new style consists mainly in the
fact that all its agitated motion, dynamic contortions, fluttering
draperies, declamatory attitudes, and flamboyant turgidity have
no internal motivation or rational justification and seem to be
produced by occult forces acting from nowhere in paroxysms

of restless emotion. The architectural structures, sacred or profane, appear as stages and side-scenes of dramatic actions performed with a rich equipment of props and ornaments by dancing, whirling, gliding, juggling, and posing images of saints, angels, heroes, and historical figures. This emphatic, exuberant, and suggestive style appears as a formal development of the grandiose artistic conceptions of the aged Michelangelo and as a revival of the static academic manner and taste standardized by such contemporary theorists of architecture and decoration as Sebastiano Serlio of Bologna and Andrea Palladio of Vicenza.

This trend gave many artists unlimited opportunities to satisfy their whims, to manifest new ideas, and to materialize their most daring inventions. It gave to artistic creation the illusion of being free and sovereign. In that era of conformity, doctrinairism, and intellectual restrictions, mechanical innovations and the love of florid oversized forms preserved the sentiment of human pride and nobility inherited from former generations. In that world of cherished illusions a multitude of talents were at work reshaping the external aspects of Italy. Rome became the capital of the new artistic realm when such popes as Sixtus V, Paulus V, and Urban VIII, maintaining the artistic traditions of their predecessors, found in Borromini and Maderna, Fontana and Bernini, suitable architects of their monumental ambitions. It is mainly these pontiffs and artists who created the rows of solemn palaces, the processions of domed churches, the superb colonnades like those of St. Peter's, the fanciful fountains, staircases, gates, and balustrades that give Rome its homogeneous character of specious magnificence.

As in antiquity, many towns in Italy aspired to become little Romes, and decorators were found to spread the new style throughout the country. In the seventeenth century, Guarino Guarini and Filippo Juvara began to transform Turin into an imposing model of monumental city planning and noble structural harmony. It was in this period that Genoa obtained its palatial splendor and architectural grandeur. Local architects made a modern town out of medieval Bologna, while Longhena completed the picturesque scene of Venice with his imposing buildings floating on the tremulous waters of the canals. The

N

same display of pomp and color embellished the smaller towns of central Italy, especially Naples and Sicily, where the more sober and substantial taste of the Tuscan renascence did not inhibit the triumphal expansion of that showy, pretentious style. While Florence never contributed to its development, a small town like Lecce in poor, far-away Apulia became the seat of its most characteristic and attractive expression.

It was in those ornate and grandiloquent forms that absolutism and the new courtly feudalism found their congruent manifestation, especially in the Low Country, where the appalling poverty of the population gave emphasis to the ambitions and isolation of the local nobility. The new setting of Italian life was created by many skilled artists. Their number and productivity leave no doubt that the arts were still of prime importance in Italian life. From Bartolomeo Ammanati to Antonio Canova, from Tintoretto to Tiepolo, in the works of Caravaggio, the Carracci, Guido Reni, Guercino, Salvator Rosa, and many other minor and provincial masters, the Italians continued to embody their traditional aesthetic predilections in sculpture and painting. They continued to adorn their towns and churches, palaces and streets, villas and gardens to such an extent that the general aspect of modern Italy seems to have been created by the monumental workmanship and decorative sense of that supposedly decadent era. The prevailing decorative style of that period became the national expression of the Italian sense of art.

Yet there is a general feeling that those common efforts of Italian towns and regions to beautify the country created mainly a splendid façade behind which only shadows of faith and power seem to have lived and moved. The architectural and ornamental grandeur was not supported by spiritual conquests, intellectual achievements, moral aspirations, public welfare, and common prosperity. The Council of Trent, especially through its completion and expansion by the Jesuit Cardinal Bellarmino, had purified the ranks of the clergy and enforced its theological system. But general conditions were at their worst during these centuries of foreign domination and papal tutelage. All that pomp and grandeur only perpetuated and intensified the vanity and frivolity of a people always inspired by formal predilections and the cult of external beauty. The humanistic traditions, resumed for educational purposes in the schools of the Jesuits but deprived of their philosophical and ethical substance, led to the same formal virtuosity and elegant juggleries that transformed the figurative arts into optical tricks, surprising effects, and theatrical illusions.

The voluptuous intemperance of Marini, the Anacreontic jocundity of Chiabrera, the seductive verbalism of innumerable rhymers were in that period general throughout Europe. But Gongora had his compensation in Cervantes and Lope de Vega, and the English Lyly was overshadowed by Shakespeare. French preciosity was ennobled by Corneille, ridiculed by Molière, and demolished by Racine. In Italy the tragic sentiment of life was suffocated by the elaborate casuistry that had been introduced into family life, schools, and confessionals in an effort to deflect thought from doubt and dissent, poetry from intimate confidence, and art from pantheistic or Platonic aspirations. For two centuries Dante was forgotten, Machiavelli silenced, Petrarca suspected, and the humanists abandoned. In the effulgence of their new churches and in the luster of their palaces, the Italians became obedient and pliable under the guidance of their 'directors of conscience' and under the golden yoke of their sovereigns, vicars, governors, and officials. They lost their sense and consciousness of the cosmic and human forces that determine the course of the world and dominate the life of man.

The necessity of entrusting their minds and inner conflicts to a trained counselor empowered to relieve sin and doubt destroyed interest in human destinies and moral problems. 'Mental reservation' was a new and easy way to escape tragic conflicts between moral duties and human passions. Italian poetry therefore lacked the tragic inspiration and dramatic conflict involved in a struggle for the sake of an idea, a sacrifice for a passion, a clash of opinions, a picture of human ambitions, errors and loneliness, a noble resistance to the demon of evil or the fatality of history and nature. A spark of that poetic fire illumines Trissino's *Sofonisba*, composed in 1515, the first real tragedy in modern literature. An effort toward tragic grandeur animates Tasso's *Torrismondo*. But the eloquence of words and gestures is more stirring than the human understanding and the dramatic effect of heroic conflicts. The whole of Italy and Europe was thrilled by the melodious sighs of the enamored shepherds of Tasso and Guarini struggling against the wicked pranks of malicious satyrs in an idyllic background of gallantry, color, and music.

The Italian tragic sentiment, still literary enough, found adequate characters and honest expression only with Vittorio Alfieri, late in the eighteenth century, when consciousness of human dignity and self-sufficiency was restored to the Italians through the worship of their own memories and the influence of the ideas of liberty and tolerance then sweeping across Europe. Until that time the Italian theater had been a display of pleasant illusions and spectacular *imbrogli* to please the ears and eyes of a refined society of privileged literary gourmets; more and more music had replaced reality and the sense of words. Literary comedy and the Italian satirical spirit had disappeared almost entirely after a promising effort toward convincing pictures of human manners and types.

Formerly the figure of a greedy and unscrupulous friar, such as appears in Machiavelli's *Mandragola,* had inspired the facetious spirit of the Italians and transformed the humanistic imitation of Plautus and Terence into a graphic caricature of contemporary realities and customs. The satire of the ignorant physicians, fraudulent astrologers, idiotic professors, grandiloquent wiseacres, as typified by Ruzzante, Cecchi, Pietro Aretino, and many other professional or occasional playwrights, expressed the feelings of broad sections of Italian society who preferred to laugh at the expense of fools, simpletons, and impostors rather than applaud the unconvincing intricacies of the literary comedies or the antiquarian revival of classical models. After Machiavelli, comic inspiration was diverted from the gross and senseless obscenity of the literary theater and directed toward a deeper appreciation of the fanciful aspects of human life and behavior. In the vernacular Italian comedy, the classical structure works as a co-ordinating framework for the representation of the eternal collision between intelligence and stupidity, common sense and eccentricity, the *buon naturale* and the folly of morons and fools.

Such an, attitude toward human wickedness and obduracy implied a philosophy and a moral instinct very similar to those that had inspired the placid jocularity of Boccaccio. It is also related to Machiavelli's conviction that a triumph over human stupidity is a virtuous deed and an act of higher justice. This philosophy engendered the specific comic sentiment of the Italians and their keen belief that ridicule kills more rapidly than failure. It is an essentially rational and practical sentiment emanating from an instinctive sense of normality and confirmed by an abstract idea of justice, fitness, and decorum. The comic sense of the Italians is far removed from the more condescending Anglo-Saxon sense of humor; it developed out of experience and practical wisdom in a long and bitter struggle between the individual and society. Its most cynical and cruel expression is contained in Giordano Bruno's *Candelaio,* a comedy with savage realism and the crude pessimism of despair.

After that the literary comedy disappeared from the Italian scene for a hundred and fifty years, until Carlo Goldoni, its classical master, revived it in the French style adapted to the festive merriment of Venice. But the satirical mood of the first Florentine playwrights or the passionate exasperation of the Neapolitan philosophers never again inspired a poet or attracted a public amid the intellectual decline, the moralistic conformity, and conventional shallowness of the new Italian society. The modern comedy was an outgrowth of humanistic civilization. It was a typically Italian manifestation of a general state of mind. Its extraordinary popularity in the sixteenth century implied the habit of expressing in poetic symbols and theatrical tricks a common philosophy and a universal concept of life. When this spiritual background and these traditions and conditions were upset and changed by an educational formalism and a normalized culture, only the professional comedy survived in the rigid schemes of the *commedia dell' arte,* in which human characters were frozen into masques, a comic plot resolved into a pretext for improvised buffooneries, puns, and allusions, and the whole action became dependent upon the skill, ready wit, and histrionic juggleries of a few popular actors.

Nevertheless, even in that uncouth, plebeian, and clownish

form, the professional comedy preserved its characteristic, unique, and national Italian character. In the stable repertory of those wandering troops, every region of the country was represented in a scurrilous human type. The facility in improvising verses and songs, the wealth of literary quotations, and the psychological insight into the most extravagant accidents and situations were not the product of routine alone, but the substance and effect of a national civilization transformed into life, instinct, and natural habit. For that reason Italian comedians were appreciated everywhere in Europe and were highly successful in their own country, where their inflated gestures and pompous declamation were in high favor and well suited to the rhetorical education of the Italian people. Comic poetry, however, ended in that skill and glitter because it can never subsist without an opinion, no matter how latent, or subsist on probation or authoritarian approbation. The Italians had ceased to laugh and had grown accustomed to the Spanish gravity of courtly manners or to the composure and duplicity of Tartuffe.

The Catholic restoration absorbed most of the national energies and intellectual capacities of the Italian people, as can be seen from the great number of prelates, priests, and abbots who excelled in every branch of learning and showed remarkable abilities in the propagation of the faith, the advancement of knowledge, and public administration. The mendicant orders continued to offer a haven to the poor and an opportunity to fanatics. The Company of Jesus distributed academic chairs to intellectuals, opened the world to explorers, and led political talents to the courts and offices where they became prominent and influential. For works of active piety new orders were added to the numerous congregations already in existence. The Oratorians of St. Philip Neri, the Salesians, the Lazarists, and some charitable orders collected men and women devoted to internal missions, popular education, and public assistance. Convents, monasteries, nunneries developed as never before and deflected widespread energies from active life and secular interests. The opportunities granted to the most diversified talents by the powerful and wealthy ecclesiastical organizations were limited in number and scope. Many gifted Italians emigrated to foreign countries and started a stream of intellectual colonization that spanned the world and made Italian art, language, and culture universal. But these energies were lost to the mother country. The spiritual vitality of Italy was quelled. From then on the national genius expanded in the only fields where it could still be free and unobstructed: first, in the scientific sphere, until a fatal clash with faith and Church clipped the wings of scientific imagination and narrowed the scope of scientific investigation; afterwards in the realm of music, where inspiration was free and thought banned. Here artistic talent was sovereign, conquering and subjugating all the spiritual forces that regulated the vital energies of the Italian people.

XV. *The Search for Truth and the Tragedy of Science*

SCIENCE has a twofold aim: the rational interpretation of phenomena and the practical application of its doctrines and notions. For many centuries during the Middle Ages the utilization of theoretical knowledge for practical purposes was the main interest and achievement of scientists. Their philosophies constituted the basis for medical theory and practice, just as their cosmology served mainly to perfect astrological procedure. Medieval science developed out of the philosophical and scientific heritage of antiquity, mainly through Arabic mediation and interpretation, and never shook the speculative foundations of the leading disciplines of medicine and astrology. During all those centuries truth was vested in authority as represented by such doctrines as Aristotelianism, or by such leading authors as Pliny, Ptolemy, Avicenna, and Galen, and finally by educational institutions such as the universities of Bologna, Padua, and Naples.

The unsurpassed advantage of Aristotelianism was that even in its imperfect, contradictory, and uncritical form it represented —as it still does, for better or worse—the most complete system of knowledge ever devised by the human mind, and was always subject to amendment by abstract reasoning and empirical evidence. The Aristotelian system was the world itself, reduced to order and clarity, to consistency and evidence, to human understanding and logical perfection. None of its numerous interpreters ever attempted to undermine that complete and conclusive organism of scientific lore. Its authority was intrinsic, arising from its fitness and scope, not merely from ecclesiastical coercion or unthinking tradition. This is proved by the dominant position and lasting influence of Aristotelianism in both the Mohammedan and the Christian spheres of thought and religion long after it had satisfied the intellectual needs of large sections of the ancient pagan world. As an aggregate of treatises on single branches of knowledge, it had the consistency of a system and the flexibility of an encyclopaedic synthesis.

Christian civilization had nothing to substitute for the Greek and Arabic authorities in such specialized disciplines as medicine, astronomy, and mathematics. In the medieval schools, those branches of knowledge did not advance by empirical research or methodical investigations, but expanded through discussion, grew by integration, and spread through an endless compilation of manuals, encyclopaedias, *specula,* and *thesauri.* The medieval system of science, learning, and education had one great advantage over modern systems: it possessed a universal theoretical foundation, without which satisfactory intellectual activity is impossible. The medieval universities were professional institutions, as are most American universities in our day, but they were organized within an intellectual framework of universal doctrines. The scientific truth taught in schools and books was embedded in a spiritual system of thought and faith that determined its authority and value. This authority was embodied in the rigid curriculum of the liberal arts, which represented the static aspect of a culture conservative in its foundations, methods, and objectives.

The main disadvantage of the medieval scientific system was that its exclusively intellectual foundation and methods prevented the direct absorption of the empirical world into that vast organization of thought and knowledge. Hence, the strictly conservative character of scientific education and literature. Just as the absence of an ethical code for practical life isolated professional activities from the medieval system of Christian morals, the empirical world found itself excluded for many centuries from the system of medieval science and culture. In Italy the tension between scholasticism and empiricism was greater and more protracted than elsewhere because the country lacked strong cultural traditions, while it was exceptionally rich in practical,

N*

secular experience. Beyond the Alps the great compilations of
Vincent de Beauvais, Guillaume de Champeaux, Bartholomew
the Englishman, Roger Bacon, and various authors specializing
in particular fields of knowledge were kept up to date by the
inclusion of recent accomplishments and discoveries. In Italy
compilatory encyclopaedism, represented mainly by Brunetto
Latini's *Trésor*, did not achieve comparable importance, while
the contributions of an empirical character were not at first accorded scientific status and dignity.

The case of Marco Polo's famous book is characteristic of this
aspect of Italian civilization. Intended as a 'Description of the
World' and containing the first systematic report of the countries
and peoples of the East, the book, written in 1298, was considered
exclusively as light and pleasant reading, not as a source of
geographical information. Only toward the middle of the fifteenth
century, and probably after the impression made in Florence by
the representatives of the Oriental sects participating in the
Council, did the leading Italian cosmographer, Paolo Toscanelli,
avail himself, still rather furtively, of Marco Polo's information
that integrated and corrected the data of Pliny and the newly
discovered *Geography* of Ptolemy, first translated into Latin in
1406. Again, it was more than a century before the reports of
medieval travelers appeared in G. B. Ramusio's famous collection
of *Navigazioni e Viaggi* [1] as contributions to geographical lore
equivalent, and sometimes superior, to those of the ancients.
The situation is clearly defined by one of the most dramatic episodes in the history of geography. A committee of mathematicians
appointed, in 1484, by the king of Portugal rejected Columbus'
project 'to reach the East by the West,' because the scientific
geographers of the time were still ignorant of the existence of
Cipangu (Japan), Cathay (China), and the Great Khans, and because they had a more correct appreciation of the circumference
of the earth than the Genoese navigator and his Florentine counselor Paolo Toscanelli. None of the parties involved in those fateful discussions had any idea of an intermediate continent between
Europe and Asia, although the knowledge of more or less fabulous

[1] Venice, 1550-56.

Atlantic islands had been for a long time the subject of tales, poems, and legends.

The characteristic development of medieval mathematics shows the same lack of interest among learned circles in the spread of algebra and other methods of calculation to the Western World. After the pioneering attempts of Leonardo Pisano, around 1200, the Italians perfected, mainly in Florence, a system of commercial arithmetic that reached scientific heights after three centuries of an independent practice in trade and money matters. The basic terms of modern bookkeeping still reveal their Italian and medieval origins. Yet the curriculum of the higher schools did not include calculation in the arithmetic of the *Quadrivium*. The separation of the liberal arts from 'mechanical' practice was so radical that advancement in mathematical studies in the late medieval schools, as marked by Prosdocimo de' Beldomandi or Biagio Pelacani, was achieved in connection with music, geometry, and astrology, i.e. in speculative disciplines, as branches of a general intellectual training, rather than in the new fields of arithmetic and algebra practiced for convenience in computation.

The cleavage between the two domains of intellectual activity is illustrated by the dramatic story of the first solution of cubic equations. This step, which marks the beginning of a new epoch in mathematical science, was accomplished by two Italians in 1535. The rules for the solution of that crucial algebraic problem were formulated in obscure verses by a practical engineer, Niccolò Tartaglia, who never enjoyed the advantages of a university training, in competition with a talented adventurer of science and medicine, Girolamo Cardano, whose role in the whole affair is as dubious as everything he undertook in private, public, and scientific life. The achievement is the more impressive and extraordinary because it was attained without the symbols and signs that make modern algebraic practice a matter of routine. To the modern mind the old intuitive and discursive methods of mathematical thinking are almost inconceivable, but the unofficial history of science reveals a succession of genuine mathematical talents at work in the most diversified branches of life, feeling their way through the intricacies of practical problems and the narrows of school education. The trend is shown in the

great *Summa de arithmetica, geometria,* etc., published in 1494
by Leonardo da Vinci's friend and collaborator, Luca Pacioli,
a Minorite who devoted his life to the didactic co-ordination of
the mathematical sciences in theory and practice and to the
popularization of this neglected branch of Italian culture. The
works of this industrious Italian mathematician grant a profound
insight into the spirit and interests of an era that showed little
inclination for scientific innovation and made scanty contributions
to the theoretical advancement of the natural sciences.

While the static character of medieval science derived from the
general opinion that truth lies in authority, the decline of scientific interests in the humanistic era was brought about by the
general feeling that truth resides in beauty. Even scientific talents
were attracted by the problems of art rather than by those of
pure science, as the activity of many artists from L. B. Alberti
to Piero della Francesca and Leonardo da Vinci eloquently
shows.[2] For half a century Luca Pacioli, the mathematician, was
the center of that large circle of experimenting, calculating, and
speculating artists and engineers. As has already been described,
it was in that spiritual environment that the geometrization of
space was developed as an aesthetic canon, a scientific method,
and a philosophical intuition entirely independent of the doctrines and teachings of the schools. The mathematical perspective elaborated as a branch of geometry and as a system of optics
far transcended artistic requirements and became an experimental science embracing the cosmic mysteries of light and
space, and the philosophical problems of reality and truth.

The geometrization of space attained by the arts and their
theorists was the empirical, theoretical, and natural premise for
the three-dimensional perception of physical phenomena in rest
and motion. Only in such a geometrical medium was a quantitative consideration of kinetic and dynamic phenomena truly scientific, that is, accessible to exact measurements and observations.
Artists and engineers became so convinced of the universal value
of mathematics for the explanation of mechanical and natural
happenings that their greatest master, Leonardo da Vinci, could

[2] See above, ch. 13.

'find proportions not only in numbers and measures but also in sounds, weight, time, and situation, whatever their magnitude.' He had the feeling that 'mechanics is the paradise of the mathematical sciences' and that the universal order was geometrical, realizing in its proportions precision and beauty in measurable perfection.

*   *   *

The belief that the world was divinely organized according to 'measure, number, and weight,' was an old one, consecrated in an impressive passage in the 'Wisdom of Solomon' where the world stands before God 'as the turning of the scale.' [3] Yet neither Christian wisdom nor Aristotelian scholasticism ever elaborated this Pythagorean vision mathematically. There is little trace in Italian school philosophy of the substitution of quantitative for qualitative conceptions of physics, as sporadically attempted by Parisian philosophers of the fourteenth century in the wake of Ockhamist suggestions. Even the Platonic revival of the Italian humanists did not promote a mathematical approach to the problems of motion and natural philosophy. The ontological concept of a natural appetite causing the general and individual phenomena of movement made a mathematical explanation superfluous or unsuitable. Therefore there are even fewer contributions to physical science in humanistic literature than in the works and discussions of contemporary scholasticism.

Yet it is a striking fact that the outstanding mathematicians and astronomers of the humanistic era, such as Georg Peurbach, Nicolaus Cusanus, and Johann Müller Regiomontanus, did not join the schools of Paris, Oxford, and Salamanca, where a long tradition of scientific studies had centralized the intellectual life of Europe and the medieval cosmology was taught by renowned professors. Nor, unlike Martin Behaim, the geographer, did those German scholars migrate to Portugal, where Henry the Navigator and King John had grouped the best specialists in their particular fields of science. The leading German mathematicians all went to Italy, although the lack of special schools of cosmography and science would at first sight make this seem surprising. What

[3] *Liber sapientiae*, xi, 21-3.

those famous foreigners sought in the Italian cultural sphere was not a direct contribution to the studies in which they were masters, but rather the inspiration, the intellectual support, and congenial interest which they later helped to create in their own country after years of personal contact with Italian cultural pioneers. What linked Nicolaus Cusanus with the Italian humanists was their unconventional approach to the problem of philosophy and science. In extending his speculations far beyond the scholastic sphere, the German prelate was linked by a sort of spiritual affinity with the humanists, who opposed to the authority of the school a veneration for the doctrines and wisdom of the ancients. Despite the wide range of his mystical and scientific speculation, Nicolaus Cusanus created no resolute system, but, like his Italian humanistic friends, he left behind him a number of intuitions, anticipations, and beginnings that made him the leading figure in the philosophical and scientific renewal of his era.

For the same reason the accomplishments of Regiomontanus in the more specialized fields of mathematics and astronomy belong to the Italian cultural sphere. His determined criticism of the Ptolemaic cosmology was grounded, to be sure, in the glaring discrepancies between astronomical calculations and current observations of the heavenly bodies. But instead of confining himself to corrections based on improved mathematical techniques, astronomical instruments, and planetary tables, as others had done even in his day, he went so far as to express his doubts about the validity of the Ptolemaic cosmology as a whole and of the geocentric system in particular. To support this critical attitude he found in Italy scholars indirectly acquainted with the various astronomical and cosmographical theories of the ancients, handed down in Greek and Latin texts which had been unknown to former generations of scientists. The names and ideas of Aristarchus of Samos, Hipparchus, and Eudoxus had a new meaning to men familiar with Lucretius and Archimedes, Plato and Vitruvius, Cicero and the Greek scientific authors brought to light by the Italian humanists. Premature death deterred Regiomontanus from undertaking a thorough revision of the cosmological system that had become unequal to the practical requirements of astronomers and navigators as well as the intellectual curiosity of the contemporary mind.

That great undertaking was the work of Nicolaus Copernicus, whose treatise on *The Revolutions of the Heavenly Bodies* (1543) marks the overturn of all the scientific and philosophical conceptions commonly accepted until his day. For an independent spirit untouched by the chauvinistic and racial madness of our time the question whether Copernicus was a Pole or a German, a Prussian or a 'Sarmatian,' is entirely irrelevant. For a modern scientist educated in the spirit and methods of general relativity, the question of the objective value of the geocentric or the heliocentric system has lost much of its interest and significance. What remains is the historical problem of the formation of the Copernican mind and the evolution of his structural vision of the universe. It cannot be doubted that the scientific education of this great man was Italian and humanistic. Beginning in 1496, he attended the universities of Bologna, Ferrara, and Padua.

It is improbable that he was particularly attracted by the fame of Italian astronomers, such as Paolo Toscanelli in Florence, Giovanni Bianchini in Ferrara, or Domenico Maria Novara in Bologna. It was the general humanistic revival of antiquity that primarily fascinated the intellectual youth of Europe and started the periodic invasion of Italy by foreign scholars that lasted until the end of the eighteenth century. Men interested in the mathematical sciences were able to profit both by the advanced methods of calculation of the Italian *abacisti* and by the geometrical Platonism of the artists and scholars united in the cult and speculations of the 'divine proportion.' Albrecht Dürer, the greatest of German painters, was in Venice while Copernicus was studying at Italian universities. Both were equally inspired by the scientific *genius loci* that found its expression in mathematical interests and artistic achievements.

It was that spiritual aura rather than any specific technical or practical problems that encouraged the development of the Copernican theory. The theoretical inadequacy and practical deficiencies of the Ptolemaic system were not the principal reasons for its abandonment by some daring spirits and able astronomers of that epoch. The reform of the calendar, promoted by several popes, and more precise astronomic and geodetic measurements, were accomplished within the old cosmological system. Almost a century after the arrival of Copernicus in Italy, the Dane, Tycho Brahe, considerably augmented the astronomic knowledge of his contemporaries without renouncing the traditional geocentric system. The first planetary tables calculated after the publication of Copernicus' great work, in 1543, show little improvement over the old ones. Nor can his heliocentric system be considered a practical simplification as compared to the Ptolemaic and Aristotelian cosmology, since it attributes three movements to the earth, implying a new complexity of mathematical relations.

The innermost causes underlying the new cosmological vision were neither mystical and speculative, like those of Nicolaus Cusanus, nor practical and technical like those of Regiomontanus, but essentially rational and aesthetic, synthesized by a great scientific enthusiasm. To a critical mind the daily rotation of the firmament around the earth had always been inconceivable, even conceding that divine power could move that immeasurable, although finite, cosmic structure with an incalculable velocity. Moreover, in the words of Copernicus, the apparent irregularities in the movements of the planets were so striking and difficult to explain because they disturbed the harmony of the universe and the symmetry of its parts. The geocentric system that tried to reconcile all the apparent incongruities of the 'world machine' appeared to him as if 'somebody had brought together from different places hands, feet, a head, and other limbs, all very fine in themselves, but not wrought in correct proportions for the same body, so that, if recomposed, they would form a monster rather than a human being.'

As his whole book shows, Copernicus rejected the old cosmological system with the same distaste that prompted the Italian humanists to turn away from the amorphous, inartistic, and abstract system of scholastic thought. Again truth was sought in beauty, and perfection attained in formal qualities of structure and style. The aesthetic and scientific temper of contemporary Italy is evident in every aspect of the work. It is written in the typical humanistic style, with a profusion of Latin and Greek quotations, and much solicitude for polished eloquence and rhythmic elegance. The conclusion is summed up in a solemn peroration praising the sun in poetical terms as master of the universe and the perfect work of a divine architect.

Intrinsically the system appears as the geometrical embodiment of a cosmic harmony. It is the product of a free scientific imagination and not of astronomical observations. The movement of the earth and planets around the sun is not caused by metaphysical influences, but by their spherical form, which determines their circular motion in the cosmic space limited by the motionless sphere of the fixed stars. In that form the Copernican vision is a courageous attempt to reconstruct in a geometrical order the system of Aristarchus of Samos and of the so-called Pythagorean cosmologists mentioned in the treatise and very much discussed in the circles of the scientific-minded humanists of that era. Actually, the Copernican system is only one of several attempts undertaken by contemporary humanists in Italy to revive the ancient cosmological doctrines opposed to the Ptolemaic concepts and criticized by Aristotle. In Aristotle's book *On Heaven*, which was a standard work of philosophical and scientific culture, Italy was indicated as the country in which the Pythagorean tradition was kept alive by influential groups of scholars and enthusiasts.[4] The Italian humanists, to whom that famous passage had always been familiar, seem to have cultivated that old tradition as a sort of cultural heritage.

While Copernicus, after almost ten years in Italy, was composing his book, the Veronese physician, poet, and scientist, Girolamo Fracastoro, was at work on an elaborate treatise reconstructing the homocentric system of Eudoxus in which the planets rotated in concentric spheres around different axes. Fracastoro surpassed Copernicus in his attempts to make astronomical observations with a rudimentary telescope, the first mentioned in the history of science.[5] At the same time, around 1520, Celio Calcagnini, a learned and widely traveled scholar from Ferrara, vied with Fracastoro in reconstructing a Pythagorean cosmology that claimed to meet the scientific requirements of a general sys-

[4] *De caelo*, Book II, ch. 13.
[5] G. Fracastoro, *De homocentricis*, 1530, sect. 3, ch. 23; sect. 2, ch. 8.

tem of the world and also to satisfy the demands of practical astronomy. The notebooks of Leonardo da Vinci reflect his interest in the same problems before they were taken up in systematic discussions and calculations aiming at a reform of the dominant cosmological views. Several dilettanti joined in devising corrections of the old theories and new explanations of planetary anomalies. Some of those amateur astronomers were popular vernacular writers' ignored by the history of science but no less symptomatic for the general scientific trends. They confirm what is indirectly known about the great popularity of astronomy in the Italian society of the Copernican era.

In Florence, around 1550, the heliocentric system was under constant discussion. It was already customary for the Italian nobility to complement their literary curriculum with a private study of astronomy and mathematics, under specially appointed masters. The scientific fervor became even greater than the philosophical curiosity that once prompted some citizens of Florence to write letters to Marsilio Ficino asking for clarification of metaphysical and moral problems. Women did not want to be inferior to men in that intellectual conquest of the skies. In 1539, before the work of Copernicus was printed, the learned and noble Alessandro Piccolomini of Siena ceased to praise his beloved Laudomia with the usual garland of nicely finished sonnets and wrote for her and the educated ladies of Italy a pleasant introduction to astronomy and cosmology, the first of the genre of polished books on science characterized by such masterpieces as Fontenelle's *Pluralité des mondes* and Algarotti's *Newtonianism for Ladies* (1733). The Italian intellectual nobility seem to have tired of courtly discussions on Platonic love, literary topics, and amorous casuistry. They had given up the dangerous reexamination of theological and dogmatical problems. The spiritual interests of the privileged classes and of large sections of the population turned to questions of science and natural philosophy.

Just as in Petrarca's time, these intellectual pastimes found a leading center in Venice, where they were favored by active publishers and booksellers, by the presence of Paduan professors, and by a conditional tolerance of the civilian authorities toward scientific studies. One of the palaces on the Grand Canal, in which scientific-minded patricians, scholars, ladies, and amateurs gathered for their discussions, became the scene of Galileo's dialogues on the principal systems of the world and the new principles and methods of physical investigation. It was, indeed, through these circles, called 'academies' and designated by odd names, strange emblems, and precious devices, that scientific interests became widespread among the cultivated public.

The reasons for the evolution of intellectual interests from the pure humanities to astronomy and cosmology were manifold. Purely scientific curiosity concurred with practical experience in directing the public favor toward the skies and a systematic knowledge of natural phenomena. The old conceptions consecrated by a long literary tradition and scholastic education were shaken by the wide geographical experience acquired in the epoch of discoveries and colonial expansion. In the astronomic field, the appearance of Halley's comet, in 1456, and its observation by Toscanelli and his contemporaries inaugurated the discussions on the sublunar or celestial course of the comets that were to endure for nearly two centuries. The appearance of the so-called 'new stars,' or *novae*, in 1572 and 1604, the systematic investigation of the southern sky, the problem of longitudes and latitudes, and, above all, the reform of the calendar drew the curiosity of numerous Italians to celestial phenomena and astronomical studies.

This general participation in a specific branch of knowledge can be compared with the popularity acquired by the physical sciences after the discovery of electricity, Montgolfier's balloons, the steam engine, Einstein's relativity, or the atomic bomb. In all these cases and in many more, questions connected with scientific views and methods inaccessible to the layman became topics of public interest, instrumental in determining cultural predilections and intellectual developments. It was probably a unique instance in the sociology of science, before or since, when in 1516, the Florentine republic ordered posted up in all public places a printed invitation to the inhabitants of its territory to express their views on the reform of the calendar decreed shortly before by the Lateran council. Every person in the town and countryside received a printed booklet instructing him in the astronomical questions involved in the papal initiative.

Such examples of scientific democracy are, of course, rare in Italy and unknown in other countries. They presuppose a high cultural level and a spirit of intellectual co-operation such as had existed until that time mainly in the field of the fine arts. The *Divina Commedia* had contributed immensely to the popularization of cosmographical views, since the poem had been publicly commented upon in churches and learned circles. The increasing vogue of cosmography is attested by the great success of Gregorio Dati's *Sfera,* a poem in popular stanzas written shortly after 1400 and followed by a scientific vernacular literature in verse and prose. The phenomena of magnetism became a renewed object of speculation and observation after Columbus' discovery of the declination of the magnetic needle during his first Atlantic crossing.

But what really lay at the root of Italian interest in astronomy was the Italian's intense passion for the practice and technique of astrology. If Pope Paul III, the very man who instituted the Holy Office and accepted the dedication of the work of Copernicus, never appointed a consistory without having one of his astrologers calculate a favorable 'conjuncture,' it should not seem surprising that every high prelate, potentate, nobleman, layman, professional, and physician regulated his life and activity by horoscopes, which many of them had learned to cast by themselves. In the sixteenth century astrology had become a public preoccupation rather than a profession, and involved a general familiarity with celestial phenomena and a skill in mathematical operations inconceivable in our era of planetaria and calculating machines. The religious scruples against this widespread astrological practice were easily overcome by the conventional opinion that the free human will is able to counteract bad astral influences when they are scientifically revealed in horoscopes and conjunctures. And since the theory and practice of astrology were an essential element of the medical curriculum, the universities were more advanced in the fields of cosmology, astronomy, and mathematics than in any other branch of professional education.

All these branches of science enjoyed comparative neutrality and independence in a period when intellectual interests and activities were becoming increasingly limited. No objections were expressed to the Copernican or other cosmological systems, to astrological practice or natural investigations. After the departure of Vesalius for Switzerland and Flanders in 1542, the medical sciences developed freely in Italian universities, especially in the activity and writings of leading anatomists, such as Bartolomeo Eustachio, Gabriele Fallopio, and Realdo Colombo, the man who, in 1556, dissected the body of Ignatius of Loyola in Rome, and published a detailed report on his findings. This professional immunity attracted many talents to science and technology and made Italy a country of naturalists, physicians, mechanics, and mathematicians, while all trends of philosophical and literary thought had to seek more favorable conditions abroad. But as soon as all those technical disciplines and professional abilities evolved into an autonomous natural philosophy and determined a new methodological approach to the fundamental problems of science and knowledge, the scientific thought and the spiritual organization of the country found themselves crippled and misled by the same limitations that brought moral apathy and intellectual disintegration to all other creative activities of Italian society.

That fateful evolution which deprived Italy of scientific leadership and destroyed so much of her intellectual energies took place as soon as a few daring spirits transcended the limits of specialized disciplines and ventured—as Giordano Bruno said—'to understand the whole truth.' This philosophical task was assumed by science immediately after the death of the Neapolitan thinker on the Roman pyre had ended all efforts toward a speculative and purely human solution of the riddles of the world. The free endeavors and achievements of an era rich in scientific talents and interests had widely shaken people's faith in authority as a source of truth. The idea that truth is a child of time—*Veritas filia temporis*—had become so popular that it was expressed and represented in many forms, as a motto, an emblem, and an allegory. The scientific fervor that fostered that vague feeling of optimism and progress also weakened the enthusiasm of the gen-

erations that had searched for truth in beauty as an image of
the cosmic proportions of a metaphysical harmony.

Giordano Bruno destroyed that harmony with the 'heroic
furor' that led his impetuous speculative imagination to demol-
ish not only the Aristotelian, Ptolemaic, and scholastic cosmology,
but also the limited universe of Copernicus and the geometrical
foundations on which it was built. He substituted the idea of an
infinite universe for the awkward machinery of a world regulated by a mathematical system of human invention and limited
by the insufficiency of human knowledge and imagination. Yet
the logical shortcomings and intrinsic deficiencies of Bruno's
doctrines contributed as much as his punishment to nullifying
their influence on Italian intellectual life. He was in fact denounced by one of those scientific-minded Venetian noblemen
who expected from the philosopher a substantial insight into the
secrets of the world and received instead volcanic outbursts of a
blasphemous Neapolitan eloquence. The time was past when
poetical fiction, mythological allegories, and striking metaphors
could satisfy the intellectual interests of unconventional spirits
and experienced men.

After the success of the Counter-Reformation, the problems
of science, which more than anything else attracted the general
curiosity and creative ingenuity of the Italians, had to be solved
by scientific procedures and reasoning compatible with the
abundance of mathematical talents characteristic of those generations. The free expansion of scientific interests had developed
a belief in the identity of truth and certitude, independent of
authority and beauty, that is, of religious and aesthetic concerns.
The concept, substantiated in Galileo's method and discoveries,
marks the turn in the evolution of science and thought from the
medieval to the modern. Leonardo da Vinci had a vague feeling
of that identity when he strove to find a common principle for
art and science. The engineers, architects, and mechanics who
observed natural phenomena for professional reasons, though
in a scientific mood—such as Tartaglia, Cardano, Guidobaldo del
Monte, Benedetti, and some of the best representatives of a
magia naturale—inherited and confirmed the opinion that the
truth can be found through a rigorous methodical procedure of

measuring, counting, and weighing, but not by a purely speculative co-ordination or a scholarly classification of facts and
data. The thinking of that new generation of speculative empiricists was dominated by the conviction that truth lies in scientific
exactness.

In considering the phenomena of motion and concussion, of
falling or floating bodies, there was as little agreement among
the theorists of mechanics as there was among astronomers and
cosmologists in interpreting the structure of the universe and
the movements of the heavenly bodies. The ontological distinction between the 'natural' circular motion of the planets and the
'violent' and accidental rectilinear motion assigned to our earthly
sphere prevented the formulation of a coherent system of physical knowledge and of a consistent methodological procedure
equally valid for the qualitative and quantitative interpretation
of natural phenomena. Moreover, as long as the Copernican and
other cosmological systems rested on speculative assumptions
and mathematical expedients, they were open to discussion and,
so to speak, were a matter of taste. In case of conflicts between
orthodox philosophy and new doctrines, the customary escape
of double truth granted the able dialecticians in universities and
'academies' enough protection against the risks that Bruno, in a
defiant attitude of intellectual self-assurance, had accepted.

After 1609, when Galileo's telescope revealed the satellites of
Jupiter, the structure of the moon, the sun-spots, the anomalies
of Saturn, the phases of Venus, and hitherto unknown astronomical phenomena, the era of conjectural and controversial discussions was closed and no loophole left for the captious expedient
of double truth. Galileo had discovered the physical unity of the
universe and the methological unity of science based, as he
taught, on 'directed experience and necessary demonstrations.'
That new insight into the secrets of nature abolished forever the
concept of immutable, ingenerable, and incorruptible celestial
spheres turned around the earth by angelical intelligences and
opposed to the sublunar region of rest and corruption. In place
of that limited, speculative, dualistic cosmology and an orderly
world of geometrical perfection, a new universe was disclosed
to the minds and eyes of men. They were taught to consider their

homely planet as a globe moving in an infinite space with all the stars and planets, and moved by the same laws that explain all measurable and calculable phenomena of motion in heaven and earth.

These laws established that the velocity of falling bodies is independent of their mass or weight and proportional to time, and that the distance traveled is proportional to the square of the time consumed in the fall. These simple notions arrived at by experiment and induction constitute the foundation of modern mechanics, and initiated the greatest of intellectual revolutions. That quantitative approach to the phenomena of motion is at once empirical, speculative, and mathematical. It abolished the customary distinction between bodies naturally heavy or light and introduced for the first time into physical speculation the two basic concepts of a new natural philosophy: namely, the principle of inertia, implying that bodies preserve their state of rest or motion indefinitely if not affected by external conditions; secondly, the assumption that 'matter is unalterable, i.e. always the same, and because of its eternal and necessary character it is possible to produce demonstrations of it no less straight and neat than those of mathematics.'

While the idea of inertia is in Galileo's mind a cosmic vision and an abstract reality of a purely physical nature, the unalterable character of matter justifies, and even requires, a mathematical procedure in the interpretation of natural phenomena. The interdependence of matter and mathematics determines the inter-dependence, if not the identity, of physics and mathematics, and consequently the submission of natural philosophy and scientific knowledge to the intuitive and inexorable veracity of the methods, principles, and conclusions of physics. Truth does not lie in the perfection of geometrical proportions, but in exact observations, correct calculations, and proper experiments. This new search for truth makes formal considerations useless, syllogistic deductions senseless, and analogical explanations meaningless. The structure of the universe, the contemplation of the wonders of nature, and the penetration of the divine mind are open now to all men who adapt their minds to sound scientific thought and submit their philosophy and cosmology to purposeful observation and experiment. Nature is like a book always open before our eyes and understandable to everybody able to spell out the mathematical language in which it is written. Celestial mechanics are only an aspect of the general rules that explain the fall or floating of bodies, the inclined plane, the movement of the pendulum, and the different forms and variations of motion. On that basis the heliocentric hypothesis was transformed into a problem of mechanics and could be considered as a part of mathematical and experimental science. With that Galileo inaugurated a new method of thinking that obliged his scientific contemporaries to substitute for a finite image of the world and a coherent system of accepted knowledge his independent 'new sciences' that represented only the first step in a new and slow conquest of the universe by the human mind.

*　　*　　*

A century of intense and widespread scientific curiosity had prepared the Italian public to understand and to appreciate the importance of Galileo's discoveries both in astronomy and mechanics. About 1590 as an instructor in Pisa he made use of the leaning tower in public experiments that substantiated his new approach to the problem of falling bodies. Only scholars unaware of the great popularity of scientific interests in that Italian society can deny the reality of this characteristic appeal to public judgment and support. Similarly, when Galileo perfected his telescope, he granted first insight into the newly discovered marvels to the notables of the Venetian republic.

The opposition to Galileo's work came from faculties and colleges. His most famous colleague at the Paduan university, Cesare Cremonini, refused to glance at the wonders of the sky just revealed by the telescope, while the highly esteemed astronomer of the University of Bologna, G. A. Magini, joined the Roman professor of philosophy, Giulio Cesare Lagalla, and the mathematicians of the Jesuit *Collegio Romano* in rejecting the results of the telescopic observations. Galileo immediately gave up his Paduan chair and put himself and his discoveries under the protection of the Tuscan Grand Duke Cosimo II, who, it is true, was

unable to save him from the humiliation and detention that concluded his life and career.

From the day of his appointment as philosopher and mathematician to the Grand Duke, the courts and 'academic' groups of
noblemen and free scholars became the centers of scientific
studies and discussions in which innumerable Italian laymen
were passionately involved. Letters flocked to Galileo's desk
from all parts of the country. His discoveries were praised in
hundreds of poems by the most celebrated and most obscure
writers. Galileo took part in many disputes on subjects that included cosmological theories, current astronomical observations,
and the new principles and experiments of mechanics and hydraulics. The number of his followers, who called themselves
Galileisti, increased from year to year and soon included, besides
an important group of learned ecclesiastics, some of the most
respectable and influential personalities of the country's public,
religious, and intellectual life.

It is an eloquent proof of the scientific passion of those years
that Galileo enjoyed the sympathetic appreciation of Cardinal
Bellarmino, the greatest contemporary theologian, who had just
re-established the authentic and canonical reality of Purgatory.
The astute and learned Cardinal Maffeo Barberini, who later, as
Pope Urban VIII, destroyed Galileo's civic existence by his direct and harsh intervention, was fascinated by his intellectual
ability and scientific accomplishments and publicly praised him
as a congenial spirit and a technical expert. No objections were
heard when, in 1611, Galileo personally presented his telescope
to the papal court, and all eyes turned toward the new wonders
of the sky. The painter Cigoli from Florence represented them
exactly after Galileo's description, in a fresco in Santa Maria
Maggiore, one of Rome's four basilicas. -

It was not in religious or scholastic circles that the ominous
question whether the new doctrines agreed with Biblical revelation and theological conclusions first came to the fore. The discussions on that ticklish point began in courtly conversations in
the Grand Duke's residence at Florence. For that reason the
arguments in favor of the autonomy of the scientific mind and
against theological interference in cosmological investigations

were first discussed in open letters printed as an appeal to the
public opinion, then as powerful in cultural questions as it previously was in matters of art. Galileo's pamphlet summarizing
and eloquently upholding the principle of total scientific independence was addressed to the Grand Duchess Christine, mother
of the reigning sovereign. A denunciation of the new doctrine
and of laical interference in divine authority was inescapable and
led finally to a condemnation of the Copernican system and to
the prohibition to teach or defend it in whatever form.

That fatal decree of 5 March 1616 did not affect the scientist
personally or the single branches of science he impersonated.
No one was prevented from making astronomical observations
and improving mathematical and physical knowledge. Ecclesiastics contributed to their development and diffusion. Galileo was
even able to write one of his masterpieces of scientific prose,
his *Saggiatore,* a highly polemical manifesto of the new methods
and objectives of natural philosophy as an entirely secular and
independent discipline. But the co-ordination of all the sciences
in his vision of a physical unity of the universe was broken and
theoretically destroyed. Without that co-ordination of earthly and
heavenly phenomena in a coherent and unequivocal system of
knowledge, all its branches were nothing more than 'sagacious
inventions for the delight of ingenious spirits,' an intellectual
game or an element of practical utility. They represented a new
and even more effective support of the 'double truth' that Galileo
had set out to replace by a science so absolute in its methods
and results that it did not admit within its sphere any contradiction between the human and the divine mind.

Supported by the public interest in scientific discussions, de-
ceived by the growing popularity of his discoveries, and encouraged by the election of his scientific-minded patron to the papal
see, Galileo resorted to a literary artifice and expounded in his
Dialogue on the Principal Systems of the World the coherent
vision of a universe dominated by the principles of his mechanics
in contrast with the contradictory and conjectural assumptions
of the Aristotelian and Ptolemaic doctrines. In that attractive literary setting the old system of knowledge and methods of
thought appeared untenable, while his own cosmological vision

and scientific procedure appeared convincing and necessary. This time the inquisitorial action promoted in 1632 by the angry Pope did not descend on the Copernican system alone, but also on Galileo's transgression in defending it, and extended to eight more censurable points in his philosophy. In that action the heliocentric system was only the *corpus delicti,* and the decree of 1616 served as the legal basis for the trial and condemnation.

The reasons for the harshness of Urban VIII in humiliating to the last his old protégé transcended by far the juridical procedure and involved a question of principle of the greatest spiritual magnitude and scientific consequence. The Pope, who, for political reasons and out of personal animosity, sided with the Protestants against the Emperor and had revived the old tradition of unscrupulous papal nepotism, could easily have avoided the scandal and cruelty of the procedure without diminishing his power and prestige. Actually, the doctrine had, in 1616, only been conditionally condemned 'until correction,' and, in 1632, Galileo's book had been published with the formal approval of the ecclesiastical authorities. The same juridical formalism that supported the condemnation of Galileo, in 1632, could have been applied in his favor. Some high prelates disapproved of the rigorous procedure, probably in view of the consequences that the suppression of an accepted scientific doctrine would have on ecclesiastical prestige. The Florentine ambassador and a few papal counselors pleaded for moderation.

Yet the Pope's resentment was inexorable. He took offense because in the dialogues some of the words he had uttered in private discussions on cosmological questions had been put by Galileo into the mouth of the fictitious adversary, represented with more or less evident intention as a comic figure and the advocate of a lost cause. This personal attitude of the pontiff did not concern the Copernican system as an astronomical doctrine and universal mechanics as a physical science, but rather the self-assurance and presumption of a scientific procedure which dared to limit divine revelation and 'to constrain the power and wisdom of God within the narrow bounds of human understanding.' Galileo, on the other hand, believed so firmly in the certitude of his method that he accorded his physical conclusions,

even when erroneous, a certain pre-eminence over all other doctrines, profane as well as divine.

These were the real and fateful terms of the great spiritual
drama of which the Pope and the scientist were the protagonists.
That mutual challenge of a divine and human philosophy inaugurated the great tragedy of mankind, of which our present generations are the spectators and victims. The insoluble dilemma
in the human search for the truth was resolved by the Pope
through an act of authority. Just as his predecessors had been
unable to absorb the Protestant movement at its beginning and
had finally to stem it by violent measures of repression, Urban
VIII—the last of the great popes up to modern times—failed to
incorporate the new sciences into the spiritual organization of
the Church and perpetuated in the intellectual field the fateful
doctrinal split of Western Christianity. Again, as in the political
struggles of the Middle Ages, as in Dante's work and life and
the mind and doctrines of Machiavelli, the religious and secular
trends and energies of Italian civilization faced each other in an
insurmountable antinomy that involved the whole spiritual life
of the nation.

After Galileo's condemnation and recantation there was no
possibility left for the search and defense of a sole independent
truth with which every divine and human form of knowledge
could agree. If an authoritative sentence could establish that
universal truth and annul the theoretical conclusions of human
accomplishments, then science could not, as Galileo wished,
represent an autonomous human approach to the knowledge of
the divine mind. Without that metaphysical ambition, science
was degraded to a mere intellectual game, or to technical specialization for practical purposes. This was, indeed, what happened in Italy after Galileo's condemnation, when many scientific talents and innumerable amateurs inspired by new scientific conquests found themselves faced with the distressing and
destructive alternative of risking their lives for a new secular
concept of truth, or of limiting their interests to the narrow
sphere of a specialized discipline. A new element of tragic conflict was added to Italian civilization together with a new inducement for moral evasion and intellectual subterfuge.

The papal policy of intimidation was indeed overwhelming. The condemnation of Italy's greatest and most popular man produced a crushing impression far beyond the circles of scientists and professionals. The sentence was submitted to all Italian professors, posted in all churches, propagated in pamphlets, and repeated with the usual warnings from all pulpits. It was read in public places and communicated to all diplomatic representatives throughout the Catholic world. The suppression of the *Dialogues*, written for a general public rather than for scientific specialists, deprived the country of a literary masterpiece that included in a cosmological vision some essential problems of natural philosophy, a survey of celestial mechanics, the basic principles of dynamics, Galileo's erroneous explanation of the tides as a consequence of the rotation of the earth, and, in countless digressions of a polemical and didactic character, his ideas, divinations, and suggestions concerning the nature and methods of science, experimental procedure, and the general progress of human knowledge.

Moreover, the book represents the sum and substance of a long cultural tradition typically Italian in trends and aspects. The pre-eminence given by Galileo to natural philosophy as a basis and nucleus of knowledge perpetuated, though with a totally new approach, an Aristotelian heritage especially familiar to medical schools and centered in the Averroistic predilections of the Paduan faculty.[6] This circumstance explains the rapidly increasing number of his adherents and the subsequent application of his methods in the medical sciences. On the other hand, the essential importance attributed to mathematics and the creation of an ideal world of physical perfection connect his thought with Italian Platonism, of which his science seemed to be the rational completion and actual realization. The geometrized space of his dynamics and cosmology had for a long time been the intuitive, three-dimensional ambient to which Italian artists and theorists had accustomed the Italian minds and eyes. While the Copernican system revived an interest in Pythagorean doctrines, Galileo's theory of matter confirmed the scientific and

[6] See above, ch. x.

speculative validity of the Democritean atomism put forward in Lucretius' poem. Finally, his prudent suggestions concerning the physical infinity and plurality of the world re-evoked in a mathematical context Giordano Bruno's speculations on those controversial topics. In the epistemological and metaphysical fields, Galileo's belief in the ultimate coincidence of divine and human knowledge seemed to conclude or to reopen the discussion on the affinity and congeniality between the divine and human mind carried on by philosophers and mystical writers of the Ficinian and Neo-Platonic school.

The definitive condemnation of the book wiped out or degraded to the level of mental reservations all these speculative problems, interests, aspirations, and traditions. With that final blow, natural philosophy was dead in Italy. In 1633, the Latin translation of the forbidden *Dialogues* was published by German scholars; the manuscript of Galileo's *Discourses on the New Sciences* was slipped out of the country and printed in Leyden in 1638. From then on natural philosophy and physical science took refuge in the Protestant lands of northern Europe, where Descartes and Spinoza, Leibniz and Newton, the British empiricists and the French encyclopaedists completed, with a gradual extension of problems and deepening of knowledge, the sketchy canvas of Galileo's scientific accomplishments and speculative suggestions.

Scientific talents certainly did not die out in Italy. They continued to prosper in circles of amateurs as well as in professional groups and educational institutions. The Florentine *Accademia del Cimento* carried on Galileo's heritage between 1658 and 1667, stimulating in the field of experimental science the same collaboration of educated noblemen and specialized professionals that was customary in literary groups and in musical performances. The accomplishments of Torricelli and Viviani in physics, Redi and Borelli in physiology, Bonaventura Cavalieri in mathematics, Malpighi in botany, Cassini in astronomy, Morgagni in pathology, and investigators and inventors in other branches of research and technology bring to full evidence the vitality of interests and the assiduous activity of the new generations in the study of natural phenomena.

The universal republic of letters established in that period among the scholars of Western Europe by private correspondence, mutual information, and critical periodicals connected Italian scientists with their colleagues abroad and made science an indispensable element of general culture. The exclusively literary education of the humanistic era had given place to an eclectic individual culture that included the knowledge of scientific developments. Italians became acquainted with the branches of physics neglected by Galileo and first developed abroad. Electricity became the most favored field of Italian curiosity. Through their work in electricity, Beccaria, Galvani, and Volta acquired in the eighteenth century a universal popularity after their inventions and discoveries, respectively, in the fields of chemistry, physiology, and electrodynamics.

The philosophical interests that animated Galileo's investigations are totally absent from the schools of research he inaugurated. The absence of fundamental ideas deprived Italian scientific practice of a common goal, a superior wisdom and aspiration. Science seemed to be restricted to phenomena and data without the transcendent consciousness that makes every single truth seem—in the words of an English mystical writer of the Galilean era—like 'a sparkle of the truth itself.'[7] None of the Italian scientists explored the theoretical foundations and the ultimate significance of his work. More or less naively, they took for true what appeared certain, with no concern for the universal truth that might lie beyond the limited truth of science.

That spiritual indifference imposed by circumstances rather than by a natural disposition was more destructive than any skepticism and libertinism. It deprived Italian life in the post-Galilean era of all the intellectual ferments and moral incentives that in France resulted from Pascal's rebellion against Jesuit casuistry and Cartesian doubts, and from Bossuet's penetrating discussions with Leibniz. No attempt was ever made in Italy to reconcile on a naturalistic or empirical basis the religious world of wonder and revelation with that of human knowledge and experimental science. Galileo's discoveries and methods of

[7] John Saltmarsh, *Sparkles of Glory,* London, 1647.

research succeeded in rendering fruitless and obsolete the last traditions of scholasticism and most of humanistic philosophy. The doctrines of Descartes, Gassendi, Malebranche filtered through the ecclesiastical and political censorship and eluded the vigilance of the customs guards of the different Italian states. But the constant threat of degrading condemnations, entailing public recantation and years of imprisonment, made the discussions of those 'atomists' and Epicureans futile and foolish. Montaigne, Descartes, and Pascal might have stimulated the curiosity of a multitude of amateurs, eccentrics, and literary bystanders, but they could never triumph where Machiavelli was execrated and Galileo condemned.

In that sanctimonious society pleasant, noncommittal conversation replaced the substantial discussions characteristic of the former era. A stubborn rather than enlightened assiduity and a mania for classification replaced the creative efforts of scientific imagination in every branch of knowledge and research, and the interest in ideas was superseded by the same realistic curiosity. Historians likewise abandoned the humanistic tradition and the philosophical approach in favor of a method that prompted them to find the truth in facts, and knowledge in abundance of detail. The generations accustomed by their educators to seek the ultimate reasons for all facts and things in Divine Providence created and refined this impersonal and technical erudition, which never searched for the ultimate causes of events and phenomena but confined itself to the critical study of sources and documents.

✻   ✻   ✻

This fact-finding scholarship, of which L. A. Muratori of Modena, Apostolo Zeno of Venice, the Veronese Scipione Maffei, and Girolamo Tiraboschi are the unforgotten and outstanding representatives, separates humanistic from modern historiography by a monumental wall of printed folios. The eloquent relation of striking events and the antiquarian evocation of the classical world were now replaced by the methodical investigation of every aspect and epoch of the past, in conjunction with a philological exploration of texts and monuments. This movement coincided with similar developments in every European

o

country, but it was only in Italy that this type of collecting and
critical erudition absorbed almost the whole intellectual life of
the nation. In the decades around 1700 every region had its
group of learned men and professional scholars, devoting their
lives to the investigation of local memories, compiling the circumstantial history of their home towns, and founding 'academies' for the promotion of antiquarian and philological research.

Deprived of political responsibility, cut off from active participation in the great current of European thought, trained in discipline and obedience, the educated classes of Italian society
expressed in these forms of intellectual endeavor their love for
their country, their pride in their past, and their sentiment of
the continuity, nobility, and stability of their customs and traditions. The immense · amount of erudition piled up in every
corner of the peninsula between 1650 and the Napoleonic era is
a dead heritage of those generations, but it still commemorates,
in miles of pigskin volumes preserved in provincial Italian libraries, the unflinching devotion and silent enthusiasm that inspired their authors and readers. These scholarly undertakings
are seldom enlivened by any inspiring idea or transcendent concept of history. Most of them are dry and stilted. They represent just what Giovanni Lami, one of the most erudite men of
that era, called *deliciae eruditorum,* or 'the scholars' delight.'

Even that impersonal, documentary revival of the past sometimes provoked suspicion and persecution. The devout, candid,
and scrupulous Muratori, Italy's greatest historian and an honorable churchman, was warned not to touch upon disciplinary
and dogmatic matters in the exercise of his immense scholarly
activity. Pietro Giannone had to pay for his celebrated *Civil
History of the Kingdom of Naples* (1723) with excommunication,
a miserable life of exile and imprisonment, and death in despair.
The pathetic story of this upright man shows the degree of intellectual abjection to which all the Italian princes, and especially the king of Sardinia, had degraded their subjects. The
whole story of the sufferings inflicted on free spirits by that
organized intellectual terror has not yet been written, although
it is partly known from the biographies of thinkers who took
refuge abroad.

Even within the prescribed limitations, however, innumerable regional and local scholars were imbued by a passion for knowledge and truth, and represented a moral force. A deep patriotism inspired Muratori's imperishable collection of the *Rerum Italicarum Scriptores* and his monumental *Annali d'Italia*, although both were undertaken from a simple desire to know 'how things had happened.' The patriotic and historical feeling of those generations was more bound up with facts and relics than with ideas and projects. Therefore, the early explorers of national and local antiquity were not regarded as mere scholarly eccentrics living far from the reality of life. On the contrary, they were admired by connoisseurs and the illiterate alike, who looked upon scholarship as a sort of superior existence and spiritual nobility. In those days a library was not only the pride of the smallest town, but an indispensable ornament of every family that could afford more than the bare necessities of everyday life. The custom disappeared early in the nineteenth century with the rise of a petty bourgeois society, and has not been resumed.

This widespread love of learned studies was the only intellectual counterbalance to the frivolous pastimes of the ecclesiastics and noblemen who represented the culture of that era. Indeed, the very authors of ponderous works of antiquarian and literary erudition often delighted in manufacturing pastoral dramas, texts for operas, courtly panegyrics, elegant love songs, languishing madrigals, pungent epigrams, and satirical poems for all occasions. The poets who, at the end of the seventeenth century, founded a nation-wide organization for the cult of the light-hearted Muse—the *Arcadia*—were the same distinguished scholars who, like Crescimbeni and Gravina, compiled learned treatises on the most varied subjects of literary, archaeological, and juridical erudition. The *Accademia dell' Arcadia*, founded in 1690 and still existing as a venerable reminder of the past, represented in its combination of religious and aesthetic formalism, ceremonious manners, and scholarly interests the trifling spirit of an emasculated civilization. Small wonder that many of the freest spirits sought fortune and freedom abroad, like the economist Galiani of Naples, the three leading poets of the eight-

eenth century, Metastasio, Goldoni, and Alfieri, the reformer of
criminal justice Cesare Beccaria, the critic Giuseppe Baretti, and
all the rhymers, adventurers, magicians, literati, artists, and
craftsmen who became favorites at the courts of Paris and
Vienna, Madrid and St. Petersburg, London and Warsaw.

The ideas of the Neapolitan Giambattista Vico, the foremost Italian philosopher of this period, represent a reaction to
this general intellectual shallowness. A pupil of the Jesuits, as
all Italian laymen were in his day, a lawyer like most of the
Neapolitan intellectuals in modern times, sharing the poverty
and domestic troubles of his condition, he was transported by
the passion of his contemporaries for polyhistoric learning. But
he surpassed every Italian scholar in the intuitive power of his
speculation and in the dialectical thoroughness of his criticism.
His writings are obscure and heterogenous, sometimes volcanic,
boisterous, and contradictory, animated by the same impetuous
eloquence and occult lyricism that flares up in the works of his
countrymen Giordano Bruno and Tommaso Campanella.

Yet the sagacity of Vico's thought penetrates those intricacies
and involutions because of the double approach in his search
for the truth. His critical insight into the methods and goals of
science and philosophy gave him a clear vision of the limited
possibilities of knowledge, while his constructive thinking succeeded in building up a system that was universal in scope and
of lasting value. His daring and fundamental achievement consisted in the negation of natural philosophy as a basis for the
speculative understanding of the world. With this negative attitude Vico detached himself from the traditions of ancient and
medieval philosophy from which all the Christian and Italian
systems and doctrines had derived. He believed and proved that
man is unable to understand the natural order of things created
by God because the human mind can only know what it has
created out of itself. Nature is not, as for Galileo, an open book
that can be read and understood by everyone provided with a
sufficient knowledge of the mathematical language. On the contrary, nature is for man a book with seven seals that can never
be completely broken and never will reveal the secrets of the
divine mind and the meaning of Divine Providence. Only God

can understand His work, and human knowledge is limited to human accomplishments. Truth is not Descartes' much-vaunted objective certitude in physics and metaphysics, but rather the fact itself in so far as it is created by the human mind, experience, and imagination.

From that consciousness a new science of man arose in a dialectical contrast to the science of nature. Its purpose was the knowledge of the world of man, that is, of the moral and social order created by him in his historical evolution. Vico traced that development with the consciousness of the spiritual unity of mankind just as Galileo had inaugurated the science of nature with the vision of the physical unity of the universe. A new humanism was created by Vico in the face of the new naturalism. His attitude toward the Cartesian method and doctrines was very much the same as Petrarca's reaction to Averroism; [8] both undertook to divert the human mind from the contemplation of the physical universe toward the appreciation of the world of man. Vico's speculative humanism was larger in scope and disclosed a deeper philosophical insight. It extended the historical, aesthetic, political, and moral trends of Italian humanism to the whole of mankind in a dynamic vision of its gradual evolution from a primitive society to a civilized social and juridical organization. Vico studied the phases of that recurrent development in the clear consciousness of an intellectual renewal and under the aspects of truth and justice. In that way he activated the inert bulk of massive and aimless erudition piled up by his contemporaries, and transformed the antiquarian knowledge of the past into an epic vision of human experience and Divine Providence.

With its appeal to the imagination, its metaphysical inadequacy and prophetic pathos, Vico's work found little favor with his cool-headed contemporaries who were satisfied with an accommodating religious formalism and thrilled by the portentous discoveries of Newton and the developments of experimental science. Apart from a few leading professional men, such as the reformers of Italian juridical thought, Genovese, Filan-

[8] See above, ch. x.

gieri, and Mario Pagano, very few of Vico's countrymen drew inspiration from his *Scienza Nuova*. His work remained surrounded by a kind of sacred aura that manifested a vague sense of its importance. A real understanding of its speculative value was only attained abroad, in spheres of thought and culture opposed to the dominant intellectualistic and naturalistic trends. At the turn of the century the German representatives of critical and absolute idealism were clearly aware of their spiritual affinity with Vico. French pioneers of modern historiography, such as Michelet, recognized in the Neapolitan philosopher a precursor and master.

Stripped of their theological implications, deprived of their transcendental meanings, and brought into a logical scheme, Vico's doctrines became, in the second half of the last century, the starting point of a philosophical revival in opposition to the naturalistic positivism deeply anchored in the minds and schools of the Upper Country. To a leading group of Neapolitan philosophers, unimpressed by the progress of a conquering material civilization, Vico's thought appeared as the revelation of a spiritual reality embodied in human history and expressed in the products of human imagination. Of this young tradition in Italian philosophy, Benedetto Croce is the living and acting representative. A moral force in the obscure and destructive vicissitudes of our century, his doctrines likewise failed to rally the active energies of the nation in a constructive effort of spiritual and political reconstruction.[9]

The intrinsic reason for this failure is that the historical vision substantiating the philosophy of Vico and Croce has no fulfillment or issue. Because of their interpretative rather than constructive character, the systems of the Neapolitan philosophers never created an inspiring or applicable ideology comparable to those derived from the leading doctrines of modern times, as, for instance, Locke's empiricism, the French sensualism and encyclopaedism, Kant's critical idealism, Hegel's speculative logic, Comte's positivism, Nietzsche's gospel of the superman, American pragmatism and its theoretical ramifications. All these and

[9] See below, ch. xvii.

other systems of thought have had a marked effect upon the
shaping of the modern world, intellectually as well as practically.
They have all acted as powerful energies in the individual consciousness and in public life, in utopias and ideologies, in political organizations and economic theories. Every one of those
leading philosophies had an ideological nucleus of universal
significance and application, such as the concept of the rights
of man or the formula of the social contract, the categorical im-
perative, the idea of evolution or the myth of progress. Liberalism, socialism, communism, even anarchism and fascism are the
political and social offspring of those theoretical systems and
maxims.

The doctrines of the Neapolitan school of thought had not
such far-reaching effects. Their influence was mainly in the
literary sphere, where they became a source of discussions, controversies, and critical criteria. It was, indeed, Vico's concept of
history and poetry that gave this school of thought its original
speculative orientation. History as a manifestation of the universal mind, and poetry as a universal form of knowledge represent the common ground of that Italian idealism, which denies
that reality resides in objective data and considers reality as
history perpetually in the making. Nature is interpreted as an
experience of the human mind, which is the only intelligible
reality. Art as its intuitive expression, as language and poetry, as
a permanent function of that spirit, is a superior form of knowledge, and aesthetics as the science of expression is a leading
discipline in the search for truth.

Since this truth is historical, the product and essence of human
life and experience, the natural sciences are merely systems of
practical and empirical concepts, consequently unfit to reveal
the essence of reality or to become the starting point of a philosophy of nature, much less a guide and standard in our quest
for ultimate knowledge and universal principles. This total and
monistic humanism, which found its most elaborate expression
in Croce's identification of philosophy and science with history,
is the distinguishing aspect of Italy's spiritual evolution, as much
akin to German idealism as it is adverse to French rationalism
embodied in 'scientific philosophy.' Thus, in more than two

centuries of latent influence and unified tradition, the Neapolitan school of thought from Vico to Croce consistently condemned the supremacy of what Vico called 'the physics of the ignorants' and, consequently, every system of philosophy developed from scientific experience and procedure.

Confined once more within the boundaries of a technical discipline, science hovers everywhere in a metaphysical vacuum. It increasingly governs man's existence, but it is discarded by philosophers as a source of truth transcending the specialized knowledge of a technical discipline. With all the other nations of the world, Italy participates in the general spiritual and moral crisis of our day. The Italian crisis is aggravated by its failure to draw full spiritual and practical advantage from the scientific humanism which grew out of its own intellectual accomplishments. The scientific enlightenment of the nation did not promote, as in Germany, technological achievements favoring a fair distribution of prosperity; nor did it develop, as in France, a national civilization substantiating political principles and cultural trends.

Equally restrained by religious limitations and philosophical objections, science has counted little in the Italian cultural and spiritual experience of the last century. It has produced its Pacinotti and Marconi, many distinguished mathematicians and physicists; but none of the great currents of modern scientific thought developed out of the Italian cultural sphere. After Galileo's condemnation, literary concerns and artistic imagination became again predominant in the interests of the Italian people. Music helped to build up a world of fascinating illusions, which became more powerful and stimulating than scientific enlightenment and intellectual speculation.

XVI. *The Triumph of Music*

THERE has always been music in Italy, ecclesiastical and secular, artful and popular. Italians have never forgotten that the first systematic reform of musical practice since antiquity was carried out, in the early eleventh century, by Guido d'Arezzo, the *inventor musicae,* whose system of notation is the basis of the modern development of that art. From the Alps to Sicily there has always been singing in churches and streets, in towns and villages, in courts and homes. From the earliest times there were certainly virtuosi in the playing of stringed and wind instruments, organs and harps. Dances accompanied by songs and poetry were a common form of entertainment, if not of expression. Since the thirteenth century the Italians had an original musical form of popular devotion, stimulated by St. Francis and practiced in Umbria and Tuscany. The simple, vernacular *lauda* competed with the more elaborate liturgical hymns and the traditional tropes and sequences of the Church. As a narrative and lyrical expression of religious instincts and sentiments, it had almost the same function and significance as the spirituals of the American Negroes.

There is little evidence of an early trend toward higher forms of art and a general interest in musical performances and compositions. As everywhere in the Middle Ages, music was a complement to poetic composition, and consequently it was interpretative and bound to the word. The absence of poetical imagination in the beginning of Italian literature implies the lack of musical inspiration and consequently the acceptance and diffu-

sion of Provençal and French motifs and forms in the courtly
and literary circles of the country. The poems recited by street-
singers seem to have been as monotonous, conventional, and conservative as the *laude* chanted in sanctuaries and congregations.
Nothing is known of the musical accompaniment to the original
Italian popular forms such as the *stanza* and the madrigals, before it attained a more or less refined artistic development. But
it is certain that the musical structure of the most elaborate and
noble poetical forms, such as the chansons, *ballate*, sonnets, and
hunting songs or *caccie*, were mainly varieties of old Provençal
or new French musical schemes, enlivened by rhythms and ornaments in repeated attempts at free inspiration and individual
style.

These were a courtly and literary genre, generally performed
by amateurs, as described by Boccaccio, and composed by professionals like Dante's friend Casella,[1] or the blind and prolific
Landini in the late fourteenth century. The same songs were
performed by singers and players employed or invited by the
Viscontis, Gonzagas, Estes, and all the princelets and vassals
of northern and central Italy. In France, Petrarca's contemporary, Guillaume de Machault, the Master of the *ars nova*, was at
the same time a poetic and a musical talent, as were all his predecessors and most of his followers. In Italy the two fields of
music and poetry were separate from the very beginning, and
poetic inspiration soon became independent of musical composition. There are hardly any examples of Italian poets who were
also the composers of songs, although their poems might have
been adapted to already existing tunes or recited with a distinct
modulation of the voice.

Despite their musical enthusiasm and some practice in lute
playing, Dante, Petrarca, and the poets of their time never set
their works to music and always consigned that task to their
professional friends. The Italian poets did not attempt to emulate the troubadours, the *minnesingers*, or the French poet-com-
posers of the 'new art.' Dante regarded all the lyrical forms de-
manding a musical accompaniment as inferior.[2] Thus, for the

[1] *Purgatorio*, ɪɪ, 91.
[2] *De vulgari eloquentia*, ɪɪ, iii.

first time in the history of poetry, a poem could live by itself and could be read, studied, and appreciated in the same way as the Latin classics. The Italians had learned to understand and admire Virgil, Statius, and even Cicero merely for their sonority and formal brilliance without ever requiring a musical support for the recitation of their works. Unlike their contemporaries in all parts of Europe, the Italians did not consider music as indispensable for the perfect attainment of a poetic effect.

The most evident reason for the emancipation of their poetic inspiration from musical invention lies in the didactic and philosophical character of the early Italian lyricism initiated by Guittone d'Arezzo and Guido Guinizelli, in contrast to the purely artistic poetry of a courtly and conventional character.[3] The supremacy of the word over the tone was definitely established by the very substance of that poetry. It was primarily composed to be read and meditated upon. Dante developed to the highest degree the expressive power of words, rhythms, and rhymes. Petrarca reduced the role of music to a simple instrumental tuning to establish an appropriate pitch and create a symbolic distinction of poetry from prose.

This trend toward the independence of poetry from music was intensified by the humanistic culture and the literary prevalence of Latin over the vernacular. The humanistic poetry had to abandon every form of musical accompaniment. While the classical style of antiquity could be revived by imitation of ancient poetry, art, and decoration, or reproduced by measurements and reconstruction, not the slightest trace of ancient musical practice had survived in a form suitable for performance and amenable to the medieval types of instruments. Thus, the humanists who composed Horatian strophes and lovely songs in the Catullan manner had to rely only upon the intrinsic music of their verses. The autonomy of the word as a means of lyrical expression was achieved during that era and extended also to the contemporary vernacular poetry.

There is no evidence that any of the lyrical poems of Lorenzo de' Medici and his circle were set to music by the poets them-

[3] See above, ch. VII.

selves, as had been customary in the era of the troubadours. Only
the more popular types of poetry, like carnival songs, texts for
dances, and *laudi* required musical support in accordance with
the unbroken traditions of popular and courtly entertainment.
When Poliziano's *Orfeo,* the first Italian attempt at secular
theater, was performed in Mantua in July 1471, the narrative
dialogues and pastoral scenes were interspersed with lyrical
songs and dancing choruses, still reminiscent of the religious
mystery plays. It was a prophetic symptom of the further development of Italian drama and music that this pleasant and
melodious pastoral poem was already pervaded by musical aspirations and characteristically devoted to the mythological symbol
of the power of music.

Yet the outstanding musicians in the Italian courts and
churches of the fifteenth century were foreigners who introduced
into Italian musical practice the highly developed technique and
the peculiar artistic interests of the leading French, Flemish,
and English schools of composition. Little remained of the lively
musical activities characteristic of the preceding era. The all but
total eclipse of music as an expression of Italian artistic sentiment may be explained by the absolute predominance of the
figurative arts in the spiritual ambient of that epoch. The creative fervor of the nation was directed and absorbed by the extro-
vert manifestations of religious feelings, profane aspirations, and
cultural ideals. Despite the frequent images of angels and children singing or playing musical instruments in the paintings
and sculptures of the time, music seems to have been little more
than an ornament and a pleasant accessory of a more substantial
and lasting artistic and intellectual production. The decline of
musical interests in contrast to the contemporary sculptural and
pictorial enthusiasm becomes evident if the frequent mention
of the power and charm of music contained in the *Divina Commedia* and in other literary monuments of the fourteenth century is compared with the learned allusions in humanistic literature and the dry and dull musical treatises then produced.

The many talented foreigners who delighted musical amateurs
and refined society with their polyphonic masses and songs were
not hampered by national traditions; they gave vent to their

inspiration, skill, and invention amidst the applause of the leading centers of Italian culture. Those composers from France and Flanders flowering at the courts of Milan, Mantua, Ferrara, Rimini, Florence, and Naples, or appointed at the basilicas of Venice and Rome, made important concessions to Italian taste, always inclined toward melodic developments and sprightly rhythms. It was a Netherlander, the famous Henricus Isaac, who gave artistic form to the old tunes of carnival songs and May dances when Lorenzo de' Medici wrote his spirited texts for those popular poetic and decorative performances. Alexander Agricola, another foreigner prominent in the same years in the musical life of Florence, introduced secular Italian motifs into the elaborate structure of his florid, sacred compositions.

It seems certain that those complicated and sophisticated polyphonic compositions of masses and motets appealed only to the groups of educated, cosmopolitan amateurs who despised the monotonous, vulgar tunes of *laude* or folk songs and had adopted secular habits and attitudes even in the expression of their religious devotion. The members of that vast cultured society were not shocked by a mass ornamented with cheerful themes from profane chansons or made unintelligible by the tearing asunder of the words to suit the capricious texture of intricate scores. The Italian situation in regard to poetry and music had developed to a unique and paradoxical climax. While, on the one hand, music counted for little or nothing in the attainment of literary expression and perfection, words, on the other hand, counted for as little, and less, for the crowd of French, Flemish, and German musicians, because the texts were simply an articulate support for musical delivery.

The result of this development was that at the beginning of the sixteenth century poetry and music were mutually independent. Vocal and instrumental parts had become interchangeable and the art of music was as professional, artistic, and removed from general understanding as were the polished Latin of the humanists and the stilted style of the contemporary courtly poets. The extreme verbal and structural artifices of skilled rhymers, like the much admired Cariteo at the Aragonese court, Antonio Tebaldeo in Ferrara, and Serafino Aquilano in Cesare

Borgia's service, somehow reflect in their stilted poems the flamboyant exaggerations of the contemporary musical style in which a maximum of technical mastery accompanied a minimum of lyrical expression. The situation around 1500 was not far different from that at the end of the nineteenth century when German orchestral and chamber music, Wagner's melodramas, the French musical impressionists and—more recently—atonal composers were appreciated by a restricted class of privileged concert-goers and imitated by a few talented musical outsiders, but failed to appeal to the general mood and taste or to penetrate the minds and consciousness of the public at large.

The first symptoms of a reaction to that foreign musical hegemony and the turgid contrapuntal intricacies of the leading masters coincide with the culminating point in the development of the figurative arts. Leonardo da Vinci astonished his contemporaries with the charm of his voice, the skill of his expressive execution, and his ingenuity in enriching and increasing the sound of instruments. Musical ecstasy along with Biblical, celestial, and mythological subjects, became a stimulus for artistic representation. Titian's famous 'Concert,' painted around 1515 and long attributed to Giorgione, is the classical image of the power of music as revealed in the exalted features and gestures of enraptured performers. Raphael's 'Santa Cecilia,' painted in the same year, transfers to the pictorial sphere the poetic and philosophic motif of the celestial and earthly music as taught by Marsilio Ficino, a musical enthusiast himself.

The general revival of musical interests and fashions is documented by a more frequent representation of instruments, players, and concerts in the figurative arts, and by such unprofessional discussions and conversations on musical subjects as those related in Castiglione's *Courtier*, or in Leonardo's notebooks. After the figurative arts had held uncontested supremacy for almost a century, music vied again with painting and poetry in the expression of artistic feeling and spiritual aspirations. How this revival of musical lyricism forced its way through the technicalities and artifices of Franco-Flemish composers is shown by the collections of contemporary songs published in the first years of the sixteenth century by Ottaviano Petrucci, the pioneer and industrialist, if not the inventor, of music printing.

These anthologies represent in many hundreds of short compositions what may be designated as the current domestic music in contrast to the more pretentious forms of liturgical and courtly performances. It is characterized by the artistic combination of simple melodic and rhythmic schemes with a fluid harmonic or contrapuntal texture, both based on a short lyrical and amorous poem. Such are the popular *fròttole,* the *strambotti,* the *villanelle,* and *canzonette,* whose very designations reveal their jocose, rustic, and sentimental character. In their original, pre-artistic form they might be compared in a way to the popular modern Italian chansons composed by obscure provincial rhymers and musicians to please the mood of the multitudes cut off from the enjoyment of higher forms of art. It was certainly in that simple and pleasing style that the municipal fiddler and fifers delighted the townspeople at festivals and public ceremonies. The foreign masters were inspired by the simple rhythms and melodies of those unpretentious songs to work out the elaborate and dignified musical structures that satisfied both the traditional inclinations of the Italian people and the artistic demands of refined connoisseurs.

This compromise between different types of music produced short, simple compositions in which the polyphonic structure developed by the Franco-Flemish schools was fused with the melodic traditions of the Italian style. Soon several native composers, such as Tromboncino, Cara, and Francesco d'Ana, tried to emulate their foreign masters by specializing in the composition of *fròttole* and other songs as vocal quartets, with the higher voice, the soprano, carrying the melody and the three lower voices furnishing a fluid support. From the Venetian musical circles and print shops, this typically Italian secular style spread rapidly over the whole country and created, shortly after 1500, the long enduring custom of domestic music that ended the courtly exclusiveness of musical practice and initiated the musical education of the Italian people.

Only a well-trained musicologist can follow the formal evolution of the individual forms and textures within the general frame

of European music. Even for specialists in the particular field of
Renaissance music, many a problem is still unsolved and the
particular style of the various schools and composers difficult
to individualize. But the intimate connection of musical practice
with other artistic and social aspects of that civilization helps an
interested outsider to appreciate the historical and symptomatic
value of its principal manifestations. Two or three marked phenomena become generally evident in their particular and universal significance: first, the importance gradually acquired by
music as a means of emotional and artistic expression, in opposition to the decline of the figurative arts and the academization
of poetry; second, the prominence attained by words over tones
in the course of that evolution; last, but not least, the development of a distinct national style that enables even an untrained
ear and eye to recognize, after a few measures and modulations,
the origin of a melody or of harmonic combinations. This gradual development of music to the rank of a dominant art took
place in Italy during the course of the sixteenth century and is
marked, on the one hand, by the increasing number of composers, musicians, and amateurs, and, on the other hand, by the
great variety of new species, types, and ornaments created in
Italy in the course of a hundred years of an enthusiastic and
masterly musical productivity.

Its great achievement was the subordination of tones to words,
or the co-ordination of these two, and the consequent return of
music to an auxiliary means of poetical expression as it was in
classical antiquity and in medieval practice, before the higher
forms of poetry became autonomous and self-sufficient. That
resumption of bygone practice and forgotten artistic traditions
stimulated creative inspiration as much as it stirred up theoretical
problems concerning the relation between words and music. This
is the reason why the flowering of new musical forms was accompanied during the entire sixteenth century by numerous treatises
and lively discussions on the essence and function of music.
Yet that revival of interpretative secular music represents only a
first tentative step, still limited in success. Not only were most
of the composers foreign adherents of the stylish contrapuntal
complexities, but even the Italian musicians, inspired by simple

songs and by the elaborate poems of contemporary Italian lyri-
cists, hardly went beyond professional routine and a conventional
musical mannerism.

The interpretative power of music was restricted by the very
conventionalism of that poetry, with its limited range of creative inspiration even in the works of the best authors, such as
Pietro Bembo, Jacopo Sannazaro, Giovanni Guidiccioni, Luigi
Alamanni, and Francesco Molza. These prolific imitators of
Petrarca's style and phraseology succeeded on their part in elicit-
ing from the intrinsic musicality of their words, rhymes, and
verses the keenest and most sagacious effects. They compensated
for their lack of sentimental imagination by an expressive refinement of poetic eloquence. Consequently, every musical attempt to enhance the formal perfection of those amorous poems
with additional accents, suitable tones, and adequate rhythms
turned out to be pleonastic and illusory. The industrialization of
poetry characterized by the publication of numerous collections
of *canzonette, fròttole, strambotti, villanelle,* et cetera, printed
'for the use of enamoured youth,' contributed to the definitive
failure of purely interpretative music in the lyrical field of art and
inspiration.

Indeed, the simple, intentionally unassuming forms of poetical
and musical entertainment were soon matched by a more refined
and elaborate structure of vocal polyphony realized in secular
madrigals and liturgical motets. Because of their artistic correct-
ness and dignified character, these musical forms represent what
was then called a 'reserved' music, both in the professional and
social sense of the word. Intended for educated amateurs and
developed to high perfection by the best foreign and native
composers, the new madrigalistic style was dominant during the
second half of the century in manifold varieties of church and
chamber music. It was characterized by an imaginative but
appropriate transfiguration of the lyrical or liturgical texts, a
dynamic intensification of sentiments and passions, an illustrative and emphatic expansion of the allusions, metaphors, and
comparisons expressed in poetical compositions and sacred
words. A perfect correlation between text and music was
achieved even in intricate polyphonic textures. In the co-ordi-

nation of parts and within the strict application of harmonic and contrapuntal rules, great liberty of musical invention was granted the composers inspired by a poem, a hymn, or a mass. The incongruous accumulation of heterogeneous texts, of ecclesiastical and secular motifs, of dignified and plebeian accents in the same polyphonic texture was abandoned by the new generations in favor of a well-balanced and rational co-ordination of effects.

This was accomplished in the sixteenth century by skilled Italian madrigalists from Costanzo Festa to Andrea and Giovanni Gabrieli, from Nicola Vicentino to Luca Marenzio, Prince Gesualdo di Venosa, Orazio Vecchi, and many other prolific professionals and amateurs. They were flanked by the no less numerous and ingenious Netherlanders from Willaert to Orlando di Lasso, from Arcadelt to Philip de Monte, whose schools, inventions, and techniques left an indelible trace in the development of Italian music. Palestrina attained the highest perfection in vocal polyphony, an almost legendary popularity as the reformer of church music, and a well-deserved place among the greatest glories of the nation.

The individual variations of all these outstanding masters and of many more remarkable composers cannot be described in words, or even adequately appreciated in revivals of their works adapted for modern performance. The involved structure of their music and the stylistic demands on a modern choir make the masterpieces of the madrigalists almost inaccessible to the general public. But if their imposing production and its importance in the life of their era is considered in connection with the artistic intentions and the general influence of those masters, the impending triumph of music over all other manifestations of Italian genius becomes evident and eloquent. The multitude of talents, the variety of styles, the continuous innovations, the enthusiastic response of the public are unmistakable symptoms of the shifting of general and creative interests toward the musical expression of lyrical feelings and artistic impulses.

Music became the only free and autonomous manifestation of the Italian artistic spirit in a period when thought, science, literature, and the figurative arts were all under strict tutelage and authoritarian control. An official reform of church music was attempted around 1580, under Gregory XIII, the pope who introduced our modern calendar and celebrated the massacre of Saint Bartholomew with public rejoicing. A clause promulgated by the Council of Trent (Section xxii) proscribed 'lascivious or impure admixtures' in church playing and singing. But in avoiding those excesses, the musicians followed their good taste and personal inspiration rather than ecclesiastical recommendations. The first emasculated male sopranos—the famous *castrati* of Italian musical tradition—entered the papal choir in 1562, when Palestrina's fame as the most inspired and skilled composer of liturgical music had reached its peak.

Of that almost unhampered freedom in the practice of music the whole nation took advantage with even greater enthusiasm and persistence than it once showed for poetry in the era of Dante and for the figurative arts in Michelangelo's day. The country seemed to be flooded by an incessant stream of music that surprised and transported even foreign travelers, from Montaigne to Stendhal, who found a country of singers and players where they expected to find a people of scholars and poets. Music is a ubiquitous aspect of 'baroque' civilization everywhere in Europe, but it is only in Italy that it became dominant, exclusive, and general. The whole creative vitality of the nation seemed to be concentrated in a collective effort to build up a magic sphere of tones and rhythms in which emotions could expand in pleasure, drowsy abandonment, and mysterious sensations.

❉   ❉   ❉

In the very years when music, at least in Italy, ceased to be an element of cosmological speculation and a metaphysical expression of a universal harmony, it became the ineffable, artistic revelation of the secret forces that dominate human feelings. Professional composers and innumerable dilettanti produced a type of music that stirred the soul and called forth ecstatic transports. They excelled, like Palestrina, in the sweetness and smoothness of melodious development; like Marenzio and Venosa in the audacity of harmonic effects, or, like Giovanni Gabrieli and the Venetian school in the dynamic agitation of chromatic tones and forced dissonances. Like the poetry of Marini and his followers, the music of those madrigalists aims at surprising impressions, startling combinations, emphatic grandiloquence. In their sonorous illustration of polished, stilted poems the vocal parts of those elaborate compositions imitate with rational ingenuity the inflated metaphors, bizarre quips, and tense antitheses of the texts. Soft, sinuous melody alternates with dramatic climaxes amid a plethora of dazzling ornaments.

This was a stupefying and morbid art that seemed to excite a vague feeling of the infinite and an illusion of mystical rapture, but in reality produced mental inertia and languid fantasies. This music was hypnotic; it dispelled disquieting thoughts and submerged troublesome conflicts. And it is this quality that made music a powerful instrument of religious propaganda when St. Philip Neri, a Florentine nobleman, settled in Rome and assembled in a sort of musical congregation the common people of the town who were unprepared for the high forms of literary and aristocratic education cultivated by the Jesuits. That organization of music for the salvation and delight of endangered souls was intended to counteract the Protestant cult of music with its community singing and vernacular chorales and carols. In this it was conspicuously successful. Neri's efforts had their counterpart in the intense practice of church music in Venice, soon re-echoed in all the numerous cathedrals of northern Italy.

The influence of that universal musical vogue and of the innovations brought forth in the course of a few decades marked the decline of the old popular singing of *laude*. This typical Florentine expression of popular devotion succumbed to higher forms of religious poetry and art. The latter were realized, after 1600, in the lyrical and dramatic *oratorio* sung in the principal Italian churches with an increasing display of choral, solo, orchestral, and even theatrical effects. The last remnants of medieval musical devotion took refuge beneath certain sacred images in the back streets of Florence and soon died out with the secularization of religious and artistic practice. Despite the efforts of Neri and other leading musicians, Italian religious music never attained the artistic importance, the devotional intensity and grandeur characteristic of Protestant sacred compositions.

It was in the secular field that Italian musical genius flowered.

There is practically no ecclesiastical influence in the whole development of Italian music, which consequently appears as the most coherent and characteristic manifestation of the laical spirit of the nation. It became the dominant and most original revelation of Italian artistic life with all its lyrical and dramatic qualities. The continuous invention of new musical varieties is an evident and lasting proof of the free creative *élan* that gave life to the classic forms of modern music. They began with the contrapuntal subtleties of the *ricercare,* a forerunner of the polyphonic fugue, and were completed by the loose variations of the *fantasia* and *toccata,* executed mainly on the organ and the first keyboard instruments, and followed in the seventeenth century by the monumental multiformity of the *sonata.* The popular verve of the *canzonetta* replaced the early vogue of the *fròttole* and similar simple forms of entertaining music. The combination of vocal or orchestral parts in a concurrent ensemble of several voices and instruments produced the different forms of *concerto* and, after Giovanni Gabrieli, a new style of polyphonic chamber and church music characterized by a fluid, dynamic, and contrasting alternation or opposition of dissimilar 'consorting' groups of performers. Although these forms are all developments of traditional forms, each one of them corresponds to an individual artistic concept. The same is true of the invention and development of new instruments that had to be adapted to the increasing differentiation of musical types and the growing autonomy of instrumental as against vocal music. It was through these trends that the keyboard instruments developed with their mechanical efficiency and acoustic fullness, climaxed by the gigantic organs in the rich Italian sanctuaries and the first pianofortes built, shortly after 1700, by the Florentine Bartolomeo Cristofori. But about 1600 the violin took the lead over all other instruments, and became the most typical expression of Italian musical growth. This newcomer was able to conquer music not so much because of its intrinsic sonority, smoothness, and flexibility, as because of its conformity to the requirements of the new style and the new ideals of musical perfection. As a matter of fact, the violin met with opposition among amateurs who objected to its harsh, shrill tones as contrasted with the soft low-pitched violas and delicate harpsichords. What decided the triumph of the violin was the supremacy of the sopranos in the compositions of the great madrigalists, finally confirmed when the invention of the thorough-bass, around 1600, made the higher voice the dominant part in every kind of polyphonic ensemble. From then on the violin became the instrument and expression of Italian preference for melody to contrapuntal and harmonic artifice.

The perfection and development of instruments coincide with the increasing complexity of orchestral structures and the growth of mixed forms of vocal and instrumental composition. The new varieties of instrumental and orchestral music, especially after 1650, mark a distinct tendency toward emancipation from words, verses, and the natural limitations of the human voice. And, indeed, after Girolamo Frescobaldi's masterpieces for organ and harpsichord and the creation of more intimate forms of instrumental polyphony by numerous other Italian composers, music attained an unprecedented inventive independence with a definite turn toward self-sufficiency, abstraction, and intrinsic development. These compositions inaugurated the great epoch of the solo virtuoso, of instrumental chamber ensemble, and full orchestral effects. Their aesthetic perfection no longer resulted from direct emotional inspiration—the so-called *affetti* of the theoretists of the period—but from purely tonal and rhythmic considerations, expressed in free melodies, capricious variations, whimsical ornaments, thematic enlargements, and involutions.

What still linked many of these instrumental works with older musical traditions and the practice of art and life was the tonal stylization of national, regional, and foreign dances, which became standard musical forms. The fondness for dance in all sections of Italian lay society during the sixteenth century laid the ground for the elaborate musical elaboration of popular rhythms like the *passemezzo*, the *pavana*, the *saltarello*, and others imported from Spain and France. These dance forms became autonomous in that movements, gestures, and figures were directed by instrumental accompaniment, without the support of words. When the *canzoni a ballo*, so popular in the period of Lorenzo de' Medici, were abandoned as a form of courtly and urban entertainment, the combination of verses, songs, and instrumental accompaniment became a purely rustic amusement and died out as an artistic genre.

They were replaced by the ballet as a more refined expression of the Italian love of the dance. While these courtly and theatrical performances maintained the mimetic character of medieval dances, entertaining dancers and spectators alike with a combination of elegant movements, significant gestures, and pleasant tunes, the purely musical adaptations of those rhythms and figures led to the most diversified types of tonal and ornamental imagination. Some of them are still appreciated in our day, especially the masterpieces of Corelli, Frescobaldi, and Scarlatti, more or less authentically reproduced by virtuosi of keyboard and stringed instruments. The works of their pupils, imitators, and successors, such as Vivaldi, Tartini, Benedetto Marcello, have never disappeared from the musical repertory. Because of the delicacy and refinement of their inventions and workmanship, they are still part of every musical curriculum.

These famous works are only scattered remnants of a prodigious musical production, and those immortal masters are only a few outstanding composers from an immense throng of highly prolific artists and dilettanti who provided the whole country with an abundance of good and bad music. Neither the extended bibliographies of printed compositions nor the bulk of unpublished scores piled up in Italian, European, and American libraries give a complete idea of the general diffusion and profound influence of music in Italian life after the spiritual and political revolution of the sixteenth century.

An even more eloquent expression of that almost delirious musical fervor is offered by the protracted vogue of vocal and instrumental improvisation. It became so popular as to represent a national habit, and not in music alone. For two centuries that sort of artistic and intellectual pastime was the typical and universal form of higher entertainment in all classes of Italian society, with poets, musicians, and even painters and comedians gaining frenzied public acclaim similar to that enjoyed in our day by boxing champions and motion-picture actors. In that era of Italian civilization the improvisation of verses and music was

a common feature of social life. It was regarded as a particular
charm and merit in women. As late as 1807, Madame de Staël
made her romantic Corinne—an imaginary improviser of sonorous
verses—the ardent symbol of Italian genius.

In life and fiction many of those extemporaneous verbal and
musical acrobats delighted the Italian public for centuries. They
treated words like music and made the Italian language an instrument of the most subtle rhythmic and acoustical impressions, extending finally to the vernacular idiom that consciousness of the intrinsic musical power of words and verses that
Petrarca and the humanists had proclaimed for the Latin of the
classics. A rhymer like Cristoforo Fiorentino, called the *altissimo*
because of his verbal ingenuity and startling presence of mind,
was the idol of those in the turbulent Italy of the Counter-
Reformation who appreciated the tricks and puns of literary
clowns infatuated with the sound of their own words. The popularity attained at the same period in northern Italy by Giulio
Cesare Croce through his mastery of poetic and musical improvisation was surpassed in the following generations by the many
who developed this particular ability to the highest degree of
formal refinement and exploited it commercially to the full. The
success of the *commedia dell' arte* was likewise due to the talent
with which its actors improvised the dialogues, repartees, and
tirades suggested by a conventional scenario or a traditional
comic cliché.

Musical improvisation was only one aspect of that general
trend that contributed so much to making Italian art and poetry
unsubstantial, formalistic, and merely entertaining. That vogue
expresses the inanity of an artistic civilization deprived of its
essential aims, of civil liberties and moral responsibilities, of the
free development of intellectual impulses and cultural trends.
For the first time art, poetry, and music served for escape rather
than creation. Escapism is an aesthetic doctrine for deserters
and runaways. Garrulous poets, word-juggling actors, and musical virtuosi co-operated in transforming the tenuous human substance of Tasso's poems and the divine inspiration of Palestrina's
music into a sweet, bewitching spell for gallant temptations, fop-

pish vagaries, and ephemeral moods. Extemporization substituted for spontaneity, virtuosity for vigor, and illusion for veracity.

The general addition to artistic improvisation led the great composers to grant the performers of their works a broad liberty of interpretation and an active collaboration in the completion of parts and scores. Much tonal ornamentation was left to the invention and skill of players and singers whose personal contributions became important and even essential to the success of the works. A last remnant of this custom still exists in 'cadenzas' interpolated into classical concerti, in which the virtuoso shows his inventive ability and ornamental skill in highly elaborate, ostensibly improvised variations on basic themes. The toccata in instrumental music and the coloratura in vocal parts, both highly developed in Italian music after 1600, are direct offshoots of the extemporaneous display of decorative effects, capricious impromptus, and birdlike trills, flows, and runs.

In these artifices of musical 'bravura' little is left of the emotional incentives, interpretive efforts, illustrative intentions, and artistic functions of music. Its essential feature was the melody, which remained the dominant expression of the musical sentiment of the Italians after their leading masters had extricated its contours from the polyphonic combinations of the past and the massive complications of the new instrumental and 'consorted' style.

*   *   *

The development of music as a leading Italian art stimulated theoretical speculations concerning its essence, function, and perfection. Music profited from the spiritual freedom and unlimited individual privileges once accorded to the figurative arts. Like some leading painters, sculptors, and architects, great composers and professional musicians tried to elaborate and impose new musical expressions and stylistic innovations through technical experiments, scientific doctrines, scholarly arguments, and aesthetic maxims. The free development of music as the only autonomous, secular art favored the expansion of natural talents, and also the continuous rise of new technical, historical, and speculative problems. Music never experienced the limitations imposed on poetry by the Florentine *Accademia della*

Crusca, organized after 1584 as an absolute tribunal for the regulation of literary taste and style. Nor did musical inspiration ever have to submit to an institution like the *Accademia del Disegno,* founded in Florence in 1562 and considered the authoritative instance in all questions relating to the arts. The history of music has no parallel to the lamentable letter of self-repudiation sent, in 1582, by the aging Bartolomeo Ammanati to that academy as a warning against the sinful display of artistic nudes. Nor is there any example of a composer systematically denuding a masterpiece of personal inspiration and poetic verve, as Tasso did with his poem in order to satisfy the fastidious pretenses of the 'flowery' Florentine academicians.

In music every composer, group, and school had to support their style and concepts in pamphlets and treatises intended to enlighten the multitudes of musical enthusiasts. At the turn of the fifteenth century the rich theoretical literature centered around Franchino Gafurio, and in the course of the successive generations around the Venetian Giuseppe Zarlino and his countryman Nicola Vicentino. The Florentine musical group joined these scholarly lucubrations and critical discussions in the person of Vincenzo Galilei, father of the founder of modern science, and, to a certain extent, himself the founder of modern Italian music.

The main theoretical concern of all these speculative and practical musicians was to establish a connection between the musical style of their schools and their vague knowledge of Greek music, and thus extend the humanistic accomplishments of poets and artists to their own field. Since nothing was left of the musical masterpieces of the ancients, these theorists felt their desperate inferiority and isolation in relation to contemporary writers, artists, scientists, and professionals, who found inspiration and models in the monuments and documents of ancient civilization. Musical authors were read and studied, but music itself did not participate in the general creative renewal of the ancient world. The traditional and foreign patterns of the dominant musical styles seemed to be the only dissonant feature in the cultural harmony of classical ideals and intellectual or artistic life.

The theories of the Italian musical renewal took pains to invoke the Platonic and geometric concept of the 'divine proportion' and the Pythagorean and arithmetical symbolism of the 'universal harmony,' but all those speculative efforts and esoteric calculations had little effect on the musical practice of those erudite theorists and composers. Their works perpetuated in many individual varieties of a national type the polyphonic artifices and contrapuntal developments of their Franco-Flemish masters. Only Vincenzo Galilei, the Florentine, was earnestly troubled by that disturbing split between theoretical ideals and artistic practice. He alone dropped all the old metaphysical and scientific criteria and approached the problem of a musical renewal from an artistic and historical standpoint. His scholarly investigations of Greek music prompted him to adapt to modern practice what he believed to have been the true musical style of the ancients.

This was a typical humanistic attitude that renewed in a new field of artistic creation the inspiring illusion of the early masters of Florentine sculpture and architecture. The idea of reviving the artistic heritage of the ancients implied the customary abandonment of foreign, or 'Gothic,' forms and spirit in favor of a typically Latin and Italian mode of expression. Vincenzo Galilei's *Dialogue on Old and New Music,* published in Florence in 1581, contains the manifesto of these trends. At the same time it provided theoretical justification for the technical artifices and aesthetic norms on which the new style of music was based. But in music as in other disciplines, the ties with ancient models and sources were a scholarly illusion or a vague historical reminiscence.

Vincenzo Galilei experimented with his supposed renewal of Greco-Roman music in two compositions as far removed as possible from any classical model or inspiration. He set to music the Ugolino episode of the *Divina Commedia* (*Inf.*, xxxiii) and the *Lamentations of Jeremiah,* thus trying his new style in a vernacular and secular text of highly dramatic and epic effect, as well as in Latin Biblical passages of lyrical and liturgical character. What he believed to be a classical monody in sharp contrast to the contemporary polyphonic style was a sort of musical speech or recitative, reminiscent of the psalmodizing tone of church singers, but now intended to follow the sense and rhythm of the words and supported by a simple instrumental accompaniment of harmonic structure.

In reality, that innovation, far from being a renewal of an ancient monodic style, derived from the medieval, single-voiced chanting of vernacular and secular poems. Music again lost its autonomy and had to adjust itself to the words and natural accents of the spoken language. In this strict adherence to a given text, music resumed the function of enhancing the sound and meaning of words. This form of emphatic recitation is a branch and offspring of elocution rather than of musical expression. The musical speech of the *recitativo* requires and provokes the accompaniment of oratorical gestures and mimicry, while the ringing harmonies of the harpsichord and the thorough-bass amplify the emotional temper of the text.

The double nature of spoken music intensifies the illusion of poetry, and at the same time gives it a realistic touch. This monodic declamation soon became a standard form of dramatic music, both secular and religious. It was as far from the technical complications of the madrigalists as from the fixed rhythms of popular poetry and music. About 1600 that peculiar style of arhythmic declamatory music was established as a definitive feature in operas and oratorios. These two new forms of art, festive and theatrical in character, perpetuated the most diversified expressions of Italian taste. For almost two centuries, music and poetry remained inseparable and interdependent.

The new style of vocal declamation appealed to a small group of Florentine literati and musical amateurs centered around Count Giovanni Bardi di Vernio and the patrician Jacopo Corsi, in whose palace the first performances of the secular melodrama took place. The group constituted a 'comradeship' of poets and musicians, a *camerata,* as they called it, in order to dissociate it from the innumerable 'academies' of scholars and literati thriving in every corner of Italy. This *camerata* inaugurated the new musical drama with *La Dafne,* words by Ottavio Rinuccini and music by Jacopo Peri, presented in 1594,[4] and soon followed by the latter's *Euridice*. In 1600, the same subject inspired a highly talented and active musician, Giulio Caccini of Rome. Some years before, Emilio de' Cavalieri had adopted the monodic style for his *Rappresentazione di Anima e Corpo,* performed in the Roman *oratorio* of St. Philip Neri, and this was the first musical religious drama of that type.

Yet it was secular inspiration and poetical refinement rather than religious devotion that led to the predominance of music over all other arts and brought forth the musical masterpieces of the new style. The great simplicity of action, text, and music in all those early attempts to create a new artistic form clearly reveals the antagonism felt by the Florentine group toward the pompous style of the Neapolitan poets and the exuberant sonority of the Venetian musicians. Florence never consented to the decorative and colorful flourish or to the monumental and hyperbolic turgidity of baroque taste and imagination. The *camerata* reacted against it in poetry with the elegant simplicity of a mythological and pastoral drama, in music with the unpretentious nobility of a musical declamation.

The sincerity of this group in reviving, even with incongruous historical artifices, the classical simplicity of the Greek drama cannot be questioned. It can be proved merely by comparing the complex action and the garrulous effusions of Guarini's *Pastor Fido,* published in 1590, with the sober style and structure of those first musical dramas. Moreover, all the composers insist in their explanatory remarks upon the concept of a *musica affettuosa* that stresses the emotional expression of music and reduces the ornamental embellishments or makes them serve expressive purposes.

This rigid, awkward, and rudimentary form gained in life, movement, and articulation when a true musical genius discovered the artistic possibilities inherent in a harmonious combination of action and lyrics, speech and melody, voice and instruments, solo and chorus. The perfect fusion of these different elements was achieved by Claudio Monteverdi of Cremona, the

---

[4] Or 1597.

town that since then has resounded with the tones of the stringed instruments of Amati and Stradivarius. That great composer was endowed with an exceptional musical imagination, a keen sense of dramatic effects, a perfect command of instrumental and vocal technique, an intimate understanding of the subtle musicality of words and verses. Not only did he introduce into 'the operatic structure the characteristic features of that hybrid type, but in his long and productive career he also extended his scope far beyond the limits of pastoral and idyllic subjects.

In his *Ritorno di Ulisse* and *Incoronazione di Poppea* (1642), musical expression was harmonized with dramatic action, poetic text, and stage setting. In those musical dramas the action was climaxed in the lyrical solo songs, *arie*, introduced by dramatic and narrative recitatives. An instrumental overture, *sinfonia*, created the musical frame and set the general temper of the work. The *arioso*—a graceful recitative, intermediate between musical speech and full melody—smoothed over the breaks between song and declamation and emphasized the musical character of the drama. The prevalence of stringed instruments in the orchestra added sweetness, richness, and density to words and tones, stressing the dramatic accents and enriching the lyrical passages.

This development of the opera to a dramatic compendium of all musical types and forms coincided with its public display in vast theaters organized as commercial enterprises and directed by composers and impresarios familiar with the public taste. After the foundation of the first opera house in Venice, in 1637, and the success of Francesco Cavalli, an able composer and commercial genius, every important Italian town built its theater and extended to larger sections of the population the enjoyment of higher forms of music previously reserved for princes and prelates. A throng of rhymers, musicians, painters, dancers, actors, singers, including *castrati*, mechanics, and art lovers of all classes swarmed around the opera houses, where the whole life of the towns now seemed to converge.

Through the co-operation of many writers and musicians, Venice, Rome, and Naples successively developed local varieties of opera that soon became national and universal. The carnival

season—the *stagione*—became the social and artistic climax of
the year, while courtly events and local festivals provided additional musical events. The general Italian love of music made
possible the commercial exploitation of both the opera with its
intense, brilliant, and eccentric dramatic effects, and comic opera
with its droll, scurrilous, and extravagant buffooneries. Opera
became a habit with the Italian people who learned to see human
situations and emotional conflicts in the magnifying and distort-
ing perspective of the musical drama. From the middle of the
seventeenth century down to our era the urban Italian civilization
has been focused on church and opera house; the pompous
solemnity of the Church had its counterpart in the profane
pageantry of the theater, while the sumptuous triviality and
melodramatic effects of the opera invaded the ritual of the divine
service. Before Giulio Rospigliosi became Pope Clement IX in
1667, he composed several texts for musical comedies, just as his
great predecessor Pius II, previous to his elevation, had written
his Latin play for the entertainment of his humanistic generation.

What was required in an opera of that period, as a contemporary author reported, was 'a crafty texture, surprising incidents,
variety of meters, frequence of inventions, shortness of recitatives, abundance of songs, deceptions, entanglements, solutions
of knots, subtleties, oddities, witticisms, allegories, metaphors,
and epigrams'[5]—and this recipe was carried out by a legion of
more or less talented and prolific composers. Two learned and
productive authors made efforts to bring order, dignity, a human
touch, and classical composure to the bizarre intrigues and
tumultuous confusion of the melodrama. The first who attempted
to curb the extravagances of poets and composers was the Venetian Apostolo Zeno, whose ten volumes of operative melodramas
embrace the most heterogeneous motifs of ancient and contemporary dramatic and narrative literature. He was surpassed
by the idolized Metastasio, trifling genius of poetry and representative of a world living under the spell of music.

His ambitious effort was stimulated by the purpose of restoring
the supremacy of poetry in the theater. He strove to transplant

[5] G. A. Bontempi, *Il Paride*, 1662, Preface.

to the Italian stage the majesty of the Greek tragedy, the turbu-
lence of the Spanish drama, the grandeur of Corneille, the
trenchant vigor of Racine, the eloquence of Voltaire, the technical ability of many forgotten French playwrights, and the
thoughtful gravity of Maffei's literary dramas.[6] The natural
facility of a light-hearted *improvvisatore* and the graceful non-
chalance of a court favorite easily mastered the technicalities
of dramatic structure and the artifices of theatrical effect. But
a tragic sense of life and poetry was as foreign to Metastasio as
to his contemporary countrymen.

His restrained, appealing dramas, characterized by a quiet
optimism, represent historical or fabulous heroes as lofty punsters
and gesticulating marionettes. The fatal heroines of myths and
history act as languid matrons or sharp-witted victims. The
conflicts between passion and fatality, between evil and good,
will and authority, reason and instinct, are resolved in quick
repartees and sprightly lyrical generalizations and couplets. The
world appears as a theatrical stage on which history unfolds as a
spectacular tournament and public divertissement. In Metastasio's
cheerful and limpid verses the flame of love crackles in sparks
of gallantry. Cataclysmic, tragic forces are kept within the bounds
of decency and dignity, which in that day represented the supreme order of the world, the basic principles of human intercourse, and the fulfillment of an aesthetic norm defined as 'poetic
reason.'[7]

Metastasio infused this spirit into the minds of his contemporaries. He molded the sentiments of his people far beyond his
courtly environment, his literary sphere, and the brilliant era in
which he acquired an unsurpassed popularity. He played in his
century the role of poetical *praeceptor Italiae* once assumed by
Petrarca and recently affected by Gabriele d'Annunzio. His great
contemporary critic, Giuseppe Baretti, extolled his poetry over
that of all the Italian classics and the greatest authors of all
times.[8] All Europe was thrown into ecstasies by his concise little
dramas and his flimsy, polished chansons. But since Metastasio

[6] *Merope*, 1714.
[7] G. V. Gravina, *Della ragion poetica*, 1700.
[8] *Lettere familiari*, x.

had written his songs and libretti with music in his ears, a stage before his eyes, and famous singers in his mind, all his skill and glory were linked with operatic music and vanished rapidly when Mozart found in Lorenzo da Ponte a more fortunate author of operatic libretti.

The wit and wisdom displayed by Metastasio in hundreds of dramas inspired many composers as able in writing music as he was in scribbling verses. Unlike Voltaire's tragedies, his melodramas offered mainly musical effects but no world-shaking philosophy. The music he inspired had the same fluid facility, superficial lucidity, and ornamental levity that characterize the contemporary compositions for chamber and church, the festive cantatas and the exuberant phrasing of a vibrant *bel canto*. None of the Italian composers of his era attained the intensity of expression, the nobility of inspiration, the grandeur of workmanship of the great German composers from Schutz to J. S. Bach, from Handel to Mozart and Haydn. But no country and era ever surpassed the number of inventive, productive, and popular musicians thriving on Italian soil and overflowing the whole of Europe with their sweet and captivating melodies. The memory of some of those prolific composers has been preserved in the pantheon of Italian glories. The names of Cesti, Carissimi, Porpora, Leonardo Leo, Scarlatti, Pergolese, Jommelli, Piccinni, Paisiello, Cimarosa, and many others still have the power of nostalgic evocation. More than the changing mood of the public, it is the difficulty and expense in staging operatic performances that has consigned the masterpieces of those excellent composers to oblivion.

In their era the whole country was caught in a musical whirlwind that shook the foundations of Italian society, shattered the traditional austerity of science and education, dissolved the serious sides of life and poetry, and swept away the substance of religion, art, and morals. With its churches and palaces, schools and convents, squares and gardens, Italy had become an arena for dancing and singing multitudes, fusing into an artistic community the pleasure-seeking aristocracy and the hard-working people, the gallant abbés and busy scholars, the clergy and the laity, the rich and the poor, natives and foreigners. Carlo Goldoni,

P

who depicted that society in his jovial comedies, succeeded in freeing the comic theater from that musical fascination, but he paid tribute to the genius of his gay century by writing at least one melodrama. At the same time, boisterous Vittorio Alfieri rediscovered in Plutarch's lives of Greek and Roman heroes, in Italian chronicles and universal history, the true and eternal measure of tragic greatness in virtues and vice, in violence and sacrifice, in lofty aspirations and crime or rebellion. His successful efforts to detach human fate and dramatic poems from operatic conventions and musical frills created Italy's heroic tragedy against the background of the country's misery and grandeur. Alfieri candidly confessed in his autobiography, however, that nothing was able to stir in his soul more 'varied and terrible emotions' than music, and that he conceived most of his tragedies 'in the very moment of listening to music, or at least a few hours afterwards.' [9]

The artistic unity of the nation was completed through music, which has remained until our day the common link and universal expression of the Italian temperament. Although most of the great Italian composers worked abroad, carrying Italian forms of music through all Europe, none of them brought back home the mark of a foreign style. The intellectual life of the country, the literary interests, even the poetical inspiration of leading authors, were directed, as in the Middle Ages, by French influence, to which the imitators of Milton and Macpherson added English trends. But music maintained in every form the genuine expression of a national art.

While instrumental music gained everywhere else in artistic interest and public favor, the opera remained the only field of creative Italian composers, especially after Luigi Boccherini. It was into that dramatic structure that the Sicilian Vincenzo Bellini poured the inexhaustible flow of his tender, swelling, radiant melodies. The hegemony of Italian opera was assured when Rossini's sparkling genius raised the old patterns of the farcical *opera buffa* to the artistic heights of his *Barbiere* and the classical *opera seria* to the adventurous charm of the romantic

[9] V. Alfieri, *Vita*, 17.

drama. He found a satellite in Gaetano Donizetti, whose insinuating tunes, cheerful arias, lyrical effusions, and pathetic ensembles appealed to the particular musical sensibility of the old-fashioned, romantic, and homely middle-class society with its traditional appreciation of musical expression and theatrical effects.

Ponchielli, Catalani, and a few other forgotten representatives of this eclectic and pathetic style of grand opera were soon overshadowed by Giuseppe Verdi, whose musical versatility, infallible knowledge of stage artifices, and profound human insight fused lyrical inspiration with dramatic passion and vocal virtuosity with instrumental sonority in an unsurpassed harmony. Up to the present time Verdi and his music represent the last universal symbols of the living genius of Italy. No poet or composer of the nineteenth century, and scarcely any earlier artist, was able to extend his inspiration over such a vast range of expressive means, to master so thoroughly all the registers of vocal effects, to transfuse so convincingly into music the heroic impulses of chivalry or citizenship, the generous emotions of fighting patriotism, all the gradations of passion and tenderness, of hatred and piety, of cynicism and benevolence, of pathos and humor. With his emphatic recitatives, agitated rhythms, and dazzling arias, with his violent contrasts and tense melodic developments, Verdi projected Victor Hugo's turgid, effervescent frenzy into a metaphorical realm of rhapsody. The fictitious absurdities and inextricable complications of dramatic nightmares and chimeric libretti, like those of *Il Trovatore* or *La Forza del Destino*, are transformed into a kaleidoscopic sequence of musical visions and romantic pictures that keep the spectators under a magic enchantment of lasting and unfaltering effect.

Of the love affair in Dumas' society play, Verdi made in *La Traviata* a more cosmic than romantic 'heart-beat of the whole universe.' [10] In his later years he abandoned the melodramatic complications, the sentimental effusions, and the spectacular exoticism of *Aïda* and his earlier masterpieces. Of this turn in his art and mind the *Requiem*, composed in 1873 in memory of

[10] 'Di quell' amor ch'è palpito
   Dell' universo intero.'
   La Traviata, Atto I, Scena 3ª (the principal *leitmotif* of the opera).

Alessandro Manzoni, was the religious, if not canonical, expression. For his operatic music he finally drew his inspiration from Shakespeare's human experience, poetic symbols, and humorous wisdom. They are condensed and intensified in *Othello* and *Falstaff*. Through these operas the Italian people learned for the first time to understand the world of Shakespeare, just as the operatic humanism of the baroque composers once made the general public familiar with the gods and heroes of classical antiquity. Verdi made of music an eloquent language expressing the ineffable in human passions and emotions, stressing the marvelous and fabulous in life and history, exalting and consoling the untrained but sensitive spirits. He did not compose his works for an élite of privileged connoisseurs, but for the masses of his countrymen and for all mankind.

Verdi's music is popular and democratic. It is sometimes trivial, but never gross or indecorous. His inspiration seems at times indiscriminate and his workmanship careless or perfunctory. But his artistic means and intentions are always honest and transparent, spontaneous and expansive. His artistic efforts were powerful enough to transmit his natural vitality to the whole nation and to make the irrational and even preposterous ambiguity of the opera seem a substantial and veracious expression of the aesthetic aspirations and artistic ideals of the Italian people. Actually, no one in Italy seeks in the hybrid form of melodrama the symbolism of a philosophy or the expression of a national hero-worship. Modern Italian lovers of opera—and they are the whole nation—have little interest in the involved dramatic plots and spectacular stage actions of Verdi's melodramas. Their dramatic structure is considered mainly as a framework for lyrical interludes. In appreciating the continuous and sometimes violent contrasts between dramatic and lyrical episodes, the average spectator is fascinated mainly by the arias, duets, trios, quartets, and sextets climaxing the dramatic development and resolving the abundant sentiments and forced eloquence of the text into agreeable and convincing musical accents.

In that artificial simultaneity of divergent expressions, drama and lyricism form an indissoluble and unique artistic unity. The Italian public is always inclined to perceive the melodious bands of dramatic polyphony rather than the dialectical antitheses of opposing sentiments and contrasting psychological situations. Purely artistic concerns usually gain ascendancy over the moral, allegorical, or edifying content. For the Italians the opera evokes a resounding dream-world in which extraordinary human beings and events appear in an artistic reality of magic structure and profane spirit.

One can understand that in the presence of so intense and complete an expression of lyrical emotions and artistic ideals, no other form of art or poetry can flourish and assert itself with equal artistic impact. The success of the over-commercialized veristic opera since the end of the last century (Mascagni, Leoncavallo, Puccini) and the subsequent revival of orchestral compositions (Pizzetti, Respighi, Casella) have not changed the general Italian approach to music. It is still embodied in Verdi's art, which contributed more than anything else to the establishment in modern times of Italy's universal reputation. This circumstance, it is true, gives many Italian patriots an uneasy feeling of national guilt and inferiority. But nations and individuals who are not satisfied with one laurel at a time run the risk of becoming unjust to their past and, in some cases, of compromising their future.

XVII. *Epilogue: The Heritage of the Past and the Problems of the Future*

WHATEVER was achieved in two millennia within the geographical and linguistic boundaries of Italy has borne the mark of universality. It seems almost as if her leading men were too great and the number of her talents too vast for the size and capacity of the country. During the first thousand years after the fall of the Roman Empire, Virgil dominated what remained of secular culture and kept alive the global image of the world reflected in the geographical, historical, philosophical, and political amplitude of his truly imperial work. Caesar became the living symbol of this world, while Cicero's works perpetuated the Stoic ideal of a universal community of peoples.

In the religious field an overwhelming majority of Italian popes, beginning with Gregory the Great, succeeded in merging the idea of Christian brotherhood in the reality of a world-wide sacerdotal, juridical, and political organization to which Thomas Aquinas gave intellectual substance and metaphysical completion. Dante's thought and vision gave poetical, and consequently incorruptible, evidence that the municipalism of medieval Italian society tended to dissolve into an ideological commonwealth, Ghibelline or Guelf, rather than into a national community. In one way or another this trend prevailed in the political structure and mentality of the country until Napoleon made it, in the name of Liberty, a province of his French Empire, and after the Congress of Vienna converted it, in the name of God, into an Austrian domain.

Likewise, the local particularism of the diverse republican or autocratic city-states was always compensated by commercial or missionary intercourse with foreign peoples and the penetration of Italian explorers and traders to all the zones of the earth. What Marco Polo achieved, in 1298, with his empirical *Description of the World* was completed for the Western Hemisphere by the reports of Columbus and Vespucci. During the two centuries of this geographical experience the humanists accomplished a new Latinization of Europe and disclosed to every potentate and princelet of the peninsula the boundless horizons of ancient conquests.

In the following period European art, poetry, and civilization underwent a renewal inspired by Italian models, and the Western World became an Italian spiritual province. Simultaneously the Italian language supplanted Latin and preceded French as an international idiom of diplomacy, correspondence, and courtly intercourse. Bruno's philosophical insight into cosmic infinity and Campanella's political vision of a universal monarchy perpetuated the traditional impulse of the Italian mind toward the superhuman dimensions of Dante's and Michelangelo's inspiration. Galileo's celestial discoveries, his scientific method, and his influence on world civilization are one more aspect of this transcendent, cosmopolitan expansion, which obtained its historical counterpart and integration through Vico's comprehensive interpretation of human destinies. Music was the last and most deceptive of those steady efforts of the Italian mind to overcome the narrow limits of the country's ordinary existence. By that time the Italian people had obtained an international outlook through the multitude of authors, scientists, musicians, singers, dancers, and adventurers who settled in courts, academies, and cultural centers all over Europe.

The traditional cosmopolitanism of the Italians and their spiritual inclination toward universal values prevented the development of a political patriotism from common cultural experiences and linguistic affinities. Outside of his native Florence, Dante felt at home everywhere, at least intellectually. The question whether the country's literary idiom is Tuscan or Italian was debated for centuries and is still discussed. Neither Petrarca nor Machiavelli, who first heralded home rule for the country, ever had a clear idea of its political organization as a national community.

The regional and municipal dismemberment of the peninsula was felt to be a taint and a disadvantage mainly by those few authors who regarded France and Spain as models of a unified state. Since Italy had never been politically united, those two nations also inspired the numerous champions of Italian independence after the French and Spanish Revolutions had expounded in the constitutional charters of 1789 and 1812 the ideal of national independence and the theory of democratic liberties. Even then no unified political system could be conceived for a country whose structure was still determined by papal suzerainty and, after the collapse of the Spanish regime and the extinction of the Medici, Estes, and Farneses, by members and vassals of the Hapsburg dynasty.

None of the Italian rulers ever followed an Italian policy, least of all the house of Savoy, despite the elevation, in 1720, of the small frontier duchy of Piedmont to the Kingdom of Sardinia. The sentimental attachment of the average Italian to his native town and district, the lack of internal migration, and a tenacious, almost superstitious, sense of legality and legitimacy contributed more than loyalty or discipline to the general, passive acceptance of a regime of political regionalism and dynastic despotism. Two centuries of Jesuit education had fixed in the Italian mind the concept of political absolutism as an instrument of Divine Providence and not, as Machiavelli taught, of national reconstruction and the common good. Everyone, down to 'barbers and craftsmen,' talked about 'reasons of state.' [1] But the clever man who made this term popular was only concerned with the power and authority of the rulers and not with the interests of the subjects.[2] Likewise, his sagacious contemporary, Traiano Boccalini, who wrote the most virulent satire against the Spanish despoliation of Italy, could give his countrymen no better advice than to accept it with resignation.[3]

Under these circumstances, neither civic virtue nor military

[1] L. Zuccolo, *Dissertatio de ratione status,* 1663.
[2] Giovanni Botero, *Della Ragion di Stato,* 1589.
[3] *I ragguagli di Parnaso,* 1612; *Pietra del paragone politico,* 1615, etc.

discipline could develop as traits of a national character. Yet neither foreign domination nor despotic regimes prevented the formation of a body of loyal and diligent functionaries who became, especially in the Upper Country, the mainstay of a respected and generally honest administration. Among public servants the post was esteemed more than opinions, and a title of nobility or, more recently, a simple decoration more than freedom and even money. Every Italian archive contains countless documents of irreproachable professional practice that persisted even in periods of open public favoritism and general corruption. When, in 1861, Italian unity was officially achieved, a national army had to be built up almost out of nothing, while a poor but trustworthy officialdom, taken over from regional and local administrations, became at once the working instrument of the new state.

This very old tradition of selfless loyalty and professional integrity is particularly striking in a country that gave the world the most vicious examples of tyranny, and where abuse of authority, misgovernment, brigandage, and fiscal extortion were customary manifestations of public life. Despite these circumstances, loyalty has not always meant blind submission and opportunistic servility. An extensive, if dull, political literature reveals the persistence of an instinctive sense of legality, handed down through many generations of notaries, chancellors, scribes, accountants, and officials of every rank and function. A respect for authority and concern for legitimacy were felt even in times of the most cruel and criminal political disorder. A formally correct administration became the substitute for civic spirit and social justice.

The bureaucracy embodied the traditional legalistic conservatism that inspired many political writers of the Counter-Reformation and the ensuing period of paternalistic, oligarchic, or despotic absolutism. In those numerous treatises, followed in the eighteenth century by no less abundant and voluminous juridical dissertations, Italy was never conceived as a political entity and the Italians never appear other than as subjects of an absolutist or oligarchic government. Nor does the word or concept of liberty ever occur in that political literature in which

p*

justice only appears as the execution of a sovereign will and not as a moral necessity or a social problem. Therefore all those discussions of public life are filled with generalizations on 'good government' and technicalities of law and administration.

It is characteristic of that Italian approach to the problems of public life that it persisted even when the influence of the French enlightenment began to creep secretly through the frivolous, bigoted, and policed Italy of singers, adventurers, and gallant abbés. Italian theorists never joined the English philosophers and French Encyclopedists in disserting publicly on tolerance, equality, human rights, and popular sovereignty, although these concepts were not unknown to the scholars and noblemen of Milan, Florence, and Naples. But their works dealt exclusively with special fields of human activity and public administration; they did not touch on fundamental questions or attempt to undermine the political structure of their country.

Many outstanding Italians took an active interest in economic theories, and Antonio Genovese, Ferdinando Galiani, and Pietro Verri were the continental pioneers in this field. Juridical literature culminated in Cesare Beccaria's immortal treatise on crime and punishment, published in 1764, which was the first effective attempt to embody the humanitarian doctrines and rational speculations of his age in legal practice. But all these learned and broad-minded professional men soon realized that economic planning and judicial improvements could not be attained without a shifting of authority, an organized system of civil liberties, official co-operation, or the storming of a Bastille. The ideas elaborated by those Italians could find acceptance in Necker's France, in Adam Smith's England, or under the enlightened despotism of Catherine the Great, but not in a country still controlled by the Inquisition and ruled by coercion, ignorance, and carnivals.

It took some time before the Italian sovereigns promoted an economic revival, fiscal reforms, and a judicial readjustment after the principles of equality, social justice, and free enterprise defended by philosophers and suggested by far-sighted functionaries. But in most cases those attempts were a matter of expediency rather than of conviction, thus bearing out Machiavelli's contention that 'men, when they are well governed, neither seek nor desire any other liberty.' [4] Be that as it may, it is a striking fact that the reforms undertaken in Italy, even after the French Revolution, were of a merely administrative character, with no ideological implications or moral assumptions such as those formulated in the American Declaration of Independence or in the Bill of Rights. And even in those cases the most radical changes were not undertaken by Italian sovereigns and republics, but by the Austrian government in Lombardy under Maria Theresa and Joseph II, or by the Austrian Grand Dukes of Tuscany.

The papal state, governed almost exclusively by ecclesiastics, remained until its end in 1870 the sore point of Europe, while misgovernment, poverty, and inertia paralyzed every activity in its fertile but depopulated territories. In the Kingdom of Naples the most depraved forms of spoliation and banditry extended the feudal rights of innumerable local barons as far as the bridal chambers of their subjects and serfs. No administrative improvement or military organization after the Prussian pattern was able to transform the Kingdom of Sardinia into a modern state. If the Piedmontese were the keenest and most successful champions of liberty it was largely because the House of Savoy stubbornly resisted every concession that might have diminished the exercise of their absolute sovereign authority. It was not until 1848 that Charles Albert of Savoy granted his subjects the constitutional rights of the *Statuto,* Italy's first national charter. He did so with a view to enlarging his territory at the expense of other Italian sovereigns who could not help yielding to an almost unanimous popular movement in favor of parliamentary governments, administrative reforms, and freedom of speech, press, and association. The first honestly liberal member of the House of Savoy was Victor Emmanuel II, who achieved Italian unity in the name of liberty, and not by dynastic claims and forced concessions.

The moral and civil renewal of Italy was not promoted by any definite social philosophy or economic and political theories. In

---

[4] *Discourses on Livy,* III, ch. 5.

that process of national regeneration, the ruling dynasties had no part. They were as absent or hostile as the Roman Church, whose spiritual exhaustion equaled its political weakness and cultural inertia. No particular class in Italian society assumed leadership in the reorganization of public life and opinion. As always in Italian history, every section of the population and every region of the country contributed their share to the common accomplishments. As individuals, many noblemen, ecclesiastics, professionals, and plebeians joined in the discussions and actions directed toward the reform of public life in accordance with moral principles rather than administrative organization.

It was possible to obtain the common consent of the active elements in a divided country, because the reaction to the new ideas of liberty and equality was not theoretical, speculative, utopian, or demagogic, or even abstract and intellectual, but essentially emotional and consequently as far from systematic planning as from skeptical criticism. Actually, the sole pioneers of national reconstruction were a few poets who gave their amorphous, emasculated, and apathetic country an inspiration for a new respectable existence. Their poems were in close harmony with the general trend of European sentiments and opinions. But none of those literary heralds of a secular Italian redemption ever deluded the minds of their countrymen with the deceptive vision of an ideal society. Never did their works become an expression of social theories or political objectives. It would even be difficult to find in their poems those accents of political patriotism which dominated Italian literature during and after the struggle for territorial unity in the nineteenth century.

This stirring unconventional poetry arose, around 1760, from moral indignation and sentimental despair over the 'fetid and dead Italy' destroyed by mental laziness and regimes of tyranny.[5] Of that social misery with its consequent disorder and injustice, Giuseppe Parini gave a graphic picture, representing in keen, polished verses the contrast between the fashionable idleness of aristocratic idlers and the toil and poverty of the working people.[6] The impact of his lyrical praise of liberty and decency,

---

[5] Vittorio Alfieri, *Vita*, ch. xv.
[6] *Il Giorno* (1763-5); *Il Bisogno* (1765); *L'Educazione* (1764), etc.

the aptness of his satirical picture of the customs of his time have given his poems a lasting popularity. In the ears of a nation lulled to dream by the melodious murmur of Arcadian verses and gallant chansons, those accents resounded like trumpet blasts. The public and the Austrian police were amazed that a humble Milanese priest should use the customary poetic schemes and mythological allusions to praise the social virtues rather than Christian charity, human dignity rather than humility, his native country rather than the ruling dynasty.

Count Vittorio Alfieri created the poetic symbols for these moral and social sentiments in a series of tragedies inspired by a furious hatred of tyranny and a fervent worship of Italy's national glories. Though imbued with the political philosophy of Montesquieu and poetically inspired by the heroes of the Roman republic and the American Revolution, he never conceived a plan for the theoretical justification or practical realization of his enthusiasm for freedom and independence. His vehement tragedies, satirical poems, and political writings are the thundering explosions of a spirited nobleman intolerant of the limitations imposed by potentates, priests, and social conventions on the personal liberty and intellectual interests of a man of his rank and temper. Hence, his violent reactions when the mob-rule of the French Revolution revealed a form of tyranny he had never contemplated. His motives were moral indignation and a passionate intellectual patriotism. He wished through his poetry to mold an Italian consciousness activated by the practice of freedom and substantiated by the worship of national glories.

Alfieri's personality and work represent the impetuous revival of the laical spirit of Italy and the sudden transfer of the national culture from literary conventicles and ecclesiastical schools to public opinion and political action. From then on the Italians—who always took their inspiration from bards rather than philosophers—filled their minds and burdened their hearts with a patriotic substance that affected their natural feelings, worked upon thoughts and emotions, and drove the universal trends of the Italians into national channels. This evolution is particularly evident in the writing of the highly sensitive and profoundly human Ugo Foscolo, a no less cosmopolitan personality than Alfieri. He was even more resolutely democratic in political action and more distinctively Italian in his lyrical classicism, in the romantic spleen of his *Jacopo Ortis,* in the contemplation of death and glory in his poetical masterpiece.[7]

*   *   *

The event that made possible that vigorous explosion of laical interests and national feelings was the suppression of the Jesuit order, in 1773. With that momentous act the whole educational system of the country, monopolized by the Jesuits during two centuries of intellectual supremacy, crumbled and dissolved without leaving behind an organized substitute. The bull *Dominus ac Redemptor Noster,* reluctantly published by Pope Clement XIV, marks the end of the Counter-Reformation and of the ecclesiastical domination of Italy's cultural and spiritual life. The move was not prompted by philosophical enlightenment or democratic convictions. On the contrary, it was an act imposed by all the Catholic potentates of Europe and their Italian vassals, who felt their absolute sovereign power threatened, weakened, and even paralyzed by the political and financial organization of the Company of Jesus.

With the suppression of its militant vanguard the papacy was unable to work directly upon the mind and conscience of foreign subjects or against the initiatives and authority of foreign sovereigns. It could contrive no counteraction against heterodox trends and revolutionary doctrines in schools and families. Without the indirect intellectual support of the Jesuits even the Inquisition could not work efficiently as a bulwark against the growing radicalism in secular thought and action. Under these circumstances, the temporary abolition of the Inquisition in Tuscany and Lombardy only placed the control of intellectual life directly and exclusively under the jurisdiction of the state. Future developments in the political organization of Europe and Italy showed the inefficiency of a purely laical absolutism. After Waterloo, Pope Pius VII successively revived the Inquisition,

[7] *I Sepolcri,* 1806.

the Index, and the Company of Jesus as the strongest supports of a Catholic reaction and of the foreign regimes re-established throughout the Italian domain.

In the cultural field, the disintegration of the Jesuit educational organization had consequences even more lasting and thorough-going than in the political sphere. The rhetorical humanism culti-vated by the Order gave way to a cultural and national classicism combining vigor and elegance in art and poetry, and stressing the Italian rather than the universal values of classical tradition. On this point Italian classicism differs essentially from both Goethe's inspired humanism and the imperial phantasms of the Napoleonic era. In Italy, after the end of Jesuit influence, Latin was abandoned as the language of science and the schools in favor of the purified national vernacular, cherished as the only living symbol of a country-wide cultural unity. Dante, Machia-velli, Galileo, the Italian classics of the sixteenth century, be-came the object of intense study, passionate interest, and critical interpretation. Alfieri's vision of a free and sovereign Italy was substantiated only by these literary reminiscences and interests. No one had a clear idea of what freedom in Italy might mean in a practical political sense.

The poetic appeal to freedom and unity could reach only a comparatively small and educated section of the Italian people, and even there it led to confusion, perplexity, tension, or isolated and improvident action. The French Revolution aroused violent indignation as well as a scattered enthusiasm for rebellion. Year after year a series of conspiracies and revolts against the old order and its legitimate custodians flared up throughout Italy, down to Sicily, Corsica, and Sardinia, provoking foreign inter-vention, bloody acts of repression, and the execution of ring-leaders and organizers. These local upheavals culminated in the short-lived Neapolitan revolution of 1799, which ended with the decimation of the local intelligentsia and the shameful hanging of Admiral Francesco Caràcciolo on the yard-arm of Lord Nelson's flagship.

From then on, countless patriots, democratic idealists, political hotheads, and desperadoes paid with their lives, with imprison-ment, or exile for premature or desultory attempts to establish regional or local constitutions. Napoleon's sweeping victories, after 1796, and his reorganization of Italy, first as a republic and then as a kingdom within the French Empire, awakened the country from its general political lethargy and obliged the entire population to accept the French conquest in place of Austrian domination. The two last vestiges of the traditional universal powers disappeared from the political scene when the abdication of Francis II, in 1805, put an end to the Holy Roman Empire, and when Pope Pius VII, a prisoner of Napoleon, lost the Papal State to the French conqueror.

The reaction of the Italian people to these portentous events was in general favorable and confident. The idea of liberty and the call for popular co-operation stirred a country in need of administrative reforms and spiritual rejuvenation. Napoleon was a hero of Italian-name and descent to whom revolutionary France had given an opportunity, a mission, and a sword. When Italy was proclaimed part of the new empire, the revived literary and artistic classicism of that era obtained a historical justification and concrete support beyond the archaeological interests of scholars or the hobbies of homeless literati and professional artists. Canova's statue of Napoleon represented in the nude dignity of an idealized Roman emperor, and Vincenzo Monti's ornate poetical praise of Bonaparte's victories were not considered opportunistic ovations to a new conqueror, but accepted as exuberant expressions of an almost delirious patriotic enthusiasm.

The success of the Napoleonic organization of Italy seemed to solve all the historical and current problems of the country. It combined the imperial idea of universality, to which the Italians had been accustomed for many centuries, with the concept of national unity, and the traditions of regional autonomy. It was that heroic and clever reconciliation of past and present that prompted Manzoni to celebrate the Emperor, after his death at St. Helena, as an arbiter of two epochs of human history and as an inspired instrument of Divine Providence.[8]

But Napoleon and Italy lost that unique opportunity when,

[8] *Il Cinque Maggio*, 1821.

between 1796 and 1814, the French administration disillusioned the whole Italian population by heaping upon it the moral burden of foreign rule and the unpopular measures of a foreign administration. The newly awakened sentiment of national dignity was offended when upstart relatives of Napoleon took over the vacant thrones of the historical dynasties. French generals and magistrates administered the Italian provinces and inaugurated liberty and equality by imposing upon an unprepared population the laws, customs, and concepts of the French Revolution and the Napoleonic government. The imposition of military conscription on an unwarlike people who had nothing to defend and even less to conquer seemed too high a price for the civil and social improvements acquired through the abolition of fiscal and juridical privileges of the clergy and nobility. The secularization of the enormous ecclesiastical domains, without agrarian reform and a new social order, deprived large sections of the poor population of a last hope to escape from indigence, and destroyed the traditional possibility of a charitable haven.

When Napoleon was overthrown and his satellites were again replaced by Austrian governors and the survivors of the old dynasties, the Italian people found themselves deprived of a great experience and thrown back into an autocratic subjection they had forgotten how to endure. As always in such circumstances, a great part of the Italians accepted the *fait accompli* passively and acquiesced in a situation they were unable to change. But the active and alert elements of the population did not yield and started an underground movement of a patriotic and democratic character that rapidly spread throughout the country and among groups of exiled intellectuals. For the first time in history a nation-wide secret organization bound together all classes and professions of Italian society, grouped in local, regional, and vocational 'cells' of conspirators and sympathizers.

That political association of the *Carbonari* imitated, after 1817, in adventurous mood and in secret conventicles the rituals, symbols, and practices of Freemasonry, but with a national rather than a humanitarian goal. The objective of that secret movement was to prevent political apathy, to undermine the armed forces and the public administration of the foreign-ruled Italian states, to disseminate in schools and families the idea of national unity and democratic liberty, and to outwit the political police in the daily struggle between conspiracy. and authority. This was a new aspect in the history of Italian public life. The adventurous spirit, odd rites, and challenging attitudes attracted the Italian youth as much as the enthusiastic devotion to the new political and patriotic ideals. Romanticism as a European literary and intellectual movement was substantiated in Italy by political action and expressed as much in secret practices as in risky and heroic undertakings.

The political mobilization of the Italian people progressed rapidly and gained recruits from all classes. To their growing insurrectionary mood the proverbial misgovernment of the Papal State and the Low Country contributed as much as the resentment of the Northerners against the Austrian annexation of Milan, Venice, and the highly civilized provinces of Lombardy and Venetia. The defiant display of power organized on every occasion by the imperial army hurt the Italian feelings more deeply than had the previous degradation of Rome, Florence, Genoa, Turin, and all the historical places of the country to mere prefectures of French administrative districts.

At the same time the industrious subjects of the King of Sardinia, who had learned to appreciate, during the Napoleonic era, the practical benefits and emotional appeal of political freedom, were unable to adapt themselves again to the stubborn dynastic absolutism of the House of Savoy and to the opportunistic vacillations of its policy. The strong impulse given everywhere to laical culture and education in the course of one generation stirred up a determined anti-clerical reaction when public and private schools again came under the tutelage of the religious orders. Laxity and ruse easily overcame restrictions and control, and no possible coercion and intimidation could dispel the memory of the revolutionary ideas of the previous era.

The seditious ferments spread throughout the country by discontent, resentment, conspiracies, and a genuine love of liberty were activated everywhere, between 1820 and 1830, by the success of the insurrectionary movements in Spain, Latin America,

Greece, and France. An era of popular revolts and tumults, of passive resistance and open mutiny, of violent repression and foreign intervention completed the psychological remolding of the Italian people into a political-minded community dominated by passions rather than doctrines and guided by sentiments rather than systems and plans.

This circumstance made the Italian *Risorgimento* a domestic affair and a tumultuous, picturesque, romantic adventure, in which heroic sacrifice, candid devotion, and political gambling counted as much as quixotism, declamation, and violence. Although large sections of the population remained politically apathetic, the whole country became sentimentally involved in a patriotic state of mind manifested in every aspect of life and culture. Just as in the Middle Ages nothing was felt, said, or done without mentioning the name of God, so in the new patriotic era, the inspiring image of a free Italy pervaded every thought and emotion of all classes. The literature of that epoch and most of the nineteenth century became predominantly patriotic in inspiration and purpose. Likewise the efforts of Italian scholars in competing with foreign methods of research, and the interests of scientists who transformed their meetings into national assemblies and political clubs. Poetry and music became the popular propagandists of that general temper, and the Italians finally ceased to conceive of, or to appreciate, a cultural or intellectual achievement for its own sake and its own intrinsic value.

Only two authors were able to overcome this spiritual insularity and patriotic provincialism by directing their minds toward universal sources of inspiration. One was Giacomo Leopardi, in whose frank atheism the laical spirit of Italy found its most disquieting and alarming expression; the other was Alessandro Manzoni, the last Italian poet inspired by a comforting belief in Divine Providence and mercy. Both surpassed the common patriotic enthusiasm of their contemporaries and the exceptional shocks and experiences of their intense and sorrowful existence by plunging their thoughts into the mystery of human destiny as disclosed in humble people or famous men, in simple events or historical and natural catastrophes. Leopardi's lyrical imagination and sentimental *élan* removed the ordinary obstacles that might have prevented his mind from rising to the contemplation of the infinite in time and space. But there he foundered, engulfed in the heart-breaking vacuum of an intellectual nihilism and dragging down in his shipwreck even the amiable aspects of this cruel world.[9]

At the same time Manzoni projected his moral anxiety and unflinching belief in the redeeming power of the Christian virtues into an imaginary historical cross-section of the old Italian society.[10] A faith without bigotry, a supreme justice without theology and decretals, a charity without worldly reward are the moral forces which, in his *Promessi Sposi*, finally overcome the human cruelty, natural calamities, and political disorder which Manzoni describes with consummate skill and an incomparable power of portraiture and evocation.

In their contrasting attitudes toward the world and transcendence, Leopardi and Manzoni represent the polarity of the Italian spiritual heritage and of contemporary European trends of thought and action. Yet both the agnostic pessimist and the Catholic optimist expressed their common conviction that no social and political renewal of mankind and of their country could ever be obtained without the revival of the moral conscience.[11] In scoffing at the cult of progress, at the doctrines of democratic equality, and at the vagaries of romantic Catholicism, Leopardi repudiated the most cherished idols of his generation for the sake of a vague poetical ideal of human fraternity. Manzoni's poetry and epic masterpiece, on the other hand, were unable to restore as an active force of national reconstruction that simple faith in God and in a better life which concludes his narrative of the hardships and adventures of Renzo and Lucia.

Because of their deep respect for poets, the Italians did not resent the spiritual inadequacy and political aloofness of the two most revered men of their era. The patriotic fervor of Leopardi's youthful poems and the stirring verses of Manzoni's historical tragedies were not forgotten. Italy of the early *Risorgi-*

[9] *L'Infinito, La Ginestra*, etc.

[10] *I Promessi Sposi*, 1827.

[11] Leopardi, *Operette morali*, 1827; Manzoni, *Osservazioni sulla morale cattolica*, 1819.

mento had enough popular poets to suit the mood and emotions of an eventful era: Berchet and Pellico, Niccolini and Giusti, Prati and Mameli, Grossi and Tommaseo, with many more in every province and patriotic group. All of them reflect the fervor, the hopes and disappointments of a rising nation stirred by blinding revolutionary passions and at the same time paralyzed by the common-sense evidence of its own weakness and unpreparedness. What the country needed under those circumstances was not only bards, conspirators, prophets, and martyrs, but political leaders provided with vision and the power of persuasion, able to transform a vague temper of mind into an effective public opinion, and lyrical effusions into determined action and a working organization.

This was the goal of 'Young Italy,' a political association founded in 1831 by Giuseppe Mazzini, an exile for most of his life but for many years the spiritual wire-puller of the Italian insurrectionary theater. His great idea was to destroy Italian particularism by achieving the political unity of the country against Austrian supremacy, and, in addition, to secure its eternal stability in a fraternal brotherhood of all mankind. He believed this utopian objective could be obtained by a nation-wide association of followers ready to devote themselves, through action and sacrifice, to the cause of 'God and the People.'

This was the first slogan in the political history of Italy. It proved powerful enough to rally in a secret movement the intellectual forces and the youthful enthusiasm of a restless generation deeply convinced of the new role of Italy in a regenerated European commonwealth. But what was *God* in a secular civilization, and without the myths and dogmas of the Church? What was the *People* without a social order and an organized nation? How could that slogan become a program of action or a reality as long as the great military powers of Europe protected the papacy and preserved its territorial patrimony? Mazzini believed that a republican movement could chase them all out of the country and by a strong and lasting effort free the vital forces of national reconstruction.

The further evolution of the *Risorgimento* proved that Mazzini was wrong in that institutional dogmatism. Nevertheless, he was not a dreamer; he was rather an agitator who, on the one hand, knew the weakness of the European system of his era and rightly appreciated the power of the new trends of thought and action, but who, on the other hand, believed that no nation, state, or institution can subsist and develop on a merely materialistic and practical foundation. Karl Marx ridiculed Mazzini's religious mind and characterized him as an apostle of a lost cause rather than the leader of a rising nation. But Italy at that time, and for many years to come, showed no interest in economic reforms, industrial collectivism, and class struggle.

A nation of peasants and artisans, intellectually ruled by a conservative bourgeoisie and traditionally educated by ecclesiastics, Italy not only remained obstinate against radical ideas, but did not even contribute in a noteworthy measure to the theoretical or practical development of socialist doctrines and trends. While in England and France a socialist order was contemplated in well-known economic systems and sociological ideologies, Mazzini continued for years to sermonize the still disenfranchised workers, and Vincenzo Gioberti conceived a federation of Italian states under the leadership of a liberal pontiff.

The immense popularity acquired for a short time by Gioberti's treatise *On the Moral and Civil Primacy of Italy* (1843) revealed the latent attachment of the Italians to their historical traditions, regional home rule, and religious institutions. A learned liberal priest living in exile, Gioberti was able to find innumerable followers who were convinced that the papacy could take the lead in liberating the Italians from foreign domination, despotism, servitude, and isolation. The delirious enthusiasm that spread through the country when Pius IX, after his election in 1846, undertook some important reforms in the political and judicial administration of the papal state seemed to fulfill Gioberti's neo-Guelf dreams. They seemed, indeed, less fantastic than the creation of an Italian kingdom or republic by dethroning the Pope and chasing the Austrians, the Bourbons, and all the other Italian sovereigns out of their legal territories and residences.

All the patriotic visionaries were soon disillusioned when Pope Pius IX revoked his concessions to modern trends and institutions, and when the libertarian revolution of 1848 provoked a determined policy of orthodox reaction and theocratic absolutism under the protection of the Austrian army in the North and of the French garrison in Rome. The general failure of the revolution everywhere in Europe struck the final blow to Mazzini's republican romanticism and to Gioberti's federalist utopia. Both doctrines survived their defeat as oratorical topics and as a temper of mind: the one contributing in our own day to the overthrow of the monarchy, the other providing Italy with an exalted nationalism based on the idea of a God-given moral and spiritual primacy.

The scattered insurrections which in 1848 shook the country from Milan to Sicily and brought large sections of the population to barricades and battlefields revealed the profound changes the intellectual and moral structure of Italy had undergone. For the first time in their history the Italians were prepared to shed their blood for an idea. Patriotism was the only faith for which they ever showed a willingness to fight and make heroic sacrifices. The insurrections were, of course, ill-prepared and amateurish in organization and strategy. The whole movement was still more constitutional than national. But it did, for the first time, reveal Italy as a political force to be reckoned with.

Despite the usual opportunism, hesitations, blunders, and theatrical gestures and episodes, the country seemed to have fallen under the spell of a political demon that led it to desperate undertakings like Milan's 'five days,' or to absurd ventures like the Tuscan revolution and the short-lived Roman republic of 1848. The importance of political thought and initiative in Italian life is documented by the unprecedented number of party leaders and statesmen who made their appearance: Balbo and D'Azeglio in Piedmont; Cesare Correnti and Carlo Cattaneo in Milan; Tommaseo and Daniele Manin in Venice; Guerrazzi in Florence; Terenzio Mamiami in Rome; Guglielmo Pepe in Naples; La Farina, the brothers Amari, and many others in Sicily. All these men survive as national heroes in the memorials of Italian glories; they are little known abroad, it is true, but are unforgotten in national and local traditions.

The more or less successful contributions of all these men to the national cause were soon overshadowed by the accomplishments of the two makers of modern Italy: Giuseppe Garibaldi, a spirited military leader, and Camillo Benso, Count of Cavour, probably the greatest political genius of the nineteenth century. For the correct appreciation of his extraordinary ability one should consider not only his talents as a parliamentarian, diplomat, statesman, and organizer of a civil and military administration. In each of these branches of public life Cavour had many remarkable competitors throughout the Western Hemisphere in an era of intense political activity. But in creating a new political community out of a nation dominated by foreign powers and torn by opposing trends and interests, he enjoyed neither the Napoleonic prestige of Talleyrand nor the cosmopolitan experience of Metternich. In his daring initiatives he was not, like the British statesmen, backed by naval power and industrial wealth, nor could he rely, like Bismarck, upon a strong army and efficient technical equipment. For uniting a nation, he lacked Lincoln's democratic traditions and the national resources of France. He had at his disposal only an exceptional intelligence inspired by a deep faith in liberal institutions, supported by a realistic appreciation of events and possibilities, and directed by a punctilious integrity and singleness of purpose.

During the ten tempestuous years of Cavour's leadership the small and defeated frontier kingdom of Sardinia acted like a great power in order to become one in fact. Such an attitude would have been ridiculous and destructive without his will power and calm dignity in handling the internal and foreign affairs of his government and, implicitly, of all Italy Although the dynasty of Savoy was disgraced by selfishness, bigotry, treachery, and defeat, he was able to impose it on the whole country. Through the unpopular Crimean expedition in 1854 and the victorious alliance with France in 1859, Cavour succeeded in rehabilitating the army, demoralized since 1849 by the humiliating capitulation of Novara. After the conquest of Lombardy with French help, Cavour challenged the public opinion of his country by ceding to France, as the price for an unfair but valuable alliance, the territories of Nice and Savoy, which would always have been a foreign body and a source of conflict within the linguistic and cultural unity of the peninsula.

That territorial cession manifested Cavour's subordination of dynastic and historical rights to national principles. In a wise move of magnanimous diplomacy he secretly entrusted the conquest of Sicily and the Neapolitan kingdom to his most popular and violent opponent, Giuseppe Garibaldi. The Bourbon army and dynasty collapsed at the first impact of his band of a thousand ill-equipped and poorly armed Red Shirt volunteers, while popular revolts, plebiscites, and the military occupation of central Italy completed the political unity of the country. When Cavour died prematurely, in June 1861, the official program of the newly proclaimed Kingdom of Italy included the annexation of Venice, still an Austrian stronghold with a prosperous and strategic hinterland, and the abolition of the temporal power of the papacy, then limited to the city of Rome and its desolate Campagna.

For the attainment of those goals Cavour left to his competent but mediocre successors the leading principles of action, covering international questions of far-reaching importance that could not be solved by local uprisings or military adventures like Garibaldi's raid, let alone his defeat at Mentana, in 1867. Venice and Rome fell to the new Italian kingdom as an aftermath of the Prussian victory over Austria in 1866, and over France in 1870. In the following era of internal and external consolidation, all national energies were concentrated on the political, financial, industrial, and military organization of the country, which was spiritually exhausted by the dramatic effort of her unification, and overwhelmed by the extent of the tasks and problems at hand.

*　　*　　*

The international situation of the Italian kingdom was determined during the entire course of its existence by the circumstance that it remained the weakest of the great European powers and the greatest of the minor nations. That ambiguous condition was the cause of all the inconsistencies and vacillations in Italy's external relations, which are frequently attributed to unscrupulous opportunism and Machiavellian perfidy interpreted as basic features of the Italian national character. Since Italy's inadequate army could not compete with those of her neighbors,

the country had to accept an unpopular alliance with the stronger
military powers of Germany and Austria, and to change sides
in critical moments in order to survive. Similarly, the Italian
navy, which had been rebuilt with pride and sacrifice after the
crushing defeats in the waters of Lissa, in 1866, could develop
only in co-operation with the unchallenged British fleet. For
these reasons Italy always counted as an unstable auxiliary in
the balance of European powers. She could never seriously aspire to a leading political position in the community of modern
nations.

The internal situation remained similarly unsettled. The ideals,
trends, passions, and forces that inspired the great drama of the
Risorgimento survived as oratorical topics for parliamentary discussions, party strife, and journalistic controversies. The organization of public life and welfare was a matter of expediency
rather than of organic planning. The administrative centralization of a highly differentiated country was accomplished after
foreign patterns, and under the auspices of a dynasty that acquired authentic and general popularity only through the charm
and intelligence of Italy's first queen, Margherita di Savoia.

Italy's liberal institutions were shaped after French and English models, but had to function in a generally conservative
country of uncomplying individualists in whom illiteracy, poverty, and submissiveness had effaced any capacity for consistent
co-operation in public life. The complex work of national reconstruction inspired no original political vision or methods of government and social organization adequate to the peculiar needs
and historical antecedents of the country. In all the manifestations of Italy's political ideas, social endeavors, and intellectual
trends it is easier to find a reflection of European currents than
any original contribution to the great contemporary stream of
thought and action. This cosmopolitan aspect of Italian national
civilization has been duly considered by enlightened patriots,
such as Benedetto Croce,[12] who were not infected by the chauvinistic narcissism of noisy politicians and fickle publicists.

---

[12] *A History of Italy* (1871-1915), transl. by C. M. Ady, Oxford, 1929;
La letteratura della nuova Italia and the review *La critica*, since 1903.

The genius of Italy did not express itself in the professorial modification or dialectical remodeling of German systems, French doctrines, English traditions, and Russian experiences. The spiritual and practical unpreparedness of large sections of the country for democratic institutions and liberal trends sustained their emotional, oratorical, and formalistic aberrations in parliament and regional or municipal councils, and lowered the interest of vast masses of people in the facts and problems of public life. In the public opinion of Italy the government—*il governo*—still remained an institution detached from the people, who continued to consider the executive authorities as exploiters and the laws as an imposition and duress. Hence the oscillation of the Italian character and mood between emotion and skepticism, devotion and anarchism, realistic intelligence and pettifogging hair-splitting.

Since the achievement of national unity simultaneously with the centralization of public life and interests, there has been everywhere in Italy a sudden revival of literary regionalism marked by such writers as Giovanni Verga and Grazia Deledda. Never has dialect literature so flourished as during the making and consolidation of political unity. But this literary and sentimental reaction to the centralization of public and intellectual life only added some provincial traits to the still unformed spiritual physiognomy of modern Italy. These are evident in the mood and works of the few poets who, like Giovanni Pascoli, drew inspiration from the charms and trials of the native soil and its simple people. Only the poet and scholar, Giosue Carducci, succeeded in creating a national Italian humanism whose pagan substance, classical forms, and patriotic vigor seemed to combine the spiritual heritage of Italy with her modern national aspirations.

However, Carducci's classicism and his belief that 'only in the past is beauty, only in death is truth' hardly satisfied and inspired generations attracted more and more by the tortuosities of party politics, spoiled by the easy success of journalism, fascinated by sports and the conquests of science and technology. While his influence remained confined to literary circles and scholarly groups, the reaction to that Olympian attitude of aesthetic retrospection assumed in life and literature the violent forms of imperialism, activism, and futurism that led the country to madness and disaster.

This development is illustrated by the adventurous career of Gabriele d'Annunzio, a master of literary craftsmanship who, at the end of the last century, started his career as a spoiled child of the corrupt Roman aristocracy and ended as a poetic herald of national heroism and triumphal conquests. With his suggestive metaphors and Byronic attitudes this last offspring of the French Parnassians filled the Italian mind with a paroxysmal imperialistic quixotism and prepared the advent of a histrionic political superman who bluffed the whole world with resounding words and menacing gestures. The war-weary people and the alarmed powers who wanted peace and order at any price allowed themselves to be misled by that deceptive display of strength and authority. It was supported by an international journalistic propaganda and an armed organization of black-shirted partisans. The authentic documents at hand and the present plight of the country show it for what it was.

*   *   *

The making of Italy and the further development of the country remained an essentially secular affair. Deprived of much of its prestige and influence, of its territories and privileges, the Catholic Church retired into an attitude of official hostility toward all political, social, and intellectual movements and achievements in modern life and thought. In spite of the patriotic devotion of a great part of the secular clergy and of the political neutrality of the monastic and mendicant orders, the estrangement of the Church from the active sections of Italian society became deep and persistent.

The attitude of uncompromising medievalism assumed by Pius IX and his successors in regard to modern trends and experiences did not stem the tide, but only strengthened the currents of more or less organized anticlericalism, which, with indifferent agnosticism, represented a strong force in the development of national life. Religious doctrines and institutions were not affected by these feelings. Even in passivity the bulk of the Italian people remained faithful to their Catholic traditions and took no part in controversies of a dogmatic and ecclesiastical character. Innumerable examples of devotion, of piety and unassuming charity, showed the undiminished appeal of the Christian virtues to a people that had never known the Puritan vigilance toward sin and had always tolerated, as a matter of routine, the most shocking neglect of the Decalogue.

The Church continued to attract into its ranks not only people desiring to renounce the world for the sake of eternal salvation, but also those who sought an opportunity for a career, though in most cases the career was quite wretched. To a substantial part of the population, ecclesiastical activity represented a profession as much as a vocation. Thus, the Vatican continued to remain what it had been for centuries, namely, a predominantly Italian power and the only active heir to old Italian universalism. Italian anticlericalism was mainly a political safeguard for the protection of laical trends and institutions in a country in which an absolute sovereign with a brilliant court, a strict hierarchy, and a world-wide accredited diplomatic corps had exerted in all times an antinational political influence.

The position of the Church was confirmed by Pius X at his first consistory, on 9 November 1903, when the political office of the pontiff was proclaimed inseparable from his religious and moral mission. Since then the Vatican has developed more and more into an international political and diplomatic center, gradually renouncing its territorial rights and ambitions. It has directed its efforts to reconquering the schools and to asserting itself in the system of national education. The final agreements between the papacy and the Fascist regime resulted as much from mutual suspicion as from mutual respect for hierarchical institutions. With the Concordat of 1929, Rome gained not the two suns fancied by Dante,[18] but two autocratic rulers, one infallible by virtue of dogmatic decree and the other by virtue of political pretension. Cavour's historic formula of 'a free Church in a free state' was eliminated from the reality of Italian life.

[18] *Purgatorio*, XVI, 106-8.

Despite the coexistence and more or less official co-operation of the two powers, the Church failed to become a source of inspiration in the intellectual, spiritual, and political life of the country. In Italian society as a whole, religion is more a matter of sentiment than of thought, more a matter of habit and practice than of controversy. The ecclesiastical authorities have crushed all attempts of a few reformers, from Antonio Rosmini to Ernesto Buonaiuti, to revive the religious life of the country by reconciling the rigid dogmatism of the Church with the trends and experience of the modern world. On the other hand, most of the intellectual leaders of Italy, from Dante to Croce, were listed in the Index of condemned authors and forbidden books, and still are.

The Italian laity, living in the ubiquitous Catholic medium of the country but resisting the dogmatic pressure of the Church, has indulged in such subterfuges, makeshifts, and aberrations as a mythless, aesthetic, cultural, socialist, or national Catholicism. These were all more or less honest and clearcut expressions of latent skepticism, expediency, and philosophical dilettantism. All those fallacies stimulated the imagination of mediocre novelists, satisfied the minds of intellectual weaklings, and served as an ideological basis for political deals.

The papal attempts after 1891 to regulate the relation between capital and labor and other social problems in a Catholic spirit came too late to be effective against the Socialist International and its influence on the Italian labor movement. The organization of active Catholic groups also came too late and carried too little constructive impulse to represent a vital contribution to the intellectual and political development of the country. The Church was helpless against the outburst of national emotion and democratic enthusiasm that prompted Italy, in the spring of 1915, to join the Allied nations in the war against her former allies. After the confusion of the postwar years these Catholic groups, split within themselves and isolated in their secular environment, were swept away, together with their left-wing opponents, by the *coup d'état* that brought an armed minority of restless soldiers and political adventurers to almost uncontested power.

The royal recognition of the supremacy of these *fasci di combattimento* over all other political groups laid the foundations for the one-party state that developed, between 1922 and 1927, into a dictatorship over the economic, social, and intellectual life of the country. The official version of the events saluted in these developments the highest and purest expression of Italian genius. In reality, Fascist doctrine and organization is only one aspect of the contemporary European tendency to subordinate all national life and the individual rights of citizens to the state as an almighty and consecrated institution. Thus the Fascist regime represents in the very person of its leader and in the organization of its power both the nationalist and the socialist movements which had developed as revolutionary forces of political and social reconstruction in the European nations shaken or disrupted by the cataclysmic aftermath of the First World War.

There are no substantial differences in structure and organization between the contemporary varieties of 'totalitarian' dictatorship. But while Russian nationalism acts according to Marxist doctrines and tenets, while German National-Socialism substantiated the idea of racial supremacy, and the Spanish autocracy presents itself, in the words of its leader, as a Catholic experience, Italian Fascism lacked a consistent ideological foundation and remained from beginning to end an unsound experiment of factious power-politics and hysterical activism. There was, indeed, little power behind that warlike façade and more resignation than active co-operation in the public acceptance of a 'perpetual revolution.'

None of the principal concepts and aspects of Fascism was in harmony with Italian traditions and predilections. The idea of 'perpetual revolution' was reminiscent of Russian Bolshevism, which also furnished the patterns of police organization and, after 1925, of totalitarian and personal dictatorship. The drive toward radical centralization opposed to regional particularism in customs and dialects was inspired by French national and revolutionary examples and the same is true of the theory and strategy of violence borrowed from Sorel and his adherents. In an era that had experienced the rise and fall of a dozen short-lived empires on four continents, the Roman phraseology of

imperial conquest and grandeur was an obsolete oratorical commonplace. Fascist imperialism was conceived in competition with
the British rather than in imitation of the Roman Empire. The
disenfranchisement and persecution of the Jewish minority, small
in number but notable for intelligence and patriotism, the goose-
stepping militarism, and the pretense of an 'ethical state' were
an imitation of German ideas and institutions.

The introduction of the 'ethical state' into the Fascist program,
and particularly the educational system, as early as 1923, was
the work of Giovanni Gentile, a subtle thinker, a good family-
man of the old Italian style, and a shrewd businessman of the
modern industrial type. He strove to inculcate in a recalcitrant
nation the belief that the state was morality in action and that
obedience to rulers was the highest civic duty and virtue. These
were the practical conclusions drawn from a remodeled version
of the Prussian philosophies of Hegel and Fichte, handed down
during the second half of the last century in the Neapolitan
school of thought opposed to the supine acceptance of French
positivistic trends and methods in North-Italian science and
scholarship. Three bullets fired by unknown partisans, in September 1943, killed the unsuspecting philosopher-politician, who
for the duration of the Fascist regime had embodied the idea
of the 'ethical state' in a band of unscrupulous adventurers and
impudent profiteers. Therefore, Gentile will live in the Italian
memory as the tragic and warning figure of a philosopher who
became the first victim of popular reaction against the forced
imposition of an alien and inadequate doctrine upon domestic
traditions of thought and knowledge.

When soon afterwards the Fascist regime collapsed under the
impact of Allied military victory and internal pressure, the eyes
of the nation and the expectations of the world were directed
toward Benedetto Croce, the only representative of the old
Italian liberalism who came through the twenty-two years of
Fascist political and intellectual oppression as an active force
of spiritual resistance. He emerged from defeat and despair as
a national hero and a spiritual leader, equally favored by conservative and liberal groups in Italy and abroad. In his sudden

rise to universal reputation, his moral personality counted more than his doctrines and deeds.

Only a few intellectuals are able to appreciate in its theoretical presuppositions and practical deductions the widely ramified system of thought elaborated by the philosopher in almost sixty years of painstaking speculative efforts, public experience, and critical discussions. But the Italian mind was indirectly affected throughout the current century by the only man of thought and letters who represented the old universalism of the Italian laity as well as the spiritual heritage of the great humanists and the national *Risorgimento*. In an era of increasing provincialism and, accordingly, of rabid nationalism, Croce embodied in his mind and writings the spiritual solidarity of the world in the search for truth and in the affirmation of human liberty and dignity.

Many Italian literati had kept the Italian public in touch with foreign currents of thought, art, and action. In so doing they acted as professional publicists, or as fellow-travelers, as snobs, profiteers, or opportunists. The critical synthesis accomplished in Croce's mind and works arose from his concept of the one and universal spirit of which history is the always changing work and the only understandable manifestation. To the organic development of that concept Machiavelli and Vico contributed as much as German idealism, American pragmatism, and, in a dialectical clarification, the English economists and Karl Marx. Absent is the French tradition of thought from Descartes and the Encyclopedists down to August Comte, Hippolyte Taine, and his Italian adherents.

It was, indeed, in opposition to them that Croce's absolute historicism developed into a system of thought in which Making and Becoming are the only thinkable and understandable categories, while Being remains outside our concrete experience and consequently inaccessible to the human mind. Thus history becomes the only absolute reality and at the same time the foundation and condition for the intelligibility of reality. This philosophy, which merges into history, logically leaves God to theologians and priests, who are accepted in their historical function but not as the repositories of an absolute, revealed truth. It acknowledges the natural and mathematical sciences in their in-

Q

strumental and practical function, but not as vehicles of objective knowledge. Politics appears in the system as an autonomous aspect of practical activity and as a possible way to morality, but not as a substantiation and activation of ethical principles existing in an abstract reality outside of economic and political life. Aesthetics, which is the nucleus and pivot of the whole doctrine, is not the discussion of the essence, forms, and effect of beauty; it is the theory of the identity of intuition and expression, of language as art and poetry as lyricism, both independent of content, types, and rules, but representing the individual manifestation of intuitive knowledge as an elemental revelation of truth and reality.

This consistent theoretical abolition of the absolute in all the basic aspects of human knowledge and experience created a troublesome unrest and an intellectual bewilderment in the Italian mind. It shook the spiritual apathy and the customary condescension of the Italians toward concrete evidence of facts and forms. In the center of Catholicism, in the home of classicism, in the country of Dante, of the Renaissance, of scientific realism and religious obedience, this renunciation of the traditional standards of truth, beauty, and knowledge produced many new ferments of thought in the restless minds of the modern generations.

But that subtle and elaborate doctrine, which secretly permeated Italy's intellectual life, carried in its methods and conclusions certain elements of confusion, perplexity, and disintegration. The emphasis on aesthetics, characteristic of the system and of Croce's unremitting literary activity, is in harmony with the old Italian predilection for art and poetry. It corresponds with the traditional, almost instinctive Italian concept of beauty as a moral category and as a source of knowledge and spiritual inspiration. Yet in making the poet and artist rationally conscious of their work and objectives, and in making a strong distinction between *poesia e non poesia*, he transformed the old Italian rhetorical aestheticism into a critical one, and made Italy a country of able dialecticians rather than of inspired artists. In that spiritual atmosphere an artistic creation or a poetic vision could never be or represent an act of faith.

This situation had its counterpart in the practical—social or political—field. For Croce the state is 'an elementary and narrow form of practical life, from every part of which the moral life comes forth and overflows, spreading out in abundant, productive streams; so productive as perpetually to make and remake political life itself and the State, that is, to compel them to renew themselves in conformity with the needs which political life creates.' [14] This opinion is intimately related to Croce's dynamic and activistic interpretation of history in its connection with man's moral and practical achievements. His conservative liberalism and its theoretical justification are based on that speculative foundation. This political philosophy regards past developments as anticipation of the future and accepts actual circumstances as a test for practical ability and moral conscience, rather than as an opportunity for an act of faith.

Consequently, when defeat and confusion disrupted the headless and divided nation after September 1943, Italy's most revered man and her living symbol of political integrity and intellectual consistency could offer his distressed countrymen little more than paternal counsels of expediency, vague hopes for the future, and eloquent appeals to the individual consciences of those who were called upon for the moral and economic reconstruction of the country. Thus, while the occupational powers clipped the wings of popular enthusiasm and prevented a wild outbreak of political passions, no one came to the fore with a program for action or a plan for liberty and order. Twenty years of oppression, of passive adjustment and profitable opportunism had atrophied the nation intellectually, morally, and politically as much as German control, Allied occupation, and the economic consequences of defeat and collapse.

After similar experiences France could revert to her national and revolutionary myth of liberty, fraternity, and equality, although it was more solidly engraved on the façades of public buildings than in the hearts and minds of most of the citizens. Italy's intellectual and political leaders had no such device to put on their banners. They started a frantic and fruitless search

[14] *Politics and Morals*, New York, 1945, p. 31.

for a myth, a slogan, or a program of action that could speed up the moral and social reconstruction of the country in accordance with its national traditions and an inspiring vision of the future. Instead, innumerable petty gazetteers and many well-meaning mentors rummaged in Italy's old and new ruins in search of an inspiration that could save the national heritage and promote a spiritual renascence of the Italian people. In that moral vacuum and intellectual confusion the elected representatives of the Italian people fought for years in a Constituent Assembly, in which political opinions were expressed as much by fists as by votes and resolutions.

In the eclectical expediency of the new Constitution, Mazzini's dream of a republican brotherhood works as an ideological and moral incentive rather than as an institutional program. It proved stronger than the conservative efforts, in Italy and abroad, in favor of a shaken and inert dynasty. However, the irreparable defeat and general disillusionment have vitiated any remnants of the intellectual and political initiatives of the *Risorgimento*. The sordid end of the gang that had staged a mock revival of the Roman *fasces* made a nightmare of the dreams of imperial grandeur evoked in a long and noisy propaganda campaign. In the impending work of reconstruction, the Italian people can no longer revert to their national traditions, and for that reason they are unable to find a way to their future. Like some other European countries, Italy is now a frontier and no more the free and sovereign nation of old.

❖   ❖   ❖

In that unsettled, indigent, disarmed, ill-policed, and widely deranged national community, the clergy represented the only intact and efficient organization. Centered in a theocratic city-state of ecclesiastics and officials, it preserves its historical function and ubiquitous influence in the private and public life of the nation. And indeed, whatever may happen to them in the future, the Italians will maintain indefinitely their saints and sanctuaries, their Catholic habits and instincts, even without faith and devotion. In the plenitude of their vitality they will always abhor the abysmal isolation of Existentialism, and shun a philosophy of anguish and despair. A widespread 'Catholic atheism' is not felt to be paradoxical, because the Italians cannot help giving a soul even to the Nothing.

But it is not from these habits and moods or from its obedient Italian flock that the militant Church draws its power and initiative in the tumult of our world. For its preservation and for new conquests the Church has now to rely upon the prosperous and free countries overseas. The Pontiff is now what St. Malachias prophesied in 1590: a *pastor et nauta,* a shepherd navigating toward a new world for the greater glory of God. With that foreign support the Church had become in a short time the leading power in Italian political life. As in the era of the Guelfs and Ghibellines it is now facing those intellectual trends and political interests which aim at an autonomous development of a secular society and civilization.

The admission of women to public life and the gradual awakening of class consciousness among peasants and farm workers helped a great deal in making the Italian people as a whole, for the first time in history, political-minded and socially active. Whether this circumstance will promote a renascence of civic spirit in the actual national community is open to question. The idea of democracy as a sovereignty of the people has never been familiar to the Italians. At present the generalization of political interests and activities appears to stimulate the emotional rather than the ideological and constructive expressions of public life. The Italian radicalism of our day has its foundation in the obsolete social structure of an impoverished and disorganized country in which all the wealth is in the hands of a comparatively small group of people who do not contribute in reasonable proportions to general prosperity or to intellectual activities. Widespread tax evasion and organized export of capital as a matter of routine are characteristic expressions of those unhealthy conditions, whereas private investments in public works and endowments of lay educational and public institutions are very rare and even exceptional.

On the other hand, the vast masses of the Italian people, to a great extent illiterate and poor and now called to active participation in civic life, have neither experience of political freedom nor confidence in an economic and cultural improvement of their plight. They cannot be indefinitely intoxicated by oratorical performances nor regimented in a gregarious organization of the Fascist type. What Italians need and are seeking in these fateful days is a faith that will release their creative energies and activate the intelligence and experience accumulated through centuries of an eventful history. Italy participates in the general decline of spiritual values characteristic of the Western World, but without the compensation of a material civilization that can improve the welfare of the nation and promote at least a decent life for the majority of the population.

Under these adverse conditions the urban middle classes, led by a small bourgeoisie of provincial intellectuals, try frantically to live up to their petty ambitions and traditional standards of outward decorum. From this picturesque but amorphous and now famishing throng of city dwellers Italy draws her functionaries and officers, engineers and magistrates, prelates and professors, lawyers, physicians, musicians, and professionals of all kinds, who together represent the conservative and largely indifferent and opportunistic bulk of Italian society. The nobility, recently augmented by many political upstarts and moneymakers, shares with those middle classes the dislike of manual work and open business, but have never developed the class morale and public ambitions which stimulate the bourgeoisie to professional activities and public responsibility.

The general absence of professional pride accounts for the characteristic aspiration of all Italians to live a gentleman's life, even in poverty. *Fare il signore* is not the pursuit of happiness, which is a concept unknown in Italy, but the appreciation of leisure as an ornament of life, and of distinction as an expression of human dignity. This gentlemanly attitude toward life, embodied in Giovanni della Casa's still popular *Galateo* (1554), is responsible for the tact, affability, and good manners of Italy's common man. But it is not likely to stimulate activity, or to inspire initiative and a dynamic impulse. On the contrary, the general unproductive tendency of the decayed aristocracy and the impecunious middle classes in keeping up appearances and in living beyond their means has a disruptive influence on the ethical substance, the social structure, the economic development, and the moral character of the nation.

Not even the totalitarian efforts and the official vulgarity of Fascism succeeded in altering the temper of the Italian people, or in breaking the traditions of family life and the structure of Italian society. In addition to their psychological substance and sociological instincts, the Italians have preserved from their historical heritage a diffuse intelligence and manual ability coupled with an instinctive sense of human values. These traditional qualities will be reactivated as soon as that shattered country is given a chance to develop its talents and to dignify its national life.

Such an opportunity was given the country by its new Constitution, but is imperiled both by the verbose and turbulent democracy practiced today, and by its legalistic formalism, which may lead to despotism established through legal procedure and foreign help. Italian history shows that such a development would soon release the internal and external forces now already mobilized against such an occurrence. A proletarian dictator has little chance of success in a country traditionally adverse to doctrinarism and fanaticism, deeply attached to family life and clans, refractory in social thinking and public spirit, and accustomed to accept individualism both in its noble and evil manifestations as an inalienable human trait rather than as a philosophical attitude.

Reflected in the Italian mind, the Marxist doctrine does not imply the total abolition or socialization of ownership, but rather the way to secure for the multitudes of destitute people a minimum of property, an escape from the hopeless poverty determined by the historical structure of Italian society and the lack of the essential natural conditions for the development of national prosperity. Radicalism is favored and supported by the widespread conviction that capitalistic methods and private enterprise are powerless to reorganize a wrecked country deprived of natural and economic resources.

Yet, none of the foreign ideologies can be properly adapted and successfully realized within the reality of Italian life. For the organization of an efficient capitalistic society Italy has always lacked the internal wealth and, accordingly, the foreign credits. A Marxist organization of national economy seems impracticable in a country unsuited for autonomous industrial production and for extensive mechanized agriculture. Nor can these foreign systems be forced upon a people yearning for liberty and a free enjoyment of life.

The realization of that aspiration in the framework of Catholic principles and with a pledge for social reforms has been the goal of Christian Democracy since its creation in July 1943. Yet the concept of Christian Democracy is a Protestant and not a Catholic one, and consequently a source of paradoxes and ambiguities, of parliamentary juggleries and political casuistry, which can never make up for 'a certain poverty of thought and uncertainty of movement,' frankly admitted by the most revered spiritual leader of the group.[15] This new and powerful Guelfism suffers from the inherent contradiction of being dogmatic in spirit and democratic in methods, conservative in temper and progressive in social action, Catholic in conception but national in policy, intransigent in principles but co-operative in practice. Christian Democracy as practiced in Italy has the disadvantage of all compounded concepts in politics, philosophy, and religion. It faces and combats with increasing success the organized laical forces directed toward the attainment of a secular or socialist society.

The intellectual and active élite of the new generations, animated by an almost exalted desire for national reconstruction, dislikes an attitude requiring dialectical proficiency and an accommodating casuistry of expedients and evasions. The Italians have always had plenty of both, generally coupled with legalistic punctilio and oratorical skill. Now they are in search of a more substantial *raison d'être* and of more positive values. Large sections of the Italian people are unwilling to accept ecclesiastical tutelage as a basis for the reorganization of modern society. On the other hand, they resist a materialistic hegemony in the discussion and solution of economic problems and national goals. They need opinions and not only compromise, action but

[15] Luigi Sturzo in *Review of Politics*, IX, 1947, no. 1, p. 15.

not bargaining, apostles and not politicians, a faith and not concessions. If our world survives in an atomic age, they will some
day get all of that through toil and struggle, but not from foreign
doctrines and partisan violence.

The tragedy of these new generations lies in the disenchant-
ing experience of liberty as a spiritual vacuum and of history
as a heap of ruins. In that confused and disrupted society there
are, of course, much talk and plenty of good intentions, as there
are anxiety, cynicism, social iniquity, and constant danger. Yet
most of the victims of that tragic situation seem to practice in
thought and deed the immortal wisdom of Voltaire's Candide
by devoting themselves, silently and patiently, to the task of
cultivating, even under most adverse conditions, what poets
have called the garden of Europe and the country of the Gods.

Bibliographical Note

THE following list refers to books and periodicals in which the reader will find ample bibliographical information on every field of Italian history and civilization. These references can be supplemented by older bibliographical works mentioned in the publications listed below.

GEOGRAPHY

Almagià, R.: *La Geografia,* 2nd edition, Rome, 1922 (Guide Bibliografiche).
Bollettino della Società Geografica Italiana, since 1868.

LANGUAGE AND DIALECTS

Hall, Robert A., Jr.: *Bibliography of Italian Linguistics,* Linguistic Society of America, Baltimore, 1941.
Lingua Nostra, Rassegna di Filologia Italiana, since 1939.

CHURCH HISTORY

Bibliographical Supplements in *Revue d'histoire ecclésiastique,* since 1900.

POLITICAL HISTORY AND ECONOMY

Bibliographical Appendix to L. Salvatorelli, *A Concise History of Italy,* trans. by B. Miall, New York, 1940, pp. 631-63.
Archivio Storico Italiano, since 1842, with index by E. Rossi, 2 vols., Firenze, 1945.
American Historical Review (especially for American contributions).

HISTORY OF LITERATURE

Prezzolini, G.: *Repertorio Bibliografico della Storia e della Critica della Letteratura Italiana dal* 1902 *al* 1942, 4 vols., Rome-New York, 1937-42.
Giornale Storico della Letteratura Italiana, since 1883.
La Critica, ed. by Benedetto Croce, since 1903.
Italica, Quarterly Bulletin of the American Association of teachers of Italian (particularly for American contributions), since 1924.

Italian Studies, A Quarterly Review (particularly for English contributions), Cambridge, England, since 1937.

CONTEMPORARY LITERATURE

L'Italia che scrive, since 1918.
Leonardo, Rassegna Bibliografica, since 1930.

ERUDITION AND RESEARCH

Mazzoni, Guido: *Avviamento allo studio delle lettere italiane,* 3rd edition, Firenze, 1923.
La Bibliofilia, Rivista di Storia del Libro, di Bibliografia ed Erudizione, since 1899.

FINE ARTS

Thieme-Becker, *Künstlerlexikon,* 33 vols., 1907-39.
Art Index, New York, since 1929.

PHILOSOPHY

Bibliographical Notes in Guido de Ruggiero, *Storia della Filosofia,* new edition, Bari, 1943 ff. (4 vols.).

SCIENCE

Singer, Charles Joseph: *A Short History of Science to the Nineteenth Century,* Oxford, 1941.
Isis, International Review to the History of Science and Civilization, since 1913.
Archeion, Archivio di Storia della Scienza, since 1919.

RENAISSANCE

A Bibliography of 'Recent Literature of the Renaissance,' in *Studies in Philology,* Chapel Hill, North Carolina, since 1906.

MUSIC

Lang, P. H.: *Music in Western Civilization,* New York, 1941.
Reese, G.: *Music in the Middle Ages,* New York, 1940.
Bukofzer, M.: *Music in the Baroque Era,* New York, 1947.
Rivista Musicale Italiana, since 1894.

Additional references may be found in the bibliographical lists added to the articles in the *Enciclopedia Italiana,* 36 vols. and Appendix, 1929-39; special bibliographies in Theodore Besterman's, *A World Bibliography of Bibliographies,* 2 vols., 2nd edition, 1947; personal bibliographies of contemporary authors in *CHI È,* Rome, 1948.